# Critical Theory

## Great Debates in Philosophy
### Series Editor: Ernest Sosa

Dialogue has always been a powerful means of philosophical exploration and exposition. By presenting important current issues in philosophy in the form of a debate, this series attempts to capture the flavour of philosophical argument and to convey the excitement generated by the exchange of ideas. Each author contributes a major, original essay. When these essays have been exchanged, the authors are each given the opportunity to respond to the opposing view.

*Personal Identity*
Sydney Shoemaker and Richard Swinburne

*Consciousness and Causality*
D M Armstrong and Norman Malcolm

*Agency and Necessity*
Anthony Flew and Godfrey Vesey

*Critical Theory*
David Couzens Hoy and Thomas McCarthy

# Critical Theory

*David Couzens Hoy
and
Thomas McCarthy*

BLACKWELL
Oxford UK & Cambridge USA

The right of David Couzens Hoy and Thomas McCarthy to be identified as
authors of this work has been asserted in accordance with the Copyright,
Designs and Patents Act 1988.

First published 1994
Reprinted 1995

Blackwell Publishers, the publishing imprint of Basil Blackwell Inc.
238 Main Street
Cambridge, Massachusetts 02142, USA

Blackwell Publishers Ltd
108 Cowley Road,
Oxford OX4 1JF
UK

Library of Congress Cataloging-in-Publication Data

Hoy, David Couzens.
   Critical theory / David Couzens Hoy and Thomas McCarthy.
     p.  cm. — (Great debates in philosophy)
     Includes bibliographical references and index.
     ISBN 1–55786–172–2. — ISBN 1–55786–173–0 (pbk.)
     1. Critical theory. 2. Reason.    I. McCarthy, Thomas A.
   II. Title    III. Series.
   B809.3.H68    1994                              93–43838
   142—dc20                                        CIP

British Library Cataloguing in Publication Data
A CIP catalogue record for this book is available from the British Library.

Typeset in 10 on 12 pt Melior by Pure Tech Corporation, Pondicherry, India.
Printed in Great Britain by T.J. Press Ltd., Padstow, Cornwall.

This book is printed on acid-free paper

for
Jenny, Justin,
and
Meredith

# Contents

Introduction                                                             1

**Part I  Philosophy and Critical Theory:
          A Reprise (*Thomas McCarthy*)**                               5

1  On the Idea of a Critical Theory and
   Its Relation to Philosophy                                            7
   *1.1  Horkheimer on Historicism*                                      9
   *1.2  Traditional and Critical Theory*                               13
   *1.3  The* Aufhebung *of Philosophy*                                 22

2  Reason in a Postmetaphysical Age                                     31
   *2.1  Deconstructionist Critiques of Reason*                         32
   *2.2  Communication and Idealization*                                38
   *2.3  Accountability and Autonomy*                                   42
   *2.4  Discourse Ethics*                                              47

3  On the Pragmatics of Communicative Reason                            63
   *3.1  The Rational Properties of Practical Activities*               64
   *3.2  Pragmatizing Communicative Rationality*                        74
   *3.3  On the Methodologies of Critical Social Theory*                81
   *3.4  Multicultural Cosmopolitanism*                                 86

**Part II  Critical Theory and Critical History
           (*David Couzens Hoy*)**                                     101

4  A Deconstructive Reading of the Early Frankfurt School              103
   *4.1  Tensions in Horkheimer*                                       103
   *4.2  Deferrals in Adorno*                                          114
   *4.3  Anticipations of Poststructuralism*                           119

5  Conflicting Conceptions of Critique:
   Foucault versus Habermas                                    144
   *5.1  Foucault and the Frankfurt School*                    144
   *5.2  Naturalizing Philosophy with Evolutionary Stories*    149
   *5.3  From Hegel to Nietzsche*                              155
   *5.4  Genealogy's Critique of Habermas*                    158
   *5.5  The Critical Potential of History and of Theory*      164

6  The Contingency of Universality:
   Critical Theory as Genealogical Hermeneutics                172
   *6.1  Genealogy, For and Against*                          172
   *6.2  Habermas's Universalism*                             177
   *6.3  Gadamer's Hermeneutical Pluralism*                   188
   *6.4  Genealogical Hermeneutics*                           200

**Part III  For and Against**                                  215

7  Rejoinder to David Hoy (*Thomas McCarthy*)                  217
   *7.1  Pragmatism*                                          217
   *7.2  Genealogy*                                           224
   *7.3  Hermeneutics*                                        230
   *7.4  Pluralism*                                           238

8  Rejoinder to Thomas McCarthy (*David Couzens Hoy*)          249
   *8.1  Rational Agents or Cultural Dopes?*                  250
   *8.2  Local Solidarity or Universal Audience?*             253
   *8.3  Pluralism or Consensus?*                            263
   *8.4  Identity in Difference?*                             266

Index                                                         274

# Introduction

A striking etching by Francisco Goya depicts a figure, presumably the artist, asleep at his desk while monstrous creatures of darkness swarm about him. On the desk itself is written the title of the etching (#43 in the series, *Los Caprichos*, dating from 1799), "*El sueño de la razón produce monstruos.*" What interests us here is the title's notorious ambiguity, which expresses a widespread ambivalence about Goya's own era, particularly about eighteenth-century ideals of enlightenment. The title can be read as either "The *sleep* of reason produces monsters" or "The *dream* of reason produces monsters." The first and primary reading says that when reason goes to sleep monsters are produced. This slogan of modern enlightenment is flatly contradicted by the second, counterenlightenment reading, which says that the monsters are themselves reason's dreams. On this latter reading, reason is not simply a light opposed to the darkness of fantasy but has its own dark side.

Whatever Goya intended, our aim in this book is to debate these alternative assessments of reason for their own sake. More specifically, we shall be discussing ways in which the ambivalence encapsulated in Goya's title structures philosophical controversies within contemporary critical theory. Our discussion will begin with critical theory as formulated in the work of the Frankfurt School in the 1930s and 1940s. Our divergent assessments of these early efforts follow from our different understandings of the trajectory of critical social theory since then. One path has been marked out by a direct descendant of the Frankfurt School, Jürgen Habermas. Thomas McCarthy is the more sympathetic of us to that. David Hoy is more sympathetic to paths taken by other thinkers with whom Habermas has had his own debates, particularly the hermeneutical philosophy of Hans-Georg Gadamer and the French poststructuralism of Michel Foucault.

There are, of course, many sides to the complex configuration of present-day critical theory. Major disagreements have arisen around

questions concerning what was traditionally referred to as "the nature, scope, and limits of human reason," especially since it has become increasingly obvious that the much-heralded linguistic turn in
twentieth-century philosophy was only a way station on a much
longer journey. Growing awareness of the practical embeddedness of
languages in "forms of life" and "lifeworlds," of the historical variability of categories of thought and principles of action, of the conven-
tionality of criteria of rationality and their involvement with power
and interests, and of the embodied and practical being of rational
subjects has inexorably eroded philosophical conceptions of "pure"
reason. However, while all parties to the contemporary debates agree
in rejecting "Cartesian" conceptions of reason and the rational subject,
they disagree considerably about what that rejection entails for the
enlightenment ideals of self-consciousness, self-determination, and
self-realization. Some (like the French poststructuralists) have emphasized the thoroughly contingent character of what counts as rational
and have called for a radical critique of Western "logocentrism."
Others (like Habermas) see this radical critique as an over-reaction that
disempowers critical reason and call instead for a continuation-through-
transformation of the Kantian approach to reason. Still others have, like
Gadamer, followed a hermeneutic path or, like Richard Rorty, a pragmatist path, heading sometimes more in the enlightenment direction, sometimes more in the counterenlightenment direction.

However enlivening in their effects on critical theory, these rather
sudden metaphilosophical storms have also proved disorienting. The
aim of this book is to bring those complex developments into sharper
focus around a set of familiar philosophical issues concerning reason and the rational subject, representation and truth, knowledge and
objectivity, identity and difference, relativism and universalism, the
right and the good. But these "perennial problems" are resituated
within a context profoundly and permanently altered by an expanding
cultural, historical, rhetorical, and practical self-consciousness and a
correlative turn to interpretive studies of social practices. Such changes
have affected the very terms in which the problems are posed: Is the
idea of truth itself subject to variation? Does the idea of a unique truth
about a given domain any longer make sense? Are the broader frameworks within which truth claims are raised and contested themselves
amenable to reason, truth, and logic? Can the traditional delimitation
of rational argument from rational persuasion be maintained in some
form? Is there any conception of rational subjectivity that can replace
the Cartesian one, or any conception of rational autonomy that can
replace the Kantian one? Should we continue to treat the ideas of
subjectivity and autonomy as theoretical starting-points? If not, what

are the implications for moral and political theory? Or for the ideas of enlightenment and emancipation that have been central to critical theory? Is there any sense at all in which history can be read as a narrative of progress? Are familiar projections of European history as the pacesetter for the history of the species anything more than rank ethnocentrism? Is ethnocentrism avoidable or is it an inescapable condition? What does that mean for the possibility of understanding other cultures? Of criticizing them? Of entering into dialogue with them? And how do the answers to these questions affect our estimation of the present state and future prospects of critical theory?

These and like issues are the subjects of the debate that follows. David Hoy develops and defends a conception of genealogical hermeneutics that builds on the thought of Michel Foucault and Hans-Georg Gadamer. His aim is to formulate an antifoundationalist, historicist approach to critical theory that avoids the extremes of relativism and nihilism. Thomas McCarthy develops and defends a conception of critical social theory that builds on the thought of Jürgen Habermas. His aim is to formulate a less transcendental, more pragmatic, but nonetheless universalist conception of communicative reason. The three parts of the two opening statements parallel each other. Thus, in chapter 4 Hoy counterposes to McCarthy's partial reconstruction of Horkheimer's original program in chapter 1 a deconstruction of the same in favor of the more "Nietzschean" ideas of the later Horkheimer and Adorno. Hoy continues on this trajectory in chapter 5, invoking a Foucaultian notion of genealogy against Habermas's renewal of the original program, thus counterbalancing McCarthy's deployment in chapter 2 of Habermasian ideas against the radical critics of modernity. Finally, Hoy's criticism in chapter 6 of Habermas's theory of communicative reason runs counter to McCarthy's effort in chapter 3 to present a "pragmaticized" version of it. It is no accident that the two statements close with contrasting discussions of universalism and pluralism, for these concerns are at the heart of the debate.

In his rejoinder to Hoy in chapter 7, McCarthy defends scaled-down versions of the types of theory criticized by Hoy: metanarratives of history, holistic accounts of society, and metatheoretical foundations. He contrasts the notion of critical history that Hoy develops with the idea of theoretically informed critique central to critical social theory since Marx. After sketching an account of interpretations that differs from Hoy's in stressing their amenability to critical examination under the aspects of consistency, coherence, truth, and justice, he defends the internal connection between rational justification and rational consensus and advances a conception of critical dialogue based on mutual respect.

In his rejoinder to McCarthy in chapter 8, Hoy concurs with a view of social agency that avoids the extremes of both cultural determinism and rational self-transparency. He then defends a notion of social criticism that relies on local solidarities rather than on the universal audience McCarthy invokes, and that renounces the ideal of universal convergence on "one right interpretation" for that of interpretive pluralism. He argues against all such "monistic" ideals in favor of a conception of hermeneutic dialogue that leaves room for both expanding solidarities and reasonable disagreements. Finally, he spells out the practical-political advantages of a model of genealogical hermeneutics that resists complacency and parochialism without relying on the sorts of regulative ideals that McCarthy regards as integral to critique.

It should be evident from even these few introductory remarks that this dialectical exercise is by no means meant to end discussion on any of the issues raised. But we do hope that our exchange can give the ongoing debates within critical theory a form and direction that will make their continuation all the more fruitful.

# Acknowledgements

This book would not have been possible without a major collaborative grant in 1989–90 from the Interpretive Research division of the National Endowment for the Humanities, an independent federal agency. David Hoy also wishes to acknowledge a fellowship for college teachers in 1987–8 from the National Endowment for the Humanities, as well as generous research support over the years from the Academic Senate and the Humanities Division of the University of California, Santa Cruz, and Berkeley's Center for German and European Studies.

*David Hoy*

*Thomas McCarthy*

# Part I
## Philosophy and Critical Theory: A Reprise

*Thomas McCarthy*

# On the Idea of a Critical Theory and Its Relation to Philosophy

The *Critique of Pure Reason*, Kant noted in his preface, arose in response to a "call to reason to undertake anew the most difficult of all its tasks, namely that of self-knowledge, and to institute a tribunal which will assure to reason its lawful claims and dismiss all groundless pretensions."[1] In his transcendental philosophy the assurance of reason's lawful claims took the form of an analytic of truth and the dismissal of groundless pretensions the form of a critique of dialectical illusions.[2] Two centuries later Foucault noted the continuity of his post-Nietzschean genealogy with the classical critique of reason: "I think that the central issue of philosophy and critical thought since the eighteenth century has been, still is, and will, I hope, remain the question: What is this reason that we use? What are its historical effects? What are its limits, and what are its dangers?"[3] But he stressed the discontinuity as well: "If the Kantian question was that of knowing what limits knowledge has to renounce transgressing, it seems to me that the critical question today . . . [is]: In what is given to us as universal, necessary, obligating, what place is occupied by whatever is singular, contingent, and the product of arbitrary constraints?"[4] Thus Foucault's "practical critique" of reason looked not for "formal structures with universal value" but for "transformable singularities"; it was interested not in "necessary limitations" but in the "possibility of no longer being, doing, or thinking, what we are, do, or think."[5] Though he occasionally acknowledged the possibility of pursuing an "analytic of truth in general,"[6] his own work centered on the genealogical deconstruction of rationalistic pretensions.

Notwithstanding the highly original form in which he cast them, the basic changes one finds in Foucault's notion of a critique of reason are not peculiar to him. They stem rather from the relentless detranscendentalization of reason and decentering of the rational subject by Marx and Darwin, Nietzsche and Freud, historicism and pragmatism – to signal only a few of the many deflationary currents of nineteenth- and twentieth-century thought. The intrinsic "impurity" of what we call "reason," its embeddedness in culture and society, and the embodied and engaged nature of its bearers, are now widely acknowledged. Thus, even critical theorists less radically deconstructionist than Foucault share his view that the basic structures of thought are not accessible to the sorts of introspective survey of the contents of consciousness favored by the classical critique of reason. They agree that examining the "nature, scope, and limits" of reason calls for modes of sociohistorical inquiry that go beyond the traditional bounds of philosophical analysis. And they also agree that the critique of impure reason has practical import. Once we have turned our attention from consciousness to culture and society, it becomes evident that there are normative and evaluative presuppositions and consequences attaching to any social practice. Rational practices – including epistemic practices like theorizing – have to be viewed in their sociocultural contexts if they are to be properly understood. In this sense, the critique of impure reason is part of the study of culture and society. As a critical endeavor, it aims to enhance and transform our self-understanding in ways that affect how we live.

   This sort of practically significant, sociohistorical critique of impure reason has been a live option for postmetaphysical thinking at least since the time of the Left-Hegelians. A variant of it dominated the philosophical scene in the United States during the heyday of American Pragmatism. The point of departure of the remarks that follow is the program for critical social theory advanced by Max Horkheimer and his colleagues at the Institute for Social Research in the early 1930s.[7] On the reading offered here, that approach has the virtue of developing by transforming both aspects of Kant's critique of reason, the assurance of reason's "lawful claims" as well as the dismissal of "groundless pretensions." In contrast to exclusively deconstructionist approaches, it allows for a critical reconstruction of Enlightenment conceptions of reason and the rational subject, a kind of "determinate negation" through which they are given sociocultural forms rather than simply dismantled. And while it is critical of overly objectivized methods in the established social sciences and sees them as abetting the one-sided rationalization of modern life, it seeks to appropriate and to develop types of sociohistorical analysis that are not tied to instrumental and strategic rationality. This has the advantage of allying the philosophical critique of reason with modes of inquiry deployed in history and the human sciences to deal reflectively with the same domains of thought and action. It is in this spirit that Horkheimer, in his inaugural lecture as Director of the Institute, characterized critical theory as an "ongoing dialectical interpenetration" of philosophy and empirical research, a form of "philosophically oriented social inquiry."[8]

## 1.1  Horkheimer on Historicism

Early in the 1930s Max Horkheimer found himself in an intellectual milieu similar to ours in one respect: it was marked by a sharp swing away from previously dominant forms of neo-Kantianism and toward pronounced forms of antirationalism. In his 1934 discussion of "The Rationalism Debate in Contemporary Philosophy," Horkheimer endorsed without reservation the historicist view that "there is no final picture of either the essence or the appearance of reality. The very idea of a supernatural subject who could comprehend it is madness . . . . It is the human being who thinks, not the Ego or Reason . . . . [And that] is not something abstract, such as the human essence, but always human beings living in a particular historical epoch."[9] It is just this embeddedness in historical life that rationalists ignored when they projected worldviews untainted by "any trace of the societal beings that produced them, rather as if they were pure mirrors of an eternal order."[10] On the other hand, Horkheimer warned, none of this warranted a swing to the opposite, antirationalist extremes represented in his day by *Lebensphilosophie* and Existentialism. To hypostatize Life or Existence was not to escape metaphysical thinking, but only to turn in the old set of fundamental categories for a new one. Critical theory required more than the simple invocation of concrete-sounding, but no less essentialistic, determinations of this sort. It called for a continuation-through-transformation of the critique of reason, a materialist account of its nature, conditions, and limits. If the subject of knowledge and action could no longer be viewed as solitary, disengaged, and disembodied, and if the structures of reason could no longer be viewed as timeless, necessary, and unconditioned, then the transformation called for carried the critique of reason in the direction of sociohistorical inquiry.

At the same time, Horkheimer repeatedly urged that this project not be viewed reductionistically. In particular, he was careful to distinguish it from the increasingly influential sociology of knowledge being developed at the time by Karl Mannheim. And with good reason: his critical social theory shared with Mannheim's sociology of knowledge a recognition of the socially conditioned character of human thought. He wished, however, to hold fast to a strong distinction between true and false consciousness and thus to avoid the relativistic implications of Mannheim's approach. Even though traditional philosophy's radical dichotomy between the ideal and the real could no longer be upheld, it was not necessary to retreat to a relativism of socially conditioned perspectives. What was needed was a new concept of truth which, while renouncing any God's-eye view, retained the dichotomy between the true and the false, albeit in a more modest, suitably human form.

Thus, in his 1930 review of Mannheim's *Ideology and Utopia*, Horkheimer argued that the historically conditioned character of thought is not *per se* incompatible with truth. Only against the background of traditional, ontological-theological conceptions of eternal, unchanging truth did that seem to be the case.[11] But there was no need of an absolute guarantee to distinguish meaningfully between truth and error. Rather, what was required was a concept of truth consistent with our finitude, with our historicity, with the dependence of thought on changing social conditions. On such a concept, failure to measure up to absolute, unconditioned standards was irrelevant. To regard this failure as leading directly to relativism was just another version of the "God is dead, everything is permitted" fallacy of disappointed expectations. As Horkheimer put it: "That all our thoughts, true and false, depend on conditions that can change . . . in no way affects the validity of science. It is not clear to me why the fact of *Seinsgebundenheit* [i.e., of being historically conditioned] should affect the truth of a judgement – why shouldn't insight be just as *seinsgebunden* as error?"[12] In the first instance, the challenge was to deontologize and detranscendentalize the notion of truth.

In his 1935 essay "On the Problem of Truth," Horkheimer attempted to do just that.[13] He argued against the equation of fallibility with relativity. To grant that there is no final and conclusive theory of reality of which we are capable, is not at all to abandon the distinction between truth and error. We make that distinction in relation to the "available means of knowledge."[14] The claim that a belief is true must stand the test of experience and practice in the present. Knowing that we are fallible, that what stands the test today may well fail to do so tomorrow or in the next century, does not prevent us, or even exempt us, from making and defending claims to truth here and now. The abstract recognition that all our beliefs are open to correction does not make a rationally warranted belief any less warranted, any less rational.

A few years later, in 1939, having emigrated to New York, Horkheimer published in the journal of the transplanted Institute for Social

Research an essay on "The Social Function of Philosophy." He stressed the ways in which philosophy did not fit neatly into the system of specialized sciences. From the time of Socrates, he wrote, it has taken on "the unpleasant task of throwing the light of consciousness upon even those human relations and modes of response which have become so deeply rooted that they seem natural, immutable, and eternal."[15] Given this interest in questioning what is normally taken for granted, in probing behind established modes of thought and action, it is no wonder, Horkheimer went on, that philosophical discussions "are so much more radical and unconciliatory than discussions in the sciences. Unlike other pursuits, philosophy does not have a field of action marked out for it within the given."[16] Rather, its function is to keep us from losing ourselves "in those ideas and activities which the existing order of society instills into its members,"[17] to help us to understand what we are doing in the interest of enabling us consciously to shape our lives. In short, philosophy is critical enlightenment, an ongoing "attempt to bring reason into the world."[18] On the other hand, as noted above, Horkheimer was fully aware that this sort of radical, practically oriented reflection on reason and its realizations could no longer be carried out in the manner of classical philosophy. There is, he argued, no way of comprehending the structures of reason that does not involve sociohistorical inquiry. And if the actualization of reason is to be more than a pious wish, philosophical utopias will have to be replaced by empirically based accounts of "concrete relations and tendencies that can lead to an improvement of human life."[19] For that purpose too, the critical mission of philosophy had to be continued in the medium of social research.

From this standpoint, Horkheimer judged Mannheim's sociology of knowledge to be practically, no less than theoretically, wrong-headed. Treating styles, methods and systems of thought merely as the expression of specific social situations promoted a skeptical deflation of philosophical notions of reason rather than their refraction in the denser medium of empirical research. "The attitude taken to philosophical ideas does not comprise objective testing and practical application, but a more or less complicated correlation to a social group. [This] merely repeats the skeptical view we have already criticized. It is not calculated to explain the social function of philosophy, but rather to perform one itself – namely, to discourage thought from its practical tendency of pointing to the future."[20] This had been a major theme of Horkheimer's earlier essays as well. In "On the Problem of Truth", for instance, he had written: "Since the recognition of the truth of particular ideas disappears behind the display of conditions, the coordination with historical unities, this impartial relativism reveals itself as the friend of what exists at any given time . . . What is coming into being needs conscious decision in its struggle, while the limitation to mere understanding and contemplation serves what is already in existence."[21]

Thus, while Horkheimer joined with the then dominant forms of antirationalism in calling for an investigation of the real conditions of thought, he distanced himself from them in refusing to celebrate the newly minted hypostatizations of History, Society, Life, and Existence.[22] What the critics of rationalism failed to appreciate is that the turn to the psychological, social, and historical roots of thought did not herald the end of reason; it was the latest and most radical phase in its ongoing self-critique. The "detachment" they announced from the subject-centered categories "originally absolutized by bourgeois liberal thought" usually went hand-in-hand with a methodological indifference to questions of validity.[23] In certain varieties of historicism, for instance, this took the form of an aestheticized tour through the *musée imaginaire* of the past, with the aim of understanding everything rather than taking sides. The claims to validity of past systems of thought were not taken seriously and rationally evaluated. Instead, critique was replaced by "reverential empathy and description."[24] What concerned Horkheimer about the methodological replacement of *sachliche Prüfung*, or critical examination, with detached contemplation, was the skepticism it generated with respect to the basic normative ideas of truth, justice, freedom, responsibility and the like. While the hegemonic forms of these ideas were all too often distorted, the aim of the materialist critique of reason was not to discard them altogether but to unmask their specific distortions so as to render them unserviceable for the justification of injustice and oppression: "Whenever in history nations or classes have secured their continued existence not only with cold steel but with moral, metaphysical, and religious ideas, these ideas were in the end exposed to attack from those being dominated. A struggle against the cultural supports of social conditions usually introduces and accompanies political rebellion . . . For this reason, devaluation of the specific ideas through which a despised state of affairs is grounded, supported, and transfigured is as old as these struggles themselves."[25]

Of course, at that time Horkheimer had particular reason to worry about the abstract negation of the conceptual repertoire of rationalist individualism in favor of its binary opposites – history and tradition, community and culture. This sort of simple inversion, combined with skepticism about any strong claims to validity, fostered and justified passivity in the midst of an increasingly irrational and dangerous world. The individual was pictured as thoroughly submerged in the social whole, and the historical movement of the whole as governed by sub- or supra-personal forces beyond the reach of reason. The idea of rationally influencing the shape of social life by attempting to put the insights of historical, social, and cultural studies into effect appeared ridiculously naive, overcome, dépassé. As Horkheimer pointed out, the peculiar reflexivity of thought about individual and social life is such that thinking something is so can help make it so. The kind of insight into the depths of existence and the shallowness of enlightenment at which German philosophy excelled was only too effective in nourishing cynical and accommodative attitudes toward a world in the process of going mad.[26]

## 1.2 Traditional and Critical Theory

In the context of contemporary critical theory, left-Hegelian formulae of "realizing reason" and promoting "a rational organization of society" have a disagreeably totalizing ring to them. And there is much in the early Horkheimer that bears criticism on this score: his tendency to conceptualize society as at least potentially a unified subject with a unified will and, hence, to marginalize considerations of social, cultural, and political pluralism; his over-reliance on Marxian political economy, particularly class analysis, in identifying the causes and conditions of injustice in existing social orders; his subscription to a philosophy of history or "grand metanarrative" that underplayed the roles of contingency, locality, and identity in struggles against oppression.[27] In fact, given the currently widespread opposition to general accounts of reason and rationalization of any sort, it may be well to begin by asking why Horkheimer's approach deserves to be taken seriously at all.

The grand "either/or" structuring much of postmodernist rhetoric sets the particular *against* the universal: either one is for the totality, necessity, authority, and homogeneity of the universal, or one rejects it in the name of the fragmentary, contingent, spontaneous, and heterogeneous particular. But that opposition simply ignores the dialectical relation between the general and the particular. I shall have more to say about this in section 3.1; in the present context, it means that the relation between constructing general accounts and analyzing particular situations should be seen as one of reciprocal influence and mutual coherence rather than as one of fixed subordination and one-way determination. More specifically, no generalizing approach to the

critique of reason can serve as the closed framework or unimpeach-
able "tribunal" that Kant thought it to be. If the end of foundationalism means anything, it signifies at least the permanent openness of
any proposed universal frame to deconstructive and reconstructive
impulses from what Adorno called the "non-identical." On the other
hand, it is implausible to suppose that social and cultural studies can
get along without general conceptions of reason and rationalization.
The interpretive and evaluative frameworks that invariably, albeit often tacitly, inform the ways in which sociocultural phenomena are selected, described, ordered, analyzed, appraised, explained, and so forth,
typically include categories and assumptions tailored to grasping the
"rationalization" of modern society. And these are usually of philosophical provenance, for the simple reason that modern philosophy
has centered around the critique of reason. This is obvious in the work
of classical social theorists like Marx, Durkheim, and Weber no less
than in that of contemporary deconstructionist critics like Foucault,
Derrida, and Rorty.[28] Accordingly, the assumption underlying the
remarks that follow is that some general, "philosophical" level of analysis of ideas of reason, rationality, truth, objectivity, subjectivity,
autonomy, and so forth, is still of fundamental importance for critical
social and cultural inquiry. This is, of course, *not* to say that it is the
only significant mode of inquiry, or that it could replace more contextually specific modes, or that it is itself unaffected by the results of the
latter.[29] The hope is that many of the objectionable features of the
classical critique of reason can be overcome by deabsolutizing ideas of
reason through stressing their relations to social practice and building
deconstructive concerns into reconstructive endeavors from the start.

  With this in mind, let us turn to Horkheimer's programmatic contrast between "Traditional and Critical Theory" and situate his approach in relation to views now current among critical theorists.[30] The
axis on which the contrast turns is the reflexivity – in both its primary
senses – of social inquiry. Horkheimer repeatedly insisted both upon
the fact that social researchers are themselves engaged in socially
situated forms of social action and upon the importance of their bringing this to conscious awareness and thinking through its implications.
The social sciences, in modelling themselves after the natural sciences,
were attempting to position themselves centrally in an industrial
society increasingly dependent on monitoring and managing key socioeconomic variables. By promoting a positivistic image of themselves
as just "telling it like it is," they could claim to offer a "view from
nowhere" with all of its rights and privileges; other approaches thereby became marginalized as prescientific, ideological, self-interested,
or the like. One of the first tasks of critical theory was to challenge the

privileged "non-position" of social-scientific knowledge by analyzing the modes of its production, the roles it played in society, the interests it served, and the historical processes through which it came to power.

Leaving aside the details of Horkheimer's analysis, which reflects in key respects the Marxian political-economic framework he took over, it is important for present purposes to note that he did not regard the deconstruction of allegedly disembodied social knowledge as entailing the delegitimation of empirical social research as such. On the contrary, processing and deploying vast bodies of "factual" knowledge useful for social reproduction within an established social framework is a requirement of any developed society (205). The problem arises from its absolutization, "as though it were grounded in the nature of knowledge as such or justified in some other ahistorical way" (194). And the solution is to recognize the sorts of interests that such knowledge serves in the present society, as well as the place it might occupy in a better society, and by thus "locating" it to leave ample space for other interests and other types of knowledge.

Unlike "traditional" theory, then, critical social theory takes as topics of investigation the reflexivity of social research, the division of labor – including scientific and scholarly labor – in which it is carried on, and its social functions; that is, it studies "what theory means in human life" (197). It reflects, in particular, on the contexts of its own genesis and application, that is, on its own embeddedness in the social matrix out of which it arises and within which it will find its uses. Unlike contemporary deconstructionists, however, Horkheimer does not understand this as prohibiting all but "local" knowledge. Rather, he seeks to locate both traditional and critical research within a broad account of contemporary society which, he wants to claim, is more adequate than any of its competitors. I shall have more to say below about how acknowledging the situatedness of knowledge is compatible with raising claims to situation-transcendent validity. For now it will be worthwhile to explore a bit further the distinctive sense in which sociocultural knowledge is reflexive knowledge, for that is the key to its differences from natural science.

While the goals and directions of research in the natural sciences are less and less a purely intrascientific matter, in the social sciences the events, structures, and processes that influence the agenda of research also belong to the subject matter of research (195–6). More generally, social inquiry is a moment of the very process of social reproduction it aims to comprehend. The social world is produced and reproduced in and through the social actions of social actors, including the activities of agents engaged in analyzing it. This peculiar reflexivity has a number of implications. For one thing, it suggests a social constructionist view of social reality, which positivism completely misses with its passive, perceptual models of subject-object relations (200). For another, it means that social subjects of knowledge are shaped by the same sorts of historical forces that shape their objects of knowledge: for them to understand something of the latter is also to understand something of themselves. Finally, it means that in some sense the topics and resources of social inquiry are the same: the social world is itself constructed in part via the very ideas that researchers employ to understand it (200–1). This is true, in particular, of the types of social research carried on within established social structures, for example, in studying business and administration. The domain of objects investigated is in some measure reproduced by activities according to the very notions used to comprehend it (202). Thus, what C. Wright Mills would later call "bureaucratic" social science could largely restrict itself to processing data with conceptual resources that were themselves operative in the very production of the phenomena being studied.

Critical social theory breaks with that type of approach by, among other things, taking the reflexivity of social inquiry explicitly into account. This entails a challenge to the traditional dichotomies between genesis and justification, justification and application, fact and value, and so forth, which were used to rope off a "neutral" field for social research (208). Critical theory is concerned precisely with the historical and social genesis of the facts it examines and with the social contexts in which its results will have their effects. It stresses that social research is itself a form of social interaction in which the objects of knowledge are potentially subjects of the very same knowledge, and thus that it is willy-nilly a potential factor in changing social relations. Consciously taking up this reflexive relation to social practice, critical social theory expressly aims at becoming a factor in social change by becoming part of the self-consciousness of oppressed social groups. It does not consider the purposes it serves to be external to the context of inquiry.

Through a social-practical reformulation of certain Kantian ideas, Horkheimer could argue that the moral-political orientation of critical social inquiry was not arbitrary but inherently rational. In the framework of the philosophy of consciousness, Kant had argued that reason was at bottom a capacity not for speculation but for freedom. Once we turn our attention from consciousness to culture and society, the privileged status that Western philosophy has generally accorded to knowledge and representation becomes even less plausible. In fact, if knowledge itself is understood to be a social product, the traditional oppositions between theory and practice, fact and value, and the like break down, for there are practical dimensions to any social activity, theorizing included. Translated into social-theoretical terms, the primacy of practical reason means, according to Horkheimer, that an interest in "reasonable conditions of life" is intrinsic to the exercise of our rational capacities. We shall have an opportunity below to consider how he connects this with an interest in a just organization of society.[31] At present it is important to note that this practical concern enters into the very construction of a critical theory and is at work in the research processes informed by the theory. It is, in fact, what lends consistency and coherency to a tradition of thought that accepts the ongoing necessity of adapting its concepts, theories, techniques, and the like to an ever-changing reality. "The transmission of critical theory in as rigorous a fashion as possible is a condition of its historical success. That transmission does not, however, take place via established practices and fixed procedures but via an interest in social change. This interest is aroused ever anew by prevailing injustices, but it must be shaped and guided by the theory and in turn react back upon it" (241).

One can, and Horkheimer sometimes does, formulate the practical interest that guides and shapes critical theory in "pragmatic" terms of striving to reduce suffering and promote happiness. In this formulation, the moral-political ideas that give expression to that interest function only regulatively, not constitutively, that is, they serve to guide and evaluate thought and action and not to represent realized or realizable states of affairs. But too often Horkheimer formulates that interest in terms of the holistic representations with which the Marxist tradition abounds. Thus he readily translates "reasonable conditions of life" into a "rational organization of society" in which an "all-embracing subject" does away with "the opposition between the individual's purposefulness, spontaneity, and rationality, and the processes and relations of social labor on which society is built" (210). The idealist conception of freedom as self-conscious self-determination is thereby projected onto a unified macrosubject of which individuals are harmonious moments. It is against just such "totalizing" representations that postmodernist thinkers have launched their most telling attacks. However, there is no need to construe the sociocultural embodiment of practical reason in those terms. As we shall see, Habermas, who pursues a similar line of thought, rejects that construal as a residue of the "philosophy of consciousness" and focuses instead on the conditions and procedures of democratic pluralism. But here I want to raise again another matter: the usefulness of grand narratives and big pictures.

Sociocultural critique is best thought of as a polymorphic, multi-layered, and multidimensional enterprise. Not all critical work need be or can be done in the same way or at the same level of specificity or generality. Moreover, determining for what purposes and in what contexts different groups occupy the same or different "positions" inevitably involves pragmatic considerations. There is no objective reason why, for certain purposes and in certain contexts, a more universal "we" should not be appropriate. It could be useful, for instance, in attacking the cultural supports of a general order of domination from which numerous groups suffer, or in analyzing the expanding global networks of symbolic and material interchange. Critics who appeal to one notion or another of encapsulated forms of life to deny that in important respects we are all in the same situation are simply living in the past. We do not have first to create a global space; that is already being done, and at breakneck speed.[32] To better understand this process, we have to go beyond local cultural studies and try to comprehend the internationalization of politics and economics, science and technology, information and communication that now affects the *inside* of every local culture.

Cultural criticism is not the self-sufficient, self-enclosed undertaking its more textualistically inclined practitioners sometimes make it appear to be. For obvious reasons, critics located in the humanities tend to foreground the sorts of phenomena they have been trained to identify and analyze and to background everything else. We can use only the tools we have at our disposal. But that need not prevent us from recognizing that such phenomena are embedded in a broader social matrix and from acknowledging the interdependence of "textual" studies with social and cultural studies of various other sorts. One of the broadest goals of a genuinely multidisciplinary research practice would be a "critical theory of the present," that is, a general view of contemporary society, its problems, and its prospects. That is what Horkheimer referred to as a "comprehensive existential judgement," which he delivered in classical Marxist terms (227). Writing in the midst of profound socioeconomic changes, however, he added an important qualifier: owing to the continuous transformation of its object, this is a judgement with an ineliminable historical dimension (239). Thus critical theory had to be understood as an *ongoing* attempt to "reflect a living totality" (238), an ever-renewed effort to comprehend contemporary society from a practically interested point of view. "It is not a metaphysics of history but rather a changing picture of the world that develops in connection with practical efforts to improve it . . . [and that] offers no clear prognosis for historical development."[33] To be sure, Horkheimer was himself convinced that this object would remain essentially the same so long as capitalism was the dominant social formation, and thus that the "essential content" of Marxist political economy would remain valid through all the necessary adaptations and adjustments (238–40). But one need not hold this position to see the value of situating local cultural practices within a larger field of relationships. It is, in fact, not difficult to show that antiholistic critics usually rely on some general view of contemporary society, its tensions, and its tendencies, in conceiving and carrying out their specific interventions. Because these big pictures are seldom openly avowed, they do not get properly scrutinized and thus function largely as sets of unexamined assumptions. To many, this is preferable, it seems, to running the risks of totalizing thought. But again, those are not the only alternatives. Critical theorists can develop and deploy practically interested, theoretically informed, general accounts in a fallibilistic and open manner, that is, without claiming closure. The point is to view big pictures and grand narratives as *ongoing accomplishments*. They are never finished, but have to be constructed, deconstructed, and reconstructed in ever-changing circumstances. If such global accounts are going to play a role in any case, it is better to put them up for discussion from the start.

Locating particular practices in a larger field is one way of gaining distance from them, of not leaving the final say about their significance to participants and their traditions. Critical theorists of very different stripes agree in seeing a need for some such "outsider's" perspective to get beyond shared meanings and their hermeneutic retrieval. Foucault's way of creating distance from the practices we live in, for instance, is to display their "lowly origins" in contingent historical circumstances, to dispel their appearance of self-evident givenness by treating them as the outcome of multiple relations of force. The Frankfurt School approach is also based on a rejection of what Marx characterized as the specific "German ideology" of understanding ideas solely in terms of other ideas. Its guiding principle is that the full significance of ideas can be grasped only by viewing them in the context of the social practices in which they figure, and by studying the genesis, structures, and functions of those practices. And its underlying intention is to transform our self-understanding in ways that affect how we live. Gaining a critical perspective on what is normally taken for granted – for instance, by showing that the genesis of what has heretofore seemed universal and necessary involves contingent relations of force and an arbitrary closing off of alternatives, or that what parades as fair and impartial actually helps to maintain unjustifiable imbalances in social benefits and burdens – can affect the way we act. Ideas and beliefs, values and norms, standards and procedures formerly accepted as purely and simply rational may come to be seen as in the service of particular interests and this may undermine the authority that derives from their presumed rationality. Whether or not this is so, and the extent to which it is so, are not matters of conceptual necessity or theoretical inference but of contingent historical conditions. The practical significance of critical insight varies with the circumstances.

While critical social theory does not take participants' views of their practices as the last word in interpreting and assessing them, it differs from exclusively deconstructionist approaches in taking them seriously, in seeking to engage them in the very process of gaining distance from them. In a word, it treats them dialectically: the dialectical critique of reason does not abstractly negate ideas of reason but seeks critically to appropriate them and to enlist them in the struggle for a better world. Thus, in an essay entitled "Philosophy and Critical Theory" and published in the *Zeitschrift für Sozialforschung* in the same year as Horkheimer's "Traditional and Critical Theory," Herbert Marcuse stressed that idealist and individualist conceptions of reason and rational practice were not *mere* ideology, for they established reason as a critical instance: "The individual was to examine and judge everything given," and this meant that "the concept of reason contained the concept of freedom as well. For such examination and judgement would be meaningless if human beings were not free to act in accordance with their insights."[34] From his perspective, it was precisely the situation-transcending import of ideas of reason – a red flag to deconstructionists – that was their saving grace. Critical theory "opposes making reality into a criterion . . . When truth cannot be realized within the established order, it always appears to the latter as mere utopia. This transcendence speaks not against, but for, its truth."[35] This interest in the "truth content" of ideas, Marcuse went on, distinguished critical theory from the type of strictly contextualist approach of the sociology of knowledge. Research that considers only "the dependent and limited nature of consciousness" betrays critical theory's "interest in the liberation of human beings." That interest "binds it to certain ancient truths" – "universal propositions whose progressive impetus derives precisely from their universality . . . for they claim that everyone . . . should be rational, free, and happy." In a society that "gives the lie to all these universals . . . adherence to universality is more important than its philosophical destruction."[36] The area of tension between an established social order and the ideas of reason it relies on is just where dialectical critique drives its wedge.

In the same spirit, Horkheimer urged critical theorists not to surrender such ideas to the regressive forces who used them to justify their privileged positions and betrayed them whenever it was in their interest to do so. They should, instead, critically reappropriate them for progressive purposes: "The battle cries of the Enlightenment and of the French Revolution are valid now more than ever. The dialectical critique of the world borne along by them consists precisely in showing that they have retained rather than lost their actuality . . . Politics should not abandon those demands, but realize them . . . not, however, by clinging in utopian fashion to historically conditioned definitions of them, but in accordance with their meaning. The content of these ideas is not eternal but subject to historical change . . . because the human impulses that demand something better take [historically] different forms."[37]

The context-transcendence of ideas of reason harbors not only a utopian but also a subversive potential, for claims to unconditional validity are permanently exposed to criticism from all sides. Understood in this way, they point in the opposite direction from those metaphysical representations that occupy deconstructionist critics, namely toward an ongoing critique of dogmatism, bias, and self-deception in their many forms. The tension between the real and the ideal that their context-transcending import builds into the constructions of social life marks a normative surplus of meaning that critical theorists can draw upon in seeking to transcend and transform the limits of their situations. In short, the dialectical critique of reason is "internal" rather than "total."

One can even question whether the latter option is really available, for we are always and inescapably participants in social life before, during, and after any critical studies in which we might engage. There is no extramundane standpoint from which we can set our social world as a whole at a distance. It is thus not surprising that would-be total critics of Western "logocentrism" invariably rely on the same idealizing presuppositions regarding meaning, reference, truth, logic, and the like that they seek to undercut, and that radical critics of modern rationalism continually draw on assumptions specific to the modern worldview, such as the disenchantment of the world and the possibility of reflectively questioning inherited beliefs and values, gaining critical distance from traditional roles and norms, and challenging ascribed individual and group identities. Nor is it surprising that the values which underlie their criticisms typically include a host of distinctively modern orientations toward pluralism, diversity, tolerance, human dignity, equal respect, and the like. There must, then, be a reconstructive as well as a deconstructive side to any critique of reason, for it will be important to identify and analyze those presuppositions to which participants in the discourse of modernity either have no alternative at all, or none they would want to defend.

## 1.3   The *Aufhebung* of Philosophy

In "Philosophy and Critical Theory" Marcuse developed variations upon the familiar theme of continuing-through-transforming the critique of reason.[38] "Reason," he wrote, "is the fundamental category of philosophical thought," the category by which "it has bound itself to human destiny" (135). In classical philosophy it "represents the highest human potential" (136). In the modern period, it comes to be represented as self-conscious self-determination, that is, as the freedom to act on one's own insight and judgement. "With this concept of freedom as reason," Marcuse wrote, echoing Marx, "philosophy seems to reach its limit. What remains outstanding to the realization of reason is not a philosophical task" (137). Any direct leap to political practice, however, would be a potentially dangerous short circuit, for there was a theoretical dimension of the outstanding task. The philosophical concept of free rational action was seriously inadequate, and not merely by way of accidental deficiencies. Rather, its inadequacies bore the character of systematic distortions that had to be understood and explained. And because the distortions in question were linked to the role that conceptions of reason and freedom played in the reproduction of the social order, understanding and explaining them required some form of critical social inquiry.

Marcuse did not mean by this simply to reduce individualistic and idealistic conceptions of reason and freedom to ideology. They were more than that; they had a truth content that critique had to preserve even while transforming. "In the bourgeois epoch the reality of reason became the task that the free individual was to fulfill . . . The material conditions of life, however, allotted freedom to reason only in pure thought and will . . . If reason means shaping life according to people's free decisions on the basis of their knowledge, then the demand for reason henceforth means the creation of a social organization in which individuals can collectively regulate their lives in accordance with their needs" (141–2). With this insight, philosophy's interest in pure reason becomes the interest of critical social theory in historically embodied reason. This interest can be pursued in several different but interrelated ways: by critically deconstructing distorted concepts of reason and freedom that serve as cultural supports of orders of unfreedom, injustice, unhappiness; by preserving the truth content of traditional ideas through reconstructing them in social–practical terms; and, of course, by using both critical and constructive ideas in the struggle against inhuman conditions of existence. And this is an interest intrinsic to reason, for practical reason is by its nature oriented toward free rational action and against what contradicts it. Thus the concept of ideology is not only a theoretical but also a practical–political concept: it is internally related to an interest in changing social conditions in which people are not free to live their lives in the light of their own experience and judgement and in accordance with their own perception of their needs. In this sense, critical social theory gives a "human form" to philosophical ideals and "incorporates" them into the struggle for a better world (142).

The fact that such ideals are not actually realized and appear to be merely utopian does not speak against them, in Marcuse's view: "The utopian element was long the only progressive element in philosophy" (143). To be sure, critical theory is not interested in *merely* utopian ideals, but in ones which, however unrealizable in the present order of things, represent actual potentials of social development. This interest in identifying potentials in the present for a more reasonable form of life in the future is built into the categories of critical social theory: they present not a view from nowhere but from the standpoint of practical reason. And this, Marcuse explains, is what distinguishes critical theory from the sociology of knowledge: it does not *reduce* philosophical ideas to social conditions. It does, to be sure, analyze "the specific social conditions at the root of philosophy's inability to pose the problem [of reason] in a more comprehensive way" (149–50). It does so, however, not in the interest of skeptically debunking all claims to truth, but in that of preserving through reconstructing truths that past generations struggled to attain:

> That man is a rational being, that this being requires freedom, and that happiness is his highest good are all universal propositions whose progressive impetus derives precisely from their universality. Universality gives them an almost revolutionary character, for they claim that all, and not merely this or that particular person should be rational, free, and happy. In a society whose reality gives the lie to all these universals, philosophy cannot make them concrete. Under such conditions, adherence to universality is more important than its philosophical destruction. (152–3)

In a "Postscript" to Marcuse's essay, Horkheimer endorsed the idea that critical social theory could be understood as inheriting philosophy's concern with the life of reason.[39] Its defining insight, he agreed, is that the possibility of giving reasonable form to individual existence depends upon the possibility of instituting reasonable conditions of social life, and thus that philosophy's concern with the life of reason has to be continued at the level of social theory. Like Marcuse, Horkheimer characterized the object of the practical interest guiding critical social inquiry as a "free, self-determining society," which he went on to specify in terms of "real agreement" in a "real democracy," whose overriding aim is "the happiness of all individuals" in a "world that satisfies the needs and powers of human beings."[40] Or, as he also put it, "concern for the abolition of injustice . . . is the materialist content of the idealist concept of reason."[41] This general strategy of linking a deindividualized conception of practical reason to the theory of justice is familiar today in the versions of neo-Kantianism developed by Rawls, Habermas, and others. A bridge from the 1930s discussion to the contemporary discussions can conveniently be constructed from elements of Horkheimer's critique of Kantian ethics in a 1933 essay entitled "Materialism and Morality."[42]

Horkheimer stresses that morality and moral theory in their current senses are historical phenomena that have to be understood in historical terms. On his account, their characteristic opposition between duty and interest, the universal and the particular, is an expression of the very real tension in capitalist society between the possessive individualism required to thrive in a market economy and a concern for the general welfare which, invisible-hand notions notwithstanding, is ill-served by market mechanisms. Against the background of the inequitable distribution of misery and happiness, burdens and pleasures, poverty and wealth that resulted from capitalist development, the move from traditional ethics to rationalist moralities of the Kantian type can be seen as shifting the burden of deep-seated social tensions to the site of the individual conscience. It is the isolated moral subject who must struggle to overcome the opposition between self-interest and the general interest, precisely by renouncing the former in the name of the latter. The spiritualized universalism that commands in the moral domain is just the other face of the narrow egoism that reigns in the market-place. It is, Horkheimer argues, just this transposition of sociostructural problems into the inner lives of individuals that is the ideological function of morality. For there is no possibility of reducing the tension between individual goods and the common good through the moral intentions of individual agents acting within the given institutional framework. A social-structural problem requires a social-structural response, which Horkheimer characterizes generally as the effective incorporation of individuals into collective decision-making processes.

To say that modern moral theory in its paradigmatic Kantian form is a contingent historical construction that has to be understood genea-logically is, for Horkheimer, not to say that it is *merely* ideology or false consciousness and should therefore be dismantled without re-mainder. It possesses a truth content as well, which it is the task of his dialectical critique to free from its ideological trappings, transform, and retain in a more adequate conception of the relation between the universal and the particular. The idea of their reconciliation that Kant elaborated under the title of "the highest good" could not, as he evidently saw, be even approximately realized within the existing order of society. In projecting its realization into the noumenal be-yond, he gave distorted expression to the truth that morality impels us to transcend the social order which gave birth to it, an order in tension with the very idea of practical reason to which it appeals for justifica-tion. It is precisely the utopian element in Kant's idea of a perfected order in which the conflict between self-interest and the general interest are overcome that dialectical critique takes as the point of transition to its reconstructive movement.

Horkheimer never discussed at any length the institutions and pro-cedures that might effectively allow individuals to have a say in the collective decision-making processes that were to replace the blind operation of market forces. He was much more concerned with re-centering the eudemonistic element of ethics that had been margin-alized in moral theory. But he repeatedly insisted that the ideals of freedom, justice, and equality not be surrendered to the regressive forces that had expropriated them to justify unnecessary suffering. Rather, they were to be reclaimed and deployed in the struggle against the causes of human misery. "Dialectical critique [is] borne along by them . . . [They] are nothing but the isolated traits of a rational society as anticipated in morality. Politics should not abandon these demands but realize them."[43] But first they had to be freed from their moralistic confines by shifting theoretical attention away from private efforts by isolated individuals to subdue unruly inclinations and toward collect-ive efforts by social groups to transform unjust relations. Though guided by universal ideals, the public politics that was thus to reclaim center stage from private morality could not cling to unchanging formulations of them. Their content was "not eternal but subject to historical change," they took different forms in different historical circumstances.[44] That is, the concrete meaning or content of abstract ideas and principles had to be continuously reinscribed into ever-changing contexts. This general commitment to political and social ideals that are universal in import but require ongoing recontextualiza-tion is common to most critical social theorists. But another element in Horkheimer's *Aufhebung* of Kantian morality distinguishes his position strongly from the one later elaborated by Habermas: he replaces Kant's "fact of pure reason" with an "ungrounded feeling" of compassion for suffering humankind.

Morality, he wrote, "admits of no grounding, either through intuition or through argument. Rather, it represents a frame of mind. To describe the latter, to make comprehensible its personal conditions and the mechanisms for transmitting it from generation to generation is the business of psychology."[45] At its center, Horkheimer ventured, is a moral sentiment or feeling [*Gefühl*] directed toward all persons as potential members of a happy human race, to their needs and capacities, to the alleviation of their suffering and the development of their powers. To this moral sentiment "it appears that all living beings have a claim to happiness, for which it asks no justification or grounds."[46] The specific form this sentiment takes in our day, "when the poverty of humanity cries out in such contradiction to its potential wealth," is sympathy or compassion [*Mitleid*].[47] It expresses itself in a "solidarity" with the wretched of the earth that motivates the critical theorist to pursue a politics aimed at realizing-while-transforming the universal ideals mentioned above.[48]

Notwithstanding the attractions of this way of avoiding problems of "grounding,"[49] Horkheimer's account creates as many problems as it solves. Granted that feelings of indignation, compassion, love, solidarity, and the like neither need nor admit of philosophical grounding in pure practical reason, the issue remains whether they are susceptible to rational criticism and justification in any sense. The fact that questions of the sorts: Sympathy with whom? Solidarity with which side? Indignation at what? can be, are, and should be repeatedly raised and critically considered suggests that the sharp split between irrational feelings and rational discourse is another untenable opposition that has to be broken down. To drop the idea of *pure* rational motivation is not *ipso facto* to deny that motives can be elaborated, criticized, defended, and shaped by reasons, particularly when these are presented in the context of communicative exchanges with other agents moved by similar or different motives. Moreover, as Horkheimer himself is at pains to insist, psychic dispositions have to be viewed in relation to established social and cultural patterns. It is in this vein, for instance, that he explains the consciousness of a pure rational ought, the feeling of being bound by absolute commands, as a sublime form of internalized social compulsion. Thus, he cannot treat the psychic disposition he calls moral feeling as an independent variable prior to and unaffected by social relations. Why should we accord such special status to a feeling for the feelings of all other human beings or an interest in the generalizability of interests? Are they and the corresponding universalist ideals any more than mere curiosities of particular historical cultures?

One source of these problems is Horkheimer's jump from the absence of *pure* rational – that is, non-empirical – motivations for morality to the absence of *any* rational justification of its basic commands. A related source is the tendency he has to equate rational justification with ultimate grounding of some sort. As we cannot have the latter, we must do without the former as well. If, however, Horkheimer had introduced into his discussion of morality the non-foundationalist sense of rational justification he appealed to in his discussion of truth, this equation could not have been sustained. As explained above, he analyzed the validation of truth claims in terms of demonstrating their rational acceptability, not absolutely, but with respect to "the available means of knowledge" and in the fallibilistic awareness that these might well change. Had he adopted a similar approach to justice claims, he could have avoided the pitfall of equating rational warrants with a priori foundations, and thus the necessity of choosing between reasons and feelings. He was, of course, not the last to fall into that crowded pit.

Adopting a more pragmatic approach to moral justification would also have fit quite well with Horkheimer's historical account, in connection with his analysis of modern ideologies, of how the appeal to generally acceptable reasons comes to play an ever greater role in legitimating social orders. With the disappearance of value-imbued cosmologies, the privatization of religion, and the growing disenchantment of the world, it is increasingly the only form of justification available. As a result, it becomes more and more difficult to convince exploited and oppressed groups that they deserve their suffering and that their tormentors deserve whatever degrees of power, privilege, and wealth they happen to enjoy. The early modern ideologies that once accomplished this improbable task have been and continue to be relentlessly shredded with the sharp tools of criticism. This increasingly leaves contemporary societies with very little else to appeal to in legitimating their laws, institutions, and policies than the free and reasoned agreement of their members. But is this state of affairs anything more than an arbitrary outcome of contingent historical processes? What, in particular, does it have to do with practical reason?

Once we get beyond the Cartesian-Hobbesian paradigm of the solitary subject as the proper framework for analyzing the structures of thought and action, once we acknowledge their intrinsically social character, agreements freely arrived at on the basis of considering reasons pro and con come to be central to rationality in theory and in practice. This has been argued in respect to truth claims from Pierce to Putnam and Habermas and in respect to justice claims from Mead to Rawls and Habermas. Whatever problems there may be with specific proposals, it is becoming increasingly difficult to think of plausible alternatives to one form or another of communicative rationality. If some such approach to practical reason could be sustained, then the gap that Horkheimer saw between ungroundable feelings of compassion and rational justification of universal ideals would not be as unbridgeable as it seemed. One could then argue *both* in a neo-Kantian vein that democratic forms of decision-making best accord with the communicative structure of practical reason *and* in a neo-Aristotelian or neo-Hegelian vein that the dispositions of character and motivation needed to sustain democratic institutions and practices can be reliably reproduced only in certain types of sociocultural settings. It is just this sort of dual-track program that Habermas has attempted to develop in his theory of communicative action.

## NOTES

1　Immanuel Kant, *Critique of Pure Reason*, trans. Norman Kemp Smith (New York: St. Martin's Press, 1961), p. 9.
2　Ibid., pp. 100–1.
3　Michel Foucault, "Space, Knowledge, and Power," in Paul Rabinow (ed.), *The Foucault Reader* (New York: Pantheon Books, 1984), p. 249.
4　Michel Foucault, "What is Enlightenment?," in *The Foucault Reader*, p. 45.
5　Ibid., p. 46.
6　See, for instance, "The Political Technology of Individuals," in Luther Martin *et al.* (eds), *Technologies of the Self* (Amherst: The University of Massachusetts Press, 1988), p. 145, where he speaks of a "formal ontology of truth."
7　I shall not discuss the quite different version of critical theory, more Nietzschean in spirit, propounded by Horkheimer and Adorno in the 1940s, particularly in their *Dialectic of Enlightenment*, trans. John Cumming (New York: Continuum, 1972). In the case of Horkheimer, on whom I shall be focussing, the changes took place gradually, after the National Socialists came to power and the Institute was moved first to Geneva and then to New York. They are already evident in his 1937 essay on "Traditional and Critical Theory," trans. Matthew J. O'Connell, in Max Horkheimer, *Critical Theory* (New York: Herder and Herder, 1972), pp. 188–243, and in his 1939 piece on "The Social Function of Philosophy," also in *Critical Theory*, pp. 253–72, both of which I shall discuss below, but without noting the shifts that are underway. In general, I shall

not be attempting to present a full and balanced interpretation of the early Frankfurt School, or even of the early Horkheimer. I shall merely select and develop points that strike me as especially relevant to contemporary debates concerning the critique of impure reason.

8  Max Horkheimer, "The State of Contemporary Social Philosophy and the Tasks of an Institute for Social Research," trans. Peter Wagner, in Stephan Bonner and Douglas Kellner (eds), *Critical Theory and Society* (New York: Routledge, 1989), p. 31 and p. 36. Translation altered. Henceforth, existing translations will be altered as required for consistency or accuracy, without special note of the fact.

9  Max Horkheimer, "Zum Rationalismusstreit in der gegenwärtigen Philosopie," in Horkheimer, *Kritische Theorie*, 2 vols. (Frankfurt: Fischer, 1968), vol. 1, p. 145.

10 Ibid., p. 149.

11 Max Horkheimer, "Ein neuer Ideologiebegriff?," in V. Meja and N. Stehr (eds), *Der Streit um die Wissenssoziologie*, 2 vols. (Frankfurt: Suhrkamp, 1982), vol. 2, p. 485.

12 Ibid., pp. 485–6.

13 Max Horkheimer, "On the Problem of Truth," in Andrew Arato and Eike Gebhardt (eds), *The Essential Frankfurt School Reader* (New York: Urizen, 1978), pp. 407–43.

14 Ibid., p. 421.

15 "The Social Function of Philosophy," p. 257.

16 Ibid., p. 261.

17 Ibid., p. 265.

18 Ibid., p. 268.

19 Ibid., p. 269.

20 Ibid., p. 264.

21 "On the Problem of Truth," p. 418.

22 "Zum Rationalismusstreit," p. 150.

23 Max Horkheimer, "Materialism and Metaphysics," in *Critical Theory*, pp. 11–12.

24 Ibid., p. 13.

25 "Ein neuer Ideologiebegriff?", p. 487.

26 "Zum Rationalismusstreit," pp. 158ff.

27 These and other related weaknesses in Horkheimer's conception of critical theory have been spelled out repeatedly, even by theorists working within the Frankfurt School tradition. For recent discussions see Axel Honneth, *The Critique of Power*, trans. K. Baynes (Cambridge, MA: The MIT Press, 1991), and Seyla Benhabib, Wolfgang Bonss, and John McCole (eds), *On Max Horkheimer* (Cambridge, MA: The MIT Press, 1993). See also the collection of critical essays edited by Alfred Schmidt and Norbert Altwicker, *Max Horkheimer heute: Werk und Wirkung* (Frankfurt: Fischer, 1986).

28 I argued this for the last three in part I of *Ideals and Illusions: On Reconstruction and Deconstruction in Contemporary Critical Theory* (Cambridge, MA: The MIT Press, 1991), pp. 11–123.

29  It goes without saying that "philosophical" critique carried on as a form
    of sociocultural analysis typically will not be as *directly* related to polit-
    ical practice – as timely, situation-specific, action-oriented, and so forth
    – as some less academic forms of cultural politics, or even as some other
    academic forms of cultural criticism. Dealing as it does with the most
    general, abstract, and thus situation-non-specific of our cultural resources,
    its analyses will not be tailored to some one particular audience – which
    is not to say that it is aimed at no audience – nor, typically, will the
    impact of its results be restricted to one particular discipline – which is
    not to say that it floats free of all disciplinary settings.

30  See note 7. Page references to this essay will appear in parentheses in the
    text.

31  On p. 213 of "Traditional and Critical Theory" he says that this interest is
    "immanent in human labor." I shall not be pursuing that line of thought,
    however, but the one developed earlier in his 1933 essay, "Materialism
    and Morality," trans. G. Frederick Hunter and John Torpey, *Telos* 69
    (1986): 85–118.

32  I shall take up this point in section 3.4.

33  "Materialism and Morality," p. 114.

34  Herbert Marcuse, "Philosophy and Critical Theory," trans. Jeremy J. Shapiro,
    in *Negations* (Boston: Beacon, 1968), p. 136.

35  Ibid., p. 143.

36  Ibid., pp. 152–3.

37  "Materialism and Morality," p. 108.

38  See note 34. Page references to this essay will appear in parentheses in the
    text.

39  Max Horkheimer, "Postscript," in *Critical Theory*, pp. 244–52.

40  Ibid., pp. 248–250.

41  "Traditional and Critical Theory," p. 242.

42  See note 31.

43  "Materialism and Morality," p. 108.

44  Ibid., p. 108.

45  Ibid., p. 104.

46  Ibid., p. 106.

47  Ibid., p. 106.

48  Ibid., p. 107.

49  Compare Richard Rorty's rejection of any sort of grounding for morality
    beyond compassion for and solidarity with those who suffer, in *Contin-
    gency, Irony, and Solidarity* (Cambridge, UK: Cambridge University Press,
    1989), and my critique of it in *Ideals and Illusions*, pp. 35–42.

# 2

# Reason in a Postmetaphysical Age

The selective interpretation of Horkheimer offered in chapter 1 had the limited aim of appropriating for present purposes some basic elements of his idea of a critical theory. There was no attempt to illuminate all the different sides of that idea. The focus was on a single aspect: continuing the philosophical critique of reason in the medium of social, cultural, and historical studies. But even after trimming and pruning the less viable parts of Horkheimer's program, we are left with a conception of critique too overgrown to survive in the contemporary philosophical climate. The source of the problem is the residue of the philosophy of consciousness present in Western Marxism from the start. This has regularly given rise to exaggerated ideas of reason and its realization which have to be cut down to proper size if critical social theory is to remain a live option. The prototype of those ideas is Hegel's attempt to reconcile reason and reality via the model of self-consciousness: spirit has to recognize its other as itself in its otherness. In Marx's *Aufhebung* this took the form of a social, laboring subject who externalized itself in a world that was of its own making but was not a free conscious product, a self-objectification of essential human powers. Rather, it was a distorted, alienated world that could be reappropriated only through critical-revolutionary activity. This figure of thought is implicitly at work in Horkheimer's account of the realization of reason in terms of a unified social subject bringing about a rational organization of society. And it is just this conception of reason as the relation-to-self of a societal macrosubject encompassing all individual subjects that deconstructionists have found so objectionable in the Hegelian-Marxist tradition. But in rightly criticizing this and other totalizing conceptions of reason, they have often gone to the opposite extreme of disempowering ideas of reason altogether. In chapter 2 I want first to indicate, very briefly, the sorts of problems encountered by theorists who take that overly negative tack,[1] and then to consider the conception of communicative reason with which Habermas tries to steer a course between the two extremes. In chapter 3 I shall attempt to sketch a more pragmatic version of that conception.

## 2.1   Deconstructionist Critiques of Reason

In *Philosophy and the Mirror of Nature* Richard Rorty proposed an "epistemological behaviorism" that views justification purely as a social phenomenon. Understanding knowledge becomes a matter of understanding the social practices in which we justify beliefs, and explicating rationality a matter of providing thick ethnographic accounts of established rational practices. We have to resist, as he puts it, "the urge to see social practices of justification as more than just such practices."[2] Instead, we should explain "rationality and epistemic authority by reference to what society lets us say," and treat truth as "conformity to the norms of the day."[3] This sort of radical historicism lands him in familiar self-referential contradictions. If he is proposing notions of reason and truth relative-to-a-framework, then he cannot claim for himself any framework-neutral metaperspective from which to depict – in absolute terms, as it were – such framework-relative truths. The God's-eye view implicitly claimed by this type of cultural relativism cannot exist, by its own account.[4]

Rorty subsequently sought to remove any ambiguity on this point by embracing a "frank ethnocentrism" which "divides the human race into people to whom one must justify one's beliefs" – one's *ethnos* – "and the others."[5] We can, he elaborates, only debate with people with whom we have enough in common to make discussion fruitful; and any justification offered in such discussions will have to rely on already shared understandings, beliefs, values, criteria, and so on. This approach, he thinks, lets the air of transcendence out of philosophically inflated ideas of reason and truth without claiming for itself any standpoint outside the world, that is to say, outside "our" world. But it leads directly to another, equally formidable set of problems. Rorty's *ethnos* is heir to centuries of distinguishing between appearance and reality, doxa and episteme, prejudice and reason, custom and morality, convention and justice, and so on. To justify his beliefs to *us*, he cannot simply appeal to communal agreement, established conventions, or the like. If being ethnocentric means using the forms of justification prevalent in our culture, then, in many pursuits at least, it will entail constructing arguments that claim to be valid transculturally; for that is what we have long been up to in areas such as philosophy, science, and morality, where one is supposed precisely not to accept views merely because they are prevalent. For us, then, frank ethnocentrism would involve the paradoxical endorsement of just the sort of universalism it is meant to undercut. One obvious lesson here is that the ideas of reason that Rorty wants to purge are deeply embedded in our culture. Dislodging them is less a matter of frank self-acceptance than of radical self-transformation.

Michel Foucault was clear on this point.[6] His genealogies seek to delegitimize such ideas by displaying their "lowly origins" in contingent historical circumstances, revealing them to be deeply implicated in multiple relations of force. He resolutely displaces the participant's perspective with an externalist perspective from which the claims of reason are not engaged but observed at work in the constellations of power in which they function. "Each society," he writes, "has its regime of truth,"[7] and genealogy is interested precisely in how we govern ourselves through its production. Thus it directs our attention to the rules, prescriptions, and procedures that are constitutive of epistemic practices, to the relations of asymmetry and hierarchy they encode, to the ways in which they include and exclude, make central and peripheral. This shift in focus makes us aware that there is something like a politics of truth already at this level of analysis: people and practices get valorized or stigmatized, rewarded or punished, dismissed or vested with authority on this basis. Foucault also examines the relations of theoretical discourses to the practical discourses in which they are applied by psychologists, physicians, judges, administrators, social workers, and the like, as well as to the institutional practices with which they are interwoven in asylums, hospitals, prisons, schools, administrative bureaucracies, and the like. In areas of inquiry ranging from psychiatry and medicine to penology and population studies, he uncovers the feedback relations that obtain between the power that is exercised over people to extract data from and about them, on the one hand, and the effects of power that attach to the qualified experts and licensed professionals who possess and deploy that knowledge, on the other.

Foucault's attempt to disempower ideas of reason by totally objectivating them is no less involved in performative contradictions than Rorty's very different approach. The activity of the genealogist is as culturally situated as that of the frank ethnocentrist. We can't be observers without at the same time being participants. That is to say, we can make a topic of our culture only by simultaneously drawing upon it as a resource. This is evident in the case of genealogy. In the first place, Foucault's analyses of truth as an effect of power themselves lay claim to truth. Admitting, as he did, to a "happy positivism" does not resolve the contradiction, for describing what a given group takes to be good grounds is itself a normatively structured activity that involves appeal to good grounds. Furthermore, as a number of commentators have pointed out, the unmistakably moral overtones of Foucault's account of our "disciplinary society," with its "docile bodies" and "confessing animals," reveal its never acknowledged, but always operative, normative presuppositions to be derived from the humanist tradition he is attacking.[8] Finally, in his critique of the subject-centeredness of modern Western culture, Foucault swings to the opposite extreme of hypostatizing wholes – grids, regimes, networks, *dispositifs*, and the like – while treating the individual merely as one of their effects. But he cannot simply drop the conceptual framework of agency and accountability that is ingrained in our usual understanding of social practices without causing problems for his own enterprise. Who practices genealogical analysis? What does it require of them? What promise does it hold out to them? If the subject is nothing but an effect of power, how are we to understand the type of reflection that takes the form of genealogy? Foucault writes as if his genealogies advanced self-understanding and promoted self-transformation. But no sense can be made of this without some notion of accountable subjects who can achieve gains in self-consciousness with a liberating effect on their lives. This is no doubt one reason why, in the last years of his life, Foucault stopped insisting that he wanted to bring the Enlightenment to an end and begin exploring ways in which to continue by transforming it.[9]

Jacques Derrida has never been under the illusion that he could place himself wholly outside of or beyond the logocentrism of Western culture. Deconstruction is not a matter of simply renouncing ideas of reason but of interrogating them, disrupting and displacing them, revealing them to be illusions that are so deep-seated as to be irremovable.[10] To begin with, it involves a radical decentering of the subject in relation to language. As signification is always a function of largely unconscious differential relations among signifiers, speakers, hearers, situations, contexts, and the like, we are never completely masters of what we say. Beyond any present meaning lies the absent, unspoken, unthought network of conditions, presuppositions, and implications on which it depends. As a result, our meaning always escapes any unitary conscious grasp we may have of it, for language, as "writing," inevitably harbors the possibility of an endless "dissemination" of sense, an indefinite multiplicity of recontextualizations and reinterpretations.

Philosophy is a kind of writing that is essentially predicated on denying all of this, that attempts to detach meanings from the "relational and differential tissue" in which they are always enmeshed.[11] Throughout its history, it has tried one device after another to freeze the play of signifiers: ideal, univocal meanings (Forms), an ultimate referent or "transcendental signified" (Being), clear and distinct ideas in self-conscious minds, absolute knowledge, the logical essence of language, and so on – all calculated to call a halt to the dissemination of meaning at the borders of this or that closed system of truth. But such closure is impossible; philosophy cannot transcend its medium. The claim to have done so always relies on excluding, ignoring, marginalizing, or assimilating whatever escapes the grids of intelligibility imposed on the movement of *différance*. And this repression of what does not fit inevitably leaves its effects, in the forms of paradoxes, internal contradictions, and systematic incoherencies, which it is the task of critical analysis to bring to light. Thus deconstruction ceaselessly undermines the pretense to theoretical mastery, the dream of a definitive grasp of basic meanings and truths, the illusion of a pure reason that could gain control over its own conditions. In Derrida's words: "It inaugurates the destruction, not the demolition but the de-sedimenting, the de-construction, of all of the significations that have their source in the logos. Particularly the signification of *truth*."[12]

This kind of totalized critique of reason has, of course, to deal with the paradoxes of self-referentiality that inevitably follow in its wake. How can one deconstruct all ideas of reason without at the same time relying on them, at least tacitly? One of Derrida's responses to this dilemma is his well-known "double gesture" or "double writing" which combines, roughly speaking, internalist and externalist tactics, uncovering implicit presuppositions in conflict with an explicit problematic *and* placing oneself outside that problematic. The difficulty for Derrida is that the former tactic does not escape the orbit of logocentrism, for it is just what philosophers have been up to all along. It is in fact the heart of the dialectic, as Derrida is aware: "Here one risks ceaselessly confirming, consolidating, relifting [*relever*, the word Derrida uses to render Hegel's *aufheben*] at an always more certain depth that which one allegedly deconstructs."[13] Nor can the other tactic, that of "changing terrain," ever amount to an absolute break with logocentrism, as Derrida acknowledges: "We can pronounce not a single deconstructive proposition which has not already had to slip into the form, the logic, and the implicit postulation of precisely what it seeks to contest."[14]

One of the explanations Derrida offers for this inevitability is interestingly reminiscent of Kant's account of the illusionary potential of ideas of reason. "Everyday language," Derrida tells us, "is not innocent or neutral . . . it carries with it . . . presuppositions inseparable from metaphysics, which, although little attended to, are knotted into a system."[15] He goes on to explain that these presuppositions are "not an accidental prejudice, but rather a kind of structural lure, what Kant would have called a transcendental illusion. The latter is modified according to the language, the era, the culture." Western metaphysics, he concludes, is "a powerful systematization of this illusion."[16] Thus Derrida seems to hold, like Kant, that ideas of reason built into thought/language inevitably give rise to illusions that we can, with difficulty, detect but never cômpletely dispel. It is those illusions, enhanced and systematized, which make up Western logocentrism. The difference from Kant is that he develops no positive, non-metaphysical employment of such ideas. And this inevitably lands him in familiar performative contradictions whenever he turns to discuss specific social and political problems. In such contexts he implicitly relies on just the sorts of ideas of reason that he elsewhere subverts.[17] Confronted with this apparent inconsistency, Derrida has acknowledged that, though such ideas are never guaranteed absolutely, they do have a role to play in "pragmatically determined situations."[18] Indeed, he allows that "norms of minimal intelligibility" belong to "the requirements of all culture."[19] The deconstructionist point is only that what has been constructed can be dismantled, every contextualization is open to recontextualization. The values of "objectivity" and "truth," for instance, "impose themselves within a context which is extremely vast, old, powerfully established, stabilized or rooted in a network of conventions (for instance, those of language) and yet still remains a context."[20] With these remarks, Derrida points in the direction of a pragmatics of communication. But he persists in his one-sidedly negative treatment of the idealizing presuppositions of meaning: whatever has been constructed can be deconstructed, destabilized, subverted. That may be, but by the same token it could also be reconstructed, reconfirmed, renewed. Derrida never develops this side of things, however.

There is marked tendency for "postmetaphysical" thinkers to engage in metaphysics of a negative sort, that is, to remain at the level of metaphysics in seeking to disrupt and displace it. When that happens, one set of hypostatizations gets traded in for another: the one for the many, the universal for the particular, identity for difference, reason for the other of reason, the structures of thought for the infrastructures of thought, the logical essence of language for the heterological essence of language, and so on. A common feature of these negative metaphysics is an abstract negation of the conceptual apparatus of rationalist individualism. The individual gets represented as thoroughly submerged in some whole – language, culture, history, *Seinsgeschick*, *différance*, power, or the like – and the movement of the whole is seen as governed by sub- or supra-personal forces beyond the reach of reason. As Horkheimer remarked in the 1930s, global contextualism of this sort, which is just the flip-side of rationalist individualism, is practically as well as theoretically debilitating. While it is true that rationalist accounts of reason, truth, autonomy, justice, and so forth stand in need of criticism, merely generating scepticism with regard to them risks disempowering critical reason altogether. Moreover, trading in grand narratives of progress for equally one-sided *Verfallsgeschichten* of Nietzschean or Heideggerian provenance mires thought in various abstract negations. Fixing on technocratization, bureaucratization, normalization, and so on tends to make invisible the hard-won gains in civil, political, social, and human rights – not to mention the positive fruits of science and technology.

If we adopt a more pragmatic approach, we can appreciate both aspects of ideas of reason: their potential for misuse and their irreplaceable function in cooperative social interaction. Under their regulative aegis, the claims we raise in communicating are intrinsically related to reasons that can be offered pro and con. The role of warranting and contesting reasons is in turn tied to the ability of competent subjects to accept and reject them, to weigh and revise them, to originate and criticize them. It is just this that fades from sight in the globalizing views we have been considering. Rather than appearing as the simultaneously dependent and independent moments of this process that they are, accountable agents get transformed into cultural dopes, nodal points in grids of power, effects of the play of *différance*, or the like. Rational criticism and the learning processes that feed on it appear to be either events of entirely local significance or incomprehensible shifts in horizons of meanings. The potential for arriving at uncoerced agreement on the basis of reasons open to intersubjective assessment – that is, the potential for reason – gets downgraded to a capacity to serve as carriers of the dominant social and cultural forms.

Exclusively deconstructionist approaches fail to appreciate that the unconditionality of ideas of reason harbors not only a dogmatic but a subversive potential: context-transcendent claims to validity are permanently exposed to criticism from all sides. Postmodernist critique is itself unintelligible without this, that is, without the supposition that the received views it criticizes claim a validity transcending the contexts in which they were put forward. Understood pragmatically, then, the unconditionality of validity claims *also* runs counter to what its postmodernist critics suppose – toward the ongoing critique of dogmatism, error, and self-deception in all their forms. The tension between the real and the ideal it builds into the construction of social facts represents an immanent potential for criticism that actors can draw upon in seeking to transcend and transform the limits of their situations. This "normative surplus" of meaning, which points beyond what we agree to here and now, is, as Habermas once put it, "a thorn in the flesh of social reality"[21]

## 2.2   Communication and Idealization

In his theory of communicative action Habermas attempts to identify and reconstruct social-practical analogues of Kant's ideas of reason. They appear there as *pragmatic presuppositions* of communication. As noted, this has the effect of relocating the Kantian opposition between the real and the ideal *within* the domain of social practice. Cooperative interaction is seen to be structured around ideas of reason which are neither fully constitutive in the Platonic sense nor merely regulative in the Kantian sense. As *idealizing suppositions* we cannot avoid making while engaged in processes of mutual understanding, they are *actually effective* in organizing communication and at the same time *counterfactual* in ways that point beyond the limits of actual situations. As a result, social-practical ideas of reason are both "immanent" in and "transcendent" to practices constitutive of forms of life. It might be helpful here to provide preliminary, rough indications of a few such ideas.

Habermas agrees with Harold Garfinkel in rejecting depictions of social agents as "cultural dopes" who simply act in compliance with preestablished patterns.[22] Such models of social action systematically ignore the agents' own understanding of social structure and their reflexive use of it. He offers an alternative account in which we orient our behavior to shared schemes of interpretation and expectation, attributing knowledge of them to one another, and holding each other accountable in terms of them. We use that knowledge to analyze, manage, and transform the very situations in which we are involved. Accordingly, in normal social interaction we reciprocally impute practical rationality to interaction partners, credit them with knowing what they are doing and why they are doing it, view their conduct as under their control and done for some purpose or reason known to them, and thus hold them responsible for it. Although this *supposition* of rational agency is frequently – strictly speaking, perhaps even always – *counterfactual*, it is of fundamental significance for the structure of human relations that we normally deal with one another as if it were the case. The accent here falls differently than in models of social practice without a subject, where the determining factors are language, culture, social roles, power relations, or the like.

The supposition of rationally accountable subjects figures, in turn, in the idealizing supposition of an independent reality known in common: competent subjects are expected to deal with conflicts of experience and testimony in ways that themselves presuppose, and thus reconfirm, the intersubjective availability of an objectively real world.[23] Discrepancies are to be attributed to errors in perception, interpretation, reporting, and the like, that is, to be resolved on the basis of the very presupposition they maintain. In this sense, the objectivity of real-world events – their validity for "consciousness in general" as Kant would say, or as we can say in a more social- practical mode, their intersubjective validity – is a pragmatic presupposition of social interaction for which social actors are held sanctionably accountable, and with good reason: it is the basis of our cooperative activities.

The idealizations of rational accountability and real-world objectivity both figure in our idealized notion of truth, for objectivity is the other side of the intersubjective validity of certain types of truth claims. Any adequate account of our practices of truth-telling has to attend not only to the situated, socially conditioned character of raising truth claims and offering warrants for them, but to the situation-transcending import of the claims themselves: this is the way things are, objectively, as any competent agent could know. While we have no ideas of standards of truth wholly independent of particular languages and practices, it remains that "truth" serves as an idea of reason with respect to which we can criticize the standards we inherit and learn to see things in a different way. Neither the particularity and context-immanence nor the universality and context-transcendence of truth claims can be ignored without doing violence to our actual practices of truth. We can, and typically do, make contextually conditioned and fallible claims to objective truth.

In Habermas's view, the potential for reason resides centrally in the capacity to arrive at uncoerced agreements concerning validity claims on the basis of reasons open to intersubjective assessment. This is a side of social interaction to which post-Nietzscheans who treat social relations as so many expressions of the will to power are peculiarly blind: the "will" to nonviolent, consensual cooperation. The theory of communicative rationality focuses on the pragmatic presuppositions of mutual understanding (*Verständigung*) of this sort. It illuminates the ways in which idealizing suppositions, even when counterfactual, are actually effective in organizing processes of reaching agreement. Social cooperation requires the *ongoing accomplishment* of shared meanings, an objective world known in common, a shared social world whose norms are recognized as legitimate, and competent subjects capable of accounting for their actions. In this sense, the objective, social, and subjective "worlds" are continually being constructed and reconstructed in ever changing situations. And it is the idealizing suppositions that normatively orient those processes that lend them their coherence.

Contemporary contextualists are, to be sure, only too happy to grant the importance of public understandings and agreements. But this is a prelude to denying any context-transcending import to the validity claims that figure in them. That is the point, for instance, of Rorty's insistence that practices of justification not be treated as anything more than social practices. He might even concede the roles that idealizing notions of agency, objectivity, and truth play in such practices; but he would then hasten to add, in a Wittgensteinian tone of voice, that these just are *our* practices. Here we arrive at the striking paradox, noted above, which seems to be endemic to radically historicist or culturalist approaches: "Our" culture is permeated with transcultural notions of validity. If, in the absence of any God's-eye view, we have to start from where we are – for instance, to use the forms of justification actually available to us – this will involve, in many pursuits at least, offering arguments that claim validity beyond the confines of our culture.[24]

That is obviously not what contextualists intend. They are moved, rather, by the ways in which historical, social, and cultural studies have gradually but inexorably eroded our cultural self-confidence, shaken our universalist self-understanding, and made us ever more aware of our own particularities and limitations. Thus the real question is what to make of the historicist self-awareness that has been developing in the West for more than 150 years now. One of the ways in which Rorty tries to deal with it is by adapting to his purpose the Kantian notion of two standpoints. "To be a behaviorist in epistemology," he tells us, is to look at inquiry in our culture "bifocally," both as "the achievement of objective truth" and as "patterns adopted for various historical reasons." From the former standpoint the results of inquiry are "the best idea we currently have about how to explain what is going on." From the latter standpoint they are "just the facts about what a given society, or profession, or other group takes to be good grounds for an assertion of a certain sort." These are incompatible standpoints in the sense that we cannot occupy both simultaneously. But there is no need to; we may shift from one point of view to the other.[25] It is important to keep in mind, however, that the standpoint of the observer of cultural practices is the viewpoint not of God but of, say, the historian of ideas or the anthropologist, and this, as we now realize, is not a view from nowhere. Interpreters inevitably bring with themselves the perspectives and concerns of their own cultures; they cannot avoid relying upon the taken-for-granted assumptions built into the languages and practices that comprise their own forms of life. In the case at hand, this means that we can distance ourselves from certain of our cultural practices only by taking others for granted. We can never be observers without at the same time being participants.

This point is worth considering with some care, for misunderstanding it gives rise to a type of fallacious reasoning that has been enormously influential: the fallacy of treating ontological conditions as normative principles. The present home of this fallacy is philosophical hermeneutics, and a paradigm case of it is Gadamer's critique of enlightenment criticism. He points out quite correctly that the traditional enlightenment consciousness of being beyond prejudice, tradition, and convention is a false consciousness. We are always and inevitably *mehr Sein als Bewußtsein*, more (historical) being than consciousness.[26] What we take for granted in any act of reflective critique is immeasurably vaster than what we call into question. From this ontological insight Gadamer tries to draw normative conclusions against enlightenment criticism and in favor of traditionalism, and that, of course, is a *non sequitur*. If we grant that we are always "more being than consciousness," as he says, this is no less true of the revolutionary critic than of the traditional conservative. Both will inevitably take much more for granted than they will consciously question, accept, or reject. But this does not tell us which we are to be or with respect to what we are to be either. Its value is as a *corrective to false consciousness* – the sense of being outside of or above history and tradition – and not as a prescription for belief or action. As a reflective participant, I can critically interrogate and reject this or that element of my culture, and ontology as such will not determine whether I am right to do so. Similarly, to acknowledge that we cannot help but debate with people with whom we share enough to make debate possible is not to say that we cannot criticize and revise features of our common background, nor does it preclude making claims that are meant to be valid beyond our "ethnos."

The fact that we can only make a topic of our culture by simultaneously drawing upon it as a resource has implications that actually run counter to Rorty's intentions. As noted earlier, the very practice of reporting "the facts about what a given group takes to be good grounds" is itself a normatively structured activity that involves appealing to good grounds. Rorty sometimes writes as if it were only when we are engaged in such dubious enterprises as epistemology that we endorse the established patterns of normal inquiry rather than simply treating them as "patterns adopted for historical reasons;" but of course we endorse them whenever we are engaged in the types of inquiry in question. And while he does characterize the two standpoints as complementary, he has a marked tendency to ignore the participant's standpoint when he is promoting his own brand of historicism. In general, it is not *because* we agree that we hold a claim to be valid; rather, we agree because we have grounds for granting its validity. Particularly in practices of reflective inquiry it is the reasons or grounds offered for a claim that comprise its warrant and, when conditions are right, lead to agreement in the relevant community. In such cases my description of my community's agreement represents my fellow members as accepting validity claims on grounds that I, as a party to the agreement, also regard as good grounds. The detached third-person description, then, does not *replace* the engaged first-person endorsement but *reports* it. And it is not the reported agreement that warrants the claim, but the warrant for the claim that grounds the agreement.

To justify his beliefs to us, Rorty has to provide just the sorts of reasons we are accustomed to receiving for claims such as he makes, reasons meant to support not merely their "truth for us" but their truth, period. Thus it is that he does not try to convince us to accept his claims about language, mind, knowledge, morality, politics, and the rest by adducing community agreement, cultural approval, or anything of the sort. Participating in recognizable forms of rational justification, he attempts to get us to agree with his views by presenting, in his own voice, a variety of supporting reasons, including philosophical arguments against received forms of foundationalism. We are clearly meant to respond to these as participants, to accept them as good reasons, reasons that warrant the positions he espouses. Throwing historical and comparative considerations into the balance does not magically absolve us from weighing claims to validity on our own. That we now understand our capacities for reasoning to be tied to culturally variable and historically changeable forms of social practice can mean the end of the Enlightenment only for thinkers who remain so captivated by absolutist conceptions of reason, truth, and right that their passing means there is nothing left that really makes a difference.

## 2.3   Accountability and Autonomy

In the third section of the *Groundwork*, to assure us that the morality he has distilled from the common moral consciousness is no mere "phantom of the mind," Kant asserts that "everybody who cannot act except *under the Idea of freedom* is by this alone – from a practical point of view – really free,"[27] and then goes on to state that this is true precisely of rational beings. As rational agents we *have to* regard ourselves as capable of acting and judging on the basis of reasons, and in this sense as free, whether or not we can prove theoretically that we are. That is to say, viewing ourselves as free to respond to the force of considerations pro and con is *practically unavoidable* for agents such as we. And since thinking is itself a form of acting on reasons, the assumptions that underlie practical rationality figure in the exercise of theoretical reason as well.[28] But that very exercise, which in the first-person perspective rests on the pragmatic presuppositions of rational agency, may be turned back on that agency itself to produce third-person accounts of its conditions. In other words, the conditions of possibility of rational agency as viewed from the participants' perspective are in constitutive tension with its causal conditions as viewed from the observers' perspective. But that, according to Kant, is precisely the predicament of finite reason, the inescapable situation in which we must act and think. There is no getting out of it, either by achieving closure in a comprehensive third-person (God's-eye) view of the whole of which we and our actions are parts, or by dispensing altogether with observational accounts of the conditions of human action.[29] What we can and must do is shift continually between the two points of view. Notwithstanding his talk of two *worlds*, Kant often characterizes the intelligible/sensible distinction in just these terms: "The concept of the intelligible is thus only *a point of view* which reason finds itself constrained to adopt outside of appearances *in order to conceive of itself as practical.*"[30] As practical reasoners we must suppose (Habermas would say: make the idealizing supposition) that we are free to respond to the rational force of evidence and argument. Even when examining just how culturally and historically situated our reasoned responses inevitably are, we cannot avoid presupposing *in actu* the capacity for autonomous reasoning.

If there is anything to be learned from this insight into the human predicament, it is surely that we can never be just observers. To think and to act is to participate, with all its attendant presuppositions, idealizing and otherwise. What heightened historical and cultural self-consciousness teaches us is not that we should – or could – avoid committing the original sin of participation, but that we should try to be observant, critical participants. It is just this notion of critical participation around which Habermas's detranscendentalized notion of autonomy revolves.

Recent attempts within analytic philosophy to remedy the inadequacies of Kant's account of rational agency have moved beyond their earlier focus on motivational structure, particularly on the hierarchical relation between "first-order" and "higher-order" preferences.[31] Higher-order preferences or values, it is now clear, can no more be attributed to a "deep self untainted by socialization" than can first-order desires.[32] Considerations like this have led to more procedural conceptions of autonomy which turn on an agent's ability to reflect critically on his or her preference structures.[33] They stress a type of deliberative competence that may well be gained *in* the process of socialization. Beyond this, the relevant notion of deliberation can itself be desubjectivized in line with recent "constructivist" accounts of practical reasoning that feature public justification and intersubjective agreement.[34] From this perspective, autonomy resides principally in a capacity for critical reflection understood, in the first instance, as a capacity to participate in discourses of a certain kind.

For present purposes, I shall use *accountability* to designate an agent's capacity to engage in *practical reasoning* of the sorts required for everyday interaction, that is, roughly speaking, her ability to offer (typically conventional) accounts of her behaviour and to assess others' accounts of theirs (usually by reference to conventional standards). Accountability in this sense is a minimum requirement for *rational agency*. I will use *autonomy* to designate an agent's capacity to engage in *critical-reflective discourse* concerning the justifiability of established or proposed norms and beliefs. Autonomy in this sense is central to the stronger sort of rational agency that Kant referred to as *Mündigkeit*, the capacity to think for oneself. Rational agents in both the weaker and stronger senses are practical reasoners and hence *participants* in public processes of criticism and justification. Accountable agents are, among other things, able to provide publicly defensible – and in this sense objective – accounts of their actions and beliefs, that is, to satisfy interaction partners that their beliefs and actions are backed by good reasons. Autonomous agents are able to do so also at a critical-reflective level of discourse. At both levels, there is an internal connection between rational justification, understood as establishing a claim's acceptability by appeal to good reasons, and rational agency, understood as the capacity to participate in public discussions aimed at reaching mutual understanding.

The same internal connection links Habermas's conceptions of rational justification and rational agency. His analysis of everyday interaction focuses on the role played therein by implicit and explicit claims to validity and by the assorted practices of reason-giving geared to challenging and vindicating them. "If we assume that the human species maintains itself through the socially coordinated activities of its members and that this coordination is established through communication, and in certain spheres of life through communication aimed at reaching agreement, then the reproduction of the species *also* requires satisfying the conditions of a rationality inherent in communicative action."[35] Communication in this sense is not merely a matter of producing linguistically well-formed sentences. In speaking we relate to the world around us, to other subjects, and to our own intentions, feelings, and desires. In each of these respects we are constantly raising claims, even if usually only implicitly, concerning the validity of what we are saying, implying, or presupposing – claims, for instance, concerning the truth of what we say in relation to *the* objective world, or concerning the rightness of what we say and do in relation to the shared norms and values of *our* social lifeworld, or concerning the sincerity of the manifest expressions of *each's own* intentional states. Naturally, claims of these sorts can be contested, criticized, discussed, defended, withdrawn, revised, and the like. There are any number of ways of settling disputed claims, including appeals to authority, threats, and brute force. One way, the weighing of reasons-for and reasons-against, has, at least since the time of Socrates, been regarded as fundamental to the idea of rationality. And it is to just this experience of arriving at mutual understanding through no other force but that of insight and argument, of relying on reasoned discussion to gain intersubjective recognition for contestable validity claims, that Habermas looks in developing his idea of communicative rationality. Accordingly, his notion of rational accountability is centered on the agent's ability to participate competently in processes of reaching understanding (*Verständigung*). While participating in such processes, and as a pragmatic presupposition thereof, communicatively competent subjects reciprocally impute to one another the capacity to act on reasons and to accept or reject with reason the validity claims that others raise.

In Habermas's conceptualization, the shift from everyday interaction and accountability to argumentative discourse and autonomy is a matter of degree, that is, of further developing practices and capacities already inculcated in daily life. To be sure, their development is not simply a matter of occasional ingenuity or individual virtuosity. It is bound up with social, cultural, and psychological conditions that undergo historical change. In modern societies conditions are such as to provide increased institutional, cultural, and motivational support for reflective modes of argumentation and critique. Forms of expert discourse have developed which are transmitted and developed within specialized cultural traditions and embodied in differentiated cultural institutions. Thus, for instance, the scientific enterprise, the legal system, and the institutions of art criticism represent enduring possibilities of discursively thematizing various types of validity claims and of productively assimilating our negative experiences with them.

It is, among other things, the extent to which modes of reflective discourse have been institutionalized, and the requisite cultural and motivational conditions for them have been satisfied, that distinguishes modern from traditional societies. In the modern context the capacity for critical reflection that is integral to rational autonomy includes an ability to participate in such discourses, to learn from them, and to be guided by them. Though as discourse participants we may and often do adopt the attitudes of observers and critics toward practices we normally live in, we also, and unavoidably, buy into the presuppositions structuring the very forms of critical discourse in which we are engaging. And these are by no means negligible. In addition to idealizing suppositions regarding truth, the intersubjective availability of the objective world and the rational competency of discourse partners, there are additional assumptions built into the very idea of free and equal participants discoursing reasonably, settling disputes in a non-coercive manner, and coming to agreements solely on the basis of reasons pro and con. Habermas has summed up the idealizing suppositions informing discursive practices that are taken to be rational in this emphatic sense in his account of the "ideal speech situation." I shall not go into the details of that model here, but I will remark briefly on its widely misunderstood status. It is meant only as a summary account of (some of) the normative presuppositions of (some) forms of critical-reflective discourse.[36] The apposite challenge, then, is not the oft-repeated observation that the ideal is not real and never can be. That is part of the point of ideals in the Kantian tradition. Another part is that they are nevertheless actually operative in organizing thought and action.

There is another aspect of the interrelated notions of critical-reflective discourse and rational autonomy worth noting at this point: their post-traditional character. It goes without saying that "post-traditional" does not mean here "floating free of tradition altogether." It alludes to changes in our relations to inherited contexts of meaning and validity, schemes of interpretation and justification, patterns of socialization and individuation, and the like. These changes are *always* a matter of degree and *never* global in their reach. But they are not without far-reaching effects on processes of cultural reproduction, social integration, and identity formation. What Habermas refers to as the "communicative thawing" of inherited patterns in ever-expanding domains of modern life exposes the authority of tradition increasingly to discursive questioning, displaces particularistic norms and values by more general and abstract ones, and supersedes traditionally ascribed identities with identities that have to be constructed and reconstructed in ever-changing situations.[37] Customary beliefs can less and less be relied upon to guarantee the reproduction of modern forms of life; context-specific norms and values are less and less adequate to the demands of social integration; concrete roles and fixed models are increasingly insufficient to secure identity. There are growing needs for discursively tested convictions, general principles of legality and morality, and highly individuated, self-directing subjects.[38] It is important to note that this heightening of reflexivity, generality, and individualism informs and structures the "discourse of modernity" itself. For instance, all of the various participants – post- and anti-modernist as well as modernist – take for granted the possibility of reflectively questioning received beliefs and values, of gaining critical distance from inherited norms and roles, and of challenging ascribed individual and group identities. Even arguments like Alasdair MacIntyre's for the superiority of premodern traditions are not themselves traditional arguments but the *traditionalistic* arguments of hyper-reflexive moderns. One can argue against these basic features of post-traditional culture only by drawing upon them, and this is a good indication that they are practically unavoidable presuppositions of contemporary discourse. One either buys into them or drops out of it.

## 2.4  Discourse Ethics

Habermas's theory of communicative action adopts the internal perspective of participants in communication and attempts to reconstruct certain general conditions of participation. More precisely, his aim is to provide an account of the pragmatic presuppositions we cannot avoid making when we adopt the first-person standpoint of communicatively competent agents, either as everyday practical reasoners or as reflective co-discussants. For my purposes here it is not necessary to decide whether some or all of these are presuppositions which only *we* must make or are presuppositions of *Verständigung überhaupt*. Given that we must start from where we are, any presuppositions that are practically indispensable for participating in communication processes to which we have no alternative will figure as preconditions of our communication – whether or not they belong to the conditions of possibility of communication as such. A reconstruction of the pragmatics of our communicative situation would, then, make clear at least where our discussions have to start. And this in itself, as we shall see, has far-reaching consequences for the discourse of modernity.

That discourse turns on what we, the participants, can and cannot make sense of, render plausible, justify, refute, effectively criticize, conceive as alternatives, and so on. If there are constraining preconditions built into the discursive situation itself, they may in turn constrain the range of possible outcomes. Consider, for instance, how we relate to worldviews in which there is no developed awareness of alternatives to the established body of beliefs and connected with this, say, a sacredness attributed to beliefs and avoidance reactions expected in the face of challenges to them. It is precisely our historically, sociologically, and anthropologically schooled view of the *diversity* of systems of belief and practice that informs our discourse about them. Hence we are constrained, on pain of performative contradiction, to regard systems of belief that do not understand themselves as interpretations of the world, subject to error and open to revision, as deficient in that respect, as not having learned something that we know. There is, to put it plainly, no going back on the experiences of cultural change and pluralism we have had or unlearning what we have learned from them about the variability of forms of life and views of the world. In the discourse of modernity we cannot sensibly argue against *that*.

There are other general presuppositions of contemporary discourse with which one might, perhaps, meaningfully take issue, but with respect to which the burden of proof on the critic is so great as to be prohibitive.[39] Consider, for instance, the distinction we draw between empirical-scientific questions and questions of religion, morality, or metaphysics. There is no easy way to go back on this and argue convincingly, for example, that the number, position, and composition of the planets could be decided by appeal to revelation, morals, or metaphysics. The same could be said for animistic and anthropomorphic accounts of nature, magical techniques that blur our distinction between instrumental control over things and moral relations among persons, or attitudes towards names and naming that contravene our distinction between the symbolic power of expression and physical efficacy. In our cultural-historical situation it would be difficult-bordering-on-impossible to produce, for instance, a *warranted* denial that there has been a significant learning process underway in regard at least to our *technical* understanding of nature, and that modern societies have learned to pursue the interest in prediction and control more effectively by differentiating it out from other concerns. But this means that from where we must start, some differences in beliefs and practices will be more than mere differences, precisely because they can only be made sense of as the results of learning. To put the point in another way, our standards of intelligibility and rationality inevitably enter into our interpretations of other cultures. In seeking to understand how strange (to us) beliefs can appear meaningful and reasonable in their contexts, we have to look for differences in circumstances that would account for the differences in belief. If we find that what we have to abstract from in our setting in order to make the beliefs understandable (to us) are practically unavoidable presuppositions of rational discourse as we understand it, then our explanation contains, at least implicitly, an evaluation. It says, in effect, that a given belief might make sense and reasonably be held in a context from which something we have learned is missing – and this amounts to saying that it is belief which can no longer reasonably be held.

I have been speaking primarily of beliefs, but it is worth remarking that our assessment of norms and values cannot remain unaffected by what we regard as learning in more narrowly cognitive domains. Traditional value systems are intimately interwoven with beliefs about how the world is. That is why the learning processes associated with names like Galileo and Darwin could have such a profound impact on normative and evaluative elements of modern life. To put the point somewhat crudely, certain ethical views could be publicly justified only by appeal to beliefs that are no longer tenable. Since the reasons we regard as warranting evaluative and normative judgements have to be compatible with what we have learned in other domains, whole classes of reasons for acting are no longer available to us – for example, that marriages must be arranged *because* ancestral spirits are affected by whom one marries; that menstruating women may not sleep in the same bed with their husbands or touch their children *because* the body is a temple which must be kept pure and menstruating women are impure; that people have souls which transmigrate in proportion to their sanctity and *thus* that received inequalities are a form of just desert; that to be a woman and to survive the death of one's husband is an indication of prior sin which must *therefore* be absolved before one dies.[40] In these and like cases it is the *kinds of reasons* that have been devalued and not just the *specific claims* about ancestral spirits or transmigrating souls. The same holds for legitimations of authority in terms of descent from the gods or justifications of unequal treatment by appeal to the natural inferiority and unfitness for self-rule of this race or that sex.

Though the elimination of broad classes of reasons does not by itself settle questions of right and wrong, good and bad, better and worse, the scope of *reasonable* disagreement gets considerably narrowed. As a result, the norms and values that could stand up to criticism and be upheld in free and open discussion are by no means coextensive with the spectrum of what has historically been valued or might arbitrarily be commanded. But neither is it uniquely determined. One of the things we have learned about values, for instance, is that reasonable people can reasonably hold different conceptions of the good, that there is no one way of life suited to all individuals and groups, and thus that a pluralistic culture within which members can pursue – within limits – their different ideas of the good life is the most reasonable societal arrangement. One source of these limits is the basic principles built into the very model of seeking reasoned agreement through open discussion, principles that must be observed if such discussion is to be at all possible. It is precisely those principles that Habermas's account of practical discourse is meant to reconstruct. With the foregoing remarks as background, let us now glance briefly at the central elements of that account.

As we have seen, Habermas shifts the focus of the "analytic" part of the critique of reason from forms of transcendental subjectivity to forms of communicative interaction. Kant, still operating within the horizon of individual consciousness, could comprehend objective validity only in terms of structures of consciousness as such; for Habermas, validity is tied to reasoned agreement concerning defeasible claims. The key to his idea of discursive rationality is the use of reasons or grounds – the unforced force of the better argument – to gain intersubjective recognition for contestable claims. In the modern period this increasingly takes place within specialized domains of critical-reflective discourse meant to deal with different types of validity claims. Against this background, Habermas's idea of a "discourse ethics" can be viewed as a communication-theoretic reconstruction of the moral standpoint that Kant differentiated from the natural standpoint: the discourse model represents a procedural reformulation of Kant's categorical imperative. Rather than ascribing to others as valid any maxim that I can will to be a universal law, I must submit my maxim to others for purposes of discursively testing its claim to validity. The emphasis shifts from what each can will without contradiction to be a general law to what all can agree to as a general norm. Accordingly, "rational will-formation" is not something that can be identified and certified privately; it is inextricably bound to communication processes in which agreements are both discovered and shaped.

For Kant, the autonomy of the will required the exclusion of all "pathological" interests from the choice of maxims of action. If my particular ends of action (which can be summed up as my happiness) are not excluded from its determining grounds, my maxim will *ipso facto* be unsuitable for universal legislation; for if a maxim is to be universalizable, valid for all rational beings, then it must be independent of my particular inclinations. This constellation alters perceptibly when we shift to Habermas's communicative framework. The aim of practical discourse is to come to a "rationally motivated" agreement about which norms are justifiable. Individual wants, needs, desires, and feelings need not, indeed cannot be excluded, for it is precisely in relation to them that agreement is sought. They belong to the content of practical discourse. What that content concretely is depends to a large extent on the specific conditions and potentials of sociocultural life at a given time and place.

Habermas is concerned above all to argue against noncognitivists that practical questions can be decided rationally, and yet to avoid the pitfalls connected with attempts to assimilate or reduce rightness claims to truth claims. With respect to both types of claims, objectivity is tied to intersubjective validity, and in a discursive context this means warranted assertability or rational acceptability not just "for us" (the actual participants) but for all competent participants.[41] True, the sorts of warranting reasons are different in the theoretical and practical domains. But the differences are not such as to exclude the latter from the realm of rationality. Practical questions can also be decided "with reason," and intersubjective recognition for practical claims can be "rationally motivated," the expression of a justified, warranted, or grounded consensus. However, the backing that is required for contested norms is not, or not merely, the sorts of observational and experimental evidence used to support general laws. The relevant evidence is first and foremost the consequences and side-effects that the general observance of a norm can be expected to have in regard to the wants, needs, desires, feelings, and interests of those likely to be affected by it. As intersubjectively binding, reciprocal expectations of behavior, "norms regulate legitimate chances for the satisfaction of needs and wants."[42] Thus, that about which agreement is sought in practical discourse is the justifiability of a proposed or existing regulation of such chances.

Norms "exist" through being intersubjectively recognized as valid. Since norms that are actually "in force" can prove upon examination to be unjustifiable, the relation of practical discourse to social reality can be critical in a way that the relation of theoretical discourse to natural reality cannot. "Objectivity" in this context is doubly dependent on rationally-motivated, intersubjective recognition. It is precisely the function of practical discourse, as Habermas conceives it, to test which norms are objectively (rationally) justifiable and thus deserve to be objectively (actually) in force. In the post-traditional cultural situation we are in, there are no good grounds for denying the title "rational" to agreements motivated by a nondeceptive recognition of common needs and interests,[43] in the light of adequate knowledge of existing and effectible conditions, and with a view to likely consequences and side-effects. Just these sorts of considerations are what we mean by saying that there are good or cogent reasons for adopting a proposed normative regulation.

Like Kant, Habermas, distinguishes the types of practical reasoning and corresponding types of "ought" proper to questions about what is pragmatically expedient, ethically prudent, and morally right.[44] Calculations of rational choice aim at recommendations relevant to the pursuit of contingent purposes in the light of given preferences. When serious questions of value arise, deliberation on who one is and who one wants to be yields insights concerning the good life. If questions of justice are involved, fair and impartial consideration of conflicting interests is required to judge what is right or just. And like Kant, Habermas regards questions of the last type, rather than specifically ethical matters, to be the proper domain of *moral theory*. This is not to say that ethical deliberation is irrational or exhibits no general structures of its own,[45] but only that the disintegration of sacred canopies has opened the question "How should I (or one, or we) live?" to the irreducible pluralism of modern life. To suppose that all the questions of the good life dealt with under the rubric of classical ethics – questions of happiness and virtue, character and ethos, community and tradition – could be answered once and for all, and by philosophers, is no longer plausible. Matters of individual or group self-understanding and self-realization, rooted as they are in particular life histories and traditions, do not admit of general theory; and prudential deliberation on the good life, moving as it does within the horizons of particular lifeworlds and forms of life, does not yield universal prescriptions. Furthermore, without its metaphysical underpinnings, phronesis can too easily coalesce with the commonsense of a given way of life – with its built-in bias for the way things are and distrust of individuals who morally criticize the accepted way of doing things.[46]

If taking modern pluralism seriously means giving up the idea that philosophy can single out a privileged way of life, or provide an answer to the question "How should I (we) live?" that is valid for everyone, it does not, in Habermas' view, preclude a general theory of a narrower sort, namely a theory of justice. Accordingly, the aim of his discourse ethics is solely to reconstruct the moral point of view as the perspective in which competing normative claims can be fairly and impartially adjudicated. As we saw, it is geared like Kant's ethics to what everyone could rationally will to be binding on everyone alike. But it shifts the frame of reference from Kant's solitary, reflecting, moral consciousness to the community of moral subjects in dialogue, and it replaces his categorical imperative with a procedure of moral argumentation aiming at reaching reasoned agreement among those subject to the norm in question. Unlike Rawls's Kantian constructivism, however, Habermas's representation of practical discourse does not feature rational egoists prudently contracting behind a veil of ignorance, a procedure that can itself be carried out monologically, but moral agents trying to put themselves in each other's shoes.[47] That is, by requiring that perspective-taking be general and reciprocal, discourse ethics builds a moment of empathy into the public procedure of coming to a reasoned agreement.

As the trajectory of argument around Rawls' notion of reflective equilibrium illustrates, the burden of proof on any moral theorist who hopes to ground a conception of justice in anything more universal than the "settled convictions" of our political culture is enormous.[48] Because Habermas wants to do just that, the links he forges to action theory are crucial; they are meant to show that our basic moral intuitions spring from something deeper and more universal than contingent features of our tradition. In his view, the task of moral theory is reflectively to articulate, refine, and elaborate the intuitive grasp of the normative presuppositions of social interaction that belongs to the repertoire of competent social actors in any society. The basic moral intuitions the theorist reconstructs are, as Aristotle noted, acquired in the process of socialization; but, Habermas argues, they include an "abstract core" that is more than culture-specific. Members of our species become individuals in and through being socialized into networks of reciprocal social relations, so that personal identity is from the start interwoven with relations of mutual recognition. This interdependence brings with it a reciprocal vulnerability that calls for guarantees of mutual consideration to preserve both the integrity of individuals and the web of interpersonal relations in which they form and maintain their identities. Both of these concerns – with the inviolability of the person and the welfare of the community – have been at the heart of traditional moralities.

In the Kantian tradition, respect for the integrity and dignity of the person has been tied to the freedom of moral subjects to act upon norms they themselves accept as binding on the basis of their own insight; and concern for the common good has been linked to the impartiality of laws that can be accepted by everyone on that basis. In Habermas's discourse ethics, which bases the justification of norms on the reasoned agreement of those subject to them, equal respect for persons is reflected in the right of each participant to respond with a "yes" or "no" to the reasons offered by way of justification. Concern for the common good is reflected in the requirement of general and reciprocal perspective-taking: in seeking mutual understanding, each must attempt to get beyond an egocentric viewpoint by taking into account the interests of others and giving them equal weight to his or her own. General norms justified from this standpoint of impartiality will of necessity abstract from many of the specific circumstances of concrete cases. They are not meant to answer questions of the type: "What should I do here and now?" And that, of course, regularly prompts neo-Aristotelian objections to the abstraction that Kantian (re-)constructivism fosters from what gives content to our ethical life. These objections seem to confront us with the choice of either returning to some version of Aristotelianism or modifying the Kantian approach so as to give them, as far as possible, their due. Discourse ethics takes the latter tack. On the one hand, in contrast to ethics of the good life, it confines itself to the limited task of reconstructing the moral point of view, leaving concrete moral and ethical judgements to participants themselves. On the other hand, locating the common core of morality in the normative presuppositions of communicative interaction, it develops a thoroughly intersubjectivist interpretation of the moral point of view; practical discourse, as a reflective continuation of communicative interaction, preserves that common core. Rather than contractual agreements among "unencumbered" individuals with arbitrarily chosen ends, it involves public discussions among socialized and situated subjects about matters of the common good. The egocentric perspective is not treated as primary but derivative; autonomy is conceptualized as competence in shared forms of communication. Thus practical discourse presupposes and draws upon the normative structures of social interaction; it does not cut the bonds of social integration as do social contract models. In this way discourse ethics attempts to capture at least the structural aspects of solidarity as a perspective complementary to that of equal treatment. But this is not the notion of solidarity that figures in traditionalistic models: "As a component of universalistic morality, solidarity loses its merely particular meaning, in which it is limited to the internal relationships of a collectivity ethnocentrically isolated from other groups – the character of forced willingness to sacrifice oneself for a collective system, which is always present in premodern forms of solidarity . . . [where] fellowship is entwined with followership . . . Justice conceived in postconventional terms can converge with solidarity, as its other side, only when solidarity has been transformed in light of the idea of a general, discursive formation of will."[49]

In discourse ethics theoretical counterparts to what Horkheimer referred to as the "bourgeois ideals" of freedom, justice, equality, tolerance, and the like are built into the model of deliberative practical reason itself. The embodiment of the latter in the institutions and practices of a democratic society would, then, require that such ideals be part of a shared political culture. They are not, on this account, merely historical curiosities of a bygone era. Furthermore, as Habermas conceives of it, practical discourse demands of participants that they take into consideration the needs and interests of all who will be affected by the outcome of their deliberations. Thus, something like what Horkheimer characterized as an ungroundable feeling of compassion and an interest in the elimination of injustice also figure in this model as preconditions of full participation. As noted in section 1.3, a feeling for the feelings of others and an interest in the common interest are not the products of pure reason. Hence, the effective embodiment of practical discourses would also require forms of socialization and cultural reproduction that could be counted on to foster such motivations and dispositions.[50]

It is, in fact, possible to read Habermas's extensive writings on politics and society as a protracted examination of the cultural, psychological, and institutional preconditions of and barriers to the historical embodiment of practical reason. Thus very early on, in *The Structural Transformation of the Public Sphere*, he presented a historical-sociological account of the emergence, transformation, and disintegration of the bourgeois public sphere in which critical public discussion of matters of general interest was to be institutionalized.[51] He noted the contradiction between the liberal public sphere's constitutive catalogue of the "basic rights of man" and their *de facto* restriction to a certain class of men. And he traced the tensions that gave rise to as, with the development of capitalism, the public body expanded beyond the bourgeoisie to include groups who were systematically disadvantaged by the economic system and demanded state regulation and compensation. The interest behind this theoretically informed history of the present becomes quite clear in the concluding analysis of the hollow public spheres of mediatized mass democracies. There are related accounts of the historical genealogy, structural dilemmas, and crisis tendencies of contemporary democratic institutions in *Legitimation Crisis, The Theory of Communicative Action*, and other writings.[52] Their focus is typically on what it has taken historically to institutionalize communicatively structured domains of public deliberation, why these institutions have been ambivalent from the start, how economic and administrative expansion has increasingly subordinated them to the dynamics of capitalist growth, and where this gives rise to new potentials for conflict and new social movements.

I am not concerned here with the details of those discussions, but only with correcting the frequent short-circuiting by Habermas's critics

of the lengthy path by which he connects the idealizations of discourse ethics with the realities of democratic politics. Though the gap
between the abstract universality of the demands of justice and the
concrete particularity of conceptions of the good can be considerably
narrowed in theory once we get beyond the atomistic individualism of
liberal approaches and the mirror-image collectivism of communitarian approaches, it can finally be bridged only in practice. For one
thing, the abstraction from particular situations and individual cases
that is an unavoidable part of justifying *general* norms has to be
undone in applying such norms to concrete circumstances.[53] For
another, the moral insights achieved in practical discourse will remain ineffective in practice if they are not somehow anchored in a
concrete way of life: apart from *Sittlichkeit, Moralität* is a pure abstraction. "Any univeralistic morality is dependent upon a form of life
that *meets it halfway*. There has to be a modicum of congruence
between morality and the practices of socialization and education . . .
[and] a modicum of fit between morality and sociopolitical institutions."[54] To the extent that this condition is met, elements of *Moralität*
themselves become part of *Sittlichkeit*.[55] Finally, moral theory cannot
itself resolve particular ethical problems or even limn the contours of
the good life. In analyzing practical reasoning and its reflective continuation in practical discourse, Habermas merely elaborates in theory
a procedure that can be put into practice only by those actually
involved with moral and political issues. "[P]hilosophy cannot absolve anyone of moral responsibility. And that includes philosophers,
for like everyone else they face moral-practical issues of great complexity, and the first thing they might profitably do is to get a clearer
view of the situation they find themselves in. The historical and social
sciences can be of greater help in this endeavor than philosophy . . .
[As] Max Horkheimer . . . [wrote in] 1933: 'What is needed to get
beyond the utopian character of Kant's idea of a perfect constitution
of humankind, is a materialist theory of society.' "[56]

This line of thought has been taken up by Claus Offe, who argues
that the utopian idea of "a perfect constitution of humankind" has to
be replaced by the more modest projects of *guaranteeing minimums*
according to the principle that no individual, social group, or society
"is to be deprived of the material means of subsistence, of human and
civil rights, or of opportunities for political and social participation,"
and of *enacting responsible self-limitations* with regard to "the dynamics
of technological, military, economic, bureaucratic, and ecological
modernization."[57] Even this more modest proposal calls for conditions of socialization and institutional arrangements that favor the
development and exercise of a capacity for autonomous moral judge-

ment. Complex modern societies cannot compensate for the weakening of traditional bonds solely by means of legal coercion, expert management, and financial incentives. They have a "functional need" for social actors to be oriented by an ethics of responsibility in such areas as socialization, education, health, transportation, and immigration, as well as in such relations as those between genders, generations, and professionals and clients.[58] On the other hand, the ethical orientation in question cannot survive in social-structural settings that systematically encourage strategic rather than cooperative behavior, or that place unreasonable risks and burdens on the exercise of autonomous moral judgement. Freedoms guaranteed in law and capacities developed in socialization are not alone sufficient to promote that exercise if institutional conditions discourage it. Thus the existence and practice of personal and collective autonomy is contingent on every side – socializatory, educational, cultural, institutional, social-structural – and these relations of dependence are not one-way and self-contained but reciprocal and interconnected. It is just this web of empirical interdependencies that critical social theory, using ideas of reason as lodestars, takes as its object of inquiry.[59]

As I am concerned here only with the more "philosophical" aspects of this project, I shall return in chapter 3 to those ideas themselves. In the current atmosphere of debate, it is not merely their sociopolitical practicability that is at issue, but their plausibility as conceptualizations of human possibilities. With this in mind, I shall offer a less "transcendental," more "pragmatic" account of their "nature, scope, and limits."

## NOTES

1  For a more detailed discussion see part I of *Ideals and Illusions*, pp. 11–123.
2  Richard Rorty, *Philosophy and the Mirror of Nature* (Princeton: Princeton University Press, 1979), p. 390.
3  Ibid., pp. 174, 367.
4  See Hilary Putnam, "Why Reason Can't Be Naturalized," in K. Baynes, J. Bohman, T. McCarthy (eds), *After Philosophy* (Cambridge, MA: The MIT Press, 1987), pp. 222–44.
5  Richard Rorty, "Solidarity or Objectivity," in J. Rajchman and C. West (eds), *Post-Analytic Philosophy* (New York: Columbia University Press, 1985), p. 13.
6  I am referring in what follows to Foucault's work from the 1970s, still his most influential in the English-speaking world, and not to the earlier or later phases of his thought.

7  Michel Foucault, "Truth and Power," in Foucault, *Power/Knowledge*, ed. and trans. C. Gordon (New York: Pantheon Books, 1980), p. 131.

8  See Nancy Fraser, "Foucault on Modern Power: Empirical Insights and Normative Confusions," in Fraser, *Unruly Practices* (Minneapolis: The University of Minnesota Press, 1989), pp. 17–34.

9  See especially Michel Foucault, "What is Enlightenment?", in P. Rabinow (ed.), *The Foucault Reader* (New York: Pantheon Books, 1984), pp. 32–50, and my discussion in *Ideals and Illusions*, pp. 60–75.

10  See, for example, the interview with Julia Kristeva, in Derrida, *Positions* (Chicago: The University of Chicago Press, 1981), pp. 15–36.

11  Ibid., p. 32.

12  Jacques Derrida, *Of Grammatology*, trans. G. Spivak (Baltimore: The Johns Hopkins University Press, 1976), p. 10.

13  Jacques Derrida, "The Ends of Man," in *Margins of Philosophy*, trans. A. Bass (Chicago: The University of Chicago Press, 1982), p. 135.

14  Jacques Derrida, "Structure, Sign and Play in the Discourse of the Human Sciences," in *Writing and Difference*, trans. A. Bass (Chicago: The University of Chicago Press, 1978), pp. 280–1.

15  *Positions*, p. 19.

16  *Positions*, p. 33.

17  See, for instance, his response to critics in "But Beyond . . . ," *Critical Inquiry* 13 (1986): 155–70.

18  Jacques Derrida, "Afterword: Toward an Ethic of Discussion," an interview with Gerald Graff, in Derrida, *Limited Inc.*, trans. S. Weber (Evanston: Northwestern University Press, 1988), p. 150.

19  Ibid., p. 147.

20  Ibid., p. 136.

21  Jürgen Habermas, *Postmetaphysical Thinking*, trans. W. Hohengarten (Cambridge, MA: The MIT Press, 1992), p. 47. See also his *Moral Consciousness and Communicative Action*, trans. C. Lenhardt and S. Nicholsen (Cambridge, MA: The MIT Press, 1990), p. 203, where he characterizes this as "the tension manifesting itself in everyday communication as the factual force of counterfactual presuppositions."

22  See Harold Garfinkel, *Studies in Ethnomethodology* (Englewood Cliffs: Prentice Hall, 1967), and Habermas's discussion of different models of social action in *The Theory of Communicative Action*, 2 vols., trans. T. McCarthy (Boston: Beacon Press, 1984, 1987), vol. 1, pp. 75–101. The ideas sketched in this and the following two paragraphs are developed further in section 3.1, below.

23  See Melvin Pollner, "Mundane Reasoning," *Philosophy of the Social Sciences* 4 (1975): 35–54, and Habermas's discussion in *The Theory of Communicative Action*, vol. 1, pp. 12–15.

24  This paradox besets, I think, even the milder form of historicism presupposed by the method of reflective equilibrium: context-transcending claims that belong to our settled convictions are represented as the context-immanent beliefs of a particular cultural tradition. It seems doubtful that *this* method could provide adequate justification for *those* beliefs.

25  *Philosophy and the Mirror of Nature*, p. 386.
26  See Hans-Georg Gadamer, *Truth and Method* (New York: The Seabury Press, 1975), esp. pp. 235ff, and Habermas's review thereof in F. Dallmayr and T. McCarthy (eds), *Understanding and Social Inquiry* (Notre Dame: University of Notre Dame Press, 1977), pp. 335–63. For an overview and discussion of their debate, see Georgia Warnke, *Gadamer: Hermeneutics, Tradition, and Reason* (Oxford: Blackwell, 1987), pp. 107–38.
27  Immanuel Kant, *Groundwork of the Metaphysic of Morals*, trans. H. J. Paton (New York: Harper and Row, 1964), p. 115. See Onora O'Neill's discussion of this section of the *Groundwork* in her *Constructions of Reason* (Cambridge: Cambridge University Press, 1989), pp. 51–77.
28  O'Neill argues ibid., p. 59, that the categorical imperative is the supreme principle of reasoning generally: it is "the principle of thinking and acting on principles that can hold for all." This approach ties objectivity to rational acceptability for all.
29  Rorty seeks to get out of it with his "frank ethnocentrism," but, as I have argued above, he thereby slips into privileging the third-person perspective: We know, as observers, that we, as participants, can't get round certain presuppositions; and this awareness, he suggests, itself suffices to distance us from, and thus to relativize, those presuppositions. But awareness of what *we must suppose* in order to speak and act in ways to which *we have no reasonable alternative* could better serve as the starting point for a reconstructive pragmatics.
30  *Groundwork*, p. 126. This is the interpretation that O'Neill develops in *Constructions of Reason*, pp. 59–63.
31  For the hierarchical approach, see Harry Frankfurt, "Freedom of the Will and the Concept of a Person," *The Journal of Philosophy* 68 (1971): 5–20.
32  Kenneth Baynes, "Autonomy, Reason, and Intersubjectivity," paper read at the Central Division Meeting of the American Philosophical Association, April 1992. I am indebted to Baynes for the line of argument I follow in this paragraph. Cf. J. Habermas, "Individuation through Socialization," in *Postmetaphysical Thinking*, pp. 149–204.
33  See, for example, Gerald Dworkin, *The Theory and Practice of Autonomy* (Cambridge: Cambridge University Press, 1988).
34  See, for instance, T. M. Scanlon, Jr., "The Significance of Choice," in *The Tanner Lectures on Human Values*, vol. 8 (Salt Lake City: University of Utah Press, 1988), pp. 149–216.
35  *The Theory of Communicative Action*, vol. 1, p. 397.
36  The forms of discourse in question have to do with claims to truth and moral rightness for which it is supposed there is only one correct answer. The presuppositions of aesthetic, evaluative, and even ethical discourse are, as Habermas recognizes, somewhat weaker.
37  See, for instance, *The Philosophical Discourse of Modernity*, trans. F. Lawrence (Cambridge, MA: The MIT Press, 1987), pp. 344–7.
38  It has been a commonplace of sociology since Durkheim, at the latest, that increased generality of norms and values and heightened individualism are *interdependent* and not opposed developments. A surprisingly large

number of "postmodern" critics seem still to be unaware of this, as they equate generality or universality with uniformity.

39  I develop this suggestion from a different angle in "Contra Relativism: A Thought Experiment," in Michael Krausz (ed.), *Relativism: Interpretation and Confrontation* (Notre Dame: University of Notre Dame Press, 1989), pp. 256–71.

40  These examples are taken from Richard A. Shweder, who is making a similar point, in "Post-Nietzschean Anthropology: The Idea of Multiple Objective Worlds," in *Relativism: Interpretation and Confrontation*, pp. 102–3. The point about *kinds* of reasons being devalued is developed by Habermas in "Legitimation Problems in the Modern State," in Habermas, *Communication and the Evolution of Society*, trans. T. McCarthy (Boston: Beacon Press, 1979), pp. 178–205.

41  "Discourse or argumentation is a more exacting type of communication . . . [It] generalizes, abstracts, and stretches the presuppositions of context-bound communicative actions by extending their range to include competent subjects beyond the provincial limits of their own particular form of life." *Moral Consciousness and Communicative Action*, p. 202.

42  Jürgen Habermas, "Wahrheitstheorien," in H. Fahrenbach (ed.), *Wirklichkeit und Reflexion* (Pfüllingen: Neske, 1973), p. 351. The focus on needs and wants is, to be sure, characteristic of modern societies, in which increasing disenchantment and pluralism have stripped reasons embedded in particular religious or cultural traditions of their consensus-producing power at a societal level. For an excellent overview and discussion of Habermas's discourse ethics, see William Rehg, *Insight and Solidarity* (Berkeley: University of California Press, 1994).

43  It should perhaps be noted that Habermas does not treat needs and interests simply as given. Always interpreted, they are simultaneously discovered and shaped in practical discourse. For a discussion of the "transformative moment" of practical discourse see Seyla Benhabib, *Critique, Norm, and Utopia* (New York: Columbia University Press, 1986), pp. 313–16.

44  See "On the Pragmatic, the Ethical, and the Moral Employments of Practical Reason," in Habermas, *Justification and Application*, trans. Ciaran Cronin (Cambridge, MA: The MIT Press, 1993), pp. 1–17.

45  Nor is it to say that it is any less important to practical reasoning in everyday life, which is normally concerned more with questions of expediency and prudence than with issues of justice. Furthermore, a given action situation may be considered from more than one of these perspectives.

46  See Habermas, "Lawrence Kohlberg and Neo Aristotelianism," in *Justification and Application, pp.* 113–32, and Cronin's "Translator's Introduction" to that work, pp. xi–xxxi.

47  For an excellent discussion of the comparative strengths and weaknesses of the two approaches see Kenneth Baynes, *The Normative Grounds of Social Criticism: Kant, Rawls, and Habermas* (Albany: State University of New York Press, 1991).

48  See especially John Rawls, "Justice as Fairness: Political Not Metaphysical," *Philosophy and Public Affairs* 14 (1985): 223–51. To appreciate how easily Rawls's approach can be given an anti-Kantian twist, see Richard Rorty, "The Priority of Democracy to Philosophy," in M. D. Peterson and R. C. Vaughan (eds), *The Virginia Statute for Religious Freedom* (Cambridge, UK: Cambridge University Press, 1988), pp. 257–82, esp. pp. 261ff. For an insightful discussion of "the hermeneutic turn" in political philosophy more generally, see Georgia Warnke, *Justice and Interpretation* (Cambridge, MA: The MIT Press, 1992).

49  Jürgen Habermas, "Justice and Solidarity: On the Discussion Concerning Stage 6," in T. Wren (ed.), *The Moral Domain* (Cambridge, MA: The MIT Press, 1990), pp. 244–5. One aspect of this transformation appears as follows: "While the degree of solidarity and the level of [general] welfare are indicators of the quality of communal life, they are not the only ones. Just as important is that *equal* consideration be given to the interests of every individual in defining the general interest." In this way, "discourse ethics extends the deontological concept of justice by including in it those structural aspects of the good life that can be distinguished from the concrete totality of specific forms of life." *Moral Consciousness and Communicative Action*, p. 203.

50  This is not, of course, to "ground" such motivations through answering the question: Why should I be moral? For Habermas, the demand for grounding is a demand for justification not motivation (and certainly not foundations), and that is a matter of producing reasons acceptable to all. This ties grounding to practical reasoning and practical discourse.

51  *The Structural Transformation of the Public Sphere*, trans. T. Burger (Cambridge, MA: The MIT Press, 1989).

52  *Legitimation Crisis*, trans. T. McCarthy (Cambridge, MA: The MIT Press, 1975).

53  For a detailed discussion of the application of general norms from a discourse-theoretical point of view, see Klaus Günther, *The Sense of Appropriateness: Application Discourses in Morality and Law*, trans. J. Farrell (Albany: SUNY Press, 1993).

54  *Moral Consciousness and Communicative Action*, pp. 207–8.

55  "The last two or three centuries have witnessed the emergence, after a long seesawing struggle, of a *directional* trend toward the realization of basic rights . . . a less and less selective reading and utilization of the universalistic meaning that fundamental-rights norms have; it testifies to the 'existence of reason,' if only in bits and pieces . . . To be sure, the gradual embodiment of moral principles in concrete forms of life is not something that can safely be left to Hegel's absolute spirit. Rather, it is chiefly a function of collective efforts and sacrifices made by sociopolitical movements," ibid., p. 208. Cf. also Habermas, "Über Moralität und Sittlichkeit – was macht eine Lebensform 'rational' ", in H. Schnädelbach (ed.), *Rationalität* (Frankfurt: Suhrkamp Verlag, 1984), pp. 218–35.

56  Ibid., p. 211.

57  Claus Offe, "Bindings, Shackles, Brakes: On Self-Limitation Strategies,"
    in A. Honneth, T. McCarthy, C. Offe and A. Wellmer (eds), *Cultural-
    Political Interventions in the Unfinished Project of Enlightenment*, trans.
    B. Fultner (Cambridge, MA: The MIT Press, 1992), p. 9.
58  Ibid., p. 20.
59  Cf. ibid., p. 35: "A close look at concrete institutions of interest-mediation
    and political will-formation may thus render the perspective of discourse
    ethics fruitful for a differentiated diagnosis showing which institutional
    arrangements, under the prevailing structures and conditions of the social
    division of labor, help agents to bear the burden of meeting the criteria of
    fairness, justice, and solidarity better than which other arrangements, and
    why."

# 3

# On the Pragmatics of Communicative Reason

In modern Western philosophy cognitive concerns with knowledge, truth, objectivity, and the like, particularly when prompted by exemplary achievements in the formal and physical sciences, have tended to predominate. The results of "theoretical" analyses have typically set the stage for the treatment of "practical" philosophical issues, even when thinkers like Kant defended the primacy of practical reason. What has been too often ignored and always underanalyzed is the pervasive normativity of social life. As a result, the deep roots of ethics and politics in the substance of human coexistence have largely remained not only out of sight but out of mind. This fateful blindness and forgetfulness are, perhaps, conditions of possibility for the astounding prevalence of cognitive-instrumental conceptions of reason in our tradition. Modeling practical reason simply as rational choice, for example, would otherwise make little sense, for it would be evident that the orientation to norms is as broad and deep as the orientation to ends, accountability as teleology, cooperation as competition. The depth and pervasiveness of normativity has, to be sure, not been entirely hidden from philosophical view. Earlier in this century, George Herbert Mead and Ludwig Wittgenstein brought it to attention in their different ways. And in more recent years the practically motivated analyses of Foucaultians and feminists have made visible a number of the ordinarily invisible ways in which the social world is constructed around normative conceptions. But for philosophical purposes, some of the conceptually richest accounts can be found extramurally, in recent contributions to the sociology of everyday life, especially in the ethnomethodological studies carried out by Harold Garfinkel and his associates. Their analyses of the pervasive normativity and accountability of social practice may serve as a fruitful point of departure for rethinking philosophical conceptions of practical reason.[1]

In chapter 3 I want to sketch some of the lessons that can be learned from ethnomethodology and then use them to plot an approach to communicative reason that steers a middle course between the inflationary aims of classical rationalism and the deflationary spirit of contemporary poststructuralism. I shall conclude by indicating some of the ways in which the paradigmatic philosophical enterprise of a critique of reason might be carried on from there.

## 3.1 The Rational Properties of Practical Activities

In the Parsonian paradigm that came to dominate sociological thought after World War II, social order was explained chiefly through the institutionalization and internalization of values and norms. Correspondingly, social action was represented as normatively regulated behavior such that deviations from institutionally established patterns would, regularly enough, be sanctioned; and social actors were depicted as psychologically committed, in consequence of the "need dispositions" instilled by socialization, to culturally shared values and normatively prescribed patterns of action. This conceptualization was effectively challenged in the 1960s by approaches to social action developed in the social interactionist tradition stemming from George Herbert Mead and in the tradition of phenomenological sociology stemming from Alfred Schutz. Particularly in the sociologies of everyday life elaborated by Erving Goffman and Harold Garfinkel and their followers, the picture of social actors as mere rule followers was rendered implausible beyond repair. Here I want only to distill a few key points from the ethnomethodological critique.[2]

In his *Studies in Ethnomethdology*, Garfinkel objects to the representation of social agents as "judgemental dopes" who simply act "in compliance with preestablished and legitimate alternatives of action that the common culture provides," or whose choices among alternatives are "compelled on the grounds of psychiatric biography, conditioning history, and the variables of mental functioning."[3] Such representations treat as epiphenomenal the agents' own knowledge of social norms and their active use of that knowledge to produce and manage the very scenes in which they are involved. As against them, Garfinkel focuses on practical reasoning in everyday settings and treats the "rational properties of practical activities" as the "ongoing accomplishments" of actors themselves.[4] The key to these accomplishments is the way we use our common-sense mastery of social organization to make situations of interaction *intelligible and ac-*

*countable.* The socially standardized understandings we bring to action settings comprise both shared background knowledge *and* common normative expectations, and thus they serve simultaneously as cognitive *and* normative presuppositions of interaction. We orient our behavior to these shared schemes of interpretation and expectation, mutually attributing awareness of them to one another and reciprocally holding one another accountable in terms of them.[5]

This altered view of the cognitive-normative basis of social order requires corresponding changes in received views of socialization and the motivation to conform. Becoming a competent social actor cannot be a matter merely of depth-psychological formation or behavioral conditioning, for the core of interactive competence is an extensive and detailed understanding of social organization, of the "natural-moral" facts of life in a society, of the rules of its different games. To be sure, the taken for granted background assumptions that enter into the production and recognition of "perceivedly normal" courses of action remain largely implicit, unformulated. We routinely bring to situations of interaction a tacit awareness of the normative expectations relevant to them and an intuitive appreciation of the consequences that might follow from breaking them. We implicitly attribute the same awareness and anticipation to our interaction partners, as they do to us, and we reciprocally hold one another accountable by reference to such shared expectations. If called to account, we may cite the relevant norms as reasons for normatively appropriate behavior, whereas violations usually require special considerations if they are to be excused or justified. Unwarranted departures from shared background expectations may be regarded as willful deviations and sanctioned by everything from negative affective responses and breakdowns in cooperation to explicit reprimands and punishments. The possibility of being called to account for what we do and our awareness of the differential accountability for behavior that deviates from, compared with that which conforms to, socially shared expectations are central to the normative constraint and motivated compliance that characterize routine interactions; as such, they are essential ingredients in any stable social order.

One aspect of the rational basis of social interaction upon which ethnomethodological studies have shed light is the way in which competent agents use their knowledge of what is normatively expected in a situation to shape their own conduct. They perform their actions with a view to how the latter will be perceived and assessed by others. Aware that they will be held accountable for what they do, they make what they do accountable; that is, a concern with accountability figures already in the "design" of their actions.[6] And the very considerations that enter into that design may, if they are called to account, be cited to explain and justify those actions. Accountability is thus "reflexive": it tacitly informs the very performance of the actions for which agents may be held accountable. Thus there is an inbuilt relation between the sorts of "reasonable consideration" that go into shaping our conduct and the sorts of "reasons" to which we may appeal in giving accounts of it. Rationally accountable agents are, in short, expected to produce accountably rational actions, that is, actions which can be described, explained, and justified as reasonable in their contexts. In the case of "perceivedly normal" courses of conduct, this may involve no more than a mention of elements of the common culture and existing institutions which serve as socially warranted grounds of inference and action, together with an indication of relevant features of the situation at hand. In the case of perceived breaches of standard expectations, something more will be required.

In either case, our accounts of our actions also contribute to the sense of the situations in which they are given. They do not merely provide "second-order" commentary on scenes of action defined independently of them. They are part and parcel of those very scenes, reflexively reconstituting the situations to which they refer. (Compare: "I didn't mean to ignore you. I just didn't hear you say 'hello'." and "I heard you, but after what you did last night I want nothing to do with you."[7]) The reflexivity of accountability and accounting means that reasons and reason-giving belong to the warp and woof of social interaction from the start. The type of critical-reflective discourse we earlier connected with the idea of autonomy thus marks a significant change in degree, but not the creation of a wholly new kind of interaction. It is, as it were, the everyday reflexivity of accounting practices become reflective.

Competent social actors are supposed to be able not only to understand what is going on and to give an account of themselves in standard situations, but to use their mastery of the rules of the game actively to manage social situations. Like Wittgenstein, Garfinkel rejects the received models of "rule-governed" behavior. On his account, social action is not simply a matter of following set rules in predefined situations, for social norms are neither exhaustive nor unambiguous, neither fully spelled out nor algorithmically applicable, and, as we have seen, social situations are not defined independently of the participants' own activities. By their very nature, general rules *must* understate the complexity of the concrete circumstance to which they apply. They are *supposed* to cover an indefinite range of specific instances, and those instances are not marked out as such in advance of any interpretive work. This is *a fortiori* true of the largely implicit, approximate, ambiguous, and open-ended norms that structure interaction in everyday life. Like any general rules, but even more so, they come without a detailed, exhaustive set of instructions for applying them. Thus they cannot determine, and hence cannot fully explain, specific, concrete actions in specific, concrete situations. Their "application" requires not unthinking conformity but competent practical reasoning to deal with contingencies as they arise and competent for-all-practical-purposes judgements in the light of concrete circumstances. And this of course means that there is always an element of the ad hoc and discretionary about their meaning-in-practice.[8] That meaning is elaborated continually as the agents whose behavior is guided by them negotiate the definitions of the ever-changing situations in which they are applied. As competent agents, they will be expected not only to know what everyone knows, but to supply the practical reasoning and good judgement required to put that knowledge into practice.

Not only "decontextualized" general rules and norms but also abstract general concepts, standards, criteria, principles, schemes, ideals, and so forth allow for an indefinite number of possible contextualizations, so that their particular, situated meaning has to be practically determined through participants' on-the-spot interpretations. This is at the root of another pervasive feature of social action, which Garfinkel, recalling the semantic properties of deictic terms, refers to as its indexicality. It is not only terms like "here" and "there," "then" and "now," "I" and "you" whose concrete sense is determined by the circumstances of utterance. This holds for general terms across the board. Thus the particular referent of typical referring terms (e.g. "the medicine," "the market") and the concrete sense of typical descriptive terms (e.g. "is expensive" as predicated of either) will also be dependent on when and where and by whom they are uttered. As a result, communication in natural language always depends on the "interpretive cooperation" of speakers and hearers. A speaker has no choice but to "trust" hearers to do the contextualizing "work" needed to make concrete sense of the terms with whose general meaning they are all familiar. Thus, mutual intelligibility is not given once and for all with socialization into a common language and culture; the latter is merely a precondition for something that has to be "ongoingly accomplished," in ever-changing circumstances, and always only "for all practical purposes."[9]

As Garfinkel points out, the indexicality of meaning holds not only for linguistic expressions but also for utterances as actions, as well as for actions generally. Their concrete sense can be understood only with reference to the who, when, where, what, and why of their performance.[10] Furthermore, the indexicality of action applies to accounting practices too. ("Why is *he* giving *this* account of *that, here* and *now*?") That is to say, everyday accounts are not merely representations of action. They may be that, but much more besides. For they are themselves practical actions with a point, designed to organize and manage social settings, and like other such actions they can function and signify in a variety of ways.

Because no two situations are exactly alike, general terms, rules, norms, standards, techniques, schemes, and the like *have to abstract* from determinate circumstances of application *if they are to be at all useful*. This is not a defect but a condition of possibility of speech and action.[11] And indexicality is just the other side of this abstract indeterminacy. Languages are spoken and understood, and actions are performed and recognized by particular individuals in particular situations. And that particularity inevitably contributes to the concrete sense that is made by and of speech and action. Contextual considerations are, then, always at play in the production and interpretation of meaning. This is the truth of contextualism – but it is not the whole truth. For it is precisely *the dialectic of the general and the particular* that sustains the play of signifiers. Some light has been thrown on just how this works by ethnomethodological studies of conversation. What seems to be required to make conversation work are formal structures with "local particularization potential," that is, abstract, general structures which are, on the one hand, relatively invariant to the parties speaking, but are also, on the other hand, able to accommodate the variations the latter introduce.[12] The dialectic of the general and the particular here takes the form of an interplay between structure and context carried through by competent actors who can orient to both. Reciprocally imputed, mutually assumed, and socially sanctioned structures of interaction are "locally" and "interactionally" managed by participants themselves through on-the-spot interpretations and judgements.[13] The key mechanism here is "recipient design," that is, the shaping of utterances and actions by participants so as to display not only a knowledge of the common culture but a sensitivity to the particular context, including the particular others involved and the history of their relationships.[14] Competent, practically rational agents are, then, the lifeblood of the dialectic. It is only through their "work" that the essential indeterminacy of language and culture can achieve the practical determinacy of speech and action in concrete contexts.

Sensitivity to context is itself exhibited in organized and accountable ways shaped by the general structures at play in a situation. The use of general referring or descriptive terms, for instance, establishes an orientation for whatever contextualizing work has to be done by a hearer to make (practically) determinate sense of a speaker's utterance of them on a particular occasion. "The description and its context elaborate each other. The description evokes a context to be searched and, in turn, the results of the search elaborate the specific sense of a description . . . The sense that is proposed by the speaker and achieved by the hearer will therefore be particular and locally situated. The [general] term elaborated by its circumstances of use will be *sufficient* [for all practical purposes, TMc]."[15] In short, the abstract indeterminacy of general terms need not be, and usually is not, a problem *in practice*. Combined with the extensive and detailed knowledge and the capacity for practical reasoning of competent language users, it is rather the wellspring of language's inexhaustible resourcefulness.

It is also important to note that the achievement of (practically) determinate sense in concrete circumstances happens over time. As social action always has a past and a future, its sense always has retrospective and prospective dimensions. What came before and what comes after are routinely understood as relevant to the sense of what is presently said or done; they figure in the determination of what is "in fact" and "really" meant by an utterance or action. (Example: "After what I said to him yesterday, his refusal to return my greeting is probably intended as a rebuke." "As it turns out, he was merely distracted and hadn't taken offence after all.") Not only the determination of an utterance's sense, but also the determination of its validity – of its truth, say, or of its sincerity – is a step-by-step affair that involves dealing with potential discrepancies, dismissing or "normalizing" them, and the like. If social interaction is to remain stable in the face of a vast and unpredictable range of potentially relevant considerations, participants must routinely adopt what Garfinkel calls a "wait-and-see" attitude toward one another's utterances and actions so as to learn "what will have been said or done." For their meaning and validity are inherently open to clarification, confirmation, alteration, and so forth by the future course of events in general and by how speakers and hearers notice and deal with various considerations in particular. For this reason too, mutual understanding and mutual agreement can only be ongoingly achieved.

As noted, this inherent openness of speech and action to reinterpretation and reevaluation places a burden of cooperation on members if mutual understanding is to be maintained in the face of the never-ending contingencies and exigencies of social life. For instance, speakers have to trust hearers to supply relevant contextualizations, and hearers are held accountable for implementing the usual methods of doing so. And as speakers' utterances reflexively contribute to the sense of the speech situations in which they are implicated, they are held accountable for employing the usual procedures to make their meanings sufficiently determinate for the purposes at hand. The "usual" methods and procedures include, as we have seen, orienting to the organizational patterns and structural features of a shared way of life, to the details of ever shifting contexts (e.g., to particular individuals, circumstances, and purposes), and to the temporal structures of sequences of interaction. This last aspect of interactional competence has been examined in some detail and to great effect by conversational analysts.[16] In designing what to say and in recognizing what is said, speakers and hearers routinely attend, tacitly but minutely, to the ways in which current speech acts form the context for subsequent speech acts. The temporal orderliness of conversation is continuously produced, displayed, recognized, and used by them as grounds for inference and action. Thus, for instance, the "proposals" contained in speech acts like questioning, inviting, requesting, and the like define situations to which subsequent speech acts will normally be, and be heard as, oriented – for instance, answering a question, accepting or declining an invitation, granting or refusing a request. The projection of relevant next activities and the orientation thereto are not merely "in the heads" of participants but "in the culture": they function as shared schemes of intelligibility and accountability. By such means, intersubjective understanding can be continually displayed and updated in and through the organizational details of conversation without having constantly to be thematized. That is to say, hearers can exhibit their understanding of prior speech acts indirectly by what they do with their "turns"; and speakers can by the same means monitor and correct how they have been understood – so that, for example, not using one's turn to correct a previously displayed understanding is normally taken to mean that one has been understood correctly.

Another feature of the cognitive/normative structures of ordinary conversation illustrates very strikingly how an orientation to mutual understanding is built into the finest details of linguistic interaction. "There is a bias intrinsic to many aspects of the organization of talk which is generally favorable to the maintenance of bonds of social solidarity."[17] For example, the types of proposal we considered above may be accepted or rejected, but the two responses are normally accomplished in quite different ways. While acceptances (e.g., of invitations, offers, requests, and the like) are normally simple and straightforward, refusals are normally delayed, qualified or mitigated, and treated as requiring an explanation. This differential patterning of "preferred" and "dispreferred" responses is relatively invariant across speakers, and even when it is not implemented it is oriented to.

Delayed acceptances, for example, are usually heard as "reluctant," and early, straightforward refusals as "hostile" or "rude." It is significant that the "preferred format responses" are "uniformly affiliative actions which are supportive of social solidarity, while dispreferred format responses are largely [disaffiliative and] destructive of social solidarity."[18] Moreover, the preferred explanations for refusals are "no fault" accounts (e.g., an inability – rather than an unwillingness – to accept) that "save face" and preserve relationships. And prefatory delays before dispreferred responses are routinely used by speakers to modify or revise their offers before rejection occurs so as to mitigate the "face-threatening" potential of the latter. Structures of this sort, through which conflict is avoided and solidarity promoted, are pervasive in conversation. And participants are not only expected to implement them, they are held accountable for doing so. Ordinary talk thus exhibits a decided normative-structural bias in favor of maintaining the intersubjectivity of mutual understanding.[19]

This analysis of the structure of social action cuts not only against explanations of social order that ignore practical reasoning altogether while emphasizing unconscious processes, conditioning, habit, custom, or the like, but also against explanations that do focus on practical reasoning but construe it exclusively in instrumental terms. To *reduce* practical reasoning to calculations of rational choice is to ignore an equally fundamental dimension of social interaction: normality is normatively provided for, stability is underwritten by accountability. In a slogan: doing the right thing is as pervasive an action orientation as doing the smart thing. Garfinkel attempts to capture this side of things in his characterization of social order as a moral order. "For Kant, the moral order 'within' was an awesome mystery; for sociologists, the moral order 'without' is a technical mystery. A society's members encounter and know the moral order as perceivedly normal courses of action."[20] The shared understandings that *constitute* the common-sense meaning of social situations are at the same time reciprocal expectations that *regulate* behavior in them. The very framework of intelligibility which is *presupposed* by any concrete representation of social interests, social conflicts, or social force, and which cannot therefore be reduced to them, is a framework of normative *accountability*. Mutual understandings and normative expectations are as basic to the structure of social action as teleological orientations to means and ends.

This last observation suggests the deep affinities between Garfinkel's account of the routine grounds of everyday activities and Habermas's account of the structure of communicative interaction. But there are important differences as well, and they turn on precisely the elements that Habermas regards as central to his conception of communicative *reason*: context-transcending validity claims and idealizing presuppositions.[21] Can the transcendence and idealization stressed by Habermas somehow be reconciled with the indexicality and practicality emphasized by Garfinkel? In the following section I shall argue that they can, that communicative rationality may be understood temporally (it is an ongoing accomplishment), pragmatically (which is never absolute but always only for all practical purposes), and contextually (in ever changing circumstances), *without surrendering* transcendence (it turns on validity claims that go beyond the particular contexts in which they are raised) or idealization (and rests on pragmatic presuppositions that function as regulative ideas). Before moving on, however, I want to follow briefly a path of reconciliation marked on the ethnomethodological terrain itself.

In section 2.2, I referred briefly to Melvin Pollner's studies of "mundane reasoning" about the real world in everyday settings.[22] The phenomena that attracted his attention were the practices through which we maintain the supposition of an objective world in the face of discrepant reports about just what belongs to it. He found that conflicts of experience and testimony are normally dealt with in ways that themselves presuppose, and thus reconfirm, the existence of a unitary, coherent, independent reality. For example, discrepancies are attributed to errors in perception owing to poor visibility, physical obstacles, weak eyesight, lack of proper equipment, optical illusions, hallucinations, and so forth; or to errors of interpretation due to the fact that the observer is inexperienced, does not have the whole story, is telling the story from a restricted vantagepoint, and the like; or to errors in reporting, ranging from unclarity and imprecision to outright lying. It is a significant feature of such "error accounts" that we are held sanctionably accountable for producing them in the appropriate circumstances. That is to say, the maintenance of a unitary objective world is normatively required by the background expectations structuring everyday interaction. We are held accountable and in turn hold our interaction partners accountable for treating the transcendent reality of this world as invariant to discrepant reports. And we meet this demand by drawing on a repertoire of procedures for resolving conflicts about "what is really the case" which are themselves based on the very presupposition they are deployed to maintain. In short, the objectivity of the real world, the basis of our cooperative activities, is both a constant presupposition and an ongoing accomplishment of everyday interaction.[23]

Pollner also notes that the idea of the world's objective reality is internally linked to the idea of its intersubjective availability.[24] That is, we assume that we are perceiving, experiencing, and reporting the same independent reality. And just as the latter is assumed to be unitary and coherent, so too all the correct accounts of it must add up in the end to one coherent account, that is, to "the truth" about the objective world. When actual accounts depart from this ideal, we do not alter it but them. To claim truth for one's statements about the objective world is thus to anticipate corroborative reports from all other competent observers. When they are not forthcoming, we resort to error accounts, which draw on "an indefinitely large and various *ceteris paribus* provision" regarding the capacities and circumstances of presumably competent agents.[25] We can point, for instance, to physical, psychological, developmental, educational, cultural, professional, or ideological factors to explain discrepancies. "The assumption of a commonly shared world does not function as a descriptive assertion. It is not falsifiable . . . On the occasion of a disjuncture, a mundane reasoner looks to the 'all other things being equal' clause implicated in the anticipation of unanimity . . . A disjuncture is compelling grounds for asserting that one or another of the conditions thought to obtain in the anticipation of unanimity did not."[26] This means that the idea of an objective world knowable in common functions not only "constitutively" – that is, as an assumption that actually informs our practices – but also, "regulatively" – that is, as a presupposition that normatively constrains and guides our practices, including our accounting practices. It is just this constitutive-regulative duality that Habermas wants to capture in his conception of ideas of reason as unavoidable *suppositions* of communicative interaction.

The key to a pragmatic conception of communicative rationality is to understand how such ideas of reason work *in practice*, for it is only in practice that the aporetic tensions between the ideal and the real, the transcendent and the immanent, the first- and third-person points of view can be, not dissolved, but put into play and rendered productive. Thus we need not, and should not *define* truth in terms, say, of warranted assertability or acceptability under ideal epistemic conditions. What is important is to grasp the *socio-logic* of truth,[27] the internal connection between truth claims and rational acceptability that is built into our practices of truth-telling. An adequate account of these practices would have to capture not only the indexical aspects of making truth claims and offering warrants for them, but the situation-transcending import of the claims themselves – such that, for instance, it makes perfectly good sense to say things like, we have good reason to believe that *p*, but of course we may be wrong. Appealing to the idea of truth, we can criticize not only particular claims but also the very standards we have inherited. Though truth as a validity claim is never divorced from social practices of justification, from the rules and warrants of this or that sociocultural context, it cannot be reduced to any particular set thereof. The context-transcendent import of the idea of truth, its regulative "surplus" of meaning, exposes us to criticism from very different points of view. Without that idealizing moment, there would be no foothold in our established beliefs and practices for the basic challenges to consensus that force us to expand our horizons and learn to see things in new ways. The claim to a validity that carries beyond the particular circumstances of utterance, indeed a validity that could be rationally acknowledged by all competent judges under ideal epistemic conditions, is precisely what opens up assertions to ongoing discursive examination.

## 3.2  Pragmatizing Communicative Rationality

Context-transcendence through the idealizing projection of a horizon of unlimited validity has always been a function of reason in our philosophical tradition. From the time of Socrates, reason has been viewed as a capacity to go beyond the immediacies of sense, place, time, upbringing, authority, convention, tradition, and the like and to appeal to considerations that any reasonable person could accept. To renounce all strong notions of reason is to forfeit this potential for self- and situation-transcendence. However, our philosophical tradition is also replete with skeptical critiques of such notions. In current practice, criticism often takes the form of countering the idealizing presuppositions we have been considering with an array of ontological presuppositions that seem to give them the lie: the former are seen to be contrary to fact when we attend to the latter. Claims to unconditional validity are everywhere found to be conditioned by factors beyond the immediate ken of the claimants and hence, it seems, in vain. Under the rubrics of "language," "power," "Being," "*différance*," and the like, deconstructionist critics have in this way heightened our awareness of the vast and heterogeneous "unconscious" that underlies all conscious practices, including such paradigmatically rational practices as theorizing, reflecting, and criticizing. Critical social theorists have certainly not been unaware of such conditionality. It was, after all, Marx who taught us that consciousness is not pure but "afflicted" from the start with the "burdens" of matter, that it is "directly interwoven with the material activity and the material intercourse of human beings."[28] And the members of the original Frankfurt School did not hesitate to add cultural and psychological "burdens" to the socioeconomic ones. Yet, as I explained in chapter 1, the partially desublimated notions of reason and rational autonomy that the early Horkheimer and his colleagues in the Institute for Social Research worked with were still too strong to withstand the latest round of attacks on Western rationalism.

I now want to argue that Habermas's account of communicative reason, if read through the sort of pragmatizing lens provided by ethnomethodology, is able to accommodate ontological as well as idealizing assumptions. Even if the former always render the latter counterfactual, that is, even if the ideal conditions supposed in the anticipation of universal agreement never in fact obtain, ideas of reason are not thereby rendered useless or inherently pernicious. One of their salutary functions, I have suggested, is to serve as ongoing correctives to actually accepted validity claims. This perspective under-scores the importance of critical traditions and the institutionalization of critical discourses. As we have seen, practical reasoning and public accounting are already pervasive in everyday interaction. Competent actors are sanctionably expected to produce accountable actions, that is, to act in ways that are publicly explicable and publicly defensible. The accounts called for typically involve nothing more than an appeal to conventional, customary, taken-for-granted warrants of various kinds – shared beliefs, standards, norms, values, and the like – and an explication of the action situation in terms of them. But conventional warrants can lose their unquestioned character and, under certain circumstances, that may result in validity claims being thematized in critical-reflective discourse.

In the context of theoretical discourse, the regulative force of the idea of truth is supposed to be given full scope and the traditional bounds of the communication community to be expanded without limit. In practice, of course, rational acceptance by all competent judges is not something we can hope to accomplish all at once or once and for all. Rather, we try to establish the warranted assertability of a truth claim *in a particular forum* and implicitly assume responsibility – Habermas might say, issue a warranty – for demonstrating its rational acceptability in other relevant forums as well.[29] The unlimited inclu-siveness of the claim to truth is, thus, never more than potential. It is a promissory note issued across the full expanse of social space and historical time.[30] Whether or not this promise can be made good always remains to be seen. As Garfinkel might put it, warranted assertability is always "until further notice"; we always have to "wait and see" whether the reasons we found compelling in discursive conditions we assumed to be ideal (or close enough) were actually so. It is because validity claims are redeemed by the grounds or reasons offered in support of them, and not by agreement as such, that any existing consensus is open to reconsideration.[31] In the end, there is no way of determining which is "the better argument" apart from how competing arguments fare over time, that is, how they stand up to the ongoing give-and-take of argumentative discourse. The redemption of truth claims, the establishment of their warranted assertability or rational acceptability, is thus an intrinsically temporal, open-ended process. Because "for us" all the evidence is never in and all the conditions are never ideal, it is a potentially misleading hypostatization to speak, as Habermas sometimes does, of "rationally motivated consensus" in anything but processual terms – all the more so once we have abandoned traditional notions of demonstrative certainty and realized that in most areas we have to make do with a "principle of insufficient reason."[32] Intersubjective recognition of truth claims has to be ongoingly accomplished through rationally persuading one audience after another that it is "reasonable" to accept them, that is, that there are good reasons for doing so, better reasons than for accepting any of the available alternatives.

Claims to scientific truth, for instance, are raised and discussed in culturally and institutionally established forums that promote their critical examination over time. Scientists have reflexively to anticipate the scrutiny of their work by others who share the cognitive, normative, and evaluative presuppositions marking them as members of the same scientific subcommunity. If they can convince that particular audience, they have reason to expect they could convince other relevant audiences as well. That is to say, in virtue of its presumed competence, that audience can plausibly stand in for the "universal audience" of all rational beings able to judge in the matter.[33] It is this temporally extended, in principle never-ending, to-and-fro of claim and criticism in institutionalized forums, vis-à-vis particular audiences authorized to represent the universal audience, that constitutes scientific discourse. And this ongoing, dialectical give-and-take lives from the universality of the truth claims raised – the implicit promise they contain to convince a universal audience. Without that, argumentative discourse would degenerate into the "I think"/"you think," "we think"/"they think" of argument in its colloquial sense. With it, the "conversation" continues, as Rorty might say – in significant part, through ever-renewed efforts of critics to discover the hidden conditions of what is allegedly unconditional and to take them explicitly into account. Scientific truth, as the continually revised outcome of this open-ended dialectic, can only be an ongoing accomplishment. But the process itself makes no sense apart from the supposition of an objective world and the repeated claims to have captured some truth about it. They are what prompt critique and fuel dialectical movement.

The unavoidability of ontological presuppositions of various sorts does entail that there will always be a gap between the ideal and the real. But it does not follow from this that we ought to keep ourselves pure by forsaking participation for the standpoint of the uninvolved spectator. As I argued above, that is not an option for us. We cannot but be participants and thus cannot avoid undertaking the presuppositions this entails.[34] Nor is ironic participation, distancing ourselves from suppositions we regard as illusory but cannot avoid making, more than an occasional possibility. In fact, the very notion that the idealizing assumptions underlying communicative interaction are "illusions" smacks of a nostalgia for presuppositionless starting-points. The post-metaphysical question is, rather, what does the gap between the ideal and the real mean *in practice*. I have argued that it is, among other things, an invitation to *critical participation*, which has to be understood in process terms. Becoming conscious of unconscious determinants of our thought and action is not a fully achievable state of affairs but an orientation for ongoing efforts to deal reflectively with real problems, actually experienced, in concrete situations: critical self-awareness is always only "for all practical purposes." This is as true of the sorts of "ontological unconscious" stressed by deconstructionists as it is of the "psychological unconscious" that interested Freud, the "cultural unconscious" attended to by hermeneutics, and the "social-structural unconscious" unearthed by Marx. In all these dimensions, even if we suppose the possibility in principle of bringing any *particular* unconscious factor to consciousness, that by no means amounts to supposing that they might all be made conscious at once. The hope for such self-transparency disappeared with German Idealism. And this means that at every moment and in every situation unconscious factors – in this very broad sense – will inevitably play a role in shaping our interpretive and evaluative schemes. The moral of this story, however, is not a deconstructionist renunciation of any non-ironic employment of ideas of reason but a critical-pragmatic warning against treating any attempt to specify them as finished, final, complete. It reminds us that universal validity claims can be only provisionally redeemed, that the – less than logically compelling – warrants which suffice to convince one audience in one set of circumstances will not suffice to convince all other audiences in all other circumstances, and thus that "convincing a universal audience" can never be anything more than an orientation to essentially open-ended discursive processes.[35]

The dialectic of the ideal and the real, like that of the general and the particular discussed in section 2.4, is borne along by the on-the-spot actions and utterances of accountable agents. It is, as we saw, only through their situated exercise of practical reasoning and judgement that the inherent – and functionally necessary – indeterminacy of linguistic and cultural patterns can achieve the practical determinacy of everyday speech and action. But competent agents can just as well render the determinate indeterminate, the unproblematic problematic, the accepted unacceptable. That is to say, since mutual intelligibility and mutual understanding have to be ongoingly accomplished by the parties to interaction themselves, the outcomes of interaction are not determined in advance by pre-existing structures of whatever sorts. Represented, as they typically are, apart from the agents that bear them, social and cultural structures may seem to be devoid of any inherent dynamic of change. It is to agency that we must look if we hope to comprehend that dynamic, and particularly if we hope to understand the indeterminacy, innovation, proliferation, and the like to which poststructuralists so often appeal in opposing the hegemony of logocentrism, while at the same time espousing holistic conceptions of language, culture, and society that leave little or no room for agency.[36] Practically reasoning agents are a condition of possibility of determinacy *and* indeterminacy, stability *and* innovation, repetition *and* proliferation. And this means, in the case of all such apparent oppositions, that you can't have one without the other. Of course, the agents in question are always socialized agents and their agency is always informed by the sociocultural lifeworlds they take for granted and, in taking for granted, renew. The circle connecting presuppositions to accomplishments is at work here as well; but it is a non-vicious circle and one that is continually being redrawn.

The critical potential of the role that the theory of communicative action reserves to autonomous agents sometimes gets obscured by the stress Habermas places on agreement and consensus. But there are repeated, unambiguous indications of the negative freedoms built into the discourse model as well, as when he underscores "the individual's inalienable right" to agree or disagree, his or her "uninfringeable freedom to respond with a 'yes' or 'no' to criticizable validity claims."[37] It was in this latter spirit that Foucault, asked to comment on the consensus model, insisted on regarding consensus as a "critical" rather than a "regulatory" principle, "because starting from the point where you say regulatory principle, you grant that it is indeed under its governance that the phenomenon has to be organized . . . I would say, rather, that it is perhaps a critical idea to maintain at all times: to ask oneself what proportion of nonconsensuality is implied in [a] power relation and whether that degree of nonconsensuality is necessary or not . . . The farthest I would go is to say that perhaps one must not be for consensuality, but one must be against nonconsensuality."[38] Habermas, of course, wants to argue that these are two sides of the same coin. Rational consensus as a regulative principle already makes agreement depend on the uncoerced "yes" or "no" of each participant, already confers upon everyone involved the right to withhold assent unless and until convinced. The threat that Foucault, with good historical reason, to be sure, sees looming behind positive versions of any such principle can be countered if we place equal stress on the negative version. Kant, it will be recalled, already balanced the universal-law formulation of his categorical imperative with a formulation interdicting the treatment of others as less than responsible subjects: "Act in such a way that you always treat humanity, whether in your own person or in the person of any other, never simply as a means, but always at the same time as an end!"[39] In explaining this formulation, he noted that it entailed respecting the competence of others to give or withhold their assent, that is, it enjoined treating them as *mündige*, mature and responsible agents capable of conducting their own lives on the basis of their own insights, deliberations, and judgements.[40]

On the other hand, the problems that ensue from thinking of freedom *only* in negative and individualistic terms, that is, only in terms of individual rights that may not be interfered with, are well known from the history of political theory and I will not rehearse them here. If human beings are essentially social beings, beings whose very individuation is the outcome of processes of socialization, then their freedom too must have a social dimension that gets expressed in the way they participate in the collective lives of their societies. This "positive" freedom comprises not merely the absence of any interference with each doing what he or she wants to do, but the ways we act together to deal with matters of common concern, particularly the ways we deliberate on and decide in public what it is we want to do. Habermas's discourse model attempts to combine both "liberal" and "civic republican" moments of democratic will-formation: the basic right of any individual to grant or withhold assent and the active participation of all individuals in the shaping of a common will. And, as we saw in section 2.4, he maintains that freedom in this dual sense can exist, as Albrecht Wellmer has put it, "only as a form of ethical life [*Sittlichkeit*], that is, as a communal practice pervading the institutions of society at all levels and habitualized in the character, the customs, and the moral sentiments of its citizens."[41] Here, however, I am interested only in the relation of positive and negative freedom that is built into the discourse model itself: the very idea of rationally motivated consensus opens up, and holds open, a space for dissent. As we would by now expect, this idea of reason both informs ("constitutes") our discursive behavior and normatively ("regulatively") constrains and guides it. The corresponding demands — for competence, good will, and openness to reason on the part of participants, say, and for reciprocity, symmetry, and the absence of force in their discursive interactions — serve precisely as avenues of criticism directed at *de facto* agreements that claim to be rationally motivated: Was the outcome of discussion somehow determined by force or threats of force, by a differential distribution of power and privilege, by consciously or unconsciously strategic motivations, by the inability of participants to know and speak their minds or to "listen to reason?"

As explained in section 3.1, the concrete, situated meaning of *any* general norm, value, ideal, standard, or the like has to be practically determined by participants' on-the-spot interpretations and judgements. This belongs to the very nature of general normative schemes; they are supposed to cover an indefinite range and variety of specific instances. And while previously accomplished applications may serve as a guide to and, in varying degrees, as a constraint upon future interpretations, they are never sufficient to determine them exhaustively and thus to remove the need for competent practical reasoning and good judgement. To repeat a point made earlier, this is not a defect of general normative structures, but a condition of their possibility. The omnipresent dialectic of the general and the particular becomes all the more central to the institutions of post-traditional, pluralistic societies. General norms have to be accepted as binding by socially and culturally heterogeneous groups. Their legitimacy can no longer rely upon a shared comprehensive view of the meaning and value of life. In binding all alike, they must at the same time allow for diversity and difference. These apparently conflicting requirements can be met only by abstract, general norms that are applied with situation-specific inflections. In this respect, abstract generality is not a threat to difference but a licence for it. The currently widespread notion that concrete, specific norms and values are somehow more respectful of difference is a "logical howler" pure and simple. There is no *need* to impose general conceptions rigidly on variegated situations. Abstraction *need* not mean homogenization, nor universality uniformity. Here, as elsewhere, everything depends on how they are put into practice. As Garfinkel has reminded us, *all* "the rational properties" of our activities have to be ongoingly accomplished by the actors themselves. If we want, for instance, to think sensibly about what "impartiality" does or should mean in the judicial system, we have to examine how it is or should be put into practice in all the different settings and by all the different actors in that domain. The same holds for "objectivity" in science, "effectiveness" in technology, "efficiency" in business, "self-determination" in politics, "self-fulfillment" in personal life, and so on. The point, in short, is to reject the either/or opposition between decontextualized-because-generalized norms and values, on the one hand, and contextualized-because-particularized judgements, on the other. Especially in modern pluralistic societies, we cannot help but have it both ways, that is, agree upon *some* decontextualized – abstract, general, formal – norms, values, principles, rights, procedures, and the like, which must then be on-goingly contextualized – interpreted, elaborated, applied – in particular situations. As there is no way of predicting the variety and multiplicity of actors, settings, purposes, and so forth that will thereby come into play, there is no possibility of fully predetermining their meaning-in-practice. It is precisely because abstract, formal structures and procedures leave a much broader scope for "local particularization potential" than do prescriptions of concrete patterns of behavior that they are so central to modern societies. And it is for the same reason that their concrete meaning-in-action is inherently open to discussion, that is to say, essentially contestable.

## 3.3   On the Methodologies of Critical Social Theory

Like its philosophical predecessor, the critique of impure reason is concerned both to "assure to reason its lawful claims" and to "dismiss groundless pretensions" made in its name.[42] But this is now seen to require sociocultural studies of reason in practice that go beyond the bounds of philosophical analysis. As Horkheimer earlier emphasized, the types of inquiry in question may not be limited to an empathetic understanding (*Verstehen*) of putatively rational practices but must take seriously claims to validity and submit them to critical evaluation (*sachliche Prüfung*).[43] Critique does not conclude merely with demonstrating the socially conditioned character of such practices, for that is not *per se* incompatible with the validity they claim, once the latter is understood in a deabsolutized sense consistent with our finitude. The key to avoiding both a pure "insider's" or participant's standpoint and a pure "outsider's" or observer's standpoint is, I have suggested, to adopt the perspective of a critical-reflective participant. As there is no God's-eye point of view available to us, we can do no better than move back and forth between the different standpoints, playing one off against the other.[44] While we cannot avoid supposing *in actu* that we are capable of acting on reasons, that assumption can be critically tested in different forms of reflective inquiry. There is a variety of such forms and I shall not try here to provide even a tentative overview of them. But I would like to mention and very briefly characterize a few of the more familiar ones. The characterizations are not meant to be definitive but suggestive, and the boundaries they draw not rigid but flexible and porous. However considerable their differences, the modes of reflective inquiry I shall mention have in common a capacity to distance us from (some of) the practices we live in, so as to open their implicit and explicit validity claims to critical examination. Insofar as the claims stand up to scrutiny, the inquiries in question can be said to have contributed to the rational reconstruction of those practices, insofar as they do not, to their critical deconstruction. Reflective affirmation of "lawful claims" and ideology critique of "groundless pretensions" remain permanent possibilities of rational criticism even after its sociocultural turn.

"Thick descriptions" from the point of view of a "stranger" may already have significant distancing and defamiliarizing effects on the participants whose practices are being rendered. Thus, for example, minute depictions of gender and racial relations in various settings have, sometimes through the sheer shock of recognition, made problematic what was heretofore taken-for-granted and transformed self-understandings in ways that have implications for practice. Similar effects have been produced by detailed accounts of how we govern ourselves and others through the production of truth in certain human sciences, by ethnographic reports on the contingencies and vagaries of laboratory life, and by ethnomethodological descriptions of the classification and interpretation of social-scientific data, the generation and use of official statistics, and the maintenance of institutional realities. In these and like inquiries, different sorts of thick descriptions already provide critical perspectives on beliefs, practices, concepts, rules, standards, procedures, techniques, and so forth, which had been unquestioningly applied and ideally represented as rational – or even as natural and immutable. And often enough the critical perspectives are sufficient to undermine the authority that derived from their presumed and idealized rationality. Of course, detailed descriptions need not undermine what they depict; they may as well show that the respect accorded certain reputedly rational practices is in fact deserved. This is true, for instance, of the central role of experimentation in the natural sciences, which is again and again reaffirmed in ethnographies of science – quite often against their express intentions. It is also true, as we saw, of the temporal orderliness and affiliative bias of turn-taking structures uncovered by conversational analysts.

The same dual potential for corroboration and critique resides in more elaborate interpretive approaches as well. As Paul Ricoeur, among others, has made clear, the hermeneutics of recovery and affirmation is shadowed at every step by a hermeneutics of suspicion and demystification.[45] Gadamer and Freud represent permanent possibilities of interpretation. And that remains true when interpretive practices draw more or less heavily on structuralist techniques. Reconstructed rule systems can turn out, as they do in Foucault's archaeological investigations, to be contingent, arbitrary, "transformable singularities," or they can turn out, as they do in Habermas's pragmatic analyses of communication, to be enabling conditions of basic practices to which there are no good alternatives. That is to say, there is nothing in the methods of ethnographic description, hermeneutic interpretation, or microstructural analysis *as such* that dictates from the start whether the distanced perspectives they offer on lived practices will contribute to the latter's rational reconstruction or their critical deconstruction.

This can also be said of historical studies of reason-in-context. Histories of the present can, like Gadamer's history of hermeneutics, take the form of *Bildungs*-narratives depicting formative learning-processes of one kind or another, or they can, like MacIntyre's history of ethics and politics, take the form of *Verfalls*-narratives depicting processes of loss and decline.[46] The spectrum of possibilities does not narrow when social histories are constructed with the help of explicitly theoretical schemes. At present that spectrum ranges from Foucault's genealogical studies – in which paradigmatically rational practices are placed in the sociocultural contexts in which they emerge, develop, and function, so as to reveal the constellations of power and desire invested in them – to Habermas's social-evolutionary accounts of the development of normative structures, and from rational reconstructions of (episodes in) the history of modern science by conventional philosophers of science to critical deconstructions of (aspects of) the history of modern biology in feminist epistemologies of sciences. Again, there is nothing in the idea of a history of the present *as such* that predetermines the outcomes of investigation. The latter will depend on which aspects of which practices are the objects of investigation, as well as on which interpretive schemes and methods of analysis prove to be most adequate to them. One would expect that the most convincing accounts will sometimes be stories of gain, sometimes stories of loss, but mostly stories of both – as were, indeed the classical social-theoretical accounts of the emergence of the modern world as a whole.

Those accounts drew heavily on macrosociological frameworks of various sorts – institutional, social-structural, functional, systems-theoretical – which provided for another level of analysis of lived practices. Macroframeworks make it possible to study conditions and consequences of action that are beyond the ken of participants. They enable the observer to situate particular practices in stable patterns of practices and in fields of interdependencies among such patterns, and thus better to understand the role they play in reproducing large-scale social systems.[47] And this provides a new and important perspective on the putative rationality of the practices in question. Apparently beneficial, or at least harmless, practices – for instance, of financial investment or of pictorial representation – may turn out to be important ingredients in sustaining orders of oppression. This recognition transforms unintended consequences into, if not exactly intended consequences, at least known side-effects that have to be taken into account when assessing the rationality of the practices in question.

Of course, that assessment will depend to an extent on the availability and preferability of alternatives. This is one of the uses to which comparative studies can be put: they can make us aware, at both micro- and macro-levels of analysis, of different ways of doing things, and thus of the peculiarities of our own ways, as well as of their relative advantages and disadvantages. And through such awareness we can come to understand better that realizing one set of values always precludes realizing others, and thus that there is no gain without loss. Comparative analysis is, then, itself a way of taking critical distance from the taken-for-granteds of our own forms of life. And, as existing studies make evident, it can be carried out in any number of dimensions – linguistic, cultural, psychological, political, economic, sociological, and so on. *How* it should be carried out is, to be sure, a hotly debated question at the moment, for it intersects with the heightened sensitivity to otherness and difference. In section 3.4, I will conclude with some observations on certain aspects of those debates. That will provide an opportunity for a last, brief look at what is perhaps the thorniest issue raised by the sociocultural transformation of the critique of reason: what to make of the cultural variability of supposedly rational practices. But first a few additional – equally brief and unsupported – remarks about the sorts of critical inquiry suited to a critique of impure reason:

- Sociocultural approaches to critique are of ethical-political import, since the conceptions of reason they interrogate are actually embodied in practices and institutions and are analyzed and assessed with that in mind.
- All such approaches rely, implicitly or explicitly, on interpretive schemes that guide the selection, description, organization, and explication of "data."[48]

- At their most elaborate, these schemes appear as the empirically and theoretically informed, historically oriented and practically interested, general interpretive frameworks that we associate with the tradition of "grand" theorizing from Marx and Weber to Habermas and Foucault.[49]
- The theoretically generalized narratives constructed in this tradition have typically employed basic categories tailored to grasping the "rationalization" of culture and society, and those categories have typically been of philosophical ancestry, precisely because modern philosophy has centered on the critique of reason.
- The appropriation of philosophically derived concepts of reason for social-theoretical purposes enabled the grand theorists to build a tension between the real and the ideal into their interpretive frameworks and thus to combine – in very different ways, to be sure – normative and empirical perspectives in systematic narratives.
- Those narratives were constructed as histories of the present, with the practical-political aim of helping us to understand better some of the central practices and institutions of our form of life – how they arose and became established, what possibilities they opened up and/or closed off, how they functioned in the larger society, what they were good and/or bad for, and of which general trends their developments were symptomatic – in ways that entailed challenges to received understandings and thus to the orders the latter supported.
- The construction of these grand narratives combined, in different ways, many of the methods mentioned above – descriptive, interpretive, genealogical, reconstructive, structuralist, functionalist, and so on. Those methods have also been used in more limited combinations and for less ambitious purposes. However, the critique of impure reason requires, in the end, that rational practices be studied both from the "inside" *and* from the "outside," synchronically *and* diachronically, locally *and* globally, structurally *and* functionally, normatively *and* empirically. None of the separate approaches, taken by itself, gives us the whole story.

Pursuing these methodological issues, however natural a continuation of the line of argument set forth there, would take us too far afield.[50] There is, however, a set of more or less methodological concerns about cross-cultural interpretation that can scarcely be avoided once the socio-logical turn has been taken, and about them I would like to make a few, brief, concluding remarks.

## 3.4   Multicultural Cosmopolitanism

The "rationality and relativism" debates surrounding anthropology have political as well as philosophical roots.[51] Anthropology as a discipline was embedded in colonialism: observers from the imperial "centers" reported on strange ways of life at the "peripheries." Once the fieldwork paradigm became firmly established earlier in this century, accounts of alien cultures were supposed to be based on "participant observation," a fragile combination of experiential nearness and analytical distance. The natural-historical ambitions of classical anthropology rested on the assumption that "they" could be accurately described in "our" terms, an epistemological confidence reflected in the realist genre conventions of its canonical texts. During the decolonization struggles following World War II, these ambitions and assumptions began to shift. New types of interpretive ethnography came to the fore, whose purpose it was to *enter into* different systems of meaning and understand how the world looked from *their points of view*. The standard metaphor of reading cultural texts for their meanings was often mixed with the metaphor of dialogue to yield an essentially hermeneutic conception of the anthropological enterprise: seriously to study another way of life amounted to a kind of virtual conversation of humankind in which the horizons of "our" form of life were expanded through sympathetically engaging with "theirs". Frequently associated with this was the cultural-political motif of recovering and redeeming authentic native traditions, customs, and identities in danger of disappearing precisely through having been "discovered" and colonized.

More recently, a new generation of anthropologists has come to the fore, conscious of writing now not only for their traditional, mostly Western audiences, but for multicultural audiences prominently including postcolonial intellectuals and scholars sophisticated in the ways of the "metropolis." The presence of this critical audience places enormous pressure on received ideas of social-scientific objectivity, which are, after all, closely linked to notions of intersubjective validation. The "community of investigators" that now has to be convinced includes a much greater variety of "competent observers," among them indigenous anthropologists who cannot be counted on to share the assumptions that have historically structured that discipline. Gaze is now met by gaze, description by description, critique by critique. The realities of writing in this increasingly decentered and multicultural public sphere have markedly heightened ethnographic self-consciousness and prompted radical experimentation with its genre conventions. Thus, for example, the virtual dialogues of hermeneutic approaches have given way to the construction of actually dialogical or "polyphonic" texts that permit those being represented to speak in their own voices, tell their own stories, challenge the ethnographers' views, offer alternative suggestions, and the like. Ethnographic accounts have always been the products of complex, situated, ambiguous, and conflictual interactions;[52] the new "reflexive" anthropologists no longer try to conceal that fact behind the smooth objectivity of realist description or the uninterrupted soliloquies of symbolic interpretation.

It is important to see that stylistic issues of this kind are closely connected with epistemological issues. The objectivity and adequacy of participant observers' "third-person" accounts of beliefs and practices that are already informed by "first-" and "second-person" accounts cannot, in the end, be warranted independently of the latter. Such representations are *in principle* contestable by the subjects whose beliefs and practices are in question. This is one of the features of subject/subject epistemic relations that distinguish them from epistemic relations between subjects and objects-pure-and-simple. Subjects can talk back, criticize observers' understandings of them, offer alternative accounts; they can even offer accounts of what it is about the observers and their home cultures that tend to make their representations misrepresentations in important respects. The one-way descriptions of classical realism disqualified their subjects as competent partners in dialogue in the very act of representing them. And though "symbols and meaning" anthropology replaced the subject/object model of description with a subject/subject model of dialogue, the "conversations" it generated were virtual, not actual.[53] The very metaphor of a text to be read simply displaced the active/passive asymmetry of classical realism. The interpreter continued to assume an ethnographic authority to represent meanings in ways that were not exposed to reciprocal contestation by those whose meanings were being represented.[54] And this, of course, raises not only stylistic and epistemological questions, but issues of morals and politics.

Who gets to represent whom, when, where, how, and for what purposes is not without political consequences. Cultural representations help form the images we have of others; if assimilated by those others, they influence the images they have of themselves as well; they get embodied in institutions and inform policies and practices. In these ways, anthropology not only grew out of the colonial situation, it reinforced it with images of the essential pastness, immaturity, and irrationality of non-Western peoples. "They" were, in the very process of representation, denied the competence to contest those representations. Asymmetries of representation thus enacted and reproduced asymmetries of power in the colonial world. Not surprisingly, in the postcolonial situation, contestation of the meaning and method of cross-cultural representation has taken on the same importance for "Third-World" intellectuals and their allies as has the contestation of established and influential representations of gender, race, and ethnic and sexual differences for the politics of the "First World." And in the process it has become clear that the non-reciprocity and asymmetry of cross-cultural representations cannot effectively be countered by textual strategies alone, for the latter do not directly address the social, economic, political, military, and cultural asymmetries of the global force fields within which such representations are *still* situated. The "crisis of representation" in contemporary anthropology could be resolved in the end only through cross-cultural communications that were actually, rather than virtually, decentered and multivocal, that is, only through the actual empowerment of "others" to participate as equal partners in the "conversation of humankind." The moral point of cultural relativism's *abstract* negation of Eurocentric universalism – to give permission to diversity – could then be preserved in the practice of multicultural universal discourse.[55]

Whatever its merits as a normative ideal, this is obviously not the situation of cultural studies today. In the postcolonial/neocolonial world, intercultural encounters are shot through with the distorting inequalities of power that mark international relations generally. This results, as Talal Asad has put it, in "strong" and "weak" languages.[56] Non-Western intellectuals who wish to participate in global public spheres have to do so, by and large, on Western terms. It is because and insofar as they have mastered hegemonic cultures that they are "qualified" as participants and given access to international media of communication. And these media, embedded in global political-economic relations, are hardly a neutral means with which to challenge that hegemony. At the same time, the globalization of culture that goes hand in hand with the growth of economic, technological, and political interdependence, the vast migrations of populations, the ever denser networks of international telecommunications, and the like, is increasingly placing all cultures in a situation of global modernity. Among other things, this has produced an outpouring of art, literature, and scholarship calling into question the West's representations of itself and its "others." Drawing on "weapons of critique" that are part of their colonial legacy, these others now offer trenchant analyses of the cultural relations of production behind those representations: the empire writes back, as Salman Rushdie has put it.[57] Moreover, voices from the periphery are increasingly entering into the cultural formation of intellectuals, artists, and scholars at the center, synergistically combining with challenges to long-established hierarchies issuing from the newly empowered voices of women and marginalized minorities. All of this has contributed to placing in question the taken-for-granted rationality of entrenched ways of seeing and doing things, thus opening public discourse to the possibility of alternative paths of development. It has also been made clear how great were the diversity and difference glossed over by the we/they dichotomies underlying conventional cross-cultural studies.[58]

On the other hand, awareness of the constructed nature of sociocultural representations does not mean that we can do without them. Everyday communication is organized around a continual shifting back and forth among first-, second-, and third-person perspectives, whereby we adopt in turn the roles of speakers, hearers, and uninvolved spectators. The idea of proscribing talk *about* other persons in favor of talking exclusively *to* them makes no sense in that context. Nor does it in the public spheres, political and cultural, of contemporary societies, nor in the disciplines of the humanities and human sciences. And in none of these domains do we feel a general need to give everyone talked or written about "equal time" *within* our accounts of them; they can contest what we say about them on their own time and in their own texts. That is, these domains are, to greater and lesser degrees, structured so as to permit challenges and rejoinders by those who think they are being mis-represented. It is basically for the same reason that claims to universal validity – e.g., to the truth of statements or the rightness of actions and norms – need not always be placed in ironic quotes in domains in which they can be contested by others. As we have seen, strong claims of this sort are key elements in keeping public conversations going. What has made objectifying representations and universalist claims particularly offensive in the anthropological context, I am suggesting, are just the inequalities of power that have prevented colonized peoples from participating in the conversation on an equal footing. The root problem is political and thus cannot be resolved by new devices of representation, however useful they may be in their own rights. It is a problem of access to international public spheres generally and not to the individual texts produced within them. To the degree that representations of others are constructed under the pressure of possible contestation by them, the very present dangers of symbolic violence are correspondingly mitigated. In global public spheres less skewed by powerful inequalities than at present, cross-cultural interpretations, generalizations, and criticisms would be no more or less problematic than the various modes of inquiry into the human world generally are. As the examples of gender and minority studies indicate, when previously subordinated groups can speak in their own voices, there are marked changes in the very construction of texts dealing with them. At the same time, such studies have also shown that new types of text can assist in the formation of new norms of public discourse. There is an interplay here between institutional and textual dynamics, between the empowerment of different voices and writing in different voices, between politics and poetics.

The moral-political perspective on cross-cultural representation has a certain priority over the methodological and poetical perspectives just because it addresses the very conditions of the public discourses in which all validity claims, including cognitive and aesthetic claims, have to be discussed and evaluated.[59] If there are important divergences in the beliefs and outlooks, desires and feelings, norms and values of peoples who have nevertheless to live together, and if there is no "view from nowhere" from which neutrally to adjudicate such differences, then there is in the end no non-coercive alternative to finding or constructing common ground in and across the diverse "views from somewhere." And the only reasonable way of doing that is through reciprocal understanding and symmetrical discussion of differences. I argued above that this sort of cross-cultural discourse itself rests on a number of practically unavoidable presuppositions – for instance, concerning the variability of forms of life and views of the world – and on other general presuppositions that, while not necessary, place a prohibitive burden of proof on anyone who would deny them – for instance, regarding the differentiation of empirical science from religion and metaphysics.[60] On the other hand, the many influential cross-cultural comparisons that turned on contrasting "our" science and technology with "their" traditional beliefs and practices skewed discussion in the direction of those areas of modern culture where there is perhaps the greatest agreement – as if Western beliefs could be equated with science and Western practices with technology. They paid little attention to the vast disagreements pulsating through most areas of modern life – social, economic, ethical, political, religious, philosophical, aesthetic, among others – that is, to the quite obvious fact that many basic questions have remained open to serious disagreements "for us" as well. This seems especially true at present, when so many of our established folkways – including deeply implanted views of, attitudes toward, and ways of dealing with nature – are being subjected to critical scrutiny, and when the increasingly felt need for a genuinely "new world order" demands a post-imperialist recounting of the *interdependent* pasts, presents, and futures of Western and non-Western worlds.

The normative idea of a multicultural universal discourse continues to be structured by the basic pragmatic presuppositions of communicative interaction, but with some different twists. The *supposition of mutual intelligibility*, for instance, can no longer be referred to a common cultural background with its shared schemes of interpretation and evaluation. But we can and must rely on the background of our common humanity as we do the "interpretive work" we are required and "trusted" to do in cross-cultural dialogue. This need not entail a "principle of charity" in interpretion so strong as to grant in advance the consistency and correctness of others' beliefs.[61] A weaker assumption will do, to the effect that whether we – whoever "we" are – come finally to judge their – whoever "they" are – beliefs as true or false, their being held must make sense. And this ties the supposition of intelligibility to the *supposition of accountability*. For the assumption that beliefs and practices generally make sense in their contexts implies that they are the beliefs and practices of knowledgeable agents who are acting accountably in those contexts, that is, of agents who by and large know what they are doing and why they are doing it. This internal connection between intelligibility and accountability means that understanding the *whats* of beliefs and practices also and inescapably involves us in ascertaining their *whys*. Meaning gets linked with validity (for example, with truth conditions) and questions of interpretation with questions of evaluation.[62] And that interlinkage places particularly powerful constraints on cross-cultural discourse about the nature of the external world. For the *supposition of an objective world*, of an independent reality that is intersubjectively available, is internally connected with the *supposition of a unique truth* about that world. The operative assumption is that conflicting reports and accounts of it cannot all be true and thus will not prove to be equally tenable over the course of critical-reflective discussion about them. Nor can all normative arrangements be placed on a par. As noted in chapter 1, fundamental inequalities which could once be justified by appeals to beliefs about the objective world that are no longer tenable will be hard put to find substitute justifications capable of withstanding critical-reflective scrutiny. Whole classes of reasons for basic inequalities have in this way lost their discursive weight. In any case, universal discourse itself can only be structured by a *supposition of normative symmetry* that requires treating all participants with equal respect. The tension between that assumption, with its attendant train of ideas of autonomy, dignity, tolerance, fairness, and so forth, and ethical views constructed around basic inequalities – whether "natural," "God-given," "time-honored," or what have you – is evident and inescapable. This too enormously increases the burden of proof on those who would discursively defend such views.

All of these assumptions are required for achieving mutual understanding in intercultural dialogue and thus are practically unavoidable presuppositions of the first-second person relations that sustain it. Putting them into practice means adding another standpoint to the first- and third-person standpoints from which comparative studies have traditionally been laid out: "we" and "they," but no "you."[63] This is not mere wordplay; it has implications for how the public spheres of intercultural discourse should be structured.[64] The active presence of the others' voices makes all the difference, not only for "them" but for "us" as well. There is no surer path to awareness of unspoken preconceptions and prejudgements than communicative encounters with others who do not share them. Awareness, as we have seen, need not mean rejection; it can as well as result in self-conscious affirmation. Or, as may also happen in cross-cultural dialogue, in ironic self-distancing, wistful yearning, or nostalgic longing.

In any case the individual and collective identities shaped through such encounters would decidedly not be the self-contained and self-enclosed identities imagined by cultural relativists. Identities are formed in and through social relations, and when the structures of those relations alter significantly, the structures of sustainable identities cannot but follow suit. Modern identities have had to become more abstract as the diversity of roles and settings, norms and institutions, subcultures and reference groups within which competent agents have had to function has grown and spread.[65] They will have to become more abstract still as the we/they dichotomies on which identity formation has continued to rely erode in the currents of globalization. The narratives through which we try to make sense of our collective histories will increasingly have to take into account the different but interrelated stories *of and by* those others, both inside and outside our groups, at whose expense our identities have been constructed. They will have to do so, that is, if we expect our narratives and the identities they express to be acknowledged by them. And, as we might have known since Hegel, identities that are not recognized by those with whom our lives and fates are interwined are inherently unstable.[66]

The stress I have been placing on the role of intercultural dialogue in the critique of impure reason is certainly not meant to deny the importance of sociocultural studies in other, more restricted, domains. And it is most emphatically not meant to deny the importance, indeed the necessity, of using objectivating approaches to putatively rational practices: the third-person standpoint can no more be dropped than can the first- or second-person standpoint if we hope to be critical participants in the discourse of modernity. But I have wanted to underscore the need for critical theory to adopt a consistently global perspective, so as to locate the received problematics of the nation state in a broader web of interconnected histories, and thus to combine a strong historical sense of who we are and who we want to be with an equally full-bodied comparative sense. To the extent that the latter is developed in a framework of critical dialogue, it will be shaped by the different experiences, perspectives, and resources of those whose full humanity has been somehow denied. It is only in the culture and institutions embodying some such cosmopolitan idea that the boundless claims of reason could finally prove themselves to be more than Eurocentric illusions.

## NOTES

1 Other fruitful, extramural points of departure might be found in the phenomenological sociology of the lifeworld and in ethnographic accounts of cultural reproduction.

2 I will be relying here on Garfinkel's earlier work, especially the essays collected in *Studies in Ethnomethodology* (Englewood Cliffs: Prentice Hall, 1967), republished by Polity Press in 1984. My reading of his work is indebted to the excellent study by John Heritage, *Garfinkel and Ethnomethodology* (Oxford: Polity Press, 1984). It should be mentioned that this line of interpretation would not be accepted by ethnomethodologists who adopt a more radically reflexive and anti-theoretical stance – including, perhaps, Garfinkel himself. On the other hand, it is akin to the line followed by the conversational analysts to whom I shall also be referring. As my concern here is solely to offer another way of thinking about practical reason, I shall ignore exegetical disputes as such.

3 *Studies*, pp. 67–8.

4 Ibid., p. 33.

5 In this section I shall leave to one side questions of cultural difference within and between cultures and focus for the moment on the basic ingredients of mutual understanding in a common culture. This may temporarily slant the discussion in a "conformist" direction, and that slant can sometimes be detected in Garfinkel's account of the "routine grounds of everyday activities." However, in my view there is nothing inherently conservative about this approach. Analyzing socially shared and sanctioned schemes of interpretation and evaluation can, as Foucault's archeological investigations make clear, be put to effective critical use. The use I want to make of the ethnomethodological perspective will become clearer in the following section. It was already foreshadowed in my discussion of the relation between accountability and autonomy in section 2.3.

6 "The activities whereby members produce and manage settings of organized everyday affairs are identical with members' procedures for making

those settings 'account-able'. The 'reflexive' or 'incarnate' character of accounting practices and accounts makes up the crux of [my program]."
*Studies*, p. 1.

7  Heritage elaborates on the reflexivity of social action generally and of accounting practices particularly by analyzing the case of greetings, in *Garfinkel and Ethnomethodology*, pp. 106–20. For instance, an initial greeting may transform a situation of disengagement into one of engagement. The greeted party is now faced with the choice of returning or not returning the greeting, and in this way or that. A return greeting ratifies the proposed engagement; failure to return the greeting admits of different accounts, which reconstitute the situation in different ways: the recipient was a preoccupied friend or a misidentified stranger, s/he did not recognize the greeter or thought s/he was making a pass, s/he deliberately snubbed the greeter to display irritation or to start a quarrel. And so forth and so on.

8  Which is not to say that it is arbitrary. Judgements of applicability are themselves accountable; they can be contested and criticized, discussed and defended.

9  Thus Garfinkel stresses that "common understanding" has an "operational structure" consisting of a "course of interpretation" (*Studies*, p. 25) and that "shared agreement" has less to do with "the intersection of overlapping sets" than with "social methods for accomplishing members' recognition" (*Studies*, p. 30).

10  Compare: "He's always so distracted, he never returns greetings. Think nothing of it." "He's usually so friendly. I wonder if what I said yesterday offended him." "He's always been so formal. Could that warm greeting have been meant flirtatiously?" What is done (not noticing, showing irritation, flirting), like what is said, depends on the context of action, including the identities and intentions of those involved and the prehistory of their relationships. The all-purpose term "context" gets used to cover everything from the very local to the very large, from the sequencing of speech acts to formal-institutional settings. Garfinkel insists that whatever its scope, "context" not be treated simply as exogenous to interaction; it is endogenously produced and reproduced in and through the details of interaction. (Cf. Heritage, p. 283.) This is one aspect of that dialectic of agency and structure that Anthony Giddens, among others, has elaborated upon. See his *The Constitution of Society* (Berkeley: University of California Press, 1984).

11  In their fixation on the homogenizing effects of logocentrism, poststructuralists sometimes miss this evident truth.

12  Cf. Harvey Sacks, Emanuel Schegloff, and Gail Jefferson, "A Simplest Semantics for the Organization of Turn-Taking for Conversation," in J. N. Schenckhein (ed.), *Studies in the Organization of Conversational Interaction* (New York: Academic Press, 1978), p. 10. Garfinkel himself would likely reject this formulation in favor of a more radically reflexive constructionist approach. See, for example, the article he co-authored with Harvey Sacks, "On the Formal Structures of Practical

Actions," in J. C. McKinney and E. A. Tiryakian (eds), *Theoretical Sociology* (New York: Appleton Century Crofts, 1970), pp. 338–66, esp. pp. 345–6.

13 "A Simplest Semantics," pp. 40–2. That is to say, "local management" means that social actors orient *both* to general – linguistic, cultural, social, etc. – structures *and* to the particulars of their situations, and that the capacity to do so is reciprocally imputed to and sanctionably expected of competent agents.

14 Ibid., p. 43.

15 Heritage, pp. 147–8.

16 On what follows, see Heritage, pp. 233–92.

17 Heritage, p. 265.

18 Ibid., p. 268.

19 Sacks, Schegloff, and Jefferson point out, for instance, that in the organization of conversational turn-taking, talk addressed to problems encountered in understanding previous utterances is given priority, so that the normal order may be superseded for that purpose (p. 33). And they note that turn-taking organization, with its reliance on cues, displays, and the like, "builds an intrinsic motivation for listening to all utterances in a conversation" and "translates a willingness or potential desire to speak into a corollary obligation to listen" (pp. 43–4).

20 *Studies*, p. 35. He is obviously using "moral" in a much wider sense than is usual in philosophy or sociology, that is, as more or less coextensive with "normative". But this is a useful rhetorical device for stressing the omnipresence of the "ought". By contrast, even when rational choice theorists do acknowledge the pervasiveness of action guided by social norms, they typically account for this phenomenon in reductionistic terms. Thus, for example, Jon Elster has conceptualized norm-guided behavior as behavior that is *not* outcome oriented but "pushed" by forces resulting from internalization processes. As such, it is not rationally motivated behavior. (See *The Cement of Society* (Cambridge, UK: Cambridge University Press, 1989) and *Nuts and Bolts for the Social Sciences* (Cambridge, UK: Cambridge University Press, 1989).) Recently, Elster has gone so far as to concede to considerations of justice an independent weight in political deliberations; but at that point he is diverging from a strictly rational-choice approach. See "The Possibility of Rational Politics," in D. Held (ed.), *Political Theory Today* (Cambridge, UK: Cambridge University Press, 1991), pp. 115–42.

21 Garfinkel does, to be sure, attend to the "rational properties of practical activities," among which he numbers efficiency, efficacy, effectiveness, intelligibility, clarity, consistency, coherency, planfulness, typicality, uniformity, reproducibility, adequate demonstration, adequate reporting, sufficient evidence, necessary inference, and "every topic of 'logic' and 'methodology' " (*Studies*, pp. 33–4). But he insists that these "contingent ongoing accomplishments of organized artful practices" (p. 11) be treated solely as "*phenomena* for ethnomethodological study but not otherwise" (p. 33); in particular that they not be described or assessed by "using a

rule or standard obtained outside [their] actual settings" (p. 33). Like its direct ancestor, phenomenological bracketing, "ethnomethodological indifference" enjoins us simply to describe members' activities and accounts "while abstaining from all judgements of their adequacy" ("On Formal Structures of Practical Actions," p. 345). This is the point at which ethnomethodology parts ways with critical theory. Habermas does not think such indifference is a live option. (See *The Theory of Communicative Action*, vol. 1 (Boston: Beacon Press, 1984), pp. 128–30.)

22  In addition to the article cited in chapter 2, note 23, see his *Mundane Reason* (Cambridge, UK: Cambridge University Press, 1987).

23  And, of course, of the institutionalized concern with limning the real we call scientific inquiry. Cf. the ethnomethodological study of the latter by G. N. Gilbert and M. Mulkay, *Opening Pandora's Box: An Analysis of Scientists' Discourse* (Cambridge, UK: Cambridge University Press, 1984).

24  Compare Kant's tying objectivity to validity for consciousness in general.

25  *Mundane Reason*, p. 51.

26  Ibid., pp. 60–1. See also ibid., p. 65: "Each explanation preserves the world as an objective and shared order of events by showing how unanimity would have been forthcoming had it not been for the absence, failure, or violation of one of the presupposed but previously unformulated conditions necessary for unanimity." That is to say, the notions of the objective world and the truth about it function as idealizations supporting counterfactual conditionals.

27  On the notion of a socio-logic of concepts, see Jeff Coulter, *Mind in Action* (Atlantic Highlands: Humanities Press, 1989).

28  Karl Marx and Friedrich Engels, *The German Ideology* (New York: International Publishers, 1947), pp. 19, 14.

29  For an elaboration of the notion of a "forum of argumentation," see S. Toulmin, R. Rieke, and A. Janik, *An Introduction to Reasoning* (New York: Macmillan, 1979). See also Habermas's discussion of it in *The Theory of Communicative Action*, vol. 1, pp. 22–42.

30  In "Individuation through Socialization" Habermas remarks that Kant's intelligible world has to be rendered both "socially concrete" and "temporally dynamic" (p. 184), and notes that temporal dynamics play an increasingly important role in modern life. For one thing, the present is "ever more plainly interpreted" in light of the future: "[T]he supposition that present action will be placed under premises that anticipate future presents . . . applies to systemic processes (such as long-term political commitments, debt-financing, and so forth) as well as to simple interactions" (p. 188). Such modes of anticipation, i.e. of reflexive accountability, more and more come to be "socially expected," i.e. culturally imputed and institutionally demanded.

31  Compare the discussion of this point on pp. 40–2, above.

32  This phrase is used by Hans Blumenberg on p. 447 of "An Anthropological Approach to the Contemporary Significance of Rhetoric," in K. Baynes, J. Bohman, and T. McCarthy (eds), *After Philosophy*, pp. 429–58. He is concerned there with "a theory of man outside the realm of Ideas,

forsaken by evidentness" (432), and with rhetoric as the theory and practice of "the production of mutual understanding [and] agreement" in that state (433). Thus, rhetoric is presented as a "rational way of coming to terms with the provisionality of reason" (452). There are similarities between his approach and the one proposed here, but the conception of reason with which he operates is also different in important respects.

33  On the notion of a "universal audience," see Ch. Perelman and L. Olbrechts-Tyteca, *The New Rhetoric* (Notre Dame: University of Notre Dame Press, 1969), and Habermas's discussion of it in *The Theory of Communicative Action*, vol. 1, pp. 22–42.

34  There is an instructive example of this in Pollner's *Mundane Reason*. He points out that familiar *modes of reflection* on everyday speech and action *rely on some of the same basic assumptions*, particularly on the idea of a unitary, coherent, determinate, independent reality of some sort that has to be captured in a true account. His own efforts to define a standpoint "outside" the circle of such "mundane" presuppositions end in an admittedly paradoxical gesture toward the dissolution of the subject/object duality in some "Eastern spiritual disciplines" (129). Once we make the turn to a critique of "impure" reason, the *empirical* description of general structures and inescapable presuppositions can no longer claim for itself the same status "outside the world" as transcendental and phenomenological inquiry once did. It is and must remain a form of "mundane" – historical, sociological, cultural, linguistic, psychological – inquiry into structures of speech and action. The idea of getting "always already there" structures descriptively right carries with it all the basic presuppositions of mundaneity. See especially chapters 6 and 7 of *Mundane Reason*. Compare also Foucault's discussion of the "empirico-transcendental doublet" in *The Order of Things* (New York: Random House, 1970), pp. 318–22.

35  Working out the relation between actually persuading particular audiences and ideally addressing a universal audience is, I think, the key to grasping the dialectic of immanence and transcendence in argumentation theory.

36  See my critiques of Rorty, Foucault, and Derrida in this regard in *Ideals and Illusions*.

37  *Moral Consciousness and Communicative Action*, p. 202.

38  "Politics and Ethics: An Interview," in P. Rabinow (ed.), *The Foucault Reader* (New York: Pantheon, 1984), p. 379.

39  Kant, *Groundwork of the Metaphysics of Morals*, p. 96.

40  Maria Herrera develops this side of Kantian moral theory in seeking to balance Habermas's stress on consensus with an equal stress on difference, in "Justification and Application in Habermas's Discourse Ethics," unpublished ms, and in "Equal Respect among Unequal Partners: Gender Difference and the Constitution of Moral Subjects," *Philosophy East and West* 42 (1992): 263–75.

41  "Models of Freedom in the Modern World," in Michael Kelly (ed.), *Hermeneutics and Critical Theory in Ethics and Politics* (Cambridge, MA:

The MIT Press, 1990), pp. 227–52, here p. 237. This essay contains an interesting discussion of the relation between positive and negative political freedom in general and in Habermas's thought specifically. It differs from the account offered here in arguing that a "principle of negative freedom can*not* conceptually be considered to be part of a communalist conception of rationality in Habermas's sense" (p. 244). But Wellmer does allow that the two are dialectically interdependent, and that would be sufficient for the line of argument I am developing here.

42 See above, pp. 7–9.

43 See above, p. 12.

44 See above, pp. 40–3.

45 Paul Ricoeur, *Freud and Philosophy*, trans. D. Savage (New Haven: Yale University Press, 1970) and *The Conflict of Interpretations*, ed. D. Ihde, trans. W. Domingo et al. (Evanston: Northwestern University Press, 1974).

46 H. G. Gadamer, *Truth and Method* (New York: Seabury Press, 1975), Alasdair MacIntyre, *After Virtue* (Notre Dame: University of Notre Dame Press, 1981).

47 See Jürgen Habermas, *On the Logic of the Social Sciences*, trans. S. Nicholsen and J. Stark (Cambridge, MA: The MIT Press, 1988) and *The Theory of Communicative Action*, vol. 2.

48 This is true even at the level of "pure" description. See, for instance, John Heritage's discussion of "description as action," on pp. 150–7 of *Garfinkel and Ethnomethodology*, and the discussions of ethnographic description in James Clifford, *The Predicament of Culture* (Cambridge, MA: Harvard University Press, 1988) and Clifford Geertz, *Works and Lives* (Stanford: Stanford University Press, 1988).

49 See Thomas McCarthy, *The Critical Theory of Jürgen Habermas* (Cambridge, MA: The MIT Press, 1978), chapter 3, pp. 126–271.

50 For a good overview and discussion of relevant issues see James Bohman, *New Philosophy of Social Science* (Cambridge, MA: The MIT Press, 1991).

51 On what follows, see Clifford, *The Predicament of Culture*, Geertz, *Works and Lives*, George Marcus and Michael Fischer, *Anthropology as Cultural Critique* (Chicago: University of Chicago Press, 1986), J. Clifford and G. Marcus (eds), *Writing Culture* (Berkeley: University of California Press, 1986), and my review essay, "Doing the Right Thing in Cross-Cultural Representation," *Ethics* 102 (1992): 635–49. I would like to thank the University of Chicago Press for allowing me to use parts of that essay here.

52 Clifford puts the problem this entails as follows: "How, precisely, is a garrulous, overdetermined, cross-cultural encounter shot through with power relations and personal cross-purposes circumscribed as an adequate version of a more or less discrete 'other world' composed by an individual author?" (*The Predicament of Culture*, p. 25). The messy realities of field work were amply documented in Malinowski's posthumously published diaries. See Geertz's discussion of him in *Works and Lives*, pp. 73–101.

53 Moreover, the horizons to be expanded through virtual dialogue were those of the interpreter and his/her home culture, not the subject/object's.

It was "we" and not "they" who were supposed to benefit from such one-sided conversations.

54  See Clifford, "On Ethnographic Authority," in *The Predicament of Culture*, pp. 21–54.

55  The phrase, "to give permission to diversity," is from Richard Shweder (see chapter 2, note 40). The idea of "universal discourse" stems from George Herbert Mead and has been developed by Jürgen Habermas as the basic idea of his discourse ethics.

56  See Asad's contribution to *Writing Culture*, pp. 141–64, and his earlier *Anthropology and the Colonial Encounter* (New York: Humanities Press, 1972).

57  See Edward Said, "Third-World Intellectuals and Metropolitan Culture," *Raritan* 9:3 (1990): 27–50.

58  An influential critique of the tendency of Western studies of non-Western cultures to "dichotomize" into we/they contrasts and to "essentialize" the resultant "Other" is Edward Said's *Orientalism* (New York: Pantheon, 1978). In his discussion of Said, Clifford makes the point that he and other critics of Eurocentrism tend to deploy an inverse "Occidentalism" (*The Predicament of Culture*, pp. 255–76).

59  This is not to say that the problems that appear from the other perspectives are any less real. Awareness of the situated and constructed nature of anthropological accounts, for instance, does not entail that there are no such things as facts and accuracy and inaccuracy in reporting them, or shared meanings and better and worse interpretations of them, or patterns of social relations and more and less adequate representations of them. But we are far from having a satisfactory understanding of the situated construction of facts, meanings, patterns, and the like. There is also the problem of "How to represent the embedding of richly described, local, cultural worlds in larger, impersonal systems of political economy," since the "outside forces" of market and state are in fact "an integral part of the construction and constitution of the 'inside' . . . even at the most intimate levels" (Marcus and Fischer, p. 77). This is only one form of a central problem for social inquiry generally: how to grasp the recursive relations between sociocultural practices situated in large-scale systems and macrohistorical processes, on the one hand, and the ongoing sociocultural reproduction of such situation-defining systems and processes, on the other. For a recent discussion, see Bohman, *New Philosophy of Social Science*, pp. 146–85. On the sorts of questions raised by the poetical aspects of ethnography as "a kind of writing," see the essays collected in *Writing Culture*.

60  See section 2.3.

61  Donald Davidson's "transcendental" argument for such a principle is thus stronger than it need or should be. (See, for instance, "The Very Idea of a Conceptual Scheme," in Davidson, *Inquiries into Truth and Interpretation* (Oxford: Clarendon Press, 1983), pp. 183–98.) But his argument has the virtue of connecting the interpretation of beliefs to the interpretation of action, and both to the necessity of presupposing the agents' rationality.

(See, for instance, his "Problems in the Explanation of Action," in P. Petit, R. Sylvan, and J. Norman (eds), *Metaphysics and Morality* (Oxford: Blackwell, 1987), pp. 35–49.) I take a similar tack below.

62  Strikingly similar "transcendental" arguments for the necessity of what Habermas calls "rational interpretation" can be found in Davidson (see the previous note) and Habermas (see *The Theory of Communicative Action*, Vol. 1, pp. 177–91). Rational interpretation is implicitly comparative, since an interpreter's beliefs and norms inevitably serve as the point from which s/he begins to draw the hermeneutic circle. See Bohman's discussion of this in *New Philosophy of Social Science*, pp. 132–9.

63  David Michael Levin documents the "oculocentrism" behind traditional subject/object models of knowledge in the human sciences and proposes instead a model based on speaking and listening, in *The Listening Self* (London: Routledge, 1989). See also D. M. Levin (ed.), *Modernity and the Hegemony of Vision* (Los Angeles: University of California Press, 1993).

64  For instance, proposals for restructuring traditional area studies programs have been developed from this perspective at the Center for Transcultural Studies (formerly the Center for Psychosocial Studies) in Chicago. They recommend collaborative research projects that, in regard both to topics and resources, cut across the usual area, disciplinary, and national boundaries and experiment with new, interculturally interactive approaches to the study of globalization processes.

65  See Habermas. "Individuation through Socialization." Michael Walzer makes some interesting remarks on how "the four mobilities" (geographic, social, marital, and political) affect the formation of individual and collective identities, in "The Communitarian Critique of Liberalism," *Political Theory* 18 (1990): 6–23. See also Eugene Gendlin, "A Philosophical Critique of the Concept of Narcissism," in D. M. Levin (ed.), *Pathologies of the Modern Self* (New York: New York University Press, 1987), pp. 251–304.

66  See Axel Honneth, *Kampf um Anerkennung* (Frankfurt: Suhrkamp Verlag, 1992).

# Part II
## Critical Theory and Critical History

*David Couzens Hoy*

# A Deconstructive Reading of the Early Frankfurt School

## 4.1 Tensions in Horkheimer

What makes a theory "critical"? To be critical must one have a theory? These two questions are provoked by the label "critical theory," which seems initially to be an oxymoron. If not a contradiction in terms, the two words are at least in tension, and pull in different directions. My entire essay will work at explaining this tension, but for now I will simply point out that ordinarily the two terms are not naturally linked. I can criticize someone else's theory without claiming to have a theory of my own that is superior. I can also object to another's practices or the injustice of a social institution without claiming that my own practices are beyond criticism. So criticism does not obviously require a theory. Correlatively, theory, insofar as it claims to be right, distinguishes between the task of formulating itself and defending itself against criticism. While always testable by criticisms, the theory has to assume that it will survive them. Furthermore, the theory does not assume that its principal value stems from its ability to raise sound criticisms of other theories. Polemics may be interesting, but a theory does not believe it will be proved superior by virtue of being polemically superior.

When Max Horkheimer defends the notion of critical theory in the essay "Traditional and Critical Theory" (1937), he has to undermine the standard assumption that theory is one thing and the testing and application of it as criticism is another. The standard conception of theory he calls "traditional theory" in contrast to critical theory. Using Henri Poincaré's idea that science is like a library that is to be constantly expanded, Horkheimer describes the traditional conception of theory as "stored-up knowledge, put in a form that makes it useful for the closest possible description of facts."[1] This conception is traditional in that it runs through modern philosophy from Descartes to Kant and Husserl. For Horkheimer its most problematic feature is not necessarily the claim by scientific realists that theory is validated by its correspondence to an independently-given reality. More crucially, this conception suggests that all theories are valid independently of the conditions under which they are formulated or of the use to which they will be put. Traditional theory suggests a picture whereby "the activity of the scholar . . . takes place alongside all the other activities of a society but in no immediately clear connection with them."[2] Standardly, the epistemological tradition maintains that neither the genesis nor the use of the scientific theory is relevant to its validity. But when the type of theory at stake is social theory, where the theory must explain its own origin and timeliness as well as how it can claim to represent adequately the society in which it is itself a particular standpoint, the genesis and use of the social theory are pertinent to its heuristic value and soundness. Unlike traditional scientific theory, critical social theory for Horkheimer must account for its own social origins and purposes.

Before examining the features of traditional and critical theories further, however, I wish to note that the contrast that Horkheimer is drawing is not obviously one that will differentiate various first-order theories. Horkheimer does not proceed by analyzing an example of a traditional theory and then an example of a critical theory (although he would maintain that a theory like Karl Mannheim's sociology of knowledge is traditional rather than critical).[3] He also does not try to prove that an example of traditional theory would be improved on by an example of critical theory.[4] The contrast is drawn not between theories, but between conceptions of theory. The conflict as depicted in "Traditional and Critical Theory" is thus more of a meta-theoretical one between different "theories of theory."

Meta-theoretical debates are detested by many on the grounds that they appear to be wastes of time. A theory should have a practical application, and should have clearly testable results. A theory of what counts as a theory is not so obviously testable and applicable. Nevertheless, philosophers like Horkheimer and Jürgen Habermas find the meta-theoretical conflicts important. In *Knowledge and Human Interests* Habermas suggests that the traditional conception of theory is too restrictive because it narrows down the range of possible theories to one kind only, an idealized conception of theory modeled on the natural sciences. This model is itself a theory of theory, since the sciences do not themselves obviously employ or conform to this exclusive model. More importantly for Habermas, however, the traditional theory of theory would discount the status of a whole range of theories in interpretive disciplines like the social sciences, or in explicitly critical disciplines like psychoanalysis or "ideology critique" (the social-historical investigation of false consciousness).

So traditional theory of theory is itself to be criticized on its own grounds if it ignores a whole range of relevant phenomena, namely, other varieties of theory. A standard criterion insisted on by traditional theory is inclusiveness, and its own systematic blindness would be a serious defect. Furthermore, these phenomena would seem to be counter-examples if there are many theories that cannot be captured by the traditional model of what a theory should look like. Theory that is critical is in the first instance critical of itself. Unlike traditional theory, which assumes its own neutrality and therefore neither does nor can investigate itself for blindness and bias, critical theory would suspect itself of both.

Of course, there is a problem if critical theory really believes that any social theory in a divided society will inevitably be blind and biased. The traditional theorist will object that in these circumstances either critical theory is futile in its attempt to be self-conscious, or it tacitly relies on traditional, unbiased and neutral theory as an ideal limit. Critical theory would be futile since it would always fail to some extent to become completely conscious of its own socially-motivated distortions. Given critical theory's assertion of the inevitability of bias, the aspects of its own bias that it fails to bring to light would vitiate its claim to have revealed and adjusted for other aspects. Furthermore, why would critical theory ever try to reveal its own biases unless it believed it was improving itself as a theory by doing so? Since this improvement suggests in the limit an ideal whereby the theory would finally be free from bias, the self-reflective effort seems to rely tacitly on the ideal of a neutral theory that is to be arrived at by gradually disengaging the theory from its social origins and purposes.

Horkheimer's essay is admirable in that it confronts these problems, but it contains remarks that leave the disturbing impression that critical theory remains parasitic on traditional theory. He recognizes that critical theory will always appear methodologically deficient from the standpoint of traditional theory. He deals with this problem by turning the tables on traditional theory and showing it to be the conception that is deficient because it leaves crucial assumptions unexamined. In contrast to the natural sciences, the social and human sciences investigate the rules of conduct and assumptions about rationality which operate in a given society, but which are also operant in the construction and investigation of social theories. Horkheimer

believes that the traditional conception of theory ignores this circularity and thinks of its own standards as universal, and as the necessary
presuppositions of objective investigation. Traditional theory thinks
of its conclusions as being arrived at neutrally, and independently of
their potential use in correcting particular social deformations and
abuses. This correction of abuses would be the separate task of social
critics, who then apply the theoretical results.

Horkheimer contrasts this traditional conception of social criticism
with a more fully self-reflective, "critical" activity.[5] His stress is on
the word "critical," but my question is why this more general process
of critical *activity* must become critical *theory*. His response would
probably be that the activity tacitly presupposes, and is thus parasitic
on, a social theory, which is better made explicit. So described, his
goal, interestingly enough, does not appear so different from the traditional philosophical task of seeking enlightenment, or, as I will call it,
avoiding parasitism. Unexamined presuppositions always undermine
a theory, and the objection to traditional theory is that it is parasitic
on social norms that it takes to be natural.

Kant's ethical theory would be an example of traditional theory in
this respect. Kant explicitly refrains from challenging the common
moral norms of his upbringing. He searches instead for an underlying
principle that will systematically unite and therefore legitimate standard moral injunctions to help others or to keep promises. Hegel challenges Kant to explain the moral rules not by constructing a moral
meta-rule, but by discovering the social basis of morality as such. In
other words, Hegel accuses Kant's theory of not explaining, but simply presupposing the given social practices of a particular time and
place, and remaining parasitic on those practices.[6]

The advantage of critical activity is that it reveals the parasitism of
traditional theory on established social norms. The methodological
superiority of critical activity is that it bites the bullet and admits
itself to be parasitic on social contexts as well. Critical activity is
different from traditional social criticism since it does not try merely
to identify and correct particular social injustices and abuses:

> The aim of this [critical] activity is not simply to eliminate one or other
> abuse, for it regards such abuses as necessarily connected with the way
> in which the social structure is organized. Although it itself emerges
> from the social structure, its purpose is not, either in its conscious
> intention or in its objective significance, the better functioning of any
> element in the structure. On the contrary, it is suspicious of the very
> categories of better, useful, appropriate, productive, and valuable as
> these are understood in the present order, and refuses to take them as
> nonscientific presuppositions about which one can do nothing.[7]

If one were to look at this description of critical activity in isolation from Horkheimer's and the Frankfurt School's other work, one might conclude that critical activity was likely to be fruitless, or even anarchistic and nihilistic. (In other words, one might take it as a description of Michel Foucault's project, as many of his critics envisage it.) The goal of this critical activity does not seem to be to improve anything, since there is no ideal in the name of which a change could be counted as an improvement. Of course, there is more than one way to think about how a standard could be used to call a change an improvement. We need not know exactly where society is going to speak of having improved itself if, for instance, we significantly decrease suffering. The argument in the passage may also seem to involve a *non sequitur*. Even if social standards emerge from particular social contexts or historical periods, it does not follow that those standards are not valid either for that period or for other contexts or periods. A standard is not invalidated by the social conditions of its formulation, and its range of application may not be limited to the context in which it originated.

As Horkheimer presents the critical activity, it seems to lack any point of purchase, that is, any standards in the name of which it can criticize the present, or any place from which to view and assess the present. Horkheimer says the critical activity or attitude (*Verhalten*) "is *wholly* distrustful of the rules of conduct with which society as presently constituted provides each of its members."[8] The next sentence then speaks of critical *theory* as relativizing what is normally taken to be the "natural" separation of individual and society. This shift from "activity" to "theory" takes place as if both words were synonymous, when in fact they suggest a move to a more explicit cognition, and an increasingly inclusive and totalizing reflection on "the overall framework which is conditioned by the blind interaction of individual activities [*Tätigkeiten*]."[9] The theory will finally move from observing the apparently contingent interaction to explaining it not blindly, but insofar as it could be "a possible object of planful decision and rational determination of goals."[10] The theory thus becomes explicit when the social whole is comprehended and compared to the social organization that could have resulted (even if only ever counterfactually) from rational planning.

What is not clear, however, is why the critical activity needs to evolve into a fully explicit theory of the social whole, or why it would need to construct a conception of an ideal social order. Is critical activity necessarily totalizing and utopian (and thus "theoretical"), or can it succeed even if it is piecemeal and pragmatic? That critical *theory* appears unable to accept the latter alternative as sufficient, or remains ambivalent about it, is what strikes its hermeneutical, post-structuralist, or pragmatist critics as mistaken.

Horkheimer's position evolved, of course, and even "Traditional and Critical Theory" cannot be labeled "totalizing" or "utopian" since it explicitly admits that critical theory will be relativistic and temporary. Traditional theory will pounce on these admissions as problems and signs of deficiency. More interesting to me, however, are the tensions produced by other remarks that play against these admissions, and that seem to aspire to something approaching universalism and utopianism.

I would have thought that only the traditional conception of theory would have emulated the ideal inclusiveness that would enable the theorist to aspire to these features. Traditional theory desires to be presuppositionless, and therefore to see through all the conditions and assumptions that have relativized previous theories. The desire to examine and ground all possible presuppositions, and thus to avoid parasitism, can be satisfied if the theory aspires to a total explanation that applies universally. When the totality being explained is social, then the goal is a utopian conception of what society as a whole would look like ideally.

In contrast, critical theory has to recognize that in a divided society no position can claim to recognize what the best state of affairs would be ideally for everybody. Horkheimer is willing to admit the paradoxical consequences for the critical attitude when stated as theory. No matter how self-consciously individuals and groups try to act in a stratified, divided, "inhuman" society, he believes that how they really function is largely unconscious and "mechanical": "The identification, then, of [people] of critical mind with their society is marked by tension, and the tension characterizes all the concepts of the critical way of thinking."[11] So "theory" cannot be totally self-conscious and self-transparent. That is, it will not be able to justify and explain its own concepts, methods, or assumptions in a systematic, coherent, and complete way.

Despite this admission, however, Horkheimer continues to try to work out a tension-free, systematic, and coherent conception of critical theory, thereby proving its superiority over traditional theory. Horkheimer also does not strike me as one who would respond to the charge that some of his own statements are in tension with others simply by pointing out that tensions are to be expected. Given his frequent appeal to logical as well as real necessity, I expect that he would feel compelled to explain or correct such tensions. If I am right, then he still accepts a sense of "theory" which characterizes both the traditional and the critical kinds, such that to be a theory the account cannot rest content with internal contradictions or systematic blind spots.

So even if critical theory is more of a meta-theory than a first-order theory, it gets into trouble if it makes claims that it should not assert, at least on its own account of what sorts of claims can or cannot be made under "inhuman" social conditions. To point out some of the tensions in Horkheimer's own essay, I want in particular to note how the frequently used and apparently unproblematic term "inhuman" functions in the text. The term is obviously not a neutral one, but normative and theory-laden from the start. Circularity threatens if the claim that present society is inhuman is both a premise and a conclusion of critical theory. Critical rather than traditional theory arises precisely in an inhuman society, but that a society as a whole is inhuman could be asserted only from the standpoint of a developed critical theory.

As I read the text, except for the word "inhuman," the distinctions between traditional and critical theory would only be differences of degree and not differences of kind. That is to say, critical theory would differ from traditional theory only in being more rather than less self-reflective, or more rather than less suspicious of everyday customs. While there might be practical limitations on traditional theory, there would be nothing in principle that would prevent traditional theory from turning its attention to a different or wider range of phenomena.

What makes traditional seem different in kind from critical theory is the thought that in an inhuman society, traditional theory is prevented from taking itself into account in principle. Since it could not account for all points of view, it must both restrict and universalize its own point of view. That is, it does not claim to be a theory about every phenomena, only a particular range of phenomena. But it also claims to be the best point of view on, and the only genuine explanation of, the particular domain it studies. Furthermore, restricted theory in this sense might not need to be self-reflective and self-critical to the extent that critical theory asserts, since it can leave that activity to a different but similarly restricted theory (as, for example, sociologists of present society might leave to historians questions either about the society's relation to prior societies, or about the history of sociology itself).

Horkheimer does not want to give a universal, unhistorical, context-free description of what would count as "inhuman." One reason is that using the term presupposes a grasp of the social whole, as well as what would count as positive or negative human traits. A gang of thieves, he says, might evince some virtues, and the tension between these virtues and the thievery points to

a deficiency in the larger community within which the gang exists. In an
unjust society criminals are not necessarily inferior as human beings,
whereas in a fully just society they would be unhuman. Only in a
context can particular judgements about what is human acquire their
correct meaning.[12]

This context-bound character of the distinction between the human and
the inhuman means that there is no such thing as fixed human nature.
Unjust social conditions are responsible, however, for forming people
in ways they cannot control, and which therefore are almost as compelling as human nature was thought to be.

Is this a claim that only a "critical" theory could make? The point
looks like one that many traditional theorists would accept. To make
the pitch for critical theory Horkheimer is forced to shift his tone from
an abstract, quasi-descriptive mode to a polemical, denunciatory
mode. In the following passage he describes how critical theory
struggles with the division between the traditional theorist's role both
as a working scientist who regards society disinterestedly from a
distance as well as a private individual who is affected by what is
studied:

> Critical thinking, on the contrary, is motivated today by the effort really
> to transcend the tension and to abolish the opposition between the
> individual's purposefulness, spontaneity, and rationality, and those
> work-process relationships on which society is built. Critical thought
> has a concept of [humanity] as in conflict with [itself] until this opposi-
> tion is removed. If activity governed by reason is proper to [humanity],
> then existent social practice, which forms the individual's life down to
> its least details, is inhuman, and this inhumanity affects everything that
> goes on in the society.[13]

"Inhuman" here has to do with socially-induced alienation, and is an
evaluative as well as a quasi-descriptive claim. The term is polemical,
of course, since many who may regret that private life and working life
are separate spheres might nevertheless balk at calling the separation
inhuman.

Horkheimer's tone becomes even more strident at this point, and he
introduces another sense of what it is to be human. He goes on to
condemn traditional theory not simply for scientific but more for
moral reasons:

> There will always be something that is extrinsic to [humanity's] intel-
> lectual and material activity, namely nature as the totality of as yet
> unmastered elements with which society must deal. But when situ-
> ations which really depend on [humanity] alone, the relationships of

[people] in their work, and the course of [humanity's] own history are also accounted part of "nature," the resultant extrinsicality is not only not a suprahistorical eternal category (even pure nature in the sense described is not that), but it is a sign of *contemptible weakness. To surrender to such weakness is nonhuman and irrational.*[14]

Critical theory will thus not let us rest content with the existent social stratification. To think that alienation and social conflict are natural or inevitable is to give up the goal of fully self-conscious, rational social planning.

This passage sounds all too traditional and "Kantian," however, in that it links the "human" to the "rational" and deplores both the social organization and the individual attitudes toward it which fall short of full rationality. "Reason" retains the status it is granted from Descartes to the German idealists. The tensions in Horkheimer's presentation arise from the vestiges of humanism, and the identification of the human with the rational, which survive his desire to break with tradition. Such tensions are to be expected given the previously cited claim that since society is in tension with itself, all the concepts of the critical way of thinking will be characterized by tension as well.[15] Nevertheless, this statement is itself in tension with Horkheimer's subsequent claim that the critical theory is a "unified whole."[16] To be unified normally would mean to be free of tensions and to satisfy the traditional criterion of rational coherence.

For the most part, however, I find that the vestiges of the idealist tradition surface in indirect ways through statements that show vagueness or ambivalence, although perhaps not outright self-contradiction. Despite Horkheimer's insistence on the social and historical basis of human character, and his rejection of the idea of suprahistorical, eternal categories traditionally ascribed to human nature, he nevertheless takes the desire to be rational as innate: he assumes that anyone would grant that rational activity is proper to humanity, and he asserts more strongly that "the thrust towards a rational society, which admittedly seems to exist today only in the realms of fantasy, is really innate in [everyone]."[17] A quality that is innate in everyone and that is what makes us essentially human certainly seems like an eternal category of human nature. The privilege that Horkheimer gives the thrust to rationality makes it seem to be the very essence of humanity, and that is in fact the rhetorical role it plays in his polemic.

Objections of both an external and an internal sort are obvious. Whether everyone does experience the thrust to a rational society is questionable, since many may really fear the thoroughly planned society. Even if they take part in the planning, they may feel that unanticipated consequences will be as likely to diminish as to increase freedom in comparison to existent society. Furthermore, Horkheimer's own essay contains thoughts that suggest that this thrust toward the rational society may also be the greatest danger to humanity. A passage cited previously suggests that there is no escape from the inhuman consequences of faulty social organization, since existent society "forms the individual's life down to its least details" and the resultant inhumanity "affects everything that goes on in the society."[18] Since the planning for a future, more humane society takes place in an existent society that is inhumane, but since this existent inhumanity would, on Horkheimer's own premises, inevitably distort the rational planning process, even the critical theorist would have good cause to fear the results.

This problem is related to another tension in critical theory. The above claim that "everything" in the society is affected by the inhumanity of the work process presupposes a standpoint from which the social whole can be observed and characterized. Yet against the traditional theory, critical theory also suggests that theory is a social function and there is no theoretical standpoint outside the social whole. In a divided society, furthermore, no theory can claim that it has access to a general criterion (including acceptance by a particular social class such as the proletariat, however generalized the interests of that class are) for judging the theory as a whole.[19] So the critical theory faces a methodological problem in that insofar as it wants to be a "theory," it is bound to make general claims about the total social configuration. But since it also wants to be "critical," it must be suspicious of such totalizing claims and of any assertions about the society implying not a partisan and partial, but an impartial and undistorted view of the whole.

The difficulties in aspiring to a total view of society despite present social tensions also arise in projecting a philosophy of history. Again, however, Horkheimer's own statements are in tension with one another. A statement quoted in part above apparently denies that it is possible in the present to have a total understanding of history: "Previous history thus cannot really be understood; only the individuals and specific groups in it are intelligible, and even these not totally, since their internal dependence on an inhuman society means that even in their conscious action such individuals and groups are still in good measure mechanical functions."[20] In the 1940s Horkheimer, along with Adorno, came to accept the consequences of this denial of universal history. But in this essay of 1937 he concludes by asserting a standard philosophy of history, one which Martin Jay associates with Rosa Luxemburg,[21] but which in any case is not obviously justifiable given the methodological reservations about the totalizing understanding just cited:

> But the critical theory of society is, in its totality, the unfolding of a single existential judgement. To put it in broad terms, the theory says that the basic form of the historically given commodity economy on which modern history rests contains in itself the internal and external tensions of the modern era; it generates these tensions over and over again in an increasingly heightened form; and after a period of progress, development of human powers, and emancipation for the individual, after an enormous extension of human control over nature, it finally hinders further development and drives humanity into a new barbarism.[22]

There is no argument, however, that this substantive theory of history is the only one entailed by the methodological attitude Horkheimer ascribes to critical theory.

Clearly the purpose this story of the collapse of capitalism serves in "Traditional and Critical Theory" is to keep critical theory from falling back into the trap of traditional idealism. Idealism makes the mistake of believing that the thinking subject acquires knowledge independently of social and historical conditions or power relations. Furthermore, the supposed cognitive freedom of thought is then confused with freedom of will and action: "Such an illusion about the thinking subject, under which idealism has lived since Descartes, is ideology in the strict sense, for in it the limited freedom of the bourgeois individual puts on the illusory form of perfect freedom and autonomy."[23] The insistence on freedom in a divided, inhuman society is illusory because it makes freedom an internal matter of the private individual and leads to indifference about the lack of real external freedom in social interaction: "But the idea of freedom as a purely interior reality which is always there even when [people] are enslaved is typical of the idealist mentality."[24] Fichte is then cited as an example of how the appeal to metaphysical freedom is used to justify social injustice and the lack of social freedoms: "The claim that events are absolutely necessary means in the last analysis the same thing as the claim to be really free here and now: resignation in practice."[25]

The critique of idealism for accepting social injustice fatalistically also applies to traditional theory, which aims at knowledge simply for the sake of knowledge, without taking into account the need for social change. Since traditional theory demurs from actively promoting social change, it remains for Horkheimer "an aimless intellectual game, half conceptual poetry, half impotent expression of states of mind."[26] Yet critical theory avoids this aimlessness and fatalistic resignation only by asserting a philosophy of history and an optimism about human reason which are vestiges of the idealist, humanist metaphysical tradition, and to which it is not obviously entitled, given its restricted methodology of suspicion. Under the influence of Adorno, critical theory moves toward abandoning both of these vestiges of metaphysical idealism, and I shall examine the reasons and means for doing so in the next sections. But Horkheimer has already pointed out the problem of such a move. If critical theory abandons this substantive picture of history, can it prevent itself from becoming in turn merely more conceptual poetry and yet another aimless, impotent intellectual game?

## 4.2  Deferrals in Adorno

In 1937 Horkheimer predicted that the commodity economy would produce the tensions of the modern era and drive humanity into "a new barbarism." The horrors of the 1940s forced him, however, to re-examine the hope that the innate rational desires of human beings would lead beyond barbarism to a more humane society. Admitting that earlier he "still trusted too greatly in modern consciousness," he now joins with Adorno, who was probably already suspicious of such trust, in asking the question of their book, the *Dialectic of Enlightenment*, "why [humanity], instead of entering into a truly human condition, is sinking into a new kind of barbarism."[27] The scope of critical theory is thereby extended. What is to be criticized is not simply a rationalistic conception of science, but the rationalism of the entire modern era. The traditional conception of science becomes merely one more manifestation of a pervasive faith in reason which Horkheimer and Adorno call "enlightenment." The reversion to barbarism by Western bourgeois civilization is explained as the result of "not merely the ideal but the practical tendency to self-destruction" that "has always been characteristic of rationalism."[28]

As enlightenment replaces the traditional conception of theory as the more general target of critical activity, the reflective self-examination of the critical theorists functions differently. Unlike the 1937 essay, the book written during the war and published in 1947 does not offer an alternative form of theory, and does not stress the idea of critical theory. Since the book on the enlightenment is itself caught up in the modern era with its faith in reason, it cannot claim to know of an alternative to enlightenment.

Although the *Dialectic of Enlightenment* is usually counted as a classic text of critical theory, I think that the respects in which it exemplifies critical theory are not so obvious. The book is certainly critical, since it proceeds by contesting diverse cultural phenomena, both modern and ancient. The authors investigate such contemporary matters as anti-Semitism and the entertainment industry, but they also find traces of the same self-destructive rationalism as far back as the *Odyssey*. Hence, the book could safely be said to exemplify what Horkheimer called critical activity. But there is no immediately self-evident sense in which it represents a new form of theory, particularly of a sort that would be distinctively critical rather than traditional.

Instead of offering a completely different alternative to enlightenment, the authors suggest that their criticisms are intended not to undercut and replace enlightenment but to lead to a more truly enlightened position. In the preface they state that their "critique of enlightenment is intended to prepare the way for a positive notion of enlightenment which will release it from entanglement in blind domination."[29] So the danger is not enlightenment as such, but its "entanglement in blind domination." What strikes many readers (including Foucault) as paradoxical about this intention is that it seems to revert to the enlightenment theory of knowledge it criticizes. Although definitely a difficulty, this charge needs to be qualified.

The authors' position is not self-refuting or self-exempting. They do not claim that their own knowledge about what is wrong with the tradition of enlightenment is not entangled in domination or entirely free of power relations. Their critique is admittedly partisan, and is intended to disrupt the established conception of knowledge as interest-free. That is, the enlightenment tradition since Bacon believes that knowledge is power in the sense that knowledge about nature gives humans the power to manipulate and control nature. Human knowledge and natural reality are assumed to be completely commensurable in principle, so that nothing about nature is in principle unknowable. Knowledge can thus aim at the goal of unified and universal science. What the critique would shatter is the enlightenment assumption that although knowledge can be put to use and is thus a powerful tool, knowledge is itself a reflection of reality and is undistorted either by the technological uses to which it is put or the social power relations into which it enters.

However, by suggesting the possibility of a "positive notion of enlightenment" that is not "entangled" in dominating power relations, the critique of enlightenment remains parasitic on enlightenment. This parasitism produces the impression that the authors have not freed themselves from the object of their criticism, namely, the utopian illusion that genuine, enlightened knowledge will lead to increased freedom and true progress.[30] Furthermore, despite the utopian vestige in this single line, the attitude of Horkheimer and Adorno in the 1940s is notably different from Horkheimer's in the mid-1930s. In the 1940s hope for historical progress as the result of theoretical self-reflection seems to them to be so remote that it is better abandoned. Horkheimer's reflections at the end of the critical theory essay antici-pate the problems that result from losing the utopian impulse pro-vided by the expectation of historical reversal in the slide into barbarism. What will be the point of finding out that enlightenment leads to self-destruction? If discovering that feature of enlightenment is itself a form of self-enlightenment, then the critical self-reflection will not hinder and may even promote destruction.

The moral tone of Horkheimer's earlier essay becomes more difficult to maintain and justify in the absence of historical hopes for progress. In that essay Horkheimer could criticize traditional theory for falling short of the potentials of human reason when fully self-reflective. Yet since the *Dialectic of Enlightenment* never specifies what the positive notion of enlightenment would be, its final effect could seem to be to cast doubt on any faith in reason, presumably even critical reason. This shortcoming points to a more general problem about basing social criticism on moral values. Moral criticism implies that a greater good is possible, and can be promoted by morally praiseworthy action. Even Kant, who founds the deontological tradition of defin-ing the morally right prior to specifying the good life, thinks that it is incoherent both to try to be moral and to believe that there is no ultimate good to be achieved by doing so, and thus no point to human existence and the world.[31] Yet if the *Dialectic of Enlighten-ment* is to be taken seriously, the collapse into barbarism would appear to have no rational antidote. This historical pessimism makes the moral condemnation of repressive practices and of barbarism seem futile.

A later passage from *Negative Dialectics* states Adorno's final view more dramatically:

> Universal history must be construed and denied. After the catastrophes that have happened, and in view of the catastrophes to come, it would be cynical to say that a plan for a better world is manifested in history and unites it. Not to be denied for that reason, however, is the unity that cements the discontinuous, chaotically splintered moments and phases of history – the unity of the control of nature, progressing to rule over [people], and finally to that over [people's] inner nature. No universal history leads from savagery to humanitarianism, but there is one leading from the slingshot to the megaton bomb. It ends in the total menace which organized [humanity] poses to organized [human beings], in the epitome of discontinuity.[32]

If the *Dialectic of Enlightenment* departs from the earlier essays on the program of critical theory by jettisoning all but the barest vestige of a philosophy of universal history pointing toward liberation and progress, this passage underscores that break and highlights the idea of historical discontinuity. An obvious question, however, is whether Adorno has really given up universal history altogether. Has he completely abandoned the totalizing view that there is such a thing as the whole of history about which one can tell a continuous, unified story? Or has he merely substituted a negative, cynical story for the traditional Kantian and Hegelian one asserting the link between reason and progress?

Part of the answer lies in understanding the different senses in which history could be moving toward an end, depending on whether one was telling the positive or the negative story. Culmination is not the same as termination. The negative account might not even be a *story* in the same sense at all, since total annihilation would show only that there was no meaning in the events after all. The events would represent merely an arbitrary sequence of miscalculations and unfortunate mistakes, since human action could not reasonably be construed as aiming deliberately at the self-destruction of the species.

If the concept of a dialectic of enlightenment suggests more strongly that the cause of our self-destruction was our faith in knowledge and reason, that would be a more continuous story. But the negative story would still be only a regulative idea, or a fiction. That is to say, unlike the positive story, the negative story could only be told because it had not yet happened. Obviously no one would be left to tell the story leading up to the total discontinuity produced by complete nuclear holocaust. Furthermore, the positive story is originally told by Kant to persuade us that our capacity to be moral agents has a purpose, and that it is rational for us to act as if that purpose were realizable in some future world, whether temporal or nontemporal. In Kantian terminology, we might say that we cannot know but nevertheless can rationally hope that historical progress is certain. So the idea of progress is only regulative for us as knowers. But as agents we must act as if we believe that our actions contribute to this progress, so the idea becomes constitutive of, and provides a reason for, our actions. The conclusion to the positive story about the gradual progress of humanity is thus not simply a fiction. The Kantian theorist reasons that if we cannot know that progress is really going to occur, we also cannot know that it is not going to occur. So we are rational if we act on the hope that a better society is likely to be the outcome. Indeed, since we are agents and must act, we must have that hope.

In contrast, the conclusion to the negative story is for us now necessarily a fiction, albeit a scary one. We cannot really believe that our total self-destruction is certain, and we cognitively entertain the possibility only by suspending this disbelief. The negative story is never constitutive of our actions in the way the positive one is, if only because the total catastrophe has not occurred. The final destruction is not constitutive because, if it really did occur, we could no longer act at all, or at least, not for long and not significantly. That occurrence would make our previous actions pointless. All we can ever do is act so that it will not occur. We could do this constructively, by destroying all nuclear weapons, or we could be more evasive and try restricting certain kinds of scientific research and technological development. But the goal and reason for our action is clearly the negative attempt to avoid an unwelcome outcome rather than the positive task of bringing about in specific ways a desirable and better world.

I therefore read Adorno's later lines as saying that we can imagine a negative universal history, but it is not "universal" in the same sense as a positive universal history. We can act only to postpone what we hope is merely a fiction and a terrible fantasy. The narrative that this fantasy makes possible is also different from the narrative of the positive universal history. The conclusion to the negative story does not pull all previous history together into a continuous development, but gives us instead accidental, arbitrary events or at most discontinuous, fragmentary histories of uncorrelated starts and stops. The story of progress is what makes it possible to talk about universal history, since that story projects a single goal for all human action. The story of annihilation would show that whatever the many goals of human beings were, the actions and efforts come to naught and there is no single, continuous story of the human species. Negative universal history is thus not really universal history at all, but disperses this totalizing conception of history.

Adorno's later reflections on the negative story could not have appeared in the *Dialectic of Enlightenment*, of course, since the first preface was signed in May of 1944, before the full implications of atomic warfare would have been realized. Nevertheless, the possibility of nuclear devastation does not add a significantly new element to Adorno's thought, which is remarkably stable throughout his career. The violence of atomic warfare is a new element only quantitatively, not qualitatively. Enlightenment and violence always accompany each other, with the former trying but failing to assuage the fear of the latter. The *Dialectic of Enlightenment* sees the smooth social functioning introduced by bureaucracy, technology, and conformism as masking a more chaotic and brutal level that constantly threatens to erupt. The threat is not decreased by the apparently rational antidote of increasing social regulation, but on the contrary, is feared all the more. The modern world is compared with earlier worlds in which the fear of nature is masked with myths:

> The noontide panic fear in which [people] suddenly became aware of nature as totality has found its like in the panic which nowadays is ready to break out at every moment: [people] expect that the world, which is without any issue, will be set on fire by a totality which they themselves are and over which they have no control.[33]

The elements for the critique of philosophy and of universal history in Adorno's later writings are thus to be found in the earlier critique of enlightenment as well. I focus on two of these elements because they point up the difference between a more traditional conception of history and the "critical" rejection of "history" in that sense. The two are first, a denial of necessity in history, and second, a correlative insistence on discontinuity and incommensurability in history. Unlike Horkheimer's contrast between traditional and critical *theory*, which is inspired by Hegel and Lukács, the contrast that I am drawing more from Adorno between traditional and critical *history* represents a partial critique of Hegel, one that is inspired initially by Nietzsche and practiced later by Michel Foucault.

## 4.3   Anticipations of Poststructuralism

### (1)  Necessity?

The *Dialectic of Enlightenment* is both an argument for and an example of critical rather than traditional historiography. The notion of critical history comes directly from Nietzsche. In the second of Nietzsche's *Unzeitgemäße Betrachtungen*, "The Use and Abuse of History for Life," he analyzes modernity's preoccupation with history as a sign of its loss of a sense of its own role in history. Modernity tries to break with its past, but to know that its achievements are creative and novel, it must look back anxiously to see whether the past has anticipated it. Thinking historically is thus a peculiarly paradigmatic feature of modernity. Nietzsche notes that the backward-looking anxiety that generates the need to think historically can become an obsession. This obsession becomes dysfunctional when it begins to stifle active, forward-looking, creative thinking.

Thinking historically means more than thinking about the methods of historiography or the events of history, for even thinking about other philosophical topics like knowledge, culture, morality, religion, or art can involve increased and perhaps even exclusive concern with their historical nature. Nietzsche blames Hegel for the propensity of the age to be preoccupied with the past, and thus to think of oneself and one's contemporaries as latecomers. Nietzsche contrasts three ways of thinking historically. The antiquarian way simply tries to recreate the past as it really was, ignoring the present as if the present did not condition how the past is perceived and understood. Monumental historiography looks to the past for models of how to act in the present, ignoring the novelty of the present and diminishing the significance of present agents by comparison with the triumphs of past heroes. While critical historiography also has its abuses, its value is that it disabuses us of the tendency not only to see the present and the past as being fundamentally alike, but also to forget that our interest in history is really an interest in our own present and future.

Horkheimer and Adorno are trying to show that what I am calling critical history will be distinctive and useful only if it exemplifies dialectical thinking instead of the standard "rational" thinking paradigmatic of enlightenment. Dialectical thinking will construe logical necessity, social interaction, and historical development differently than rationalistic thinking does. Before explaining this difference, I should note that the authors' fixation on this difference between dialectical and rationalistic thinking now seems dated. Today there is no longer a live or productive debate about whether dialectic represents a distinctive and superior "logic" or method. Adorno's preoccupation with explaining and justifying negative dialectic as a distinctive philosophical method is on his own terms an odd obsession. His insistence on self-reflection and the historical conditionedness of theory should have led him to suspect that there was something wrong with the meta-theoretical project of depicting a superior philosophical method or a uniquely privileged "dialectical" thinking. Or perhaps he would not be surprised by the general agreement among even the more sympathetic commentators (like Fredric Jameson, Martin Jay, or Raymond Geuss) that as a methodological treatise *Negative Dialectics* is a failure. Perhaps the best explanation for the compulsive concern with method is that it is symptomatic of philosophy in general in this period. For highly self-conscious writers like Adorno and Heidegger there is both a desire to differentiate their own projects from others, and a need to confront polemical attacks on the intelligibility of their texts. Also, as self-reflective thinkers who insist that thought is historically and contextually limited by its time and context, they move away from a conception of philosophy as advancing new substantive theories about what was supposedly true ahistorically. As a result, they are left with methodological questions about how philosophy is possible *except* as the meta-theoretical enterprise concerned with method.

Despite the influence of Nietzsche, when Adorno tries to justify dialectic he is clearly debating with himself the influence of Hegel. As arguments about truths give way to arguments about method, what appears important about Hegel's approach to both philosophy and history is less Hegel's own story about history and more the dialectical method for thinking historically. Hegel is notorious for claiming that the transitions between various stages of his philosophy are necessary. Horkheimer and Adorno recognize that there is a difference between what Hegel is claiming and what the enlightenment conception of necessity involves. The enlightenment conception is supposedly linked to the narrative assumption of mythology about the necessary connection of events. Both enlightenment and mythology are said to have a static and fatalistic view of the world. Events are repetitive, in that no new types of events are ever really introduced, and human actions that try to break fate's grip inevitably fail and are requited. As an example not only of "immanent critique," but also of a characteristically speculative leap, the authors try to undercut enlightenment's belief in its own rationality by showing that in this respect enlightenment is no less irrational than mythology:

> Mythology itself set off the unending process of enlightenment in which ever and again, with the inevitability of necessity, every specific theoretic view succumbs to the destructive criticism that it is only a belief – until even the very notions of spirit, of truth and, indeed, enlightenment itself, have become animistic magic. The principle of fatal necessity, which brings low the heroes of myth and derives as a logical consequence from the pronouncement of the oracle, does not merely, when refined to the stringency of formal logic, rule in every rationalistic system of Western philosophy, but itself dominates the series of systems which begins with the hierarchy of the gods and, in a permanent twilight of the idols, hands down an identical content: anger against insufficient righteousness. Just as the myths already realize enlightenment, so enlightenment with every step becomes more deeply engulfed in mythology.[34]

While two distinct senses of necessity (deductive and historical) are run together in this passage, the polemical purpose of the analysis is clearly to distinguish between deterministic historical necessity and a nondeterministic, dialectical sense of necessity. In the rationalistic vocabulary of enlightenment, necessity is spoken of in at least two contexts: logically, to mean that there is a strict entailment between premises and a conclusion, and empirically (in both scientific and historical events, for instance) to mean that one event necessarily follows others, with no alternative possibilities or exceptions. In contrast, Hegel's dialectic is not talking about either logical entailments or deterministic connections between singular events. Instead, he is concerned in the *Phenomenology of Spirit* with "shapes of consciousness," with what I would describe as sets of beliefs, assumptions, and practices as they appear in different epistemological, moral, cultural, and historical configurations.

Hegel is interested in how individuals and groups change their beliefs, and this change appears not as the deliberate substitution of one belief for another, but as the reconfiguration of an entire set of attitudes, dispositions, and comportments. A reconfigured set is not a totally different set, since many of the same beliefs will be retained. But it is a different set in that it now comprehends why the previous configuration was inadequate and "necessarily" had to break down. Insofar as the reconfiguration comprehends the breakdown, and sees itself as having overcome the causes of that breakdown, it can think of itself as the "necessary" successor to its precursor. Hegel (in paragraph 7 of the *"Einleitung"* to the *Phänomenologie des Geistes*) calls this type of change "determinate negation," a notion Horkheimer and Adorno adapt to their own purposes. To express the idea in my terms, the prior set of beliefs is not simply negated and done away with so that any other set could take its place. Instead, the set breaks down for specific reasons internal to itself, and the effort to rectify itself leads to the particular reconfiguration that follows.

The question is whether *only* one particular reconfigured set would follow. Hegel's story in the *Phenomenology* is intended to have a single conclusion, and the narrative is structured to require readers to move to Hegel's system as the only true philosophy. But since the book ends and there is a conceptual gap between the story as told in the *Phenomenology* and the independently evolved system starting with the *Logic*, Hegel's inference about the necessity of the sequence of transitions is underdetermined. As Horkheimer and Adorno think is obvious, "by ultimately making the conscious result of the whole process of negation – totality in system and in history – into an absolute, he of course contravened the prohibition and himself lapsed into mythology."[35]

They thus prefer Hegel without the absolute. Hegel's insistence on a single story and a single system strikes them as failing to recognize the dialectical "prohibition" against taking one's own theory too seriously and thereby forgetting its historical limitations (and eventual "falsity"). A more plausible reading of Hegel's method (one later interpreters like Charles Taylor identify as "hermeneutical") gives up the insistence on necessity. Instead, alternative self-interpretations of a set's (or shape's) breakdown would lead to alternative reconfigurations. Given the number of shapes of consciousness described in the *Phenomenology* (and even that number appears arbitrary), the alternative reconfigurations would enable the number of possible alternative narratives to proliferate rapidly. Removing the absolute from the conclusion to Hegel's phenomenological narrative would quickly generate a pluralism that would be difficult to limit. The result would come close to the French poststructuralist claim that any text is involved with other texts in an infinite network of readings.

Rejecting the dialectical method, French poststructuralism after 1968 is a movement away from Hegel and toward Nietzsche. However, Adorno and Horkheimer anticipate this rejection of dialectic by characterizing dialectic in a postmodern way that is remarkably close to, for instance, Derrida's method of deconstruction and dissemination. The reason for this unexpected rapprochement may be due largely to Adorno's own fascination with Nietzsche. In thinking of dialectic as a method not for closing the distance between theory and the absolute, but for keeping any theory (including Hegel's) from "idolizing" itself as the absolute truth, the use and value of dialectical philosophy lies in its iconoclastic potential.

Like Nietzsche, who wanted to philosophize with a hammer, Adorno and Horkheimer wish to shatter any "rigoristic" conception of philosophy that is exclusively concerned with the replacement of falsities by truths. Enlightenment philosophy also tries to break the idols of superstitious belief, but "determinate negation rejects the defective ideas of the absolute, the idols, differently than does rigorism, which confronts them with the Idea that they cannot match up to."[36] Just as Nietzsche would think that enlightenment philosophy, by assuming that its own truths are indubitable, merely replaces one dogmatic falsity with another, Horkheimer and Adorno suggest that any philosophical configuration or "image" is a form of writing that contains within itself the signs of its own illusoriness: "Dialectic, on the contrary, interprets every image as writing. It shows how the admission of its falsity is to be read in the lines of its features – a confession that deprives it of its power and appropriates it for truth."[37] This critique of enlightenment seems misguided insofar as the empiricist tradition holds that supposedly proved facts can always be re-examined. But I think that what the authors really want to stress is that since no thought can be absolutely certain, the attitude of absolute conviction must be hiding some other purposes that, if made explicit, would diminish the sense of being absolutely right.

On my reading, this infusion of skepticism into dialectic serves to lessen the aspiration to "critical *theory*" and to leave the critics of enlightenment with what Horkheimer earlier called the critical activity. This critical activity manifests itself in the book not through the creation of a new social or philosophical theory but through doing what I have been calling critical history. The attraction of abstract theorizing about method gives way to concrete historical analysis because the abandonment of claims to absolute correctness implies giving up the right to claim to have the only possible explanation of the necessity of particular developments. Theoretical explanations appear to be not so different from practical interpretations. Since different interpretations are possible, the term "necessary" has less of a role, and the aspiration to "theory" becomes less elevated. Instead of a conception of theory as supplying the only explanation of the necessary occurrence of events, we are left with an interpretation of how the events were possible. If the interpretation is a good one, it will give an account that seems highly likely, but it cannot claim to be the only possible account.

The *Dialectic of Enlightenment* is thus on my interpretation not a philosophical theory of history or of reason or of knowledge, but a history of how the traditional conception of theory originates, and how it runs amok. This "immanent criticism" does not amount to offering a new conception of theory in place of the traditional one. I take the authors' vague assertion that the only antidote to Enlightenment is more enlightenment to be an admission of the parasitism of the critical activity on the traditional conception of theory. Furthermore, I think that the activity undertaken in the book points toward abandoning the hopes for a special and distinctive critical theory in favor of "immanent criticism" or practical critical history. Adorno does continue doing this kind of critical history in his essays on music and aesthetics. But the vestige of an aspiration to work out a "theory of theory" makes him want to write *Negative Dialectics*, although in full awareness of the possibility of parasitism.

One way to make sense out of his later philosophical writings and to avoid unnecessary paradox is, I believe, to take these writings not as a new philosophy of a superior way to think about thinking, which would be the traditional program for philosophy Adorno should be abandoning. Instead, these writings should be read as an account of how critical history is possible, and how immanent criticism can be effective without having to aspire to the status of theory in an ahistorical sense. In Adorno's efforts to give such an account and to avoid making claims that exempt themselves from historical uncertainty, a crucial step that I shall now discuss involves taking more seriously than does traditional theory the problem of historical discontinuity and the possibility of incommensurable gaps between different conceptual frameworks.

## (ii) Conformism and discontinuity

Because the attitude of being right can degenerate into self-righteousness, the dialectical confession of uncertainty is intended to deprive the attitude of self-righteous dogmatism of its power. While the dialectical attitude cannot claim to reveal directly dimensions that the dogmatic attitude is hiding from itself, it can show how misguided the purpose of the search for absolute certainty is. The claim of the dialectical critique of the enlightenment is that the enlightenment narrows down the range of the rational to what can be known with specific methods, thereby excluding whatever does not fit into this domain. What enlightenment thinking would not admit is that it does this not for rational reasons, but from irrational fear:

> [Humanity] imagines [itself] free from fear when there is no longer anything unknown . . . Enlightenment is mythic fear turned radical. The pure immanence of positivism, its ultimate product, is no more than a so to speak universal taboo. Nothing at all may remain outside, because the mere idea of outsidedness is the very source of fear.[38]

While positivism is not accurately described by this account, the analysis is interesting as an example of what the dialectical critique would like to be able to show. Through "immanent critique" a position would be shown to have an origin that is radically different from what it thinks its origin is. So here the origin of enlightenment is said to be fear rather than reason. The effect is also different, for instead of eliminating fear, enlightenment institutionalizes it, and risks being destroyed by it eventually. By insisting on rationality, enlightenment excludes the discontinuous and the incommensurable as "outside" reason, but this outside nevertheless threatens to prove its reality in unforeseeable and perhaps violent ways.

Dialectical philosophy cannot assert, however, that it has a correct perception of the "outside" that others fail to see, and it cannot even aspire to a distinct social vision of its own. Traditionally, the term "theory" is paired with "reality," the correct theory supposedly capturing reality as it really is. If I am right that Adorno moves in the direction of obviating the use of the term "theory," then it is not surprising if in his vocabulary "reality" has less of a determinate use, particularly when the type of reality in question is social reality. Adorno often implies that social reality, or reality of any sort, is never a given, and is not something of which any theory could claim to be a correct perception. He is aware that Nietzsche is tempted by a Schopenhauerian urge to say that reality is really chaos, and all perception therefore an abstract illusion and falsification. I think that Adorno should not be construed as asserting any such problematic ontology, since the point of the dialectical confession of the limitations of thought is to admit the inadequacies of dialectic and philosophy as a positive, constructive social-historical force. Giving up the absolute means that dialectical thinking must resign itself to serving a negative or critical function. Its difficult project is to show us some of our socially-induced illusions, but without claiming to have, or aspiring to, or perhaps even admitting the sense in talking of an undistorted grasp of reality.

Claims to have a superior grasp of reality would be in bad faith from at least two perspectives. While dialectical thinking can posit a better society or state of affairs, it cannot claim either superior *knowledge* of how social improvement is really possible, or a superior *moral* position through exemption from the distortions of unjust social division and oppression. Because of the incommensurable conceptual gap between the real and the ideal states of affairs, positing a better world becomes utopian. Utopian visions are the product more of fantasy than of theory. They are speculative and fictive rather than heuristic and literal, although in the social sphere these distinctions may be differences of degree rather than of kind. The critical historian who has any glimpses of a better future must admit them to be tainted by vestiges of an unjust past and by distortions of present struggles. The inability to claim to know how history will necessarily unfold means that these glimpses will be *merely* utopian, that is, independent of any particular, concrete social program for change.

In the light of this confession, what happens to Horkheimer's earlier worry that the critical attitude toward the present might degenerate into an attitude of social resignation and political withdrawal? Adorno maintains that his own theory does not lead to political apathy, even if it refrains from stating explicit utopian goals. He avoids detailed utopian speculations because he believes that such speculations will be seen as so different from what is really the case that they are more likely to be what leads to resignation: "The utopian impulse in thinking is all the stronger, the less it objectifies itself as utopia – a further form of regression – whereby it sabotages its own realization. Open thinking points beyond itself."[39] For Adorno the paradigm of a philosopher of resignation is Heidegger. Adorno's criticism of Heidegger centers on the charge that Heidegger's philosophy simply confirms the social status quo, and thus works to preserve arbitrary social division and discord. Yet can Adorno prevent this charge from applying to his own approach as well? To put the question in another way, do Adorno's pessimistic alterations of the original conception of critical theory strengthen the case for critical over traditional theory, or do they deflate the aspirations of critical theory to be both theoretical and critical?

The denial of necessity in the flow of historical events toward a progressive goal certainly threatens to make criticism pointless and ineffective. The reflection that restores some potential to criticism of the present turns on the question whether giving up universal history and a belief in progress leaves us mired permanently in the status quo, as Adorno thinks Heidegger's philosophy does. That the utopian hope can even survive depends on recognizing that if historical events are not strictly determined, and if there is no totalizing standpoint that comprehends all that is actual or possible at any one time, then it seems possible that history is not fated to endless repetition of the same, as both mythology and enlightenment supposedly believe. Instead of historical periods always repeating the same types of events and patterns, there can be abrupt discontinuities and profound incommensurabilities.

In underlining "the discontinuous, chaotically splintered moments and phases of history,"[40] Adorno again goes against the usual understanding of Hegelian dialectic and anticipates French poststructuralist writers like the early Foucault with his notion of abrupt historical ruptures and epistemological paradigm shifts. Adorno is not as willing as Foucault to ignore materialist historical explanations so he cannot be a straightforward advocate of discontinuity. In *Negative Dialectics* he thus shows his ambivalence by saying that "history is the unity of continuity and discontinuity" (p. 320). This statement is only apparently paradoxical, since it is intended to be deeply ironic. He would grant not only that "profit interest and thus the class relationship make up the objective motor of the production process which the life of all . . . hangs by," but also that social history runs on the antagonism of social division. However, the antagonism is likely to lead not to a better world but to disaster. Adorno's bitter joke is thus that the unity of history or "world spirit" is best defined not as progressive social emancipation but instead as "permanent catastrophe."

What is the effect of insisting on historical discontinuity rather than on the more traditional conception of history as either repeating itself or improving itself in a gradual but continuous process? A price must be paid, and the most obvious one is that the present loses its central role in the story of the gradual progression toward a better future, since the present can no longer be thought to be an especially significant or typical moment of history. The present's structures and values suddenly appear arbitrary and temporary. If our own discourse may be incommensurable with future discourses, its value is diminished even for us since we can no longer believe ourselves to be communicating effectively with our future selves. As Adorno is probably well aware, a view insisting on discontinuity and incommensurability may finally be unintelligible, even to itself.

This price is paid, however, to achieve a specific effect (and I shall discuss later whether the effect could be achieved for a lesser price). The effect is to show a causal and conceptual link between the rationalistic assumptions of enlightenment thinking and social conformism. An assumption of what Adorno and Horkheimer call "identity thinking" is that everything everywhere must be commensurable. What they are opposed to is the reduction of things to abstract signs, that is, concepts of properties and relations, the network of which allows rational thinking (and science) to put everything that exists on a grid that can then serve to compare everything with everything else. Criticizing the abstract thinking that remains exclusively on this level where everything is reduced to a system of universally interchangeable signs, Horkheimer and Adorno (echoing Hegel in the sections of the *Phenomenology* on "Legal Status" and the Enlightenment) object that identity thinking "excises the incommensurable. Not only are qualities dissolved in thought, but [people] are brought to actual conformity."[41]

An adamant critic of critical theory would charge that this move from epistemological incommensurability to social conformism is a speculative leap between two unconnected and indeed incommensurable matters. However, to argue a priori that there is no link between the suppression of social unorthodoxy and the reduction of social phenomena to statistically quantifiable relations would be to stick too obviously to "identity thinking." More empirical books from the Frankfurt School, such as the study of the prison by Rusche and Kirchheimer (which Foucault uses as a foil in *Discipline and Punish*), suggest that the development of modern social institutions is indeed accompanied and aided by the simultaneous development of the social sciences. A more sympathetic query is therefore to ask whether the critique of conformism requires such a strong notion of discursive incommensurability and historical discontinuity.

The analysis of conformism is, after all, probably what made *Dialectic of Enlightenment* so famous in the 1960s when it was widely read for the first time (the second time being in the early to mid-1980s). The critique of conformism is not unique to Horkheimer and Adorno, of course. Another, earlier example is Heidegger's description in *Being and Time* (1927) of "das Man," the anonymous third-person ("one" or "they") who does everything that is expected but who can never be called to account. Horkheimer and Adorno wish to keep their distance from Heidegger because they believe that Heidegger's appeal to authenticity is an asocial, bourgeois reversion to an empty individualism. As a clue to their real precursor, they mention Durkheim instead, although they draw contrasting conclusions: "But of course this social character of categories of thought is not, as Durkheim asserts, an expression of social solidarity, but evidence of the inscrutable unity of society and domination. Domination lends increased consistency and force to the social whole in which it establishes itself."[42] Domination is not thought of as something that some particular people do to some other people, but as what people do to themselves even though it is not in their real interest to do so.

Horkheimer and Adorno thus tell a story that anticipates Foucault's *Discipline and Punish* (although Foucault claims not to have been aware of it until after most of his own work was completed). As power is taken out of the hands of a few and supposedly taken up by all, what happens is that people must learn to "model their body and soul according to the technical apparatus" if they are to earn and survive.[43] Society becomes a self-perpetuating machine:

> Where the evolution of the machine has already turned into that of the machinery of domination (so that technical and social tendencies, always interwoven, converge in the total schematization of [human beings]), untruth is not represented merely by the outdistanced. As against that, adaptation to the power of progress involves the progress of power, and each time anew brings about those degenerations which show not unsuccessful but successful progress to be its contrary. The curse of irresistible progress is irresistible regression.[44]

The appearance of this irresistible machine is the source of the misguided "ideological" belief in both the necessity of the system as well as the value of the system's historical realization.

Anticipating Foucault, Horkheimer and Adorno reverse Bacon's dream that power will pass over to the many rather than the few: "While bourgeois economy multiplied power through the mediation of the market, it also multiplied its objects and powers to such an extent that for their administration not just the kings, not even the middle classes are no longer necessary, but all [people]."[45] Instead of dispensing with power, however, this deceptive development leads to wholesale domination. Horkheimer and Adorno cite Nietzsche as the one who already sees that Bacon's utopian dream of the enlightened spread of power into everyone's hands has the inverse effect of spreading power more efficaciously over everyone. They cite Nietzsche's anti-democratic claim that the masses are fooled insofar as "the reduction and malleability of [human beings] are worked for as 'progress'!"[46] They have to be careful, however, since they do not share his elitism, and they want to give a different assessment and explanation of the deception. In contrast to Heidegger, whom they associate with Nietzsche as an anti-proletarian philosopher offering ontological redescriptions rather than causal explanations of conformism, Horkheimer and Adorno stress the economic dimension to explain rather than to denigrate the masses' lack of self-comprehension. Unlike the rulers, who supposedly do not believe in objective necessity, "only the ruled accept as unquestionable necessity the course of development that with every decreed rise in the standard of living makes them so much more powerless."[47] The masses come to depend on either social welfare or the success of the economy for their survival and subsistence. This dependence is gradually transformed into an identification with the forces that oppress them. Of course, if this identification is the result of oppression, it is a false sense of where their real interests lie. In times of economic unrest glimpses by the masses of the illusory status of this identification can become the source of the threat of social violence (as Gramsci was to argue in more detail).

Since conformism is interpreted as the symptom of the necessity of the spread of power and domination into all aspects of society, the insistence on an incommensurable "outside" and on discontinuous shifts rather than progress in history works as an antidote to the spread of social orthodoxy. However, if Horkheimer and Adorno are right that we have outgrown the enlightenment belief in necessity anyway, then the antidote would not have to be as extreme. Pointing to the fear inside us as the sign of a mysterious and threatening "outside" reverts to an unnecessary and obscurantist polemic. Unhelpful and unintelligible, the authors' critique of conformism could be effective without implying that there is a reverse necessity to history or that the spread of domination is like the growth of an irremediable cancer. If Kantians are criticized for the belief in the necessity of progress because there is no such historical necessity, then the belief in the necessity of regress should be rejected as well. If Adorno's theory says as much, then he is not entitled to his darker polemical pronouncements.

## (iii)  Critical theory versus critical history

Reading the *Dialectic of Enlightenment* as fragments not of a critical theory, but instead as critical history removes the need for some of the polemics in which Adorno himself was unproductively embroiled. Disputes with Popperians and positivists about the nature of truth, natural science, and language seem tangential if instead of pretending to offer a different theory of rationality, the critical account limits itself to showing that the actual history of the effects of enlightenment runs counter to what the theory of enlightenment projects. While Adorno's texts would not support any contention that this is all he is trying to do, they do imply that he is at least trying to do this much. Foucault is as well, and is perhaps not trying to do anything more grandiose such as generating a different theory of reason or of social power or of the human subject. By pointing out this common denominator of their projects, I am suggesting that this is the better part of those projects. Ambitions to confront enlightenment with an alternative philosophy thereby appear exaggerated and paradoxical.

To defuse controversy about grand theory in this respect is not to say that critical history is without effect. Critical history can reveal misunderstandings of how we got to be where we are, and therefore about what we are. As an effort in self-understanding, critical history can unmask illusions perpetrated by traditional theory of theory, which misreads its own preconceptions into the historical record. Critical history can also challenge the reliance on tradition in general as well as on misconceptions of what is good or bad in the specific institutions and practices we inherit.

Adorno, however, could not have fully embraced the rejection of critical theory in favor of the practice of writing only critical histories because of his two-sided polemics. In addition to his attack on the rationalism of positivist theory of science, which is the most obvious target of the critique of enlightenment, he has to fend off the accusation by positivists that his own views are relativistic or historicistic. To anticipate this objection, but also to distance himself from Heidegger's anti-positivist philosophy, Adorno is as critical of relativism as he is of rationalism. Whereas the critique of positivism as a late culmination of the Enlightenment seems to suggest that Adorno's own standpoint would be somewhere outside that tradition, his critique of Heidegger is that it is Heidegger who wrongly desires a mysterious standpoint "beyond" our philosophical tradition. By trying to invent a new language out of the ashes of a supposedly worn-out philosophical vocabulary with vestiges in ordinary language, Heidegger becomes unintelligible. Adorno does not want to start from scratch, and thinks that we cannot avoid using inherited dualisms such as those between subject and object, nature and history, or identity and non-identity.[48] However, Adorno's texts are not any easier to read than Heidegger's. Adorno's complex, aphoristic, and fragmented style is consistent with his view that the language within which we must think and work is not a transparent mirror of reality. What the plain speech of easy and efficacious everyday communication reproduces is the illusion of social harmony and intelligibility. Adorno's highly self-conscious constructions are designed to disrupt the disguised interest in smooth social functioning presupposed by most verbal interchange.[49]

In *Negative Dialectics* Adorno insists that dialectic is not a middle ground between the absolutism and relativism it criticizes immanently (p. 35). He also thinks that the standard objection to relativism, namely, that it presupposes at least one absolute (its own truth), is facile. The objection supposedly confuses the denial of a principle with an assertion of the opposite principle. This response will not work if the principle and its negation are the only alternatives, and if a double negation formally entails the affirmative.[50] But I think that the logical dispute is not the real issue that Adorno should be addressing, and he may be simply trying to waive it to get on to a more substantive defect in relativism. The relativity of all cognition cannot be asserted from within a set of beliefs about what counts as true or false. Relativism is not really a first-order cognitive standpoint at all, and *Negative Dialectics* charges that relativism does not take seriously enough its own thought that beliefs are the product not of a heaven of eternal verities but of a social world:

> Consciousness no sooner enters into some definite thing, no sooner faces its immanent claim to be true or false, than the thought's allegedly subjective accidentality will dissolve. Relativism is nugatory for another reason: the things it considers random and accidental, on the one hand, and irreducible on the other – those things themselves are brought forth by an objectivity, by an objective individualist society, and can be deduced from it as socially necessary phenomena. (p. 36).

This critique of relativism is said by Adorno to be a paradigm of the technique of determinate negation and thus of immanent criticism. However, as a critique of Heidegger it would have to count as external criticism. The claim that Heidegger's philosophy is the typical product of a late industrialist society presupposes a theory of history Heidegger does not share. Also, from Heidegger's standpoint, what

Adorno is attacking is a special case of relativism, namely, subjectiv-
ism, or the view that human subjectivity can somehow will or constitute the objects of its knowledge. Heidegger is as opposed to that
view as is Adorno. The difference is that Heidegger thinks that the
rejection of the emphasis of modern Cartesian and Kantian philosophy on the constituting consciousness implies that the subject–
object distinction should be avoided altogether, whereas Adorno retains it, stressing the resistance of objectivity and nature to human
subjectivity and history.

Attacking relativism in others does not prove that one's position is
not itself relativistic. These attacks make it more rather than less
important that Adorno salvage his own enterprise from the charge of
relativism. Does he do so? Susan Buck-Morss argues that Adorno is
successful at avoiding relativism, since Adorno insists that the present cannot be relativistic about its own beliefs but must take itself as
a repository of significant truths. Discussing Adorno's acceptance of
the "historicization of truth," she presents Adorno as solving the
worries about relativism that plagued Dilthey: "But whereas Dilthey
had found the very concept of truth threatened by such historicity,
Adorno turned this problem into a virtue. For if the present was the
unavoidable point of reference, then it was in the present that the
concept of truth found its concrete meaning."[51] While I would also
agree that Adorno's concern for the present is a virtue, Dilthey seems
to me to be right not to have settled for this resolution of the problem
of truth. "True, at least for now" is not a notion of truth that could
withstand the charge of relativism for very long.

However, Adorno may have been wrong to think that he needed to
address the semantical issues about truth. The theory of truth, at least
as it is discussed by more recent analytic philosophers than those
with whom Adorno was arguing, may not be central to his purposes.
He could admit that there are historical shifts in what count as the
important things to say without implying that different sets of beliefs
at different historical times are radically incommensurable. What is
crucial is whether the focus of the critic is on the past, the present, or
the future. The problem is not an epistemological but a temporal one.
The critical activity can presuppose that the best theory of truth,
whatever it is, must warrant the critical historian's true beliefs, whatever they are. Certainly a philosophical theory of truth will not say
which particular beliefs are true. A theory of truth will not even
supply a criterion for doing so. First-order theories will have internal
criteria about how to test specific assertions, but there is no general
criterion of truth that all such theories must wield. What the critical
historian needs to reflect on is not truth in general, but on what the

object of criticism is, and this reflection should take seriously its strategic relation to time.

Nietzsche sees the point, for while he did not publish his problematic reflections on truth written shortly after "The Use and Abuse of History," he does see that the distinguishing feature of the critical historian is a recognition of the temporal priority of the present. Unlike the antiquarian who is interested only in the past, the critical historian wishes to understand history as an indispensable means to a better understanding of the present. As Heidegger also says when commenting on Nietzsche's essay in section 76 of *Sein und Zeit*, there is no point to criticizing the past, since we can no longer change it. What we want is to assess and if necessary to criticize the present. A critical assessment could show, for instance, either that the present preserves undesirable features left over from past forms of life, or that the present has fallen away from some of the better possibilities that our tradition has at least envisioned if not achieved.

Horkheimer and Adorno reflect on the temporality of historical thinking in their introduction to the *Dialectic of Enlightenment* (p. xv): "The task to be accomplished is not the conservation of the past, but the redemption of the hopes of the past. Today, however, the past is preserved as the destruction of the past." The appeal to the past can be used, as by fascism, to freeze society into a divided and rigid structure and thus precisely to destroy the hopes for possible social improvement which we also inherit. These hoped-for possibilities are easy to forget because they may not have been concretely embodied in existing social institutions. So a critical history that returns to the past to redeem its hopes by generating a critique of the present is not neoconservative or reactionary.

In *Being and Time* Heidegger argues that human beings are fundamentally oriented toward the future but thoroughly enmeshed in their traditions. He is thus criticized by some for being an apologist for the social status quo and by others for being a prophet of a mysterious and unintelligible future way of thinking. He can be defended by arguing that in fact he is giving a priority to the present, and insisting that neither the past nor the future should be the exclusive direction of reflection.[52] A better example of the mistake of an exclusively futural reflection can be found in Nietzsche's essay on history. The essay is not itself a concrete example of what a critical history would look like, but is more of a meta-theoretical polemic. As a result, when he must offer his own suggestions about how to cure the modern age of its sickly preoccupation with the past, he ends lamely with the abstract hope that the "youth" of a new generation will be able to think differently, although he cannot tell us anything about this thinking.[53]

In contrast to critical history, I would characterize this thought as an example of utopian thinking. Future-oriented but vague, utopian specu- lation about a new attitude, cured of the illnesses of the present, does not say much for the present. The thought does not tell us how we can be any different, and it is counter-productive if it implies that the present is a self-contained whole that must be transcended entirely. That a vague future will be better than the present is an empty suggestion compared to detailed reminders through critical histories of how the present has evolved contrary to intentions and in dir- ections that, if foreseen, would have been better avoided.

Nietzsche gets trapped in the same rhetorical dead-end that he is exposing in others because of the compelling pull on all moderns of the "new" in contrast to the "old." Later he has Zarathustra preach the idea of the eternal recurrence, which is supposed to free us not only from our preoccupation with the future (and with our salvation), but also from the resulting self-denial in the present. Nevertheless, his imagery is still future-oriented or utopian in its suggestion of the brighter noon that will be brought about by the substitution of this present-oriented idea for the Judeo-Christian conception of eschato- logical temporality. In paragraph 150 of *Minima Moralia* Adorno con- siders the interplay of the ideas of the new and the old, tracing the fascination with the new not to Nietzsche but to Baudelaire. The new for Adorno, who is arguing implicitly against Walter Benjamin, gets transformed by modern culture into the "sensational," to which mod- erns get addicted. This addiction can never be fully satisfied, how- ever, and the eventual effect on the senses is to dull rather than sharpen them. This is the paradox of modernity that Nietzsche both revealed and embodied, since, as Adorno writes, "everything modern, because of its never-changing core, has scarcely aged than it takes on a look of the archaic."[54] The continual craving for the new becomes the eternal recurrence of the same, but in a satanic rather than re- demptive way. The social analogue for the aesthetic concern with the new is the gradual tendency to become accustomed to the horrors, wars, and mass murders of the modern period. Adorno considers those who counter criticism of the tendencies in modern society by suggesting that history has always had its horrors. The apologists for modern times take disaster as being inevitable, and become resigned to being ineffective. Adorno believes that the sensationalism of the news media has produced an insensitivity to the real suffering being reported. What is missed by the apologists for the present is that although suffering is an inevitable feature of history and thus of the present as well, there is a satanic "progress towards hell" in the way the newer forms of suffering outdo the old. Those who relinquish "awareness of the growth of horror" succumb, says Adorno, to "cold-hearted contemplation."[55]

This analysis of the temporal focus of critical activity carries back to Horkheimer and Adorno's remark in the *Dialectic of Enlightenment* that the past can be either redeemed or destroyed by the reflection that tries to align the present with the past. An implication is that critical history does more than simply describe the past the way it really was. Historiographical understanding is not just detached contemplation of already-constituted facts about the past, and critical history recognizes that understanding the past involves something like "backward causation." Antiquarian historiography proceeds as if once events occur, they do so in a way that can be captured in a single, objective description. In contrast, critical historiography realizes that present interests color our interpretations of the past. The past events later perceived as significant for later developments may not have been perceivable at the earlier time. If this characterization of historical understanding is correct, further reflection should lead the critical historian to investigate not simply the past, but rather those phenomena of the present that have become problematic for us and that make us wonder about their origins and necessity.

What is most appealing to me in Adorno's position is thus not some view about truth, but his focus on the present. Susan Buck-Morss captures this focus aptly when she writes, "For Adorno, the present did not receive its meaning from history; rather, history received its meaning from the present . . . To use an expression of Baudelaire which Adorno quoted often: '*Il faut être absolutement* [sic] *moderne*' – in the sense, not of following the demands of the time, but of criticizing the modern, and hence rubbing history against the grain."[56] However, because Adorno asserts the absolutism of the demand that we be modern through quotation, the irony of the position must be emphasized. The irony comes from insisting on being completely modern while criticizing all that is modern. Irony is, of course, essential to the *modernistic* attitude (in contrast to the playful pastiche of the postmoderns).[57]

Is irony any different from resignation in its practical effect? Adorno's method is to avoid going beyond critique toward positive, constructive advice for action. Concluding a late essay entitled "Kritik" (1969), he attacks those who link the ideas of the "positive" and the "constructive," deriding the collective compulsion to action for the sake of action alone. This *Aktionismus* fails to see that the demonstration of the wrongness of an understanding (presumably through the method of immanent criticism or determinate negation) is already an index of what would be a better understanding.[58] The construction of a positive theory would fall back into the self-destructive desire to control everything.

Resignation also prescinds from positive suggestions, so how is it different? I think that even without any utopian assumptions or anti-Heideggerian dialectical maneuvers, Adorno's best answer would be that resignation carried to its natural conclusions could not be critical. Resignation would lead to acceptance of the positive, of whatever society has become. Resignation may regret the existing social structures, thinking them to be for the worse rather than for the better. But resignation is quietistic or fatalistic if it implies that social change would lead to even worse conditions. Irony is destructive rather than constructive, but if what is destroyed are frozen, oppressive conventions, then that activity is in itself beneficial. Unlike resignation the critical activity is conducive to social change, even without a constructive social program or philosophical theory. That the social change will be welcomed because it leaves some repression behind does not entail, of course, that the resulting social configuration will not require further critical activity. The need for critical activity is never outgrown.

### (iv)  Temporal deferrals

Criticism entails self-criticism, and admittedly the reading of Adorno just proffered, for polemical purposes of course, leaves out much that Adorno would have considered central to his own conception of philosophy. His dialectical account of identity and non-identity, and particularly his insistence on the ineffability of the non-identical, plays no role in the account of his critical practice I have been explicating. If the critical practice can be defended without bringing in the dialectical apparatus, then there is no need to do so unless one is interested in the apparatus for its own theoretical sake. Adorno himself could not have claimed completeness and consistency for his thought, such that every aspect of it requires every other aspect.

An account of Adorno's and Horkheimer's practice in their method of critical social history does not entail the problematic claims about science, truth, and language advanced by Adorno in his polemics against positivism and relativism. Against the latter, however, Adorno urges that the traditional dualisms cannot be ignored. In particular, the distinction between nature and history, between what human beings can change and what they cannot, is not to be dissolved into the claim that every feature of ourselves and our world is socially produced, and therefore historically relative.[59] Adorno will not specify what counts as natural or what counts as historical, since he does not think that there are eternal features of the former that could be specified. But he insists that because our social endeavours always meet with resistance, we will always find ourselves up against some in-variant nature.

By refusing to specify the contents that count as part of nature rather than of history, however, Adorno's retention of the distinction is no more compelling than the phenomenological truism that the exercise of our will always meets with some resistance, frequently from unex-pected quarters. The critical force of the distinctions between nature and history or subject and object is to allow critical theory to distin-guish between apparent human interests and real human interests. Unlike standard sociological observations that take people's state-ments about their interests at face value, critical social philosophy believes that people can misperceive their interests as the result of oppressive social institutions. Desires for certain consumer items, for instance, are not the expression of real needs, but of false wants induced by the advertising media. Furthermore, critical theory main-tains that since the apparent interests have been acquired only as the result of deception, people would disavow them in coming to perceive themselves as having the interests only as the result of oppression. In other words, they would see that the interests acquired through re-pressive social forces are not their *real* interests.[60]

The appeal to real interests is not like the more traditional appeal to natural rights, since "nature" is not a static repository of human qualities that are eternal and perhaps divine. Critical history shows that "real" means "historically emergent," such that the interests are not interests that we would have in the absence of societal organiza-tion, but are the products of specific human communities. Since critical theory admits that real interests are context-relative, however, the difference between real and apparent interests cannot be as sharp as the terms suggest. The difference will be one of degree, and not one of kind. The only way to discover the real interests is through the process of interpretation I have been calling critical history. But since a particular critical history emerges from a specific context of con-cerns, it can only claim to be one possible interpretation. Critical history cannot claim to give the only possible picture of what it portrays. As a result, its identification of real interests will be internal to its own interpretive framework, and not the final, rock-bottom identification of what people's real interests are absolutely.

The appeal to real interests is particularly misleading because it veils what makes critical history effective. To insist on capturing "real" interests more "truly" than some other "theory" makes the issue sound like an epistemological one. "Real" connotes "everywhere and always the same," or if not universal, then at least "atemporal." If my reading is at all plausible, however, what makes critical history effective is not any epistemological claim to have captured otherwise inaccessible verities about the human condition. Its effect is a temporal one: it focuses our attention on the present. Critical history, however, does this with neither the rationalist intent of making the present seem the culmination of all that has gone before, nor the neoconservative intent of preserving the status quo. Instead, following Nietzsche's (and Heidegger's) account of the advantage of critical history, the intent is to make certain that the present is still open to the future despite its problematic connection to the past.

A preoccupation with theory leads to the epistemological vocabulary of truth and reality, obscuring the focus of practice, which is temporal. Adorno's practice of critical history makes the temporal dimension more prominent, and his attempt to develop an account of the dialectical method is his way to preserve the focus on temporality at the level of theory. Adorno's differences with the present seem to be without solution, because he defers on all questions about what should be done. These deferrals, however, do not necessarily detract from the force of immanent critique, for reasons that I have just mentioned and will consider further when turning to Foucault's similar strategy. Reflecting on Adorno's own temporal sense, however, I think that what is most remarkable are not the vestiges of utopian thinking, but of negative philosophy of history. The examples concerning the history of the increase of human suffering serve to motivate us to do what we can to keep the fiction of our self-destruction from becoming real. Certainly doing so is in our real interest if anything is. But Adorno's vision can be at times so strongly dystopian that it can enervate our ability to hope, as Kant thought we must, that our actions are genuinely purposeful. Our activity would appear to be simply a temporary stopgap that is probably doomed in any case. Adorno thus uses a negative philosophy of history to achieve a critical effect, but that story makes critical activity seem hopeless and directionless. In the following chapter I shall investigate other ways of achieving the critical effect both with and without the remnants of philosophy of history. The issue is whether critical activity can occur not only without a traditional philosophical conception of theory, but also without either a utopian or a dystopian philosophy of history.

NOTES

1 Max Horkheimer, "Traditional and Critical Theory," in *Critical Theory: Selected Essays*, trans. Matthew J. O'Connell et al. (New York: Seabury Press, 1972), p. 188.

2  Ibid., p. 197.

3  See Martin Jay, *Marxism and Totality: The Adventures of a Concept from Lukács to Habermas* (Berkeley: University of California Press, 1984), p. 208.

4  As, for example, Steven Lukes does for his conception of social theory in *Power: A Radical View* (London: Macmillan Press, 1974).

5  Horkheimer, "Traditional and Critical Theory," p. 206, note 14.

6  For further discussion see my essay, "Hegel's Critique of Kantian Morality," *History of Philosophy Quarterly* VI (2) (1989): 207–32.

7  Horkheimer, "Traditional and Critical Theory," pp. 206–7.

8  Ibid., p. 207 (emphasis added).

9  Ibid.

10  Ibid.

11  Ibid., p. 208.

12  Ibid., p. 242.

13  Ibid., p. 210.

14  Ibid., p. 210 (emphasis added).

15  Ibid., p. 208.

16  Ibid., p. 238.

17  Horkheimer, "Postscript" (to "Traditional and Critical Theory"), in *Critical Theory: Selected Essays*, p. 251.

18  "Traditional and Critical Theory," p. 210.

19  Ibid., p. 242.

20  Ibid., p. 208.

21  In *Marxism and Totality* Martin Jay infers from the passage that follows that Horkheimer "still maintained a Luxemburgist confidence in the breakdown of capitalism and the subsequent alternative of barbarism or socialism, an outcome to be decided on the basis of collective human will" (p. 210).

22  "Traditional and Critical Theory," p. 227.

23  Ibid., p. 211.

24  Ibid., pp. 230–1.

25  Ibid., p. 231.

26  Ibid., p. 209.

27  Max Horkheimer and Theodor W. Adorno, *Dialectic of Enlightenment*, trans. John Cumming (New York: Seabury Press, 1972), p. xi.

28  Ibid., p. xvii.

29  Ibid., p. xvi.

30  For further evidence of the persistence of this "utopian impulse" in Adorno's thinking see Martin Jay, *Marxism and Totality*, p. 264. In a review of the English translation of *Negative Dialectics* Raymond Geuss argues that although nothing positive can be said about the utopia that contrasts to our own "antagonistic" social totality, the "utopian element is still quite strong in Adorno" (see *The Journal of Philosophy*, 72, no. 6 (March 27, 1975): 169). Geuss suggests that the force of the appeal to utopia is to show that positivistic social science, while perhaps appropriate in a utopia where human desires are not distorted by repressive social

institutions, is inappropriate for our present, divided society where one cannot take data at face value.

31  For a succinct statement of Kant's critique of moral atheism see the *Critique of Teleological Judgement*, German page 472, or page 147 in Part Two of the English translation of *The Critique of Judgement* by James Creed Meredith (Oxford: Oxford University Press, 1952): "But a dogmatic unbelief cannot stand side by side with a moral maxim governing the attitude of the mind – for reason cannot command one to pursue an end that is recognized to be nothing but a fiction of the brain." Further, see the "Dialectic" of the *Critique of Practical Reason*.

32  T. Adorno, *Negative Dialectics*, trans. E. B. Ashton (New York: Seabury Press, 1979), p. 320. Also cited and discussed by Martin Jay in *Marxism and Totality*, p. 263 and p. 536.

33  *Dialectic of Enlightenment*, p. 29.

34  Ibid., pp. 11–12.

35  Ibid., p. 24.

36  Ibid.

37  Ibid.

38  Ibid., p. 16.

39  Adorno, "Resignation," *Telos* 35 (Spring, 1975): 168. Martin Jay cites this 1969 essay in *Marxism and Totality* (pp. 264–5), but recognizes that Adorno could still be reproached for political quietism since "a vague hope for the sudden collapse of the system as a whole provides little real impetus to political action of any kind either now or in the future." Jay states the difficulty in Adorno's attitude as follows: "Adorno, therefore, seemed to be open to the charge of inconsistency because he combined an increasingly gloomy analysis of the totality on the macrological level with a call for theoretical and artistic resistance to it on the micrological. Either the totality was completely watertight in its reifying power and resistance could only be co-opted, or the totality still contained negations and Adorno's descriptions of its Satanic 'falseness' were exaggerations." Jay stresses that Adorno rejected the idea of a watertight totality and believed that even in the most totalitarian of worlds there would always be open possibilities for resistance to co-optation. As for the opposite, utopian totality, Jay maintains that Adorno also "generally tended to deny that it would appear in the form of a fully integrated community without aliena-tion" (p. 266). Foucault makes a similar but more strongly anti-utopian argument that there are no societies without power relations. My argu-ment in the following chapters is intended to show that Jay's line of defense of Adorno can be turned against Jay's (and Habermas's) criticism of Foucault. Foucault's claim entails not the political quietism that Jay, Habermas, and others fear in Foucault's view, but instead micrological resistances to specific oppressions.

40  Adorno, *Negative Dialectics*, p. 320.

41  Horkheimer and Adorno, *Dialectic of Enlightenment*, p. 12.

42  Ibid., p. 21.

43  Ibid., pp. 29–30.

44	Ibid., pp. 35–6.

45	Ibid., p. 42.

46	Ibid., p. 44.

47	Ibid., p. 38.

48	In *The Origin of Negative Dialectics: Theodore W. Adorno, Walter Benjamin, and the Frankfurt Institute* (New York: The Free Press, 1977; pp. 93–4), Susan Buck-Morss points out that in criticizing Heidegger's technique of inventing new terms Adorno is following Benjamin, who preferred the renewal of the old philosophical language to the creation of a new vocabulary. She cites early essays of Adorno as criticisms of the effort to start philosophy again "from scratch," including the following unpublished passage from "Thesen über die Sprache des Philosophen": "Heidegger's language takes flight from history, yet without escaping it . . . The traditional terminology, no matter how shattered, is to be preserved, and new words of philosophers arise today solely out of changing the configuration of the words which stand within history, not by inventing a language." A word ought to be said in Heidegger's defense, however. Heidegger himself criticizes philosophies like Husserl's that want to start "from scratch" and he rejects the Cartesian tradition of creating a presuppositionless philosophy. He also does not try to create a single new vocabulary, but experiments with different words and locutions. Finally, Heidegger's use of etymology, however inaccurate, and his deliberate "misuses" of traditional terms like essence (*Wesen*) show that his project could well be described as "changing the configurations of the words which stand within history." After all, despite moments where he seems to hope for new beginnings, he also recognizes how deeply entrenched metaphysics is in our tradition and suggests that metaphysics cannot be simply "overcome" by a critical *Überwindung* that then steps entirely beyond the history of metaphysics, but only by a less radical and indefinitely long-lasting *Verwindung*, a recuperation, that recovers lost possibilities.

49	On Adorno's hostility to easy communication see Martin Jay, *Marxism and Totality*, p. 272. For an account of the rationale for Adorno's style see also Albrecht Wellmer, "Adorno, Anwalt des Nicht-Identischen: Eine Einführung" in his *Zur Dialektik von Moderne und Postmoderne: Vernunftkritik nach Adorno* (Frankfurt: Suhrkamp, 1985), pp. 135–7.

50	For further criticisms of Adorno's attempt to work out a dialectical "logic" of contradiction see Raymond Geuss's previously cited review of *Negative Dialectics*.

51	Susan Buck-Morss, *The Origin of Negative Dialectics*, p. 51.

52	For further discussion see my essay, "History, Historicity, and Historiography in *Being and Time*," in *Heidegger and Modern Philosophy: Critical Essays*, ed. Michael Murray (New Haven: Yale University Press, 1978), pp. 329–53.

53	Paul de Man accuses Nietzsche of bad faith in thus recommending to "a mythical entity called 'youth' " the effort of self-forgetting through self-knowledge, when self-knowledge is the source of the illness of the pre-

occupation with the past. See "Literary History and Literary Modernity,"
in *Blindness and Insight: Essays in the Rhetoric of Contemporary Criticism* (New York: Oxford University Press, 1971), p. 151.

54  Adorno, *Minima Moralia: Reflections from Damaged Life*, trans. E. F. N.
Jephcott (London: NLB, 1974), p. 237.
55  Ibid., pp. 234–5.
56  Susan Buck-Morss, *The Origin of Negative Dialectics*, p. 51.
57  See my discussion of postmodern pastiche in "Foucault: Modern or
Postmodern?" in *After Foucault: Humanistic Knowledge, Postmodern
Challenges*, ed. Jonathan Arac (New Brunswick, N.J.: Rutgers University
Press, 1988).
58  Adorno, *Kritik: Kleine Schriften zur Gesellschaft*, ed. Rolf Tiedemann
(Frankfurt: Suhrkamp, 1971), pp. 18–19.
59  The dialectic of nature and spirit is illustrated in the *Dialectic of Enlightenment* by the story of Odysseus and Circe (p. 70), and stated more
abstractly on page 39: "In thought, [people] distance themselves from
nature in order thus imaginatively to present it to themselves – but only
in order to determine how it is to be dominated. . . . And so thought
becomes illusionary whenever it seeks to deny the divisive function,
distancing and objectification. All mystic unification remains deception,
the impotently inward trace of the absolved revolution." In *Zur Dialektik
von Moderne und Postmoderne* (p. 151), Albrecht Wellmer describes how
the self in forgetting its links to nature becomes blind, with the moral for
Enlightenment being that it loses sight of its goal, such that rationality
becomes irrational.
60  See Raymond Geuss's discussion of real interests in chapter 2 of *The Idea
of Critical Theory: Habermas and the Frankfurt School* (Cambridge, UK:
Cambridge University Press, 1981). See also Bernard Williams, who aptly
shows the difficulties in verifying which interests are real, in *Ethics and
the Limits of Philosophy* (Cambridge, MA: Harvard University Press,
1985), pp. 40–3.

# 5

# Conflicting Conceptions of Critique: Foucault versus Habermas

## 5.1 Foucault and the Frankfurt School

The tensions and deferrals in Horkheimer's and Adorno's conceptions of critical theory required later philosophers to take critical theory in different directions. The direct inheritor of the early critical theorists is, of course, Jürgen Habermas. But what I wish to argue is that French poststructuralism is an alternative way of continuing the tradition of critical theory. To make a case for the continuation of critical theory in poststructuralism is difficult since the connections are not obvious. From the perspective of history there is no direct tutelage between the founders of the Frankfurt School and the French, as there is between Adorno and Habermas. From the perspective of theory the case is even more complex because of the poststructuralist refusal of theory (that is, of systematic construction and argumentation). Yet insofar as Habermas tries to rescue critical theory by eliminating the tensions and deferrals of the early critical theorists, he appears to continue critical theory only by proposing a philosophical program that is really more akin to what Horkheimer called traditional theory. These refusals of traditional theory are precisely what characterize the French poststructuralists and "postmoderns," and it is therefore not surprising that in *The Philosophical Discourse of Modernity* Habermas extends his criticism of his predecessors into a polemic against his French contemporaries. This wrestling over how best to "inherit" the tradition of critical theory may be the most pressing controversy in the recent decade of European philosophy.

Speaking of the connections between the Frankfurt School and French poststructuralism requires one to reconstruct affinities instead of influences since the historical interactions were tangential. Of course, as Martin Jay points out, Walter Benjamin did have contacts with the "proto-deconstructionists" of the Collège de Sociologie in Paris in the 1930s, and there is an essay by Jacques Derrida on Benjamin implying parallels.[1] Michel Foucault also sees that there are marked parallels between his own work and the Frankfurt School. But the early critical theorists could not have played much of a role in the formation of his thought since Foucault maintains that they were almost unknown in his student days or through most of his intellectual life. When the early Frankfurt School appears in his work, it does so as a study of the prison by two adherents to the Frankfurt School, Rusche and Kirchheimer, a study that Foucault uses as a foil for his own position in *Discipline and Punish*.[2] In an interview with Gérard Raulet, published in 1983, Foucault shows that he wished that there had been direct historical connections. "Now obviously," he says, commenting on his own intellectual path, "if I had been familiar with the Frankfurt School, if I had been aware of it at the time, I would not have said a number of stupid things that I did say and I would have avoided many of the detours which I made." But he is certain that the Frankfurt School did not have an influence on French thought, although he is puzzled as to why it did not:

Now, the striking thing is that France knew absolutely nothing – or only vaguely, only very indirectly – about the current of Weberian thought. Critical Theory was hardly known in France and the Frankfurt School was practically unheard of. This, by the way, raises a minor historical problem which fascinates me and which I have not been able to resolve at all. It is common knowledge that many representatives of the Frankfurt School came to Paris in 1935, seeking refuge, and left very hastily, sickened presumably – some even said as much – but saddened anyhow not to have found more of an echo. Then came 1940, but they had already left for England and the US, where they were actually much better received. The understanding that might have been established between the Frankfurt School and French philosophical thought – by way of the history of science and therefore the question of the history of rationality – never occurred. And when I was a student, I can assure you that I never once heard the name of the Frankfurt School mentioned by any of my professors.[3]

What Foucault sees as the virtue and promise of the Frankfurt School contrasts markedly to what Habermas sees there. What Foucault values in the Frankfurt School theorists is that they avoided the "blackmail" involved in traditional theory's conception of reason. According to the traditional conception, one must be either for reason or else be irrational. Foucault calls this blackmail because it seems to make a "rational critique of rationality" impossible. What the Frankfurt School projected, and what Foucault in this interview suggests is the point of his histories, is the task of showing that a conception of rationality that appeared to be the one and only possible form of reason has a history, with a beginning and an actual or possible end. This conception of rationality is to be shown as "only *one* possible form" of reason among others (p. 201). In contrast to Habermas, Foucault does not think that to undertake a rational critique of rationality one must construct a theory of what rationality *really* is as the counterpoint to the conception that took itself as rational but that is shown by critical investigation to be veiling deep irrationality. For Foucault, "reason is self-created," which means that humans develop forms or conceptions of rationality as part of their larger project of evolving an understanding of themselves given specific historical conditions.

Whereas Foucault is thus interested in the *historicity* of reason, Habermas is interested in the *theory* of reason. Each sees his question as the only possible way out of what Horkheimer and Adorno called the dialectic of enlightenment. That is, the modern search for knowledge promised enlightenment and freedom but has produced domination and barbarism as well. Foucault himself traces this problem of writing a history of reason back to Kant, and positions himself as a direct inheritor of Kant. Foucault is not referring, of course, to the Kant who projected a "history of pure reason" that would show the *Critique of Pure Reason* as the only possible conclusion to the history of philosophy. Foucault does not mention the last section of the *Critique*, which is called "The History of Pure Reason," and which is essentially a thumbnail sketch of the history of philosophy, an enterprise Kant leaves to others to work out in detail. Kant sees the history of philosophy as a succession of what appear to be "stately structures" that are in his opinion only "ruins"; but he hopes that it will be possible to achieve "before the end of the present century what many centuries have not been able to accomplish," namely, the satisfaction of human reason.[4]

Kant's conception of the history of reason in the first *Critique* is Whiggish, that is, the history would show Kant's own philosophy as the truth of all that came before, and as the only valid conception of reason. A famous example of this is Kant's own claim to understand Plato "better than he has understood himself" (A314/B370). In contrast to this Whiggish conception of history, Foucault sees in a little essay of Kant's called "What Is Enlightenment?" the possibility of thinking about history differently. Foucault thinks that Kant in this essay is not asking the Whiggish question of how the present represents the culmination of all the past, or the dawning promise of an enlightened future age, but simply, "What difference does today introduce with respect to yesterday?"[5] This question is not an apocalyptic one, and does not privilege the present over the past. Thus, it does not assert the superiority of present rationality over past conceptions and practices of rationality. In the interview with Raulet in *Telos* (1983) Foucault shows that at that point in time he does not really understand the talk about a conflict between moderns and postmoderns. Foucault seems not even to have heard of postmodernism and he admits that he does not understand what the Germans like Habermas mean by the problem of modernity. Habermas wants to cast Foucault as a postmodern in contrast to Habermas's own modernism, but the interview suggests that the strategy of contrasting modernism and postmodernism is a mistake. Foucault can make no sense of the thought of a "collapse of reason" and he maintains in this interview with Raulet that "there is no sense at all to the proposition that reason is a long narrative which is now finished, and that another narrative is under way" (p. 205).

Foucault's initial reaction to the confrontation between a modern like Habermas and a self-avowed postmodern like Jean-François Lyotard, before Foucault really knows much about the details of the controversy, is thus to say that both are guilty of "one of the most harmful habits in contemporary thought: . . . the analysis of the present as being precisely, in history, a present of rupture, or of high point, or of completion or of a returning dawn, etc." While he admits that he has himself been guilty of this habit earlier, he suggests in this Raulet interview that the analysis of the present must be undertaken "with the proviso that we do not allow ourselves the facile, rather theatrical declaration that this moment in which we exist is one of total perdition, in the abyss of darkness, or a triumphant daybreak, etc. It is a time like any other, or rather, a time which is never quite like any other" (p. 206).

What he means is that the present is always like any other present in being problematic, but it is always different in that it involves different problems. The investigation of this question about the unique but problematic present Foucault will then call genealogy, following Nietzsche, but without the apocalyptic tone sometimes heard not only in Nietzsche but also in Adorno. The point of Foucault's genealogical historiographies is not to destroy reason. Instead, they remind us that reason's assumption of its own necessity and universality may be an illusion that ignores its historical formation in the past, its precariousness in the present, and its fragility in the future.

Correlatively, genealogy analyzes practices that were instituted in the name of reason but that threaten to harden into unquestioned but oppressive necessity. The genealogical diagnosis itself implies that there is still room for thinking about the possibility of transforming these practices. Foucault puts this point succinctly in the interview by suggesting that the value of genealogy is that it "serves to show how that-which-is has not always been," and thereby shows "why and how that-which-is might no longer be that-which-is" (p. 206). That is to say, by "following lines of fragility in the present," genealogy helps us to see how what we take as necessary was not always the case. The point is not to show that historical forms of rationality are in fact irrational, or what an ideal form of rationality would be. Instead, the goal is to realize that because these forms of rationality have been made, they can be unmade. So genealogy does not deny rationality as such. Instead, it investigates rationality not as abstract theory, but as enmeshed in the background web of concrete practices. Foucault's focus on different, historically-changing forms of rationality is thus a preference for inquiry that is substantive, concrete, and specific instead of abstract, general, and purely procedural.

The question for us today, though, is whether his substantive genealogical histories need to be supplemented by an abstract, universal, and procedural conception of reason that is validated solely by philosophical arguments (for instance, transcendental ones) instead of by historiographical and sociological data. This is the central question posed by the opposition between Habermas and Foucault.

In contrast to Foucault, Habermas sees as the essential task of philosophy today the construction of a systematic theory of reason, that is, the formulation of a single conception of rationality that will allow us to see the irrationality not only of other theoretical conceptions of rationality but also of concrete social practices. He thinks that philosophy can avoid metaphysical accounts of reason by showing how rationality is embedded not in metaphysical principles, but in the assumptions embodied in the activity of discursive communication. Habermas tries to go beyond Hegel and the "ballast" of the metaphysical tradition by "(i) abstracting the development of cognitive structures from the historical dynamic of events, and (ii) abstracting the evolution of society from the historical concretion of forms of life."[6]

Habermas's account of philosophy is opposed rhetorically to the supposedly irrational poststructuralists who fail to recognize not only the universalizing aspects of communication but also the social learning processes that accompany problem-solving through communication. On his view the poststructuralists would either fail to qualify as philosophers, or if they qualify marginally, their philosophy succeeds only in refuting itself, since they repeat the mistake of anti-metaphysical skeptics who take metaphysics all too seriously in the act of opposing it.

I would like to point out in what follows, however, that Habermas's description of philosophy is thin enough to let the poststructuralists counter that they do fit under his characterization of philosophy. First, they are not opposed to reason and truth *per se*. Second, they are proposing procedural, systematic approaches to analysis, for instance, Derrida's method of deconstruction or Foucault's method of genealogy. In this chapter I shall limit my analysis of poststructuralism mainly to Foucault, and will discuss whether Habermas's method of rational reconstruction is more effective than the countervailing strategy of genealogy, which represents an alternative way of going beyond Hegel and continuing the tradition of the early critical theorists. To begin, I want to speculate about why developmental, evolutionary accounts become central in postmetaphysical philosophy, and why Habermas's strong account of evolution nevertheless may preserve a vestige of metaphysics. I will paint in contrast a different conception of evolution, one that I develop from the Nietzschean perspective of Foucault's genealogical method.

## 5.2  Naturalizing Philosophy with Evolutionary Stories[7]

I share what I think is a standard Anglo-American picture of what philosophy becomes after metaphysics loses its iron grip. In a word, philosophy becomes naturalistic. Naturalism is at least minimally construed as philosophy that no longer thinks of itself as attaining to knowledge that is not somehow compatible with empirical science. Naturalistic philosophy starts from the assumption that human beings do not have a metaphysical essence, and are not essentially different from other natural beings. Richard Rorty thus commends naturalistic philosophy of a Deweyan sort for helping us to "avoid the self-deception of thinking that we possess a deep, hidden, metaphysically significant nature which makes us 'irreducibly' different from inkwells or atoms."[8] Naturalism is not necessarily "reductionist," since human activity must be described in the way it appears to humans even if it is also at some other level a physical process. People's values, aspirations, and moral ideals in particular are the result of *social* processes, which is also to say that for naturalists these ideals are not divine, innate, or eternal essences. As Charles Taylor remarks, "What has been argued in the different theories of the social nature of [human beings] is not just that [they] cannot physically survive alone, but much more that they only develop their characteristically human capacities in society. The claim is that living in society is a necessary condition of the development of rationality, in some sense of this property, or of becoming a moral agent in the full sense of the term, or of becoming a fully responsible, autonomous being."[9] In moral philosophy, then, naturalistic ethics can be contrasted by Bernard Williams to supernaturalistic views. Naturalism here means simply "a view according to which ethics was to be understood in worldly terms, without reference to God or any transcendental authority."[10] Socialization and moral development can be thought of, furthermore, as an evolutionary process.

Evolutionary stories enable naturalistic social and moral philosophy (as opposed to the philosophy of natural science, which is not my concern in these chapters) to account for features previously explained metaphysically as resulting from supernatural or at least nonnatural sources. But what I wish to bring out in the present context is that there are different ways in which evolution can be conceived. In biology, for instance, there is currently debate about whether evolution is gradual and progressive, or whether it is the result of events that are sudden, discontinuous, and not necessarily an advance.[11] As for the question of human and cultural evolution, we are aware of the mistakes of social Darwinists. I take Nietzsche to be among the first attempts to do philosophy naturalistically, and to avoid the metaphysical optimism that masked the ethnocentric Whiggishness of social Darwinism. I shall depict some themes in French poststructuralism as inheriting and continuing this naturalistic conception of philosophy. I shall do so, however, primarily to explain the contrast between poststructuralist genealogy and Habermasian rational reconstruction.

Habermas may also be construed as "naturalizing" philosophy because of his claim that philosophy must be closely tied to empirical social science. However, there are elements of his earlier thinking which resemble a quasi-transcendental conception of philosophy. Transcendental philosophy is somewhere between metaphysical and naturalistic philosophy, and recently Habermas has emphasized that his theory is more empirical than transcendental, thus showing what I would describe as a further move in the direction of naturalism. But my account here should show that Continental philosophy (from an American perspective) includes at least two different and even conflicting conceptions of how to naturalize philosophy.

I shall mention briefly only those elements of Habermas's theory that are relevant to the contrast I am developing. Habermas generates his conception of evolutionary theory as a non-metaphysical alternative to philosophy of history, since philosophy of history is a vestige of metaphysics. Like many philosophers he also thinks that history and theory are adversaries. Thus, in his essay "Geschichte und Evolution" Habermas contrasts history and theory by remarking that "history as such is not capable of theory [*nicht theoriefähig*]."[12] He means two things here. First, history (as opposed to historiography) is not capable of being represented teleologically in one theory. He wants to abandon the philosophical tradition of universal history, which posits reason in history by formulating a conception of the progress of humanity toward a utopian society. Second, he thinks that historiographical narratives are only ever retrospective. They therefore do not lead to the formulation of a theory from which any predictions could be made about the future. Historians are thus apparently barred not only from making claims about the future, but also from giving a critical diagnosis of the present. Social scientists, in contrast, do work from social theories and therefore might be expected to make conditional predictions of future events.

When questioned about these claims in a more recent interview, Habermas explains that he recognizes both that "the prognostic capacity of social theories was and is very limited" and that "a shrewd and politically-seasoned historian . . . often judges contemporary developmental tendencies with an astonishing sureness of touch."[13] He continues, however, to make a distinction between historiography and social-scientific theory. In particular, the social theory he envisions is evolutionary or developmental theory explaining why some social formations are more advanced than others. Habermas's purpose is to keep the evolutionary *theory* distinct from a universal *history*, and from any form of historical teleology. The evolutionary theory can explain in what respects things are better or more advanced now than before, and how they might develop further. But it does not claim that history necessarily progresses in this manner.

Why is distinguishing so sharply between historiography and evolutionary social theory so important to Habermas? Whatever his own polemical purposes were originally, there are two reasons that I can see now for thinking that a sharp distinction is required. The first concerns what I would call his "internal" connection to the Frankfurt School tradition of critical theory. The second concerns his principal, contemporary, "external" opponents, those followers of Nietzsche such as the French poststructuralists who seem to reject the modern tradition with its faith in progress toward enlightenment and reason.

Habermas thinks that critical theory can be critical only if there are universal standards for criticism of the present. Horkheimer and Adorno failed to distinguish, however, between the story that could be told from the historical agents' points of view about the progress of historical events on the one hand, and on the other, the theoretical account of social evolution provided by sociologists. Whereas historical backsliding (even into barbarism) always seems possible, evolutionary backsliding is supposedly not possible because the earlier social systems with their mythological world views and communal or feudal economic arrangements are no longer alternatives for the present, given its highly complex social organization. If I understand Habermas correctly, by eliminating the worry about backsliding, he believes that he can restore the idea of critical social theory. He tries to accomplish this, furthermore, by grounding social theory not in a philosophy of history, but in a philosophy of language. By identifying the necessary presuppositions of communicative action and showing that these are ingredient in the learning processes of social evolution, he believes that he has identified universal procedural (not substantive) standards that can be used to criticize past and present events and institutions. A crucial feature of Habermas's theory is that he claims to take the linguistic turn, emphasizing not psychological features of conscious experience, but supposedly necessary features of communicative action. These features are not historically relative, and do not require him to follow Adorno in despairing about the ability of philosophy to provide a positive, constructive account of cognitive and moral reasoning.[14]

The method for the formulation of the evolutionary explanation of social development is "rational reconstruction." Habermas thus tries to have a theory that can claim universal standards at the same time that it recognizes that historical change takes place, and that as a theory it is tied to empirical claims that may be false.[15] The theory supposedly recognizes its own potential fallibility as well as its own limitation to a particular historical context. Although the theory has itself evolved from the philosophy of the enlightenment in general, and Kant in particular, it takes seriously the Hegelian critique that Kantian transcendental and moral philosophy ignores the social context of moral principles and the changing practical conditions for the acquisition of knowledge, particularly knowledge about ourselves. Hegel institutes a critique of the enlightenment, but he still represents enlightened modernity insofar as he preserves Kant's conception of historical progress by positing reason in history. Habermas corrects both Kant and Hegel by seeing reason not in the historical actions as such, but in the learning process by which society has evolved from

preconventional to conventional to post-conventional stages. He takes
the developmental models applied by Piaget to children's cognitive
development and by Kohlberg to their moral development and extends it in turn to society's development. He is not claiming that
society is a macro-subject, but he believes that society consists of
individuals who go through the learning process. "It is primarily
subjects who learn," he remarks in an interview, "while societies can
take a step forward in the evolutionary learning-process only in a
metaphorical sense."[16] So he thinks that he can extend psychological
models for individual development to social theory as well, at least to
some degree.

Whereas Habermas tries to salvage the rational kernel of modern
philosophy through his linguistic turn, he thinks that French philosophers like Derrida and Foucault abandon this kernel. Polemics are
aggravated when Lyotard attempts to defend an avowedly postmodern
philosophy.[17] Whereas Habermas takes the linguistic turn to restore
and legitimate reason and philosophy, he sees the French poststructuralists' version of the linguistic turn as threatening the preeminence
of both reason and philosophy.

Part of this picture of the poststructuralists as painted by Habermas
is correct. As naturalists, they do abandon historical teleology, including both the hope in the progress of the species and any nostalgia for
the ideals of the past. Their affinity is no longer exclusively with the
modern tradition of enlightenment running through Kant and Hegel
and Habermas, but also with a "postmodern" current going back to
Nietzsche. Although Nietzsche is not the first to abandon belief in the
ultimate rationality of human endeavors and the teleology of human
history, he exemplifies the counter-enlightenment, postmodern belief
that the human species is only a temporary accident in an uncaring
universe. The following "fable" by Nietzsche (in an early, 1873 frag-
ment) epitomizes this attitude:

> In some remote corner of the universe, poured out and glittering in
> innumerable solar systems, there once was a star on which clever an-
> imals invented knowledge. That was the haughtiest and most mendacious
> minute of "world history" – yet only a minute. After nature had drawn a
> few breaths the star grew cold, and the clever animals had to die.[18]

Thus, Nietzsche is incredulous about Kant's belief that the human
species is not temporary, and we are now only too aware that Kant was
wrong to think that the species could not destroy itself. Furthermore,
Nietzsche's reflections on social Darwinism suggest reasons for thinking that Whiggish evolutionary social theory is even more pernicious

than the empty hopes of the enlightenment for universal history and perpetual peace.[19]

The French Nietzscheans need *not* be opposed to evolutionary accounts, but they could construe evolution differently than "rational reconstructionists" do. Evolution for Nietzsche is largely a matter of chance, producing different types, but not "better" ones, for the later types are not superior to earlier ones. Humans have no intrinsic superiority over animals, only different potentials. Only a few humans, furthermore, exploit these potentials. Nietzsche's way of talking about types also suggests that higher types are not the products of gradual developments, but are instead "lucky strokes," sudden and unexpected novelties. So while Nietzsche does praise the higher types of human beings, the rare genius is but a fortunate, momentary accident and not a sign of human progress. The higher types are higher because more complex, but they are less adaptive, and therefore temporary.

To Nietzscheans rational reconstruction as a method thus appears irrelevant. The emergence of rare geniuses cannot be reconstructed if their appearance is underdetermined by the historical and cultural conditions of their times. Moreover, Nietzsche tends to think of artists as the exemplars of the higher types, and it seems futile to argue about who was superior, Leonardo or Goethe, or even Caesar or Socrates. So the enlightenment's ideal of self-conscious attainment of universal rationality plays little role in the comparison of these various expressions of power, each of which seems to be superior precisely because of its incommensurability either with the other exceptional ones or with its unexceptional contemporaries.

The new Nietzscheans abandon the optimism of the enlightenment and its rationalist projection of standards of universal commensurability. For Habermas the price they pay is too great. The enlightenment assumption is that without universal standards, criticism of the past and present seems impossible. Also, without the deliberate transformation of such standards into optimistic aspirations guiding moral, social, and political action, the most that could be expected would seem to be a losing battle to preserve the status quo. Defenders of enlightenment will surely suspect that the most probable outcome of the Nietzscheans' pessimism is that the gloomy prognosis will be self-fulfilling. Despairing resignation to sickness is likely to make the sickness worse, whereas there seems to be a better prognosis for those who somehow manage not to give in to disease emotionally.

Yet I would point out in response that Nietzsche's real position is not nihilistic or despairing, and his writings are certainly not uncritical. So perhaps criticism is possible on different assumptions than the enlightenment's rationalistic ones. That is at least the intention of critical

history and genealogy. In what follows I shall therefore paint a different picture from Habermas's of the critical potential of genealogy. To
test the critical potential of genealogy, I will then see whether Habermas's own arguments can be subjected to a genealogical critique.

## 5.3   From Hegel to Nietzsche

First, I want to note a stronger and a weaker version of rational
reconstruction, with the intention of suggesting that Habermas's version is still transcendental, and not completely naturalized. Habermas
distinguishes evolution from universal history, social theory from historiography, the logic of development from the concrete dynamics of
development, and rationality from utopia. All these distinctions are
made so that social criticism will be possible. Criticism is possible, he
believes, only if there are rational, universal standards to which all
affected parties could agree. Habermas is trying to develop a method
that can take history and historical change seriously but that can avoid
relativism. The method is "reconstructive" insofar as it takes historical practices seriously, but is "rational" insofar as what it reconstructs
is a logical development from less good to better and better theories.
There are, however, at least two assessments that could be made of
the outcome of this development. The stronger assessment, which I
attribute to Habermas, is that the rationality that emerges is universal,
transcending the inadequacies of previous theories, and not itself
capable of being relativized by further development in either historical practice or socio-philosophical theory. This strong assessment
perpetuates the enlightenment's projection of reason emerging from
the contingencies of history, and showing itself to be logically independent of history.[20]

In contrast, I note that the American scene includes at least one
philosopher, Alasdair MacIntyre, who would give a weaker (because
more naturalistic instead of transcendental) assessment, one leading
to a more historicist understanding of rationality. In his postscript to
the second edition of *After Virtue* he rebuts the rejoinder by his critics
that in his philosophical history of moral theories he tacitly relies
on nonhistorical standards (which require nonhistorical, rational justification) in the very act of chronicling the defeats of some theories and
the victories of others.

> This rejoinder fails. For our situation in respect of theories about
> what makes one theory rationally superior to another is no different

from our situation in regard to scientific theories or to moralities-and-moral-philosophies. In the former as in the latter case what we have to aspire to is not a perfect theory, one necessarily to be assented to by any rational being, because invulnerable or almost invulnerable to objections, but rather the best theory to emerge so far in the history of this class of theories. So we ought to aspire to provide the best theory so far as to what type of theory the best theory so far must be: no more, but no less.

It follows that the writing of this kind of philosophical history can never be brought to completion.[21]

This is a weaker assessment than Habermas's since rationality is relative to its history, and depends on that history to a much greater degree than the stronger assessment implies. There is no logic of development such that the stages of the historical emergence of rationality can be shown by independent argument to be rationally required. If a later theory can be said to be superior to an earlier one, this superiority can be shown only by arguing that in the earlier stage's specific terms the later stage would have to be conceded to be an improvement. This is a weak claim, however, because the later theory cannot claim to be a necessary requirement of the development of reason, but only a historically-relative and partial improvement over its particular predecessor. If there had been a different predecessor, then there would have been no need for the specific improvements supplied by the later theory, and thus no independent justification for that later theory. The later theory does not deny, but indeed assumes, that it too is inadequate in some respects (which it may not yet have perceived), and that it may have to revise its conception of rationality (or its theory of theory) in favor of an alternative conception when these inadequacies surface.

Habermas's stronger evolutionary model implies that once the later theory emerges, a logical justification independent of the accidents of the historical emergence of the theory also becomes possible. Habermas admits that the evolution of nature is a matter of mutation and chance, and he explicitly ascribes the idea of developmental evolution only to the human level. His model for the evolution of society is reminiscent of the organic individual, with its growth from youth to maturity, such that it seems natural to say that the learning process leads to progress and advance that we cannot imagine wanting to reverse, or to order in any different way.

The Nietzscheans go beyond both Habermas and MacIntyre in rejecting a Hegelian or Whiggish story altogether. They could maintain that Habermas's distinction between the evolution of nature and of humanity preserves the quintessentially metaphysical distinction between nature and spirit. For the Nietzscheans, if the evolution of nature (instead of the organism) is the model, and if evolutionary changes are the result of sudden genetic mutations or environmental accidents, then the "ranking" of species has a different effect than the modern rationalist expects. While some species may be "cleverer," it is difficult to say in what sense they are "better" than other species. Conceivably, most species might have been better off if the most clever species had not emerged (especially if that species annihilates many other species and perhaps all life on the planet). Furthermore, there is no reason to think that the clever species itself had to be as it is, for it could have been much better off lacking certain abilities it has or possessing abilities it lacks. The Nietzscheans might argue that just as dogs lack the ability to do mathematics, or some species lack the desire to harm members of their own or other species, so humans may lack certain cognitive abilities, and they could have had a more kindly disposition.

I doubt that there is a fact of the matter about which of these evolutionary models is true. The question is which of them is more useful, and for what purposes. I suggest that the Nietzschean model is not nihilistic, and it has at least some advantages over the more Whiggish implications of rational reconstruction and evolutionary, developmental theory. The Nietzschean model challenges us not to be arrogant about the superiority of the present over the past, or of our own point of view in contrast to competing contemporary points of view. Instead of assuming that viewpoints other than our own must finally converge with ours, Nietzschean perspectivism holds open the difference between our viewpoint and other possible ones. Whereas the Whiggish model maintains that there are features of ourselves that we could not imagine wanting to be any different, the Nietzschean model challenges us to imagine ourselves as having different features than we normally take for granted both in ourselves and in others.

Of course, the danger of the Nietzschean model is that pushing it to the extreme would disrupt our sense of our own identity. There might appear to be no real justification for what we believe to be our best features, and no convincing standards that we could urge on others who seemed not to recognize these features. The model of rational reconstruction may be an over-reaction to this danger, however, if it implies that just as all individuals grow from youth to maturity, there are evolutionary standards that must come to be universally recognized in human development, even by people with extremely different historical circumstances and traditions. The rationalist, evolutionary model thus opens itself to the charge of being ethnocentric and Whiggish, that is, of seeing itself as the highest and best expression so far of human history, even if it does not claim to be the ideal culmination of that history.[22]

## 5.4  Genealogy's Critique of Habermas

Having set up this confrontation, I can now turn to the details of Habermas's position and construct a critique of it from the genealogical perspective. Habermas's view depends on an opposition he sees between history and theory. By theory he means evolutionary social theory, and by history he means not only the writing of historical narratives, but the writing of universal history (or of what Lyotard calls meta-narrative). He seems to think that only social theory or universal history can supply the basis for criticism of the past and present. Since he abandons the idea of universal history, only social theory and not historical writing by itself can evaluate, criticize, and supply the goals for practical action.

What I question is why genealogy or critical historiography could not be used for the purposes of what Horkheimer and Adorno called critical theory, without needing the stronger evolutionary account that Habermas envisions. So I will need to say more about Nietzsche's method of critical history or genealogy with an eye to the more recent examples supplied by Foucault's histories, particularly those of the prison and of sexuality. Genealogy does not attempt to construct a meta-narrative for all history, and it does not presuppose either an overarching teleology in history or a necessary evolutionary development of society. Yet it does manage to be critical. I would therefore like to review Habermas's arguments for the distinction between history and theory, testing them to see if he has ruled out or simply ignored the possibility of genealogy. Then I shall suggest some of the methodological advantages of genealogy over rational reconstruction.

To be fair to Habermas, the first thing to say about his shift from philosophy of history to philosophy of language, and thus from universal historical meta-narrative to evolutionary theory is that he shares with those he identifies as postmoderns their rejection of historical continuity, necessity, and teleology. Hence, much of Lyotard's attack on Habermas in *The Postmodern Condition* is off target. Habermas himself abandons the metaphysical postulates of the continuity, necessity, irreversibility, or univocity of history.[23]

I find Habermas's appeal to evolutionary theory unconvincing, however, because he strikes me as abandoning one set of empty speculations, those of universal history, for another, those of his evolutionary vision. Instead of finding progressive structures in history, he tries to find them in pre-history, in "anthropologically deep-seated general structures."[24] Since language precedes humans,[25] the structure of language conditions human interaction. Historiography can chart these *interactions*, but only theory, according to Habermas's adaptation of Piaget, can reach more deeply and describe the development of universal *competences* that underlie these interactions.[26] Habermas insists that the evolutionary theory that reconstructs competences should not be used as a universal history since the events leading to the historical emergence of the developmental stages are contingent. Also, judgements that later stages are higher and earlier ones lower should not be misconstrued as a totalizing judgement about the society as a whole. In an interview Habermas remarks, "One society may be superior to another with reference to the level of differentiation of its economic or administrative system, or with reference to technologies and legal institutions. But it does not follow that we are entitled to value this society more highly *as a whole*, as a concrete totality, as a form of life."[27]

I agree with this admission that society as a whole cannot be evaluated as better or worse, but then the supposed advantages of evolutionary theory over genealogy become less pronounced. Genealogy is often criticized for lacking the standards for showing how social advance can be made, and how change can be preferred to the status quo. Since genealogy can only be applied piecemeal to particular social formations and their history, it is thought to lack the overview necessary for constructive, positive social transformation. Yet Habermas himself admits the inability of theory to bring new forms of life into being, and he suggests that to confuse theory with a utopian reality is dangerous. Thus, in a recent essay, "The New Obscurity," he remarks in apparent agreement with Foucault that "generating forms of life exceeds the capacities of the medium of [political, legal, and administrative] power."[28] His own theory could thus be no more effective socially than genealogical historiography, for both can aspire to no more than criticism of particular (past or present) social arrangements. Readers have taken Habermas's projection of the ideal speech situation as an anticipation of a utopian future that could be the model for present social transformation. Yet in this same essay Habermas rejects that reading. He acknowledges that his expression, "the ideal speech situation," is misleading if it seems to suggest "a concrete form of life." He thus agrees that it would be a utopistic mistake "to confuse a highly developed communicative infrastructure of *possible* forms of life with a specific totality, in the singular, representing the successful life."[29] The "ideal" envisioned in the analysis of speech situations is only a formal, not a substantive ideal.

These qualifications of his view seem to me to undermine any arguments for the practical superiority of evolutionary theory over critical history. The supposed advantage of rational reconstruction over genealogy disappears when Habermas weakens his claims about what evolutionary theory can really do. Such qualifications lead me to challenge four further features of his theory of "theory": (1) his distinction between interaction and competence, (2) his appeal to the background of the lifeworld, (3) his insistence on the unforced force of the better argument, and (4) his theory of development as a learning process resulting from solving problems.

*(1)* Habermas's distinction between history and theory depends on the distinction adapted from Piaget between the *competences* that theory reconstructs, and the *interactions* that history charts. The idea of competence suggests that there is a statable rule involved in a performance, even if the performer is not able to state the rule explicitly. The theory (for instance, Noam Chomsky's linguistics) reconstructs this rule. Habermas then reasons analogously from Chomsky's method to his own program of universal pragmatics, which will be the basis for a theory of ethical reasoning as well. But as Bernard Williams argues, ethical competence bears little resemblance to linguistic competence in Chomsky's sense:

> In the ethical case, inasmuch as the problem is seen as the explanatory problem of representing people's ability to make judgements about new cases, we do not need to suppose that there is some clear discursive rule underlying that capacity. Aristotle supposed that there was no such rule and that a kind of inexplicit judgement was essentially involved, an ability that a group of people similarly brought up would share of seeing certain cases as like certain others.[30]

Aristotle emphasizes that moral judgement involves *phronesis*, or practical wisdom. Even if Kantians are right that ethical action requires some knowledge of moral principles, knowing some moral principles could not be all that is required in ethical action. Aristotle could also be right in stressing that there must be something like the skill of seeing what is called for in a practical situation. This skill might include a sense for which principles are relevant and which are not.

Williams suggests that the Wittgensteinian critique of rule-governedness can be extended beyond the case of ethical action to all human learning. If Wittgenstein is right about how understanding works, all human learning may lack such rule-governedness, and may not be explainable by "theory" in the Habermasian sense whereby conclusions are to be derived from Chomskian rules. In contrast to

Habermas, I could see a genealogist arguing plausibly that since judge-ments, especially ethical judgements, depend on social and historical factors like upbringing, a method of critical history will work more effectively than a Whiggishly evolutionary theory.[31]

(2) Habermas himself suggests that theory is itself always condi-tioned by a *background* that cannot be completely represented in the theory. He stresses this point to make clear that he is not a foundation-alist. Different lifeworlds are different because they have different backgrounds, but they all involve the presuppositions of communica-tive action. Insofar as we make claims that we believe to be valid, we have to set forth from the pragmatic presupposition of consensus. There is always a risk of dissent, but consensus is possible because the background of the lifeworld constitutes a conservative counterweight to this risk.[32]

This appeal to the background is in tension in at least one respect, however, with his stress on consensus and reason. If the background can never be fully articulated, the ideal of attaining agreement as the result of the unforced force of the best argument under ideal condi-tions appears to be impossible. Given the inexhaustibility and indeter-minacy of the background, we could never have all the evidence in front of us that we would need to know that the agreement reached could claim universal validity.

The indeterminacy of the background also undercuts Habermas's claim that evolutionary theory is superior to genealogical historiog-raphy. His claim depends on thinking that there is always only one right theory, "nur eine einzige richtige Theorie."[33] Genealogical histo-riography, in contrast to theory, is always a matter of interpretation, such that having different hermeneutical standpoints would lead interpreters to different conclusions. Against his theory of theory I would argue that if the background is indeterminate, and if theory is always underdetermined by the evidence, Habermas's expectation of all theories converging on the exclusively correct theory is illusory. Furthermore, when the kind of theory at stake is *social* theory, this assumption of convergence on one's own theory seems ethnocentric.

(3) The indeterminacy of the background also takes much of the force out of Habermas's appeal to the unforced force of the better argument. Arguments never "win" in the way Habermas implies since it is always possible to challenge the truth of premises, and to ask for further evidence and argumentation. Arguments only have force when there seems to be no further reason to investigate the background. However, this decision to stop further challenges to the premises cannot be itself the result only of an argument. Arguments depend on interpretations of what the problems even are, and interpretations do

not "win" or have "unforced force," but only greater or lesser degrees of plausibility.

*(4)* These same considerations challenge the claim of evolutionary theory to have shown that problems have been solved in such a way that the learning process can be reconstituted as leading in a single, irreversible direction. Habermas's argument for the rational advantage of theory over critical historiography is the basis for his claim that the French postmoderns fail to understand that social evolution has been the result of learning through problem-solving. However, the notion of making cognitive advance in science through problem-solving does not seem readily applicable to social developments. Take, for example, legal problem-solving.[34] Judges may be thought to be solving problems created by social change or technological developments, for instance, in cases of civil rights or the medical prolongation of life. While we may consider legal doctrine on civil rights to have evolved, this evolution does not seem irreversible, given change in the make-up of the court or increased tension in social relations. Also, the advance may be mainly on procedural problems, and whether this advance has been connected significantly with substantive equality is questionable.

Habermas's move from the earlier Frankfurt School's philosophy of history is, he says, a move from substantive doctrine to procedural issues. Procedure is a thin dimension, however, and may be only distantly connected to substance. This thinness is illustrated by Habermas's own insistence that the ideal speech situation does not apply to a single concrete form of life, but is more of a condition of possibility of form of life in general. In general, problem-solving strikes me as an unlikely criterion on which to base either the case for rationality or a conception of philosophical method. For one thing, the idea of the history of philosophy as solving standard problems is a neo-Kantian idea (see, for instance, Wilhelm Windelband's *History of Philosophy*) that has not been current for a long time. The cliché that philosophical problems do not change, but only the answers, has been superseded by a recognition that new problems do arise, and old ones either fall away or change their character markedly. A Kuhnian conception of history could add, furthermore, that even natural science does not progress by cumulative problem-solving alone. Whether Kuhn is right about natural science, his theory may have even better application to areas like the human sciences (such as Foucault studies) or to philosophy itself. While what Kuhn calls puzzle-solving does play a major role in the advancement of *normal* inquiry, there are also larger shifts when entire conceptions of the discipline change, as then do the puzzles themselves.

So the solution of particular problems cannot be the only sign of the development of inquiry. Instead, I would suggest, science (for instance, the social sciences but also social theory and philosophy itself) might progress by what could be called problem-*dis*solving, that is, by changing the meaning of terms or by shifting attention from some problems to others. I think that this process can be seen in twentieth-century philosophy itself, which has changed from its earlier positivist outlook. Indeed, Habermas's insistence on problem-solving seems to be a throwback to these earlier days. One major difference between analytic philosophy and Continental philosophy has been, at least in the United States, that analytic philosophy was said to be oriented more toward problem-solving, whereas Continental philosophy preferred to *generate* paradoxical problems. Both had the right to think that each was doing what philosophy really ought to be doing, I believe, because philosophy has always manifested both the drive to solve its perennial problems, and to raise new problems about the shallowness introduced by the supposed solutions. The poststructuralists in general, and Foucault in particular, seem uninterested in "solving problems." Instead, they are more interested in *raising new problems*, ones of which we were previously aware only subliminally, and for which we lack not only the appropriate analytic tools but also any obvious solutions. Now, however, Habermas is urging what older, more positivistic philosophers were saying all along, namely, that Continental philosophy must return to the paradigm of problem-solving. He thinks that philosophy has been beyond metaphysics for long enough, that we no longer need to fear the attempt to solve problems through the construction of systematic accounts. Philosophy can now be systematic without being metaphysical. The solutions, though, will be more procedural than substantive, and they risk appearing formal and empty.

But a Foucaultian approach to the history of the human sciences would seem effectively to show that Habermas's paradigm of problem-solving is too narrow. Genealogy asks the prior question of how the problems that are supposedly to be solved come to be perceived as problems in the first place. Foucault's genealogical method is applied by writing the "history of problematizations."[35] Genealogy thus does not reconstruct the solutions to problems, but reconstructs instead how the problems were possible in the first place. More than one response is always possible to any difficulty, so the question is how the difficulty came to be perceived and why certain solutions instead of others obtained. "One is not dealing with a formal system that has reference only to itself," says Foucault.[36] So "the work of a history of thought would be to rediscover at the root of these diverse [possible] solutions the general form of problematization that has made them possible – even in their very opposition; or what has made possible the transformations of the difficulties and obstacles of a practice into a general problem for which one proposes diverse practical solutions."[37] Instead of approaching the history of problems with a theory that assumes the developmental superiority of the present, genealogy reconstructs the "development of the given into a question" to show from the history how the problems could even have come to be perceived as such.[38] Genealogy is a form of developmental theory and proceeds reconstructively, but unlike Habermas's projected model, genealogy is reconstruction without the assumption of the necessity of progress.

## 5.5  The Critical Potential of History and of Theory

Whereas rational reconstruction posits in a curiously unreflective, uncritical way the triumph of reason in the present, genealogy is self-critical, no more than temporary, and thus, I believe, the genuine inheritor of Hegelian phenomenology and the Frankfurt School tradition of critical theory. Genealogical history appears to me to be a better tool than rational reconstruction of evolutionary development for investigating the background of the historical life world. The purpose of genealogy is to make us aware of the dangers of the subliminal processes of socialization that we have learned, but may want to "unlearn" as a result of the genealogical analysis. Unlike Habermasian evolutionary theory, which tells us that we cannot want to unlearn what we have learned through problem-solving, genealogy makes us aware of problems that we did not know we had. Once we discover these problems, we may well become motivated to unlearn patterns of thought and action that have become second nature.

While genealogy is of course theoretically interesting, its real work requires the medium of historiography. Foucault's difficulties in working out the theory involved in his critical histories sometimes led him to deny that he was proposing any theories at all. This move might seem to suggest that genealogy presupposes the same opposition between history and theory that Habermas does when he says that history is not capable of theory. But I propose that a better line is to argue that genealogy shows in effect that theory and history are connected, even if in a different manner than theory itself projects. Thus, genealogy often uses history to show that particular theories are self-deceptive.

Does genealogy only ever apply a previously formulated theory, or could it lead to positing a theory for the first time? If Foucault were any indication, genealogy could lead to discovery of unsuspected processes, such as the disciplinary practices that lead Foucault to start theorizing power in a new way. Of course, theory is always under-determined by the historical evidence, but it can remain tied empiric-ally to the historical evidence. Genealogy, which involves sifting the historical data, seems more closely linked to empirical evidence than evolutionary theory.

I should allow for Habermas, however, to be heard for his own defense of theory. Habermas does suggest that although evolutionary theory should not be confused with universal history, it may have some implications for historiography. But, I note, these implications leave historiography with a derivative status. For instance, Habermas draws a distinction between historiographical *research*, which can be used by evolutionary theory in its reconstructions, and historiograph-ical *writing*, which is only the result of applying a theory. But I find this distinction between researching and writing history to be artifi-cial and unsupported by any account of how to make the distinction. Research, as I understand it, involves not simply combing through the documents, but ordering them in a significant way, or ordering them in a different way than they order themselves. Research is already interpretation, and always already a writing of history.

Habermas speculates further that the evolutionary theory could per-haps be used in the writing of history as a meta-theory for evaluating competing histories of the same phenomena.[39] He denies that his-torians can project themselves into the future and then write history from that fictional perspective, since he believes that history is only ever affirmative, and can only account for what has happened, not for what could have happened.[40] Foucault's genealogical "history of the present" would thus be ruled out. Habermas does think, however, that the evolutionary theory lends itself to critical diagnosis of the present, and can be employed in arguments about the practical im-plications for the present of different strategies of social and political action.

He thus thinks that only theory and not history has critical potential. Where he finds historiography having a practical effect is only by its presupposing and applying a theory, not by generating a theory. Habermas thus thinks the historian works from a presupposed con-sensus.[41] Even the critical historian like Walter Benjamin, who brushes history against the grain to write a history of the victims, is simply presupposing the consensus of a different group, the victims instead of the victors. But for Habermas history only ever applies the theory on which there is already consensus as the result of rational argument. Historiography does not lay out theory.

Evolutionary theory is said not to have a similar problem. There is no naturalistic fallacy involved, for instance, in saying that the direction of evolution is something good. The choice of Habermas's version of historical materialism is not arbitrary. As a theoretician Habermas cannot believe that the presuppositions that make theory possible can be shown to be invalid theoretically, and this leads him to argue that the denial of "reason," in the enlightenment sense, is impossible:

> For a living being that maintains itself in the structures of ordinary language communication, the validity basis of speech has the binding force of universal and unavoidable – in this sense transcendental – presuppositions. The *theoretician* does not have the same possibility of choice in relation to the validity claims immanent in speech as he [or she] does in relation to the basic biological value of health. Otherwise he [or she] would have to deny the very presuppositions without which the theory of evolution would be meaningless. If we are not free then to reject or to accept the validity claims bound up with the cognitive potential of the human species, it is senseless to want to "decide" for or against reason, for or against the expansion of the potential of reasoned action.[42]

Defending consensus and reason leads Habermas to see the post-structuralist French thinkers as defenders of unreason. As Foucault remarked, however, this may be a false reading, since Foucault agrees that one cannot be *against* reason.[43] More like Horkheimer and Adorno in the 1940s, Foucault is simply hesitant to be unabashedly *for* reason. What an affirmation of reason would amount to is far from clear, and his histories are intended to show historically that affirming reason has not helped to prevent barbarous consequences.

If one cannot be against reason, can one be against consensus? Lyotard has tried to defend dissensus over consensus in *The Postmodern Condition*, but thereby puts himself in the weak position of seeming to ask paradoxically for consensus on his claim that dissensus is indeed the higher good. Critical history may aim at producing dissent, but not necessarily as an end in itself. Producing dissent would instead have the effect of disrupting an overly complacent sense of the superiority of the present and of the dominant traditions. Genealogy works to show that supposedly necessary and unquestionable assumptions about what is good and just have a historical origin in contingent circumstances, and do not have the transcendental status (as universal and unavoidable) usually attributed to them. Aimed less at showing us that our principles are false than that our practices are not in conformity with our principles, genealogy may not be a theory in Habermas's sense. By showing cases, as in Foucault's study of the prison, where theory in that supposedly stronger sense has little connection with practice, genealogy shows that consensus on theoretical principles is often obtained only because the theory has become too thin to have effective content.

Genealogy may indeed be more historiographical than theoretical in Habermas's sense, but the genealogist can resist Habermas's preference for developmental theory over critical, narrative history. The genealogist can challenge Habermas's assumption that theory when thinned out enough to assert universal and unavoidable claims has the normative force Habermas implies. Even if Foucault's own theoretical self-interpretation is defective, one could still conclude that genealogical history, and not evolutionary theory modeled on Piaget and Kohlberg, is the more feasible path for a naturalized philosophy that envisions effective social criticism.

## NOTES

1 See Martin Jay, *Adorno* (Cambridge, MA: Harvard University Press, 1984), pp. 21–2.
2 For a detailed discussion of Foucault on power in contrast to the Frankfurt School conception, see my essay "Power, Repression, Progress: Foucault, Lukes, and the Frankfurt School," in my anthology, *Foucault: A Critical Reader* (Oxford and Cambridge, MA: Blackwell, 1986).
3 See "Interview with Gérard Raulet," *Telos* 55 (Spring, 1983): 200. Similar remarks can be found in the 1978 interview on "Adorno, Horkheimer, and Marcuse" with the Italian journalist, Duccio Trombadori, in Michel Foucault, *Remarks on Marx: Conversations with Duccio Trombadori*, trans. R. James Goldstein and James Cascaito (New York: Semiotext(e), 1991), pp. 115–29.
4 Immanuel Kant, *Critique of Pure Reason*, trans. Norman Kemp Smith (New York: St. Martin's Press, 1963), pp. 666–9 (A852/B880-A856/B884).
5 Michel Foucault, "What Is Enlightenment?," in Paul Rabinow (ed.), *The Foucault Reader* (New York: Pantheon, 1984), p. 34.
6 Jürgen Habermas, *The Theory of Communicative Action, volume 2, Lifeworld and System: A Critique of Functionalist Reason*, trans. Thomas McCarthy (Boston: Beacon Press, 1987), p. 383. For the sake of argument I will not challenge the thesis that philosophy should avoid metaphysics, where "metaphysics" means broadly a systematic set of foundationalist and nonempirical postulates about ultimate reality. Dieter Henrich has challenged that thesis in his essay, "Was ist Metaphysik – was Moderne? Zwölf Thesen Gegen Jürgen Habermas," and my essay here differs from his in arguing more positively for naturalistic philosophy. See Dieter Henrich, *Konzepte: Essays zur Philosophie in der Zeit* (Frankfurt:

Suhrkamp, 1987), pp. 11–43. Of course, metaphysics is still an active branch of philosophy in Anglo-American universities, but it is a radically different enterprise from the kind of metaphysics that Europeans from Heidegger (or even from Nietzsche, and perhaps even from Kant and Hegel) to Habermas believe to be no longer viable.

7  An earlier version of the remainder of this chapter forms part of a lecture given at the 1987 congress of the Internationalen Hegel-Vereinigung in Stuttgart, Germany; see the Proceedings (volume 17): *Metaphysik nach Kant?*, ed. Dieter Henrich and Rolf-Peter Horstmann (Stuttgart: Klett-Cotta, 1988), pp. 743–66.

8  Richard Rorty, *Philosophy and the Mirror of Nature* (Princeton: Princeton University Press, 1979), p. 373.

9  Charles Taylor, *Philosophy and the Human Sciences: Philosophical Papers 2* (Cambridge, UK: Cambridge University Press, 1985), pp. 190–1.

10 Bernard Williams, *Ethics and the Limits of Philosophy* (Cambridge, MA: Harvard University Press, 1985), p. 121.

11 I am influenced by Stephen Jay Gould's reflections on natural history, which debunk the progressivist assumptions of some evolutionary theorists. See, for instance, *Hen's Teeth and Horse's Toes* (1983) or *The Flamingo's Smile* (1985), published by Norton and Company (New York).

12 Jürgen Habermas, "Geschichte und Evolution," in *Zur Rekonstruktion des Historischen Materialismus* (Frankfurt: Suhrkamp, 1976), p. 204.

13 Peter Dews (ed.), *Autonomy and Solidarity: Interviews with Jürgen Habermas* (London: New Left Books, 1986), p. 167.

14 See Axel Honneth, "Communication and Reconciliation: Habermas's Critique of Adorno," *Telos* 39 (1979): 45–61; and his book, *The Critique of Power: Reflective Stages in a Critical Social Theory*, trans. Kenneth Baynes (Cambridge, MA: MIT Press, 1991).

15 In *Philosophy and the Mirror of Nature* (pp. 373–89) Richard Rorty criticizes the earlier, avowedly transcendental program of rational reconstruction set out in the "Nachwort" to the second edition of Habermas's *Erkenntnis und Interesse*. My discussion extends this line of criticism to Habermas's more recent, less transcendental writings. For Rorty's own further reflections on Habermas see his essay, "Habermas and Lyotard on Postmodernity," in *Habermas and Modernity*, ed. Richard J. Bernstein (Cambridge, MA: MIT Press, 1985), plus his review of Habermas's *Philosophical Discourse of Modernity* in the *London Review of Books* (September 3, 1987).

16 Habermas, in Peter Dews (ed.), *Autonomy and Solidarity: Interviews*, p. 168. While his claim may cause some to accuse him of psychologism or methodological individualism, I believe that he can rebut such charges through his linguistic turn. Because he also argues here that "subjects capable of speech and action cannot help but learn," the basic features of communicative action are not themselves psychological, but are unavoidable linguistic aspects of social development. These features are not relative to the intentions or purposes of particular individuals, but can be used to evaluate the extent to which their actions reflect the degree of social learning.

17  Jean-François Lyotard, *The Postmodern Condition: A Report on Knowledge*, trans. Geoff Bennington and Brian Massumi (Minneapolis: University of Minnesota Press, 1984).

18  F. Nietzsche, "On Truth and Lie in an Extra-Moral Sense," in *The Portable Nietzsche*, trans. Walter Kaufmann (New York: Viking Press, 1954), p. 42.

19  See Nietzsche, "Anti-Darwin," *The Will to Power*, trans. Walter Kaufmann (New York: Random House, 1967), section 684, p. 328; "Meine Gesamtansicht," in *Werke*, volume 3, ed. Karl Schlechta (München: Carl Hanser Verlag, 1965), p. 741.

20  One could suggest that Habermas avoids this stronger version. For instance, he insists that his approach is fallibilistic, and that it recognizes its dependence on falsifiable empirical research. Yet I continue to attribute the stronger position to him because his conception of rationality, including his theory of theory, is not itself open to empirical falsification.

21  Quoted from Alasdair MacIntyre, "The Relationship of Philosophy to History," in *After Philosophy: End or Transformation?*, eds. Kenneth Baynes, James Bohman, and Thomas McCarthy (Cambridge, MA: MIT Press, 1987); pp. 418–19.

22  Habermas would resist the charge of ethnocentrism on the grounds that the universalistic reasoning abilities emerge, he believes, in *all* cultures between 800 and 300 BC, and not simply in the West. See Habermas, "Geschichte und Evolution," in *Zur Rekonstruktion des Historischen Materialismus*, p. 241.

23  Ibid., p. 248.

24  Ibid.

25  These structures go back before humans to pre-humans who supposedly developed language and labor before they evolved beyond the hunt stage into the specifically human form of familial social structure. *"Labor and language,"* says Habermas, *"are older than man and society."* See Habermas, *Communication and the Evolution of Society*, trans. Thomas McCarthy (Boston: Beacon Press, 1979), p. 137.

26  "Such a competence has no *history*, but a *development* (which takes place in the given case 'logically,' i.e., via reconstructible stages). Every history is, in principle, open; it assumes that its theme can fall under a new light because of later events (and changed narrative perspectives). For the development of a competence whose possibilities of realization are transparent, there is on the contrary only one single correct theory – and whether an initially valid theory is replaced by a better one, depends neither on the progress of events nor on changed retrospectives. A history is, in principle, a context of interactions; in it actors create something through their activity. A competence, however, is *acquired*; structures of consciousness *emerge*, so that the degree of freedom posited with the ability to act and the alternatives of action that make a historical interest possible are not at all given. A narrative always deals with particular events; essentially individual-constants appear in it. A generic competence [*Gattungskompetenz*], however, which lays claim to universality does not even fall under the category of an event that could attract

historical attention. Thus, the emergence of such a competence is only accidentally connected with identifiable persons and groups. These comprise the substratum of learning processes that are made possible by a corresponding learning level. This means that with the transition from rational reconstructions of limited innovative events to the developmental logic of a general competence, the boundary of the narrative reference system is excluded." Jürgen Habermas, "History and Evolution," trans. David J. Parent, *Telos* 39 (1979): 18.

27   Habermas, in *Autonomy and Solidarity: Interviews*, ed. Peter Dews, p. 169.

28   Jürgen Habermas, "The New Obscurity: The Crisis of the Welfare State and the Exhaustion of Utopian Energies," *The New Conservatism: Cultural Criticism and the Historians' Debate*, trans. Shierry Weber Nicholsen (Cambridge, MA: MIT Press, 1989), p. 59.

29   Ibid., p. 69.

30   Williams, *Ethics and the Limits of Philosophy*, p. 97.

31   Habermas tries to deal with this general criticism of his "discourse ethics" for being formalistic and empty in a series of writings on the connection of *Moralität* and *Sittlichkeit*. See pages 113–18 of Habermas, *Moralbewußtsein und kommunikatives Handeln* (Frankfurt: Suhrkamp, 1983); pages 218–35 of Herbert Schnädelbach (ed.), *Rationalität* (Frankfurt: Suhrkamp, 1984); and pages 16–37 of Wolfgang Kuhlmann (ed.), *Moralität und Sittlichkeit* (Frankfurt: Suhrkamp, 1986). For a summary, see Peter Dews's "Introduction" to his collection of interviews with Habermas, *Autonomy and Solidarity*, especially pp. 18–22.

32   See Jürgen Habermas, *The Philosophical Discourse of Modernity: Twelve Lectures*, trans. Frederick Lawrence (Cambridge, MA: The MIT Press, 1987), chapter 11.

33   Habermas, "Geschichte und Evolution," *Zur Rekonstruktion des Historischen Materialismus*, p. 217.

34   Among Habermas's reactions to criticisms like these is to maintain that rules and principles do guide their application, and he thinks that constitutional law provides clear examples of such a progressive learning process. Habermas has Ronald Dworkin on his side on this point, but many other legal scholars, especially those in the Critical Legal Studies movement, are skeptical. I discuss constitutional law with particular reference to Habermas in other essays, including "Interpreting the Law: Hermeneutical and Poststructuralist Perspectives," *Southern California Law Review* 58 (January, 1985): 135–76, and "Dworkin's Constructive Optimism v. Deconstructive Legal Nihilism," *Law and Philosophy* 6 (1987): 321–56.

35   Michel Foucault, "Polemics, Politics, and Problematizations: An Interview," in Paul Rabinow, ed., *The Foucault Reader*, p. 388.

36   Ibid.

37   Ibid., p. 389.

38   Ibid.

39   Habermas, "Geschichte und Evolution," *Zur Rekonstruktion des Historischen Materialismus*, p. 250.

40  Ibid., p. 245.

41  "But as soon as the historian begins with the description, he [or she] assumes a consensus about the decisions to narrate, in the light of the chosen interpretation framework, how the history 'really' or 'in fact' happened. That he [or she] assumes this consensus is not so unnatural; for the more a historian agrees with the respectively applicable tradition, the more directly he [or she] can produce action-oriented knowledge by articulating, continuing, expanding, and making more precise a consciousness of history that is a source of identity." Habermas, "History and Evolution," p. 41.

42  Habermas, *Communication and the Evolution of Society*, p. 177.

43  See Foucault, "What Is Enlightenment?," in Paul Rabinow, ed., *The Foucault Reader*, p. 43.

# The Contingency of Universality: Critical Theory as Genealogical Hermeneutics

## 6.1 Genealogy, For and Against

Is critical theory still to be contrasted today to traditional theory, or has it been subsumed by traditional theory? I pose the question as if these are the only two alternatives, but of course there is also the possibility that critical theory has triumphed over traditional theory. In philosophy today one hears much about the abandonment of positivism, foundationalism, and any search for apodictic certainty. Such a search is a vestige of Cartesianism, for it seeks to guarantee the claims of the theory by appeal to theory-independent facts or self-evident principles. If philosophy in general has abandoned this Cartesian desire, the expected corollary of this change for social theory in particular would then be that no one should aspire any longer to a social theory that transcends its own socio-historical context and makes universal validity claims. Social theory like general philosophy should insist on its own contingency instead of projecting its universality.

So conceived, critical theory would be supported by philosophical hermeneutics, which insists on the context-boundedness of understanding and sees theories as interpretations, not as pictures. Instead of picturing an independent reality, social-theoretical interpretations are seen as contingent social actions themselves. The interpretive activity of constructing a social theory also interacts with and feeds back on the social reality that it interprets. On this methodological conception all social theory would limit itself to the contingency of critical theory, and no meta-theorist would aspire to construct the universalistic philosophical picture of the conditions of the possibility for any and every valid social theory.

However, there is an obvious counter-example to this projection of critical theory's triumph over traditional theory. Jürgen Habermas's theory of communicative action does construct an account of what makes any epistemological or ethical claim valid, and he thus can be seen as "grounding," or showing the foundations of, social theory. Of course, he does not see himself reverting to what Horkheimer called traditional theory, but instead, he sees himself as making critical theory possible, that is, as showing the social potential of critical theory by explaining how a social activity such as theorizing can itself be valid. Habermas's meta-theory is intended to bridge the gap between traditional and critical theory by showing how social explanations can be valid beyond their own social context even if they could have arisen only within the contingencies of that social context.

Habermas's meta-theory is not only a counter-example to the alleged triumph of critical theory, it strikes me as also implying that there is no longer a need to follow Horkheimer in thinking that critical theory is opposed to traditional theory. Instead, I see Habermas's meta-theory as subsuming critical theory under the aegis of traditional theory. Habermas does so by granting the claim of critical theory that there are many lifeworlds and that perceptions of social life are distorted by impersonal social systems, such as money and power. But Habermas grounds critical theory in a philosophical construction of a single phenomenon, communication, that is common to any lifeworld and to any social formation. For Habermas communicative action is the universal that is presupposed by every social contingency.

Although this philosophy of communication breaks with traditional philosophy on many points, it shares at least one aspiration of traditional philosophy, namely, the project of showing that reason can rationally justify itself, and thereby resist any doubts about the possibility of coming to agreement on claims that are universally valid. Given Habermas's belief that claims can be both socially conditioned and universally valid, he would see efforts to abandon traditional theory or to limit social theory to internal, situated critique as misconceived.

Foucault's genealogical method is such an internal critique because it interprets and criticizes contingent social formations from the inside, without positing a transcendent perspective or transcendentally necessary universal standards. One technique of this critique might appear to involve what Habermas would call a performative contradiction.[1] The genealogist tries to observe the social phenomena from the inside, much as a cultural anthropologist does. Of course, the genealogist is not from another culture, as the ethnographer supposedly is in those increasingly rare cases where the ethnographer observes cultures that have not yet undergone modernization. The genealogist may thus be trying to practice a contradiction, and to occupy a standpoint that is simultaneously inside and outside. From Habermas's standpoint, the genealogist's social critique would seem to be positing its own critical claims as valid at the same time that it tried to suspend the very idea of validity. Genealogical critique would be asking for everyone's agreement that its critical claims were justified at the same time that it was putting the idea of social agreement and consensus into doubt.

This objection to genealogy may misunderstand the practice of cultural anthropology when practiced by ethnographers on their own culture.[2] The techniques of anthropological observation are being used more and more by modern society on itself. This research shows that people are often unaware of their behavior and motivation, as they are themselves frequently surprised by this behavior when they are questioned about why they said or did certain things. The genealogist thus tries to see as strange what the culture takes to be familiar. "Insiders" reading a genealogical investigation come to see for the first time subliminal aspects of their own social behavior. Simply becoming conscious of social practices that were previously unconscious often leads to difficulty in continuing to engage in those social practices. Even if one did not reject such practices, one might still feel awkward about them, and be less skillful at engaging in them. So genealogy is not performing a contradiction by trying to estrange itself *from within*. Becoming aware of social behavior that is normally unconscious often does lead to the insiders' becoming critical of that behavior.

Furthermore, the genealogist need not believe that this process of critical self-estrangement from certain social practices is possible or valid only because of some ideal outside where everyone would agree that the social practice should be abandoned. Finding one's own previous behavior to be strange simply means that one cannot engage in it any longer in the same way, not that one thinks that no rational being should engage in it. Those who are skeptical about consensus and social agreement being able to serve as the universal arbitrators of validity often point to the pluralism of society, its many, different, contingent points of view. Genealogical pluralists may not only be skeptical about achieving consensus between these points of view, they may also think that it would be wrong to do so. They see plurality as a social good. Correlatively, any attempt to eliminate social difference or to promote a homogeneous culture would represent a social evil.

Habermasians are not impressed by the pluralist's meta-theory. They see pluralism as caught in the performative contradiction whereby the pluralist cannot be a pluralist about pluralism itself. That is, the pluralist supposedly must think that pluralism is the correct view, and universally valid insofar as society really ought to be pluralistic. This contradiction shows up in two problems with pluralism. The first is a practical problem: how pluralistic can a society be? There will be some groups with some values that could not be allowed if other groups are to be able to pursue their ends. So in the very effort to be pluralistic a society would undoubtedly have to draw limits on pluralism and to forbid certain possibilities. This practical problem points out, according to Habermasians, the need for some standards transcending any particular plurality. The presupposition, at least ideally, of a single community seems required for the particular groups to be able to pursue their particular ends. This practical problem thus points to the second, more theoretical aspect of the performative contradiction. Pluralists cannot really oppose the ideal of social consensus since there must be an implied consensus on how much dissent is allowed. "The affirmation of pluralism" leads to a paradox, according to David Ingram, a noted interpreter of Habermas, in that it "implies the idea of a community wherein *everyone agrees to disagree.*"[3]

Universal reason is reconstituted on Habermas's account by those principles to which everyone would or could agree. These principles are supposedly procedural, not substantive. Habermas can thus recognize that there will be substantive social disagreement because different groups will have different conceptions of what they believe to be good. Despite these contingent differences, universality is retained at least procedurally by the ideal of uncoerced consensus. A claim is valid or morally right if it is agreed to under conditions where no one is forced to agree, and all have enough time and information to reflect rationally and to arrive at a considered judgement. This model does not tell us *what* we will arrive at (substantively). It is not even *procedural* in the thick sense of telling us *how* to go about achieving such consensus practically. (The model only tells us that certain practical procedures, such as voting, will *not* count as a rational solution, since voting implies bargaining, and even a unanimous vote does not guarantee that everyone voted the same way for the same reasons.) I therefore would call it a *meta-procedural* point about the philosophical status that any practical agreement must have, whatever substantive claim was made and by whatever practical procedures it was achieved.

The pluralist may find that it is hard to disagree with such a meta-procedural point. The Habermasian should not take this concession as a triumph, however, since the pluralist is not necessarily agreeing with the model, but simply finding the result so thin and abstract as to be empty. Granting that the ideal of uncoerced consensus is attractive does not entail conceding that it is a *necessary* ideal. Habermas claims both necessity and universality for his notion of uncoerced consensus because he thinks that it is entailed by the pluralist's (or anyone's) effort to formulate, communicate, and vindicate a view.

Foucault exemplifies the pluralists' agnosticism about Habermas's consensus model. When asked in a late interview about this model, Foucault remarked, "The farthest I would go is to say that perhaps one must not be for consensuality, but one must be against nonconsensuality."[4] His point here, I believe, is that being *for consensuality* is a stronger position than merely being against nonconsensuality. In other words, the *for* and the *against* here do not represent a simple case of either *p* or *not-p*. Being *for consensuality* connotes for him the danger of an intolerance of difference. He probably believes that normally when one states what one believes to be true, one does not add the claim that others must agree. One simply says, "*p*." Saying "you must agree that *p* is true" suggests a stronger claim. Conceptually, analyzing truth (or the assertion *that p*) as consensus (or the assertion that *everyone must agree that p*) seems misguided. Practically, Foucault may also be wary that being explicitly *for consensuality* may mean that insofar as one needs to insist that one's own position is right, one will be unable to believe that anyone could hold an opposing position rationally.

In contrast, being *against nonconsensuality* means only that when we encounter others who seem to have radically different views from our own, we should try to find out why this difference obtains, and whether there is any mutual ground for discussion. But this negative concession does not entail granting the stronger positive claim that all discussion presupposes necessarily that understanding between the two parties will result in agreement. Pluralists believe that they can enter discussion in good faith without necessarily believing that the discussion of social problems will result in a univocal assessment of the empirical situation and consensus on the best solution. (Thus, I myself believe that Thomas McCarthy and I are engaged in this debate in good faith. I also believe that we understand each other well, and that we will learn which of our arguments need to be improved or discarded. I sincerely doubt, however, that there is an imaginary focal point on which we are converging, or that there is likely to be a final consensus at the outcome of our present and future exchanges.)

Given this disagreement between Habermas and pluralists like Foucault, or between Thomas McCarthy and myself, I shall therefore turn to what I consider the philosophical heart of Habermas's theory, his analysis of communicative action (in volume 1 of his *Theory of Communicative Action*).[5] There are other parts of his theory that, while interesting, do not seem as crucial as this part. Thus, in the previous chapter I have discussed Habermas's attempt to replace a universal philosophy of history with a model of evolutionary learning processes drawing on such social researchers as Piaget and Kohlberg. While this evolutionary model seems to follow naturally from Habermas's notion of validity and moral rightness as being founded on consensus, a defender of Habermas could conceivably jettison his attachment to this style of social research and still retain the main outline of his philosophy. Similarly, his attempts to do justice to the plurality of lifeworlds (in volume 2 of his *Theory of Communicative Action*) could be welcomed without buying his account of evolutionary learning processes in the moral and social spheres. But I cannot imagine Habermas without his philosophy of language, that is, his program of universal pragmatics and his notion of the ideal speech situation.[6]

So I will be looking closely at his argument that the contingencies built into the background of our communicative speech acts are transcended at least in principle by the necessity of *reaching agreement*. After this critical assessment of Habermas's position, I will then want to conclude with some reflections on what follows for critical theory if his notion of reaching agreement is neither a necessary presupposition nor a universal ideal. I do not want to propose a better "theory," but I will suggest that a "genealogical hermeneutics" (drawing on aspects of Michel Foucault and Hans-Georg Gadamer) will serve to explain how a critical history that reveals our own social and philosophical contingencies is a sufficiently rich and concrete aspiration for social philosophy today.

## 6.2 Habermas's Universalism

Pluralism is a word that is used in many ways, and may be overworked of late. I cannot avoid using it, however, since it features so centrally in many debates today. What I can try to do, though, is to clarify at the outset the senses in which I will be understanding pluralism, hoping thereby to capture the spirit of the contemporary conflicts while at the same time adding some clarity and perhaps a new twist. This twist comes from discussing the connection between pluralism as used in both hermeneutics and social theory. At first there seems to be no connection between the hermeneutical question whether a text is susceptible to more than one right interpretation, and the social question whether a community can consist of a plurality of groups without homogenizing the cultural differences that each group wishes to preserve. Presumably the same person could believe in the possibility of there being only one right interpretation of a given text and at the same time oppose either political homogenization or what Foucault calls disciplinary normalization. That is, the issue whether ideally there is or is not only one right understanding of a text has no obvious connection with the issue whether or not social differences presuppose a higher community with at least one universally shared principle (for instance, that everyone must agree to disagree) from which other social, moral, and political principles could be derived.

Again, however, Habermas's philosophy as I read it has the effect of suggesting that there is a connection between the hermeneutical and the social issues. Of course, there are intermediate steps, and his theory articulates much more subtle and technical analyses of the problems. Nevertheless, my point in starting by contrasting the hermeneutical and the social issues is twofold. First, I want to praise Habermas's theory for having the surprising result of being able to connect two important theoretical stances that are usually not seen as related. Second, however, I want to stress the *contingency* of the connection. If one starts with a sense that these views may be *arbitrarily* connected merely because the same word, "pluralism," is used for two different matters, and then through a reading of Habermas comes to see that the matters are more closely connected, that will be a positive result. But Habermas's theory may be so convincing that some people may start to believe that the connection is so strong as to be natural or even *necessary*. I prefer, in contrast, to stress that even if there is some connection here, it is a highly *contingent* one. I want to argue for pluralism in both a hermeneutical sense and a social or cultural sense. But I do not want to be understood as arguing that there is a necessary conceptual entailment between the pluralism defended by hermeneutics, whereby there can be more than one right interpretation of a text, and the cultural-social pluralism defended by genealogy, which resists the universalization of present standards and focuses instead on historical diversity and differences.

Habermas's philosophy forces the connection here, I shall argue, because it is still driven by an older, Kantian (or perhaps even German idealist) paradigm of *systematic* philosophy whereby a stance on theoretical reason entails a similar stance on practical reason. In contrast, a genealogical hermeneutics tries to be *consistent*, but it does not try to be *systematic*. Correlatively, hermeneutical philosophy does not entail a particular political stance, just as deconstruction does not. The reason for this separation of philosophy and politics is that philosophy no longer understands itself as being able to ground every human activity. The social theorist Ernesto Laclau is correct, I believe, in his explanation of why there is no direct connection between poststructuralist philosophy and a particular practical politics:

> there is nothing that can be called a "politics of poststructuralism." The idea that theoretical approaches constitute philosophical "systems" with an unbroken continuity that goes from metaphysics to politics is an idea of the past, [one] that corresponds to a rationalistic and ultimately idealistic conception of knowledge.[7]

Of course, this is not to say that poststructuralism is apolitical, for, as I will be arguing, genealogy is like hermeneutics in insisting that social understanding is formed through an awareness of what the most pressing political problems and needs are. The point is rather that philosophy need not be seen as grounding and legitimating only one particular approach to practical politics from among the many competitors.

There may thus be central points of agreement between Habermas and Foucault, since Habermas is certainly not an opponent of social diversity and his theory allows for a plurality of lifeworlds. If Habermas and Foucault converge on this political point, however, they are coming from markedly different philosophical directions. Habermas thinks that a philosophical theory of rationality must identify and preserve the universal structures shared by all these lifeworlds. From Foucault's viewpoint, even if such structures were identified, they would be so thin as to lack any epistemological or normative import. Insisting on them would be more likely to mask than to support diversity.

So a principal meta-theoretical issue dividing Habermas and Foucault concerns what philosophy can be today. Habermas revives the Cartesian-Kantian project of defending reason and developing a *theory of rationality*. There are, of course, important differences between his theory and the traditional, enlightenment conception. The central difference is his abandonment of the paradigm of the conscious subject, a paradigm that sees reason as the essence of individual human subjectivity (as in the Cartesian cogito or the Kantian ego). Instead, Habermas develops a philosophy of intersubjectivity, one that starts from language rather than consciousness, but from language conceived as communicative interaction, not as an abstract, formal system. The rationality that Habermas envisions is no longer the instrumental reason that limits itself only to means instead of ends. If instrumental reason was exposed as contradictory by the early Frankfurt School, that critique does not apply to the communicative reason that Habermas analyzes and projects as universal.

Reason for Habermas is said not to be the pure reason of Kant, and not a nonsituated reason now dressed up in fashionable linguistic clothing. Communication always arises in specific contexts and is tied to everyday social practices. Nevertheless, Habermas thinks that because some communicative action involves asserting particular claims as valid, these validity claims transcend the contingencies of their genesis. Discourse where rational argumentation makes and assesses validity claims is thus a special case, not the general rule, of communicative interaction. But it is also a paradigm case, for although raised in the "here and now," these valid propositions "transcend" and even "blot out" spaces and times: "The transcendent moment of *universal* validity bursts every provinciality asunder."[8] Contingency is at the origin of communication and understanding, but it is left behind for Habermas in that any genuine act of intersubjective understanding must necessarily seek to be more than internal, situated critique by claiming universal validity for itself.

Just as Habermas's project grows out of and overcomes the limitations of earlier critical theory, it also starts from but supposedly overcomes another tradition, philosophical hermeneutics. Indeed, despite Habermas's famous criticisms of hermeneutics and his early debate with Gadamer, the crucial premise of Habermas's more recent theory of communication is drawn from hermeneutics. For Habermas the primary purpose of language is not to refer to reality, but to reach understanding. Reaching understanding, furthermore, is not a subjective but an intersubjective matter, so Habermas follows Gadamer in connecting understanding with agreement.

This link is easier to see in German because of the verbal similarity between "understanding" (*Verständigung*) and "agreement" (*Einverständnis*). Habermas's analysis of reaching understanding occurs in volume 1 of his *Theory of Communicative Action* (pp. 286ff). He does not explicitly cite Gadamer at this particular point, but it should be obvious from earlier pages that he is working from Gadamer's assertion that "Verstehen heißt zunächst, sich miteinander verstehen. Verständnis is zunächst Einverständnis."[9] Habermas adds elements to Gadamer's account, however, and in context Gadamer's own point is to emphasize not the agreement *per se*, but the further fact that agreement is always on some subject matter or *Sache:* "Verständigung ist also immer: Verständigung über etwas."[10]

I will reflect later on the differences between Gadamer's emphasis on the *Sache* and Habermas's emphasis on consensus, but for now I will follow Habermas's claim that reaching understanding is also an *Einigung*, a coming together into one, a unifying. That Habermas takes this formation of oneness out of an intersubjective plurality to be so fundamental to language is what leads me to identify him as a hermeneutical *universalist*. That he also sees this action as the fundamental *social* action is what enables him to extend his hermeneutical theory of language into the ground for his social philosophy. He substitutes this philosophy of language for the philosophy of history that anchored the theory of rationality in Horkheimer's early conception of critical theory.

For Habermas a rational unity emerges from a social plurality of forms of life insofar as any form of life must contain "universal structures" that are revealed in communicative action. These universal structures are not present by chance, or by haphazard evolutionary luck, but are transcendentally necessary presuppositions, no matter how mired they are in contingent motives and compulsions. These universal structures are not only presupposed by but also ascertainable through the practice of rational argumentation in the cognitive discourse that must feature in any and every form of life. Such discourse requires, on Habermas's account, the presupposition of an ideal speech situation, one where agreement entails that the conclusions of the discourse can be taken as completely warranted, either cognitively or morally.

There are two respects in which Habermas's account of the link between his theory of language and his social philosophy may sound strange to anglophone ears. First, he seems to be claiming both that participants must believe that they have "sufficiently met" the conditions of an ideal speech situation,[11] and that because the speech situation is ideal, there never has been and never will be a real situation in which the ideal conditions are satisfied. Second, Habermas's linking of understanding and agreement may appear somewhat arbitrary to anglophone ears. The verbal similarity that Habermas hears in German is not an argument for making agreement the paradigm of understanding. I hasten to add that Habermas is not making this bald a claim, since he is talking only about the understanding that is reached in the special and rarefied case of pure cognitive (or moral) discourse. But I resist the elevation of agreement into the paradigm case of understanding, when it is only a particular and limited case of one kind of understanding. I often think that I understand what a text is saying or what another person means without agreeing with that text or that person. Understanding another person or text can occur even if the interpreter's attitude is one of hermeneutical agnosticism, where one neither affirms nor denies, but simply does not participate enough in the discourse or context to utter affirmations or denials.

Habermas might urge that insofar as I think that I am right in cases where I do think I understand correctly, I must believe that the others would agree with me in the long run. Here I could resist the presupposition of the ideal speech situation by suggesting that real discourse is never ideal, and there may be good reasons that I could attribute to the others for not agreeing with me. The pluralist can maintain that even if there are universal structures such as rational argumentation, these are thin, and do not entail that substantive agreement must be achieved. Pluralists resist Habermas's connecting of understanding and consensus, maintaining in contrast that interpreters can believe that their understanding is reasonable and right without also believing that everyone else will or even should agree with them.

Of course, Habermas is talking about *Verständigung*, which is a more specific phenomenon than *Verstehen* generally. He is trying to capture the difference between exerting an influence on others (which is not the sense that he means) and coming to an understanding *with* them. The agreement or *Einverständnis* that is reached is thus neither a *Gleichgestimmtheit* (like-mindedness) nor an *Übereinstimmung* (de facto accord). Instead, it is a *Zustimmung*, an assent that is motivated not by calculation of potential gains and losses, but a straightforward "yes" or "no" depending on whether one thinks the point is true or right.[12] Habermas wants the "yes" or "no" to be motivated *rationally* as opposed to self-interestedly, and he may feel that hermeneutical pluralism and Foucaultian genealogy fail to perceive this distinction.

In my view, however, this distinction between rational motivation and motivation by coercive power or a hidden agenda may be at most a matter of degree rather than a difference in kind. Habermas's stipulative definition gives the appearance of maintaining that a claim is valid if it is rationally motivated, and it is rationally motivated if the reasons are valid. If this stipulation is not simply circular, it at least appears to be in tension with his own insistence that he is not returning to a Kantian notion of pure reason. Thinking that there is a difference in kind between claims motivated by reason alone and those motivated by power interests returns to the tenets of traditional theory that Horkheimer was trying to deconstruct.

Furthermore, Habermas's response still does not show that when I say "yes, I understand" that I am agreeing with a person as well as understanding what that person is saying. Again, there are many cases where I may understand what others are saying, and believe that they understand what I am saying, without also agreeing with them, or expecting them to agree with me.[13] Habermas's case, where I am not only trying to understand others but to come to an agreement with them as well, is a special case of understanding. I see no reason to take it as the essence of language or the "*original mode* of language use,"[14] mainly because I do not know why any particular type of language use should be singled out as the essential or even the paradigmatic case.

So what is even more problematic than the Habermasian identification of understanding and agreement is that there is no real argument for the axiom that reaching understanding and agreement is so essential to all language. "Reaching understanding," Habermas asserts boldly, "is the inherent telos of human speech."[15] Perhaps he thinks that the argument is already given in Gadamer's *Truth and Method* or in Heidegger's *Being and Time*, which are the sources he gives for the notion of *Verständigung*.[16] I shall try to show later, however, that Habermas reads universalistic premises into Gadamer, and that Gadamer is better read as a hermeneutical pluralist. For now I will point out that Gadamer has nothing akin to Habermas's quasi-foundationalist project of showing that not only is "reaching understanding" fundamental to all speech, but that other forms of social action such as conflict, competition, and "strategic action in general" are *derived* from it.[17] Habermas's strategy here is to make clear that since strategic action covers the means-ends reasoning involved in what the early Frankfurt School called instrumental reason, his own notion of communicative reason need not be construed as simply a variant of strategic action. So when we communicate to reach understanding we are not bargaining or compromising, but trying to ascertain what is right and true. Furthermore, not only is strategic use of language different from genuine communication, the former is derived from the latter. In other words, reason trumps power. Reason as achieved through communication is not merely the "winning side" in a power struggle. We could not even make sense of the idea of a power struggle unless there were something beyond the power struggle, something more than sheer power, something that we would have to think of as reason, agreement, or mutual understanding: "A communicatively achieved agreement," asserts Habermas, "has a rational basis; it cannot be imposed by either party. . . . Agreement rests on common *convictions*."[18]

According to Habermas, then, for disagreeing parties even to begin to debate, they must share many, perhaps even most, of the same beliefs. In the philosophy of language this semantic principle that most of our beliefs must be shared for us even to be talking to one another, or to think that our translation of another language is successful, is called the principle of charity. This semantic principle of translation is often extended into a methodological principle of interpretation.

Such an extension appears to be made by Habermas, for whom the background of shared belief is the "conservative counterweight" that prevents the "risk of dissent" from ever totally destroying the web of beliefs that forms the fabric of a lifeworld, the common cloth of the background social practices that make society possible.[19] With this principle any talk of plurality will presuppose that difference is really minimal, and that for the most part there must be tacit consensus. The appearance of plurality will result from a few striking differences, but these differences are assumed to be observable only insofar as they stand out from the shared ground of a common humanity, or in Habermas's terms, a universal communicative rationality.

Here again the hermeneutical pluralist will find the sentiments hard to disagree with, but not because the case is convincing. The pluralist may think that a few striking differences about the other should not lead us to assume that the other is in most respects like ourselves and shares the essential assumptions of *our* lifeworld. The pluralist may adopt the alternative interpretive hypothesis that even things that remind us of ourselves may turn out to be different in central respects when manifested by the other. We may even turn out to be our own "other," for instance, when we find in our own society marginalized groups that experience our social practices differently than the mainstream does. For the hermeneutical pluralist, interpretation can bracket the principle of charity, at least as a substantive thesis.[20] In concrete textual, social, and cross-cultural interpretation the semantic principle of charity can be unduly extended into a substantive axiom of familiarity. Gadamer cites Friedrich Schlegel's ironic "axiom of familiarity" in typical historiography, which assumes that "things must always have been just as they are for us, for things are naturally like this."[21] Hermeneutics does not assume this axiom itself (and deconstructionists are wrong to criticize it for doing so). Instead, hermeneutics can urge that suspending the axiom of familiarity is a useful heuristic strategy that prevents the interpreter from too easily suppressing difference in favor of the familiar.

Defending the pluralist strategy need not involve the spelling out of an alternative theory to Habermas's, but simply showing that there are grounds for skepticism about Habermas's theory of the telos of language. In particular, pluralists need not object to the basic idea that validity claims have a universal structure. But they could resist Habermas's particular arguments for construing validity claims as he does. Pluralists may regard validity as universal, but only in a formal or thin sense that will not get the much stronger results that Habermas claims. From the pluralist viewpoint Habermas is overextending the formal or logical notion of validity. Normally validity is simply a matter of whether the logical form of an argument is fallacious or not. An argument can thus be valid, but unsound. Habermas does not distinguish validity and soundness, and since he considers the truth of a claim to be part of what he means by its validity, he is already starting from a strong, substantive sense of validity.

But by validity he does not mean only truth. He also wants to say that a claim is valid not only if it is true, but also if it is uttered *truthfully* (that is, sincerely), and if it is normatively *right* (that is, if it satisfies the normative or moral expectations of utterance). The pluralist could object that running these separate matters together is a confusion in two respects. First, there are other kinds of utterances than constative assertions of the form *that p*, and it is hard to see what factual truth has to do with performatives such as commands, promises, and greetings, which are not making explicit truth claims. Second, it is hard to see why sincerity and moral-normative rightness are relevant to the soundness of constative, cognitive assertions.

Habermas's arguments against these objections do not seem convincing in themselves. I will review his rebuttals briefly, since what interests me more is *why* he is so committed to making validity a matter of these three factors in *every* speech act *all at once*. To respond to the first example Habermas claims that even in simply saying "hello" certain existential presuppositions are made (for instance, that there is someone there who can be greeted).[22] So Habermas believes that saying "hello" can be said to be *valid*. In contrast, I think that he thereby strains the normal philosophical usage of the word "valid," and that his argument for doing so is unclear. To say that "hello" also "contains a propositional component" of the form *that p* seems to be using the word "contain" in only a metaphorical way. By "contain" he may mean "presuppose," but even if one were to grant some intelligibility to this extension, it still remains ambiguous as to whether what is presupposed is (a) some particular state of affairs, *p*, or (b) that in general there are states of affairs, *p, q, r, etc.*, that obtain in a non-enumerable way.

Habermas sometimes argues as if (a) were what he meant. But then he is not convincing, since one does not seem to be asserting any particular proposition, *p*, when one says "hello." One can even say hello to a non-person (for instance, one's favorite house plant, or a computer that calls one on the telephone) in a way that could thus not be "intersubjectively redeemed," but that nevertheless seems "valid." However, Habermas might only mean (b), and he does cite John Searle's view that the truth conditions of simple assertions and commands cannot be determined independently of a background context. But as Habermas recognizes, this background includes "*implicit* knowledge that cannot be represented in a finite number of propositions; it is a *holistically structured* knowledge . . . that *does not stand at our disposition*, inasmuch as we cannot make it conscious and place it in doubt as we please."[23] But if (b) is what is presupposed, then Habermas's analysis of validity is uninformative, since every utterance, even a false one, presupposes that there are *some* states of affairs that obtain, where "some" does not specify any particular states of affairs but leaves undetermined what states of affairs there really are. To redeem a truth claim we would supposedly require more determinacy than this, since we should also be committed to some particular proposition, *p*, claiming that some particular state of affairs obtained.

Given Habermas's appeal to the background, it also seems unclear exactly what he is claiming about the second problem that I mentioned. He believes that even assertions of the form *that p* are valid only if in addition to their truth they are also said "rightly." That is, there are normative constraints on when and in what contexts they can be uttered, for otherwise they are said to be "inappropriate" or "out of place."[24] However, even if an assertion is uttered under awkward circumstances, it can still be true. Similarly, I might try to say something insincerely, or even to lie, but what I say might turn out to be true, even if I were lying. So the use to which the assertion is put might be an interesting matter, but it seems to be a sufficiently different matter not to be confused with truth-value by lumping truth-value, sincerity, and normative rightness together under the single concept of "validity."

If analytical clarity is not what is gained by Habermas's notion of "validity claim," why pay the price of insisting on it? Why does he make it the keystone of his system? Here I think that the answer is his drive toward systematic philosophy, and perhaps even toward the strong systematization reminiscent of philosophical *Aufbau*. In any case, he certainly makes his analysis of validity the foundation for the bridge he builds between the hermeneutical and the social spheres. I have been suggesting that Habermas is running together three separate matters, the cognitive, the moral, and the aesthetic. Kant maintained, however, that these three areas should not be confused, and philosophers have continued to agree with him and with Hume that "is" and "ought" are not connected. Other philosophers find it a difficulty in Kant that these three spheres are spheres of one thing, and that he leaves unexplained how they could be parts of one transcendental subject.

Habermas is offering a new solution to this problem. He agrees with Kant that these three spheres should be kept separate, or "differentiated" as he says. An objection to Derrida is precisely that when Derrida denies the distinction between philosophy and literature, Derrida is "dedifferentiating" these spheres and therefore trashing a major accomplishment of modern rationality. But Habermas also agrees with Kant's critics that the unity of these spheres needs an explanation. Habermas thinks that Kant's mistake was to try to ground these separate spheres in an individualized transcendental conscious-ness. Hegel correctly criticized Kant's account of transcendental con-sciousness, but made the mistake of finding the ground in an absolute subjectivity instead of giving up the idea of subjectivity altogether. As I read Habermas, he is now showing that the ground from which this rational differentiation arises is the universal form of validity claims. Insofar as any and every validity claim involves a formal schema of each of these three areas, Habermas himself has "dedifferentiated" the cognitive, the moral, and the aesthetic. Although philosophy must now keep these areas separate, philosophy does not have to worry that "reason" is trifurcated, with the unity of the three separate branches remaining philosophically incomprehensible. Whereas Kant thought a satisfactory solution was to comprehend the incomprehensibility of the connection between reason and reality,[25] Habermas finds the unity in communicative reason, and in particular, in the co-presence of the true, the right, and the truthful in any and every validity claim.

Habermas bridges the hermeneutical and the social with this ac-count of validity claims, since he is describing not only logic or semantics, but also communication. On his model validity claims have to do with relations between persons, not just with relations between sentences and the world. The universalism at the level of the linguistic or hermeneutical analysis of validity is extended to the social level since Habermas believes that the "social-life context re-produces itself" at least in part through "the common will anchored in the communicative practice of all individuals."[26]

Valid communication is thus for him more than a matter of logic or of truth-conditions, and includes all social interaction in which dis-course is involved. One might think that this domain is too large to be represented adequately in a form of theory modeled on Chomskian linguistics, formal semantics, or even speech act theory. Habermas claims to transcend all these, even though he aspires to a theory that is comparable to these in precision and rigor. He believes that his analysis of validity claims requires more than monological verifica-tion, and is social and intersubjective. That is, a person could pre-sumably not satisfy himself or herself alone that the three conditions of validity had been satisfied, but would have to have others agree to this as well.

I find this claim problematic, however, mainly because Habermas relies on the distinction between the real and the ideal. I would think that someone could decide that she had satisfied all three conditions for a particular cognitive claim, and therefore be certain that her claim was valid. A real consensus would not gain her anything more than she already had, since each person so consenting would presumably go through the process of satisfying the conditions independently. So a real consensus is not a further condition. If others dissented, that would still not show our hypothetical inquirer that she was wrong, since she could continue to believe that under conditions of ideal consensus (which, Habermas grants, are *never* achieved) her claim was valid. If Habermas's theory of discursive practice is this abstract, and if it could be satisfied by an interior or subjective monologue equally as well as by intersubjective dialogue,[27] it no longer is sufficiently concrete to serve the needs of a renewal of critical theory today.

## 6.3 Gadamer's Hermeneutical Pluralism

In the preceding account of Habermas I noted that Habermas acknowledges Gadamer's *Truth and Method* as the source for Habermas's thesis that the telos of human language is reaching understanding and agreement. In this section I want to look more closely at Gadamer to see whether his account really does serve Habermas's universalistic theory of rationality. I will grant that Habermas's reading is a possible one, but I will argue here for another reading of Gadamer, one that sees him as a hermeneutical pluralist. Then in the concluding section I shall explore the connections of this hermeneutical pluralism with the social pluralism that I have been implicitly arguing for in the previous chapter on Foucault.

Habermas's appropriation of Gadamer's theory rests on the claim that reaching understanding or *Verständigung* means reaching agreement or *Einverständnis*. Habermas develops this Gadamerian claim into a consensus theory of truth, according to which truth is not a function of reference to reality, but of the outcome of a discourse situation. In recent writings Habermas tends to present Gadamer as agreeing to a general version of consensus theory. For instance, in Habermas's polemical critique of deconstruction, Habermas allies himself with Gadamer against deconstruction by affirming that "[a]s Gadamer has shown, the hermeneutic effort that would bridge over temporal and cultural distances remains oriented toward the idea of a possible consensus being brought about in the present."[28]

This reading of Gadamer is misleading in two major respects. First, it portrays hermeneutics as polemically opposed to deconstruction. Of course, insofar as Derrida and other deconstructionists have pitted themselves against hermeneutics, Habermas may appear vindicated on this second point. However, the connections between deconstruction and hermeneutics run deeper than superficial polemics often suggest, and a hermeneutical pluralism may offer a sympathetic account of the interpretive strategies of deconstruction. However, my main concern here is less with the relation of hermeneutics and deconstruction, which I have written about in other places,[29] than with the second feature that I find misleading in Habermas's appropriation of Gadamer, namely, its omission of Gadamer's opposition to Habermas's consensus theory of truth, and more generally of Gadamer's pluralistic stress on finitude, historicity, and multiple interpretations.

Although Gadamer's model of understanding as a dialogue does make consensus a goal, that model also offers an account of consensus that is different from Habermas's own model. The Habermasian model tends to ignore what Gadamer calls the *Sache*. Gadamer's idea of the *Sache* is tied to a long tradition of philosophers claiming to return to the *Sache selbst*. The word *Sache* is difficult to translate because in English we might use words like "subject matter," "topic," "substance," "thing," "object," or "phenomenon" to capture Gadamer's idea that the *Sache* is what a dialogue is *about*. This stress on *aboutness* makes Gadamer sound more like a realist than Habermas, whose insistence on truth as reaching agreement is explicitly opposed to philosophical semantics and its analysis of truth as reference to reality. Whereas a consensus theory of truth suggests that agreeing to something makes it true, Gadamer's sense is more that we agree to something because it is true. So truth is not the result of agreement, but agreement the result of truth.

Of course, the problem is more complex than this, but I phrase Gadamer's position in this way to underline that his position is not a subjectivistic one, and that intersubjective agreement, although important, is not the foundation of his theory. Although he believes that interpretations are always bound to a particular context, he does not think that we can interpret things any way we want. Interpretations are always guided by the *Sache*, and thus by a sense that there are right and wrong ways to say things that ought to be said. Getting others to agree with one's interpretation is a related but distinct matter. For Gadamer the obligation to get others to agree follows from the need to exist cooperatively with others, and is thus better explained not by the theoretical model of an ideal, universal discourse community, but by the social requirement of showing others that agreeing and cooperating is in their particular interests.[30]

A consensus theorist might object that separating the *Sache* from consensus by giving the *Sache* logical priority over consensus overlooks the interpreters' expectation that others will agree to their interpretation, even when the interpreters themselves are disagreeing with previous interpreters. So the consensus theorist maintains that the interpreter who believes that the interpretation is right necessarily believes that it would be accepted by an ideal community of interpreters.

However, Gadamer's theory is more historical than this idealization, maintaining instead that interpretation is always open-ended, that no interpretation is ever final (even ideally), and that new interpretations will always be needed. On his account, understanding is always *application*. This claim means that understanding grows out of a particular context, and as the context changes (perhaps even as a result of the new self-understanding brought about by the new interpretation), the need for re-interpretation arises.

So for Gadamer even though the *Sache* guides the interpretation, the *Sache* is not eternal, but is itself evolving with the history of interpretation. There is no need to ask the metaphysical question whether the *Sache* remains the same or changes, since the *Sache* is not some external reality that exists independently of the process of interpretation.[31] Interpreting is not picturing, and we should not think that insofar as we believe that we understand the *Sache* better, we need to believe that we are working toward a grasp of it as it really is *an sich*, or in-itself. The ideal of a complete or final representation of all the features of any particular *Sache* is an illusion, if only because the idea of completely representing all the features of anything does not really make sense.

Since interpretation is tied to a history of interpretations, what is being interpreted is itself already an interpretation. Interpreting is thus re-interpreting, or coming up with new ways to think about both the object of interpretation and ourselves, since changes in our interpretations are tied to changes in our self-interpretations. By describing ourselves differently, we do not need to think that we are getting a better picture of ourselves as we truly are, independently of any interpretation. Instead, we are coming up with new ways not only of thinking about ourselves, but of being who we are. As we change, so will our interpretations, and these interpretations will continually need to be reinterpreted.

This more pluralistic reading of Gadamer thus contrasts to the Habermasian reading. Which is right? There are four central Gadamerian concepts that may be principally responsible for Habermas's reading, so I will now investigate the details of Gadamer's position more closely to adjudicate this conflict of interpretation. These four concepts are: (i) the *fusion* or *melting* of *horizons*; (ii) the inevitability of *prejudice*; (iii) Gadamer's problematic claim that interpretation always appeals to *authority*, and that the Enlightenment ideal of complete transparency is an illusion; and (iv) the emphasis on *Vollkommenheit*, or the completeness of interpretation. I shall offer a reading of these points that suggests that they really support pluralism instead of universalism, and that they yield a conception of interpretation that does not depend on the model of communication constructed by Habermas.

## (i) The fusion of horizons

In explicating these notions, I must stress that some confusion may result if they are understood as part of a model of perception instead of an account of *linguistic* understanding. Unlike physical objects that could be said to persist independently of any perception of them, texts come to be only in acts of reading (with writing also always involving reading). Gadamer's most general statement of this point is his claim that "*Sein, das verstanden werden kann, ist Sprache.*"[32] At various times he has glossed this sentence slightly differently, and these different paraphrases may suggest the contrast between the universalistic and pluralistic readings of his theory. Thus, in an essay published in 1967 he suggests that his claim that "being that can be understood is language" means that "we should try to understand everything that can be understood."[33] In an essay published in 1984, however, the sentence is paraphrased as implying that "that which is can never be completely understood."[34] Taken out of context, the first paraphrase might suggest that interpretation must aim at mirroring an independent reality in a complete, correct representation. But the stress should fall on the "can," and in context Gadamer's point is that language is not to be thought of as a "mirror." The second paraphrase suggests more aptly that the task of interpretation is always open-ended. An interpretation can only illuminate at the cost of shading over or leaving out other considerations. This claim, which Gadamer develops from Heidegger's account of truth, does not imply, however, that all interpretations misrepresent what they are about. They capture aspects of the *Sache* correctly, but the *Sache* is more complex than any single interpretation can possibly be. The *Sache* inheres in a background context that cannot be made fully explicit.

Both Heidegger and Gadamer work with a model in which language as such is not different from and in a representational relation to an independent reality, but where it would not make sense to speak of language and reality or Being as separate realms. In other words, the terms "reality" and "being" would not refer except within a language, and Gadamer is best understood as an "internal realist."[35] That understanding is a linguistic phenomenon can be lost from sight if one gets misled by the quasi-perceptual metaphor of the fusion of horizons. Gadamer uses the phenomenological notion of a horizon and then asks the apparently epistemological question how it is possible for us to represent within our own horizon the horizon of another time or culture that we find speaking to us from a text. He then characterizes his solution as a *Horizontverschmelzung*, a fusion or melting of horizons. The question Gadamer poses is a classic one in traditional hermeneutics: if the understanding is *ours*, how do we discover differences between the text (or the tribe, or the culture) and ourselves?

His immediate answer consists of two phenomenological observations. The first is that meanings cannot be understood arbitrarily.[36] Thus, we cannot avoid hearing sentences as making sense in particular ways, and we cannot simply will to hear them differently than we do. The second observation is that we often do find that the text either does not make sense or seems to be saying something that strikes us as false. Gadamer cites the experience of the text's giving us a shock or even an offense (*Anstoß*).[37]

Taken together, these observations suggest more generally that some of what we read, hear, and encounter will seem familiar, and some particular things will strike us as being strange and unlike what we expected. The point is not then to translate the strangeness into something with which we are already familiar. Instead, the *Anstoß* may force us to question whether what seemed familiar might instead be hiding further strangeness. So although understanding is always "our" understanding, we can recognize differences between "other" understandings and "our" understanding.

But we should not fall into the historicist illusion that we can entirely recreate that past understanding and contrast it totally to our own. Though Gadamer uses the notion of horizons, he does not want us to think of the past and present as separate horizons that are closed off from each other. When we understand the past, with its many differences, we are expanding our horizon, not stepping out of our horizon into the other horizon. Unfortunately, the idea of a *fusion* or *melting* of horizons (*Horizontverschmelzung*) has misled some readers to project the image of two countable horizons flowing into one another. If the past horizon were totally reconstructible, then there would be a historical *Gegenstand an sich*, an object-in-itself, that the historical sciences could aim to recover. But this picture is precisely the one that Gadamer intends to destroy with his insistence on the circularity of understanding and the multifariousness of possible historical voices instead of a single privileged one.

The notion of the multifariousness (*Vielfachheit*) of possible historical voices is a point that Gadamer raises to describe the difference between the natural and the human sciences. But I bring it up now more to show that Gadamer does recognize diversity and plurality, and that he does not posit these as transcended through an ideal consensus, as the Habermasian theory of communicative action suggests. Of course, some of Gadamer's deconstructionist critics read him as saying that our understanding is always conditioned by our tradition, and they accuse him of thinking that the tradition is always a single thing, or a unified whole. In contrast, they insist that a tradition or a culture is often divided against itself, or even many-sided and diverse to such an extent that it becomes impossible to know that there is *a* tradition or culture behind our understanding.

These critics would thus find the notion of a "fusion" of horizons to be insidiously hegemonic if it insisted on the unity or singleness of tradition. But I think that hermeneutics can recognize that complexity and tensions are always to be found in a tradition or culture. Gadamer's point that the difference between the natural and the human sciences is the *multifariousness* of possible historical voices suggests to me that he would not accept a belief in the unidirectional, developmental, or hegemonic character of *history*. The mistake that Gadamer's critics make may be to turn the horizon into an object. Gadamer wants to distinguish between human and natural science because if history is the object (*Sache*) of the human science, it is not the sort of object (*Gegenstand*) that scientific research can posit as its telos. There is no object-in-itself (*Gegenstand an sich*) for historical research, presumably unlike the physical sciences' research into nature. Thus, a difference between the natural and the human sciences is that "whereas the object [*Gegenstand*] of the natural sciences can be described *idealiter* as what would be known in the perfect, complete [*vollendeten*] knowledge of nature, it is senseless to speak of a perfect or complete knowledge of history [*einer vollendeten Geschichtserkenntnis*], and for this reason it is not possible to speak of an object-in-itself [*Gegenstand an sich*] toward which its research is directed."[38]

This notion of the circularity of understanding underscores the contextuality and contingency of understanding. Gadamer says that he often prefers to read the great old historians (for example, Theodor Mommsen and Johann Gustav Droysen) instead of the latest accounts.

His reason is that since there is no historical thing-in-itself, and no ideal knowledge of history, what each historian's voice reflects is a particular grasp of tradition. These different ways of grasping the tradition form the complex tradition in which our own understanding emerges. Let me express this point by speaking of background contexts. Although our context conditions our understanding (of the past, for instance), that understanding also conditions the context. There is a circular or feedback relation between the background out of which a particular interpretation emerges, such that the interpretation also changes the background. Understanding this feedback relation helps in properly assessing Gadamer's critique of the Enlightenment, and his problematic claims about prejudice and authority.

## (ii)  Prejudice or prejudgement

A second point of Gadamer's that has misled his critics is his notion that the Enlightenment belief that prejudice must be eliminated is itself a prejudice. Gadamer's account of prejudice may suggest misleadingly that understanding consists exclusively of judgements, most of which remain tacit *Vorurteile*, prejudgements or prejudices. Our understanding would then be a belief system, which we do not give up as a whole even if we abandon or revise particular beliefs. Any particular prejudgement *could* be examined on this model, but our finitude prevents us from examining them all and from positing an ideal consensus as an achievable goal. Hubert Dreyfus therefore concludes that Gadamer's view is nihilistic in the long run, since "it bases its claims that pervasive 'prejudices' are unchallengeable simply on their inaccessibility to the people who hold them, which runs the risk of making a virtue of obscure, pervasive obsessions and compulsions."[39]

There are two central features of Gadamer's hermeneutics that seem incompatible with the label of *theoretical* holism that Dreyfus therefore attaches to Gadamer, in contrast to the practical holism that Dreyfus prefers. The first is Gadamer's account of understanding as *phronesis*, and the second is his claim that understanding is always already *application*. These concepts are closely connected, since by application Gadamer does not mean applying something (like a general principle) to something (for instance, a specific situation). Instead, by application he means that we see a text or a situation as already significant. There are already meanings, issues, or principles at stake in ways presenting us with or even forcing on us "live" options (even if the text is from a remote past). Similarly, Gadamer draws on Aristotle's notion of *phronesis* to argue that understanding is more like practical everyday reasoning than like theoretical reasoning (or at least a certain picture of theoretical reasoning as deducing conclusions from general principles, rules, or laws).

Although Gadamer's account of the correction of prejudice might seem to lead to a model in which understanding ourselves involves examining our prejudices one by one and therefore working toward (but never achieving) total self-knowledge, that is not what he projects. That would be the Enlightenment model whereby communicative consensus is posited as the goal of interpretation. Gadamer gives his account of prejudice as part of his characterization of the historical conflict between the Enlightenment and its romanticist critics, a conflict that he wants to get beyond by rejecting both positions. So the account that Dreyfus criticizes is really an account that Gadamer is criticizing as well, and not finally his own. Gadamer himself echoes Heidegger's critique of modern "theory," which Gadamer describes in *Truth and Method* as "the will to dominate what exists" (p. 454). Returning to a different notion of "theory" he finds in the ancient Greeks, Gadamer also gives a different account of what we learn from experience, that is, from the process of questioning our assumptions. What we acquire is not more "justified beliefs," but, instead, what Gadamer calls "openness to experience" (p. 355). He illustrates this with a reference to Aeschylus and "learning through suffering," where what we learn is not definitive knowledge. Instead, we learn more generally that we are finite, that nothing returns, and (following Leopold von Ranke) that reality is "what cannot be destroyed" (p. 357).

## (iii)  Authority

Gadamer's account of prejudice is tied, however, to a third notion that has been problematic for his interpreters: his appeal to *authority*. Gadamer's critique of the Enlightenment is that it thinks that reflection is capable of seeing through prejudice, and thus, of making our reasons for belief and action completely transparent to ourselves. Gadamer believes that reflection is conceived too abstractly not only by earlier Enlightenment theorists, but also by Habermas. Gadamer insists more concretely that what we are doing is re-interpreting ourselves in a feedback relation. Re-interpreting ourselves may lead to changes in our situation, but we cannot rationally aspire to free ourselves completely from our given tradition and situation.

Of course, as we have seen, Habermas does not claim that reflection can completely illuminate the background context. He could even agree that sometimes we might decide that the tradition is right, and that we should adhere to it on particular points. But Habermas's central claim is that even if we decide to adhere to traditional standards and practices, we do so not because they are authoritative, but because they turn out to be, when judged reflectively, rationally acceptable.

Gadamer thus appears to be in a weak position. Habermas is arguing that a traditional standard is right only if it can be judged reflectively to be right. In contrast, Gadamer appears to be saying that a traditional standard is right simply because it is traditional. Even a sympathetic interpreter of Gadamer like Georgia Warnke finds a "conservatism" in Gadamer that she believes to be inconsistent with the rest of his hermeneutical theory:

> Gadamer's thesis here is the fundamentally conservative one that since we are historically finite, since we have no concept of rationality that is independent of the tradition to which we belong and hence no universal norms and principles to which we can appeal, we ought not even to attempt to overthrow the authority of that tradition. . . . In equating the lack of an ultimate foundation for our beliefs with the necessity of submitting to authority Gadamer reinforces the conservative dimension of his "anticipation of completeness" [*Vorgriff der Vollkommenheit*]. In *Truth and Method* . . . it usually appears as a condition of the possibility of our modifying or overcoming our prejudices about a text, work of art or the tradition as a whole and involves a provisional acceptance of the truth or authority of a work. . . . [I]n Gadamer's comments on Habermas's views such provisional acceptance becomes a political commitment. We must accept the authority of the tradition because we cannot know enough to be certain of our criticism of it.[40]

Certainly if Gadamer's thesis about authority is taken as a political thesis as well as a methodological one, it would be reactionary. But Gadamer has argued repeatedly that we can criticize the tradition, so to interpret him as urging submission to the tradition seems to misinterpret what he is claiming with his admittedly unclear appeal to the inevitability of authority playing a role in our cognitive inquiries and social practices. So I read Gadamer's point not as a political thesis, but as a methodological thesis. The methodological point is partly to show the incorrectness of the picture of inquiry as aiming at an ideal speech situation in which everyone knows as much as everyone else and in which all are equally capable of digesting all the relevant information. In reality, acquiring knowledge is a social activity, and as is often noted, it takes more than a single person to do science. There are always other interpretations, theories, or discursive practices that must be provisionally accepted. In contemporary science, for instance, given the specialization of inquiry, we presuppose a background of knowledge that is relatively stable. We expect other specialists to do their share of the work, and we take over the results provided by others (as long as the results seem plausible, or can be replicated by others if not necessarily by ourselves). Knowledge is not a set of isolated facts, but a network of assumptions and practices. Gadamer's conception of "authority," I suggest, is not a political claim, but the methodological recognition that no single person or "discourse situation" can completely illuminate or justify the entire network.

This methodological point need not have the political consequence that we cannot criticize the tradition. If we take seriously the suggestion that the tradition is *multifarious*, then there is a sense in which there is no such thing as *the* tradition. Contemporary society is not unified by a single cultural tradition, but is instead more like the conflict of many traditions, which refuse to "melt" together. While Gadamer does speak of the tradition, his theory also recognizes that it is multifarious, or better, many-voiced. So instead of reading Gadamer's theory as concluding from the absence of universal norms that we must submit to the authority of tradition, I read the theory as implying that tradition is precisely a conflict of critical voices. The absence of a standpoint above or outside the many-voiced tradition does not make criticism impossible. On the contrary, criticism becomes an inevitable and desirable feature of culture and society. The source and ground of criticism is not some standpoint beyond our context, but other voices within our context. Furthermore, these other voices will be raised especially against any voice claiming to be the only authoritative one because it alone represents the truth of *the* tradition.

## (iv)  The anticipation of completeness

My way of reading Gadamer's notions of the "fusion of horizons," prejudice, and authority is deliberately intended to make him seem more of a pluralist than a "universalist." But I must acknowledge that there are moments when he does sound like a universalist, and these are especially pronounced when he claims that there is an expectation or anticipation (*Vorgriff*) of completeness (*Vollkommenheit*) in every interpretation. Some places in *Truth and Method* where he sounds like a universalist include the following. In a gloss on Heidegger he affirms that there is no pure knowledge of discrete (*vorhanden*) facts in which the totality of understanding is not also functioning (p. 262).

In explicating the hermeneutic circle as movement back and forth between part and whole, Gadamer suggests that the "criterion of correct understanding" is "the harmony of all the details with the whole" (p. 291). Of course, the whole here is not the metaphysical whole ("everything"), but only the whole of a given text. However, theorists like Derrida and Roland Barthes have suggested that even the belief that a work is a whole and has a unity or harmony is a vestige of metaphysics. So even this limited "textual holism" may be problematic. Gadamer seems to build a universalistic telos into his model of understanding through his notion that understanding must always anticipate the completeness of the text through the *Vorgriff der Vollkommenheit*, in which we anticipate the truth of what the text says (p. 293). In a later essay he underlines the term *Vorgriff*, insisting that we only ever anticipate the final harmony and never grasp it fully. So this telos seems at best a regulative principle that guides our interpretive activity but that we never achieve.

Gadamer does seem to think that language and meaning form a whole that is invoked with any particular use of language. But he qualifies this view by saying that language is not an *existing* whole, but an "infinity of discourse" opened up with any single utterance (p. 549). So his picture is not one where the infinity comes together in a final (and therefore finite) consensus, or where the whole exists prior to the part. If one can speak of a whole at all, it is only ever as a projected possibility by which to make sense of the connection between particular details. Thus, he does claim for hermeneutics, as a "speculative" activity in his special sense, "the task of revealing a totality of meaning in all its relations" (p. 471). (The speculative activity, of which both poetry and philosophical hermeneutics are examples, tries to envision the whole of being instead of particular beings [p. 469].) But this totality cannot be captured in only one way, since the task arises in specific ways and differently at different times. So unlike the ideal of pure, theoretical inquiry, interpretation is always motivated by some particular needs, and the results of interpretation will always be configured by the special need that motivated the interpretation: "Only because the text calls for it does interpretation take place, and only in the way called for" (p. 472).

Thus, he insists that we are always in a situation and therefore can never have objective knowledge of it in its entirety. As a result *total, complete* self-knowledge is never really possible (p. 301). He does speak of "our whole being" (or more precisely, "*unser im Ganzen unsrer Geschicke gewirktes sein*"),[41] but only to insist that our knowledge of ourselves is never adequate. Similarly, although he does say that the historian's object is "the unity of the whole tradition" (p. 339), he also insists against earlier hermeneutical theorists of historiography that there is no reader before whose eyes "the great book of world history" lies open (p. 340). He is also ironical about the ideal of such a great book, and thus about the historical whole. In the foreword to the second edition of *Truth and Method* he criticizes Droysen and Wilhelm Dilthey for having been "seduced" by the model of "reading history as a book," one that is "intelligible down to the smallest letter" (p. xxxv). He repeatedly rejects the Hegelian projection of a universal history, insisting instead on the fragmentary character of history. In a response to critics he writes:

> The experience of history is not the experience of meaning, plan, and reason, and the claim to grasp reason in history could be raised only under the externalizing view of the philosopher of absolute knowledge. In truth, the experience of history returns the hermeneutic task to its own place. It always has to decipher the meaning of fragments of history anew, fragments that are limited by, and shipwreck on, the dark contingency of the factual and, above all, on the twilight into which for each present consciousness the future disappears.[42]

So if the interpreter projects a whole, the interpreter must also be aware that this projection is at best only a *Vorgriff*, an expectation. Moreover, the projection is always tied to the interpreter's own standpoint, not to a universal or "God's eye" point of view. As Gadamer says in *Truth and Method*, "The concept of the whole is itself to be understood only relatively. The whole of meaning that has to be understood in history or tradition is never the meaning of the whole of history" (p. xxxv). This passage makes the important point that Gadamer is talking about the conditions not of historical reality, but of the conditions for our *understanding* of ourselves as historical. On this account, furthermore, there is no need to think that there are determinate objects (such as isolated events or "the whole of history") that have a determinate meaning independent of any interpretation of them. This latter position would be a *metaphysical-realist* position, asserting that even the best interpretations that anyone could ever produce could still be wrong about the reality being interpreted, since this metaphysically-external reality was completely independent of interpretation. Gadamer's position, as I read it, is not a metaphysical position but a *critical*, internal one. It addresses itself to the conditions of understanding and interpretation, and is not an ontology of what really exists independently of our interpretations.

If I am right in how I interpret these central hermeneutic notions, there is no reason to think that hermeneutics is hiding deep within itself a *metaphysical* yearning for the telos of the one universally-correct interpretation to which everyone would agree ideally. Let me call this yearning *metaphysical monism*. However, I do see that someone might wish reasonably to attribute to hermeneutics a *critical monism*. This attribution might follow, for instance, if there is a regulative ideal of unity or completeness built into every act of understanding. I myself find the insistence on such regulative ideals empty, and prefer to push hermeneutics toward critical pluralism. The emptiness can be seen from the failure of such a regulative ideal to undercut deconstructionist readings, for instance, which do have a unity of approach, method, or style even if their point is that the text is not itself a unity. So the ideal should not be invoked to distinguish (contentiously and incorrectly, in my view) two different kinds of interpretations, "deconstructive" versus "hermeneutical" ones. On my understanding, deconstruction as an approach can be explained with the tenets of hermeneutics, and need not be a practical rival to hermeneutics.

From Kant one learns that what makes an ideal regulative instead of constitutive is that there could never be proof that the ideal had been empirically attained. So the expectation of completeness would simply amount to the recommendation that interpreters avoid inconsistency and keep testing their interpretations against other interpretations with more readings that take more aspects of the text into account. But there is no reason to think that there is a final end to this process, or that monism is the only rational stance. Hermeneutics is not forced to go beyond its pluralistic account of understanding and interpretation by adding the additional, much stronger requirements of ideal consensus and evolutionary reason posited in Habermas's theory of communicative action. I shall now conclude by explaining and provisionally defending this pluralism, fully expecting that Thomas McCarthy will raise many further objections to it.

## 6.4  Genealogical Hermeneutics

At the beginning of this chapter I pointed out two paradoxes of self-reference that a defense of pluralism must face. There is first the practical problem that social pluralism encounters insofar as it seems to presuppose that the community will agree to and permit the disagreement and the social plurality that the pluralist prefers. The "universalist" (a label that I shall now use for the Habermasian opponents to pluralism) infers that the pluralist tacitly presupposes a higher, single community that allows for the possibility of dissent between various groups and cultures in that community. The universalist believes that there is a tension between, on the one hand, the pluralist's supposed picture of society as irrational and as always at war with itself, and on the other hand, the pluralist's tacit appeal to a more rational society that tolerates dissent and agrees to disagree. Universalism believes itself to be on stronger moral and political ground than pluralism insofar as it recognizes the need for rational community and solidarity. Pluralism's denial of consensus seems to entail a picture of society as consisting only of hungry hordes in competition. In this picture there is no redeeming legitimation of any of the competing political strategies, and thus the triumph of even a liberal elite would be paid for only by marginalizing and silencing potential dissenters.

This problem for social pluralism is the practical manifestation of a second problem, a meta-theoretical paradox of self-reference. A methodological objection to genealogical hermeneutics is that it seems forced to abandon its pluralism insofar as it asserts its own theoretical superiority.[43] That is, genealogical hermeneutics must think of itself as *the* correct view insofar as it excludes its universalistic opponent.

The practical paradox is more difficult for the pluralist than the meta-theoretical one. The best response at the meta-theoretical level is to point out that the objection fails to distinguish between first-order and second-order theories (or between theories and meta-theories). Universalism and pluralism are contesting whether conflicts between first-order theories about object domains are resolvable in the long run through an uncoerced consensus modeled on the ideal speech situation. The universalist believes that these conflicts necessarily presuppose convergence on a single *focus imaginarius*, a focal point that is beyond the present field of vision, but without which we could not even speak of a single field of vision. Universalism thus posits two necessary presuppositions of rational discourse and inquiry: *consensus* and *convergence*.

Pluralism contests the universalist's claim that without these two presuppositions the goal of engaging in *rational* discussion becomes incoherent. Pluralism is thus more of a negative meta-position, and is not setting itself up as offering positive claims to replace the universalist's axioms. Since its conflict with universalism takes place at a second-order level, it can consistently allow for a plurality of first-order interpretations without contradicting its own contention that a second-order theory like universalism is too strong as a reconstruction of what is required at the level of first-order inquiry. (Universalism is not pluralism's only opponent. Pluralism is also opposed to methodological *nihilism*, the view that *anything* goes. That is, pluralism is not opposed to reason and does not defend irrationality or nonconsensuality. Only nihilism goes this far, and pluralism resists this extreme as well.)

If I am right that genealogical, hermeneutical pluralism can avoid the meta-theoretical paradox of self-reference, then this strategy may help with the practical paradox as well. Genealogical pluralism certainly should not oppose the possibility of social solidarity and community. Pluralism might grant that these values could trump any attempt to destroy them. But it does not thereby have to grant that these values are eternal or universal. Solidarity and community mean little as universal abstractions, and are not simply meta-procedural idealizations. They rest on substantive conceptions of the social good, and are binding not in the abstract, but only insofar as they are practiced concretely. Solidarity is thus not the imaginary focal point of an evolutionary learning process, but is binding only for contingent, historical moments. Solidarity and community may be the highest achievements of these contingent moments, and they may serve as inspiration for later moments. But they cannot be repeated, and slavish imitation by a later moment may only lead to a reactionary blindness to the new problems that a later moment faces.

This answer, I believe, is one toward which Foucault was working in his last writings. Contrary to Habermas's reading, Foucault did not see himself as a counter-enlightenment thinker attacking "the essential kernel of rationality." In the posthumously published essay, "What Is Enlightenment?," Foucault suggests that this kernel "would have to be preserved in any event."[44] The implication that I draw from this remark is that for Foucault Habermas's project of generating a meta-theory of rationality is not the critical activity that is most needed today. Instead of critical *theory*, redescribing the ideal of rational autonomy in the current vocabulary of speech act theory and evolutionary social science, what is needed is the more concrete practice of critical *history*, that is, genealogical critiques of the specific, concrete ways in which we have been socialized subliminally.

Foucault's late studies of changes between the ways human beings have understood themselves in Greek, early Christian, and modern times suggest that we can learn that our present self-understanding is not universal and eternal. These earlier self-understandings are not *alternatives* for us, since we cannot now go back to them. But they are also not *inferior* to ours, as a Habermasian evolutionary model might imply. The Habermasian model would suggest that the earlier self-understandings learned from their mistakes and "matured" into the present one. Foucault's genealogies suggest in contrast that these different self-understandings are different *interpretations*. Seeing that other peoples lived successfully with different self-interpretations from our own should suggest that we can criticize regrettable aspects of ourselves that might have seemed universal and eternal. Seeing our own self-understanding as an interpretation instead of as the best or most highly-evolved self-representation allows us to begin to criticize it. Self-criticism is more likely as the result of concrete genealogical histories than abstract, utopian projections of ideal uncoerced consensus.

Genealogical critical history shifts the methodological focus away from the postulation of a single meta-community. In contrast, genealogy sees human beings as participating in multiple communities at once, with each of these communities arising from different concrete contingencies. To criticize one community or set of social practices, we do not need to imagine some ideal standpoint that is independent of any contingent concrete standpoint. More substantively, we may judge that community, not from outside our own standpoint (since there is no such outside), but from the standpoint of other communities, or other self-understandings, that we know to be, or to have been, viable.[45]

If one gave up a sharp distinction between history and theory, I think that critical history and critical theory could be seen more usefully as mutually reinforcing aspects of the same activity. One other central feature of Habermas's theory of communicative action would have to be given up as well, however, and that is the presupposition of *convergence*. In the act of entering into discursive communication where we try to decide what is true or morally right, we presuppose, on his account, the ideal of uncoerced consensus. Of course, the consensus could show us that "we" are wrong and that the "other" is right. However, I believe that the suggestion of ethnocentrism, or more generally, of our own epistemic and moral superiority, is hard to avoid on the Habermasian model. Insofar as we believe that we do have good reasons for our beliefs, and insofar as we operate on the assumption of the principle of charity (where most of our beliefs must be true), we have to enter any *real* discourse with the assumption that we are right, and that the other should converge with us.

In other words, *consensus* combined with the principle of *charity* yields the expectation of *convergence* on one's own point of view. I find at least two places where this formula seems to be at work in Habermas's own hands, even if it is not explicitly stated in his theory. The first is in volume 1 of the *Theory of Communicative Action*, where he accuses Gadamer's interpretation model of being unable to explain how *criticism* of the other's position is possible. The second is the Eurocentrism that Habermas seems to espouse at the conclusion to his lectures on modernity.

To take up the first instance, Habermas challenges Gadamer's position for allegedly granting that the text must always be in a superior epistemic position to the interpreter, such that we can learn from it, but we do not assume that the author could learn from us. On Habermas's reading of Gadamer, "The knowledge embodied in the text is, Gadamer believes, fundamentally superior to the interpreter's."[46] Habermas suggests that anthropology is a counter-example and an antidote to Gadamer's philological position. Habermas believes that an evolutionary theory of the development of rationality structures allows the anthropologist to criticize the practices of a less-developed culture. Only such a strong theory of rationality, according to Habermas, would block a sheer relativism.

He also believes that this theory will keep us from positing our own standards as absolute, but here I find that his reasoning is still Whiggish. To be Whiggish is to assume the superiority of a later or "higher" stance over an earlier or more "primitive" one. The Habermasian claim is that with the evolution of the procedure of rationally redeeming validity claims we do not assert our own superiority without warranted reasons. This claim strikes me as empty, however, since who decides in such a case but the anthropologists? Habermas's bifurcation of anthropology is itself suspect, for increasingly there are fewer and fewer cultures that are not already altered by technological modernization. Also, the non-Western cultures (like Bali) that were the classic objects of study now have produced their own anthropologists, who can study the Western anthropologists studying the non-Western cultures. These "native" anthropologists can see the Western anthropologists as epistemic "primitives." But that is what the natives may have been doing all along anyway.

The general problem here is that contact between cultures may seem to produce a new language, which Charles Taylor in his essay "Understanding and Ethnocentricity" calls the "language of perspicuous contrast."[47] The universalist assumption is that there will be a convergence between the languages of the two cultures into a single new language that will burst the provinciality of *both* of the earlier languages. The question that the genealogical pluralist will ask, however, is why is only *one* language of perspicuous contrast the inevitable result? What seems more likely is that each culture will formulate a new language in which it now sees itself as seen by the other. But these languages need not converge. Each language may have valid reasons for preserving its own differences from the other.[48]

Ethnocentrism is thus not simply the claim that we always see things from our own perspective, or that our interpretations always flow from our own tradition. This benign hermeneutical insistence that interpretations always arise from a particular substantive context does not entail that the provinciality of that context cannot be overcome to some degree. But it also does not entail that the contingency of context can be overcome altogether by evolving substantive universal principles. What is ethnocentric is the assumption that we have become less and less context-bound, and more and more universal. This Whiggish view entails that others will have to become more like us, and is thus ethnocentric.[49]

The alternative view is that even if other cultures are following patterns first exemplified in the West, these non-Western cultures are not therefore slightly delayed in becoming just like the West. It may well be that although other countries, like Japan, look structurally like the West, and even if they seem to have adopted democratic *procedures* like those of the West, they may be interpreting and developing these procedural or structural similarities in concrete ways that differ substantively from the way the West typically does. The appearance of convergence would thus be an illusion that is fostered by stressing procedural similarities and remaining blind to substantive divergence.

Some observers might even suggest that the West is now the culture that is "behind" instead of "ahead." I would think that a better assessment would result from giving up altogether the teleological notion of convergence implied by the words "behind" and "ahead." Ernesto Laclau, the South American social theorist, suggests instead that there are different ways that technological, economic, and cultural changes are interpreted, and that ethnocentrism results only from the assumption that Europe's interpretation is the highest and most advanced one simply because the changes started there:

> That there has been throughout the last centuries a "Westernization" of the world through a technological, economic and cultural revolution that started in Europe is an obvious enough fact; that those transformations are intrinsically Western and that other peoples can only oppose a purely external and defensive resistance by way of defense of their national and cultural identity, seems to me essentially false and reactionary. The true ethnocentrism does not lie in asserting that the "universalization" of values, techniques, scientific control of the environment, etc., is an irreversible process, but in sustaining that this process is linked by an essential bond, immanent to the "ethnia of the West."[50]

The pernicious ethnocentrism that Laclau fears will arise from an overly abstract assessment of the direction of universalization lurks dangerously close to Habermas's conclusion to his *Philosophical Discourse of Modernity*. There Habermas grants that Europe generated not only the theory of rationality that culminates in his own model of the intersubjective redemption of validity claims. Europe also gave

birth to an instrumental mentality resulting from the blind compulsion to meet force with more force and culminating in phenomena like
the arms race and Star Wars. Habermas deplores this latter mentality,
of course, but he also seems to think that only Europe has the resources to criticize and ameliorate this mentality:

> Modern Europe has created the spiritual presuppositions and the ma-
> terial foundations for a world in which this mentality has taken the
> place of reason. That is the real heart of the critique of reason since
> Nietzsche. Who else but Europe could draw from *its own* traditions the
> insight, the energy, the courage of vision – everything that would be
> necessary to strip from the (no longer metaphysical, but metabiological)
> premises of a blind compulsion to system maintenance and system
> expansion their power to shape our mentality.[51]

Why Habermas attributes the blame, but also the hope for redemption,
only to Europe is not clear. I infer that his own model of the teleological evolution of rationality is what leads him to adopt this metaphor
of Europe being not only the origin but also the end of social evil. His
model may not be a full-fledged philosophy of history, but it seems
to be at least a vestige of such a philosophy. As such it signals the
remnants in Habermas's theory of a Eurocentric philosophy of rational
subjectivity that he has not succeeded in avoiding. "Reason" on his
theory is still preeminently European.

   In contrast to the universalist's insistence on convergence, the
pluralist should not overreact and insist only on divergence. Certainly
an anti-universalist theorist like Laclau is not denying that in some
technological, economic, and cultural respects there is convergence.
The anti-universalist could even grant that the model of communication is right to insist that in the modern world all countries and
cultures are able to talk with one another.[52] Provinciality must be
deplored, and the anti-universalist need not go to the extreme of
asserting that communication is impossible because the different languages and forms of life in the modern world are incommensurable.
Gadamer makes the point, for instance, that communication is often
much easier with our contemporaries from extremely different traditions than it is with texts from the distant past of our own tradition.
Communication with contemporaries is always with other people.
Even if these people seem to inhabit radically different worlds, we can
still converse about and come to an understanding of these differences. This admission does not entail, however, that we can bridge or
resolve these differences, even ideally in the long run.

   To defend pluralism, genealogical hermeneutics need not celebrate
divergence in contrast to convergence. However, it can insist that the

appearance of convergence, especially when that convergence is only at an abstract level, should not *mask* substantive divergence. Furthermore, genealogical hermeneutics can urge that divergence be tolerated even in the absence of a universal set of values or standards for the assessment of differences. Communicative discussion of these differences is certainly good, but such communication is not what makes interpretation possible. On the contrary, communication would not be necessary unless there were differences in interpretation, and interpretation is thus what first makes communication possible.

If genealogical hermeneutics is a viable version of critical theory, there will be some differences from the way that critical theory is traditionally construed. Inquiry is no longer conceived as the search for certainty, nor even as the search for transcultural validity. Instead, inquiry is the reinterpretation of what was already an interpretation. Methodologically then, these critical interpretations are explained too abstractly as simply a matter of coming up with the best arguments, as if all that is involved is procedural argumentation from premises to conclusions. Argumentation will be involved in genealogical research, but the goal is more substantive, namely, finding new descriptions of ourselves that locate new possibilities in our situation. These reinterpretations may even change what the premises are. So while formal validity alone is always a necessary condition of good interpretation, it is not a sufficient condition, since good interpretation can alter our conception of what is to be argued and what our premises mean.

Critical theory conceived as genealogical hermeneutics may unmask substantive injustice, but it need not justify this unmasking through the methodological picture of inquiry presented by traditional theory. It need not construe itself as seeing through illusions and showing us how society really is. Instead, it can present itself as offering new interpretations. Along the way it may be unmasking previous interpretations. Since what is unmasked is self-interpretation, this unmasking through genealogical critical history can now be seen not simply in traditional epistemological terms as "revealing reality," but also modally as "deconstructing necessity." That is, genealogical research will show that self-understandings that are taken as universal, eternal, and necessary have a history, with a beginning, and therefore, possibly, an end. Genealogy thus shows that self-understandings are interpretations, and it can bring us to suspect that conceptions of ourselves that we have taken to be necessary are only contingent. In making this contingency manifest, genealogy makes it possible for people to see how they could want to be different from how they are.

We can learn to live with contingency, of course, and we may also find that we like features of our self-interpretation. However, even if

we like our own self-interpretation, we need not automatically assume that everybody else should interpret themselves in the same
way. Genealogy may subvert this assumption, but in contrast to earlier
formulations of critical theory, genealogy need not be construed as
proving that the self-interpretation is "false." Interpretations are not
true or false in the same sense that particular assertions within an
interpretation are. A genealogical study of a social self-interpretation
will be valuable if it serves as a reminder of the contingencies and
problems of one interpretation, and the possibility or even desirability
of other interpretations. If genealogy shows the "falsity" of anything,
it may be only of the meta-theoretical illusion that ideally there are no
genuine conflicts of interpretation.

A pluralistic hermeneutics thus implies that we can live without the
ideal of a universal meta-interpretation that could serve as a criterion
for adjudicating differences between interpretations. An interpretation should not assume that it can ascend to a non-interpretive
standpoint from which its superiority over all other interpretations
can be decisively adjudicated. An interpretation should remain open
to other possible interpretations, and recognize that it enriches
itself by confronting other perspectives. Correlatively, a philosophy of
interpretation need not restrict itself to the Cartesian project of the
self-validation of reason. Critical theory should not be preoccupied
exclusively with justifying itself, and with worrying about abstract
self-referential paradoxes. Instead, as social theory it should try to be
more than merely the "theory of (social) theory." Critical theory should
not see itself as divorced from critical history, but must be willing to
get its hands dirty by going out and doing some concrete, historical
genealogies.

Obviously my own chapters in this book do not live up to this last
imperative. At most they represent a genealogical history of recent
social *theory*, when what is really called for are genealogical histories
of social *practices*. The only justification for these abstract chapters is
that they serve as an alternative to Habermas's reading of the history
of critical theory. They would not be necessary except to ensure that
there is more than one way to read this history. They also do not claim
for themselves any final authority. They point not to definitive solutions, but to open-ended possibilities. Deconstruction and genealogy,
for instance, are not yet well-defined research programs that provide
the concrete studies that could vindicate the pluralistic reading offered here in contrast to Habermas's universalism. These chapters will
therefore need to be rewritten as future research confirms or discon-
firms their argument that there is a will-to-interpret and to do critical
history in a genealogical, hermeneutical way. For now, however, this

argument may have an emancipatory effect if it convinces critical historians that the will-to-interpret can rationally resist the model of ideal consensus and universal convergence.

## NOTES

1 Habermas derives the notion of performative contradiction from Karl-Otto Apel, who in turn was following Jaakko Hintikka. As an example, consider a skeptic who says, "I doubt that I exist." The skeptic's act of utterance presupposes the very existence that is to be doubted. Habermas thus defines a performative contradiction as occurring when "a constative speech act *k(p)* rests on noncontingent presuppositions whose propositional content contradicts the asserted proposition *p*." See Habermas, "Discourse Ethics," in *Moral Consciousness and Communicative Action*, trans. Christian Lenhardt and Shierry Weber Nicholsen (Cambridge, MA: MIT Press, 1990), p. 80. See also Martin Jay, "The Debate over Performative Contradiction: Habermas versus the Poststructuralists," *Force Fields: Between Intellectual History and Cultural Critique* (New York: Routledge, 1993).

2 My remarks on ethnography in this chapter are influenced by recent writings by Clifford Geertz as well as by my colleague, James Clifford, whom Thomas McCarthy discusses at length in chapter 3.

3 David Ingram, "The Postmodern Kantianism of Arendt and Lyotard," *The Review of Metaphysics* 42 (September, 1988): 52 (emphasis added).

4 Michel Foucault, "Politics and Ethics: An Interview," in Paul Rabinow, ed., *The Foucault Reader*, p. 379.

5 Jürgen Habermas, *The Theory of Communicative Action, volume 1, Reason and the Rationalization of Society*, trans. Thomas McCarthy (Boston: Beacon Press, 1984).

6 David Ingram would disagree, since he implies that Habermas would be better off without the analysis of speech acts, of which Ingram says, "The abstractness of [Habermas's] model raises serious doubts about its value for empirical research. . . . Furthermore, it remains unclear why a formal pragmatic analysis of speech action is needed in the first place" (*Habermas and the Dialectic of Reason*; New Haven: Yale University Press, 1987; p. 40). Habermas's interpreters often try to defend his theory by jettisoning elements of it that they do not find plausible. All that critics like myself can do, therefore, is to object to the arguments as they stand, and remain open to revisionist readings. However, my answer to David Ingram here would be that the formal pragmatic analysis is necessary because Habermas is a *systematic* philosopher in a style going back to Kant, a style that preserves the foundationalist drive of traditional theory and modern philosophy. Habermas thinks that a correct philosophy of language (or what he calls "universal pragmatics") can serve as the

unifying ground for his social philosophy. This social philosophy may be more pluralistic than I am allowing, but on my reading, Habermas's defense of pluralistic politics, with which I agree, is so deeply embedded in his analysis of speech acts, which in turn is what enables him to insist on the universalistic ideal of uncoerced consensus, that I take his analysis of language and understanding as the keystone of his theory. For a defender of Habermas to remove this keystone would seem to have the unintended effect of reducing Habermas's *Aufbau*, his carefully constructed edifice, to an eclectic pile of rubble, or at best, a postmodern architectural collage.

7 See "Building a New Left: An Interview with Ernesto Laclau," *Strategies: A Journal of Theory, Culture and Politics* 1 (Fall, 1988): 23.

8 Habermas, *The Philosophical Discourse of Modernity*, p. 322.

9 Hans-Georg Gadamer, *Wahrheit und Methode: Grundzüge einer philosophischen Hermeneutik*, second edition (Tübingen: J. C. B. Mohr, 1965), p. 168. These lines are translated by Joel Weinsheimer and Donald G. Marshall in the second, revised edition of *Truth and Method* (New York: Crossroad, 1989) as follows: " 'to understand means to come to an understanding with each other.' Understanding is, primarily, agreement" (p. 180).

10 "Coming to an understanding, then, is always coming to an understanding about something." *Truth and Method*, p. 180.

11 Habermas, *The Philosophical Discourse of Modernity*, pp. 323–6.

12 Habermas, *The Theory of Communicative Action*, volume 1, p. 287.

13 In response to Habermas Gadamer remarks that "*Wer verstehen will, braucht das, was er versteht, nicht zu bejahen.*" ("One does not need to agree to that which one would understand.") Gadamer, "Replik," in Karl-Otto Apel, et al., *Hermeneutik und Ideologiekritik* (Frankfurt: Suhrkamp, 1971), p. 313.

14 Habermas, *The Theory of Communicative Action*, volume 1, p. 280.

15 Ibid., p. 287. See Allen W. Wood, "Habermas' Defense of Rationalism," *New German Critique* 35 (1985): 157, who also objects that there is no argument for this claim, and that such an argument could only result from the (unlikely) completion of Habermas's philosophical construction of "universal pragmatics." Wood argues cogently that Habermas's analysis of perlocutionary speech acts is flawed, and that Habermas is mistaken to think that perlocutionary intentions to bring something about can never be announced in the explicit utterance by which I intend to bring about these results.

16 Habermas, *The Theory of Communicative Action*, volume 1, p. 107.

17 Habermas, *Communication and the Evolution of Society*, p. 1.

18 Habermas, *The Theory of Communicative Action*, volume 1, p. 287.

19 Habermas, *The Philosophical Discourse of Modernity*, p. 326.

20 For a more detailed discussion of the relevance of Donald Davidson's principle of charity to hermeneutics, see my essay, "Post-Cartesian Interpretation: Hans-Georg Gadamer and Donald Davidson," forthcoming from the Library of Living Philosophers in *The Philosophy of Hans-Georg Gadamer*, ed. Lewis E. Hahn (LaSalle, IL: Open Court Publishing Company).

21  Cited by Gadamer in *Truth and Method*, p. 361.

22  Habermas, *The Theory of Communicative Action*, volume 1, p. 311.

23  Ibid., p. 336.

24  Ibid., p. 311.

25  Kant, *Groundwork of the Metaphysic of Morals*, trans. H. J. Paton (New York: Harper & Row, 1964), p. 131.

26  Habermas, *The Theory of Communicative Action*, volume 1, p. 398.

27  Habermas might resist this charge by suggesting that what he is formalizing is what happens whenever there is genuine communication, even if we can never know of any particular act of discursive communication whether it is genuine or not. The argument would thus be transcendental in form, suggesting that if there is genuine discursive communication, these conditions of validity would have to be satisfied. This transcendental argument would save him from the task of identifying any particular consensus as genuine communication. But it would generate difficulties for him since it does not entail that there ever is any genuine communication. At most we learn that these conditions are what *we would have to believe* to obtain. Even that result may be too strong, however, since a transcendental argument for necessary belief always depends on an "if" clause, and this clause can be rephrased to yield different conceptual entailments. For critical discussion of transcendental arguments see Robert C. Solomon, *In the Spirit of Hegel* (New York: Oxford University Press, 1983), pp. 351–60.

28  Habermas, *The Philosophical Discourse of Modernity*, p. 198.

29  See, for instance, "Heidegger and the Hermeneutic Turn," in *The Cambridge Companion to Heidegger*, ed. Charles B. Guignon (Cambridge, UK: Cambridge University Press, 1993), pp. 170–94; "Splitting the Difference: Habermas's Critique of Derrida," in *Working Through Derrida*, ed. Gary B. Madison (Evanston, IL: Northwestern University Press, 1993), pp. 230–51; "Must We Say What We Mean? The Grammatological Critique of Hermeneutics," in *Hermeneutics and Modern Philosophy*, ed. Brice R. Wachterhauser (Albany: SUNY Press, 1986), pp. 397–415.

30  See Gadamer, "Replik," p. 316.

31  Lawrence Kennedy Schmidt does a helpful job of puzzling through Gadamer's various statements about the *Sache* in *The Epistemology of Hans-Georg Gadamer* (Frankfurt: Peter Lang, 1985), especially pp. 199–215.

32  "Being that can be understood is language." Gadamer, *Wahrheit und Methode*, p. xxi; *Truth and Method*, p. xxxiv.

33  Gadamer, "On the Scope and Function of Hermeneutical Reflection," in *Hermeneutics and Modern Philosophy*, ed. Brice R. Wachterhauser, pp. 288–289. The German reads, "alles verstehen wollen, was sich verstehen läßt." See "Rhetorik, Hermeneutik und Ideologiekritik," in H.-G. Gadamer, *Kleine Schriften I* (Tübingen: J. C. B. Mohr, 1967), p. 123.

34  Gadamer, "Text and Interpretation," in *Hermeneutics and Modern Philosophy*, p. 382. The German reads, "das, was ist, nie ganz verstanden werden kann." See "Text und Interpretation," in *Text und Interpretation*, ed. Philippe Forget (Munich: Wilhelm Fink Verlag, 1984), p. 29.

35  See Hilary Putnam, *Reason, Truth and History* (Cambridge, UK: Cambridge University Press, 1981), pp. 49ff, 134–47. In this chapter I shall follow Putnam's distinction between *metaphysical* and *internal* views about realism and objectivity. This distinction retraces Kant's distinction between the noumenal and the phenomenal. If the phenomenal is all there is and all we need, then philosophy ceases to be "metaphysical" since it does not posit a two-world view. Instead, it becomes naturalized, and it is internal to the world it describes. Other terms that I shall use for the naturalized, internal perspective are "critical" and "methodological" (in contrast to "ontological").

36  Gadamer, *Truth and Method*, p. 268.

37  See Gadamer, *Wahrheit und Methode*, p. 252.

38  Ibid., p. 269; translation modified from *Truth and Method*, p. 285.

39  Hubert L. Dreyfus, "Holism and Hermeneutics," *Review of Metaphysics* 34 (1980): 21.

40  Georgia Warnke, *Gadamer: Hermeneutics, Tradition and Reason* (Stanford: Stanford University Press, 1987), p. 136.

41  Gadamer, *Wahrheit und Methode*, p. xx.

42  Gadamer, "Replik," p. 302; cited (with a slight modification) from Georgia Warnke's eloquent translation in *Gadamer: Hermeneutics, Tradition and Reason*, p. 123.

43  Hugh Silverman pursued this objection with me, and I thank him for the discussion.

44  Michel Foucault, "What Is Enlightenment?" in *The Foucault Reader*, p. 43.

45  Alexander Nehamas makes this point against Habermas while reviewing Habermas's *Philosophical Discourse of Modernity* in the May 30, 1988 issue of *The New Republic* 198 (22), pp. 34–5: "We acquire our beliefs, our desires, our values at different times, in different circumstances, from various sources. Each one of us belongs to a number of distinct but overlapping communities, and each community has its own but overlapping standards of rationality – or, if you prefer, standards of communicative competence. We don't need to stand outside *everything* in order to criticize and evaluate the standards and practices, the 'reason,' of any particular community. All we need is a position outside *it*. This position is provided by the many other communities of which we are all members."

46  Habermas, *The Theory of Communicative Action*, volume 1, p. 134.

47  Charles Taylor, *Philosophy and the Human Sciences: Philosophical Papers 2* (Cambridge, UK: Cambridge University Press, 1985), p. 125.

48  In a response to Habermas Gadamer argues that differences in experiences lead to political and cultural differences that may not be resolvable. This lack of resolvability does not imply that communication has broken down, but simply that the commonality of political will is lacking to find some common synthesis. Political competence is thus a different matter from communicative competence, and communication about political and cultural differences may not lead to agreement. See Gadamer, "Replik," pp. 304–7.

49  I investigate ethnocentrism in more detail in two essays: "Is Hermeneutics Ethnocentric?" in *The Interpretive Turn: Philosophy, Science, Culture,* ed. David R. Hiley, James F. Bohman, and Richard Shusterman (Ithaca: Cornell University Press, 1991; some paragraphs from this version are reprinted here with permission), pp. 155–75; and "Significant Others: Objectivity and Ethnocentrism," forthcoming in *Objectivity,* ed. John Paul Jones, Theodore Schatzki, and Wolfgang Natter (New York: Guilford Publications).

50  "Building a New Left: An Interview with Ernesto Laclau," *Strategies,* p. 20.

51  Habermas, *The Philosophical Discourse of Modernity,* p. 367.

52  Laclau's own objection to Habermas (conveyed to me in conversation) is that communication is never free from power plays, i.e., that it only ever serves hegemonic interests. This is a stronger response than is necessary, however, and Gadamer's more moderate response, which I describe below, is enough to make the pluralistic case.

# Part III
## For and Against

# 7

# Rejoinder to David Hoy

The criticisms marshalled by David Hoy in his opening statement are so numerous and various that any attempt on my part to provide a point-by-point rejoinder would soon collapse from overload. Fortunately, many of the most important of them can be grouped together under one or another of four principal themes: (1) pragmatism, (2) genealogy, (3) hermeneutics, and (4) pluralism. In what follows, I will comment briefly on each of the complexes of argumentation signified by these headings, that is, on Hoy's arguments against theory, for critical history, for interpretation, and against universalism.

## 7.1 Pragmatism

One of the disconcerting features of the otherwise welcome renewal of interest in American Pragmatism is the suggestion by some "new pragmatists" that Peirce, James, Dewey, and Mead were actually much closer in spirit to Nietzsche, Heidegger, and the French poststructuralists than to Kant and the German Idealists – whom, unlike the former, they encountered as students and continued to draw inspiration from throughout their lives. In fact, the classical pragmatists were given to theory on a grand scale, and in all the senses decried by neopragmatists, from Peirce's metaphysical realism to Dewey's and Mead's metanarratives of scientific and social progress. Moreover, their thought was marked by the holism, universalism, and utopianism that Hoy rejects in the name of "piecemeal and pragmatic" criticism (p. 107 above). This is not merely to dispute legitimate ancestry or to reclaim the rhetorical high ground arrogated by Rorty and others. It raises the important question of whether one might not be naturalistic and pragmatic and still aspire to "theory" in one or more of the senses at

issue. For, despite the repeated denunciation of all "binary oppositions" and every "critical tribunal," postmodernist discourse actually
relies quite heavily on a series of stark "either/or"s to justify a strin-
gent list of "do"s and "don't"s: thou shalt not spin grand historical
metanarratives, construct big societal pictures, entertain high utopian
ideals, or think deep philosophical thoughts. The supreme opposition, which structures all the rest, is that between *Reason* – that is,
foundationalist and absolutist conceptions of reason – and whatever
in a given context is identified as *The Other of Reason* – sensibility,
imagination, desire, the body, women, nature, history, the non-Western
world, language, culture, art, rhetoric, and so on. I argued in my
opening statement that these alternatives are not exhaustive. It is only
when one accepts an extreme diagnosis of modernity as everywhere
corrupted by "ontotheology" or the like, that the extreme remedy of
deconstruction seems necessary. Otherwise it is difficult to see why
one could not, in a fallibilist, naturalist, and pragmatist spirit, still
pursue theory in one or another of the relevant senses.

Which are the relevant senses in the present context? Hoy zeroes in
on just the senses that have been central to critical social theory from
Marx to Habermas. In the first place, (a) an overarching "metanarrative" of historical development, that is, of large-scale social, economic,
political, and cultural changes, which in Marx takes the form of a
materialist theory of history and in Habermas that of a theory of social
evolution. Then, (b) a "totalizing" account of contemporary society, of
its emergence, growth, tensions, and tendencies, of its basic structures
and processes, which in Marx takes the form of a critique of political
economy and in Habermas that of a critique of system–lifeworld
relations. And, finally, (c) a treatment of the conceptual and normative
foundations (but not in the foundationalist sense) of critical social
theory, which in Marx takes the form of a materialist appropriation
of Hegelian philosophy by way of a never fully elaborated notion of
social *praxis* and in Habermas that of a theory of communicative
action.[1] I will address each of these in turn.

(a) Hoy underplays the *critical* orientation and *practical* intention of
critical social theory and treats its general accounts of societal transformation simply as "grand metanarratives" of progress, ignoring the
*use* to which those developmental schemes are put in the critique of
contemporary society. To be sure, there are grounds for this reading
within the history of critical theory. The young Marx wanted to
distance himself from the philosophy of history, with its pretense to a
contemplative view of a whole whose meaning could be rendered in
terms of necessary progress. He insisted that the movement of history
was not a matter of metaphysical necessity but was contingent in

regard to both the empirical conditions of change and the practical engagement of social actors, and that the meaning of history was not a subject for metaphysical hypostatization but for political action. But the mature Marx, in his efforts to distinguish himself from merely philosophical critics and purely utopian socialists, sometimes ascribed to his own conception of history a necessity and scientificity that echoed earlier claims for the philosophy of history. Subsequently, especially in the hands of his "orthodox" followers, the importance of critical self-reflection and emancipatory political practice regularly receded behind the solid, objective necessity of inexorable laws of history. The spectacle of that regression prompted the Frankfurt School's renewed stress on the critical and practical dimensions of Marxism. And yet, as Hoy has indicated, they did not always resist the temptation to treat their own general historical schemes as philosophies of history. I do not think, however, that it is correct to place Habermas's theory of social evolution in the same category. Distinguishing structural patterns from empirical processes under contingent conditions, he attributes neither unilinearity, nor necessity, nor continuity, nor irreversibility to history.[2] But I will not debate Habermas interpretation here. I want, rather, to emphasize the practical motivation behind critical social theory's interest in "grand metanarratives": their point is to aid in the construction of critical histories of the present. That is to say, the *theoretically generalized narratives* of societal transformation characteristic of this tradition are meant to serve as *interpretive frameworks* for historically oriented, critical analyses of contemporary society. Their underlying purpose is to enhance our understanding of capitalist modernization, with its vast consequences, positive and negative, for traditional social orders. If they are viewed naturalistically and fallibilistically, there is nothing "in principle" impossible about such general schemes. From a pragmatic point of view, the proof of the pudding can only be in the eating, that is, in how well or badly they fare as interpretive frameworks for critical accounts of the contemporary world. As Marx strikingly illustrated in *The Eighteenth Brumaire of Louis Bonaparte*, "metanarratives" of societal change may also serve as narrative foils for the construction of critical histories of particular events, situations, and processes. That use will be discussed in considering Hoy's treatment of genealogy. For now, suffice it to say that claiming "a priori," as it were, that general historical schemes could never be of any use in any context, or that even if they were, it would be wrong to use them, would be a decidedly unpragmatic way of dealing with these issues.

Finally, it should be noted that in the tradition of critical social theory, the historical critiques framed by these general accounts of societal change have typically not been directed at "them" – that is, at other cultures and societies – but at "us" – that is, at our own. The overriding aim has been *self*-criticism, but self-criticism informed by a general sense of how we got where we are and which are the real alternatives and possibilities for change. To be sure, critical theorists from Marx to Habermas have made "invidious comparisons" with traditional societies, both in Europe and elsewhere. But they are mild compared to their trenchant criticisms of the deep pathologies of their own societies. As that is evident, the only issue may be whether social critics should be discouraged from saying or implying anything un-flattering about any society – or culture, or group – other than their own. I will discuss the wisdom of that policy under "pluralism."

(b) What is true of "grand metanarratives" of historical change holds also for "big pictures" of contemporary society. As I argued in my opening statement, there is no need to claim a God's-eye view of the whole; a reflective participant's view will do just fine. The strengths and weaknesses of competing general accounts of contemporary so-ciety can certainly be discussed in a naturalistic and fallibilistic spirit. And their usefulness for understanding and explaining particular features of our world surely has to prove itself in practice. Before dismissing them out of hand, it would be well to recall that histori-cally oriented, general accounts of modern society were the stock-in-trade of classical social theorists from Smith and Ferguson, through Marx and Mill, to Durkheim and Weber, and beyond. Is it plausible to assume that we can learn nothing of value from this type of grand theorizing? More likely, without it we would be left with an ever-growing heap of fragmented analyses and interpretations.

One element of Hoy's case against "totalizing" theories of society is the suggestion that they aim at accounting for every detail of every aspect of everything, which would of course be a hopeless task. But if we were to understand the aim of general social theory in the more pragmatic sense of "seeing how things hang together" at a societal level of analysis, it might seem less hopeless. We do, in fact, constant-ly face questions concerning how what happens in one area of social life or one part of the world or one period of history affects or is affected by what happens in others. If social theorists were to abandon the effort to construct coherent, empirically based accounts of macro-historical processes and macrosocietal interconnections, then the field would simply be left to the army of journalists, pundits, politicians, and pop-theorists who are always more than willing to supply that need. Furthermore, interpretive practices themselves would be se-verely limited by the inability, as George Marcus and Michael Fischer have put it, "to represent the embedding of richly described, local, cultural worlds in larger, impersonal systems," for those worlds cannot plausibly be represented as "isolate[s] with outside forces of market and state impinging on [them]." Rather, such forces are "an integral part of the construction and the constitution of the 'inside,' the cultural unit itself, and must be so registered at the most intimate levels of the cultural process.'[3]

Another feature of Hoy's attack on "totalizing" social theory is his depiction of it as a continuation of metaphysics by other means, that is, as aiming at the kind of totality and finality that Kant demolished, one would like to say "once and for all," in the "Dialectic" of the *First Critique*. It is important to recall in this connection what was said in my opening statement about the *ongoing* character of such constructions and the *practical* interest of critical social theory. In ongoingly constructing, deconstructing, and reconstructing "big pictures" of basic structures, processes, and interdependencies, no less than in ongoingly fashioning "grand metanarratives" of macrohistorical transformations, the critical social theorist is guided by the aim of enhancing our self-understanding in ways that have implications for practice. Trying to understand, for instance, how investment policies in the industrialized world affect development and underdevelopment in the rest of the world is surely no less a critical activity than trying to understand the self-images of particular cultural units in either, and it is surely of no less practical-political import.

(c) Critical studies of modernization processes, with their deeply ambivalent record of gains and losses, have, at least since Max Weber, *also* been configured as studies of rationalization processes. Basic social-theoretical concepts and assumptions have been tailored to highlight the rationalizable aspects of social action and to provide a framework for interpreting modernization as rationalization, however ambiguous, one-sided, or distorted. It is here that Habermas's theory of communicative rationality belongs. He understands it as a "metatheoretical framework for action theory," on the same level as and competing with Weber's account of rationality in means–ends terms and its currently influential rational-choice reformulations.[4] He stresses its empirical-theoretical, in contradistinction to ontological or transcendental, character.[5] Hoy's remarks regarding this level of theorizing are ambivalent. On the one hand, he seems to be against any attempt to revive strong theoretical approaches to reason or to continue them by other means. On the other hand, in defending himself against charges of performative self-contradiction, he allows for the possibility of a "metatheory," in contrast to a "first-order theory," of reason (p. 201). But he also suggests that any such metatheory would be too "thin" to support substantive conclusions of any import (pp. 176, 179).

I find this position unconvincing, for a number of reasons. To begin with, neopragmatists like Rorty, genealogists like Foucault, and hermeneuticists like Gadamer have their own theories of reason, truth, objectivity, and the like. To be sure, their accounts are opposed to rationalism at many points. But having a different account – one, say, that stresses history, culture, practice, or power – is not the same as having no account. Nor are these accounts any less general than Habermas's; they are simply different – typically deflationary – general accounts. Nor, finally, do such general, deflationary accounts of reason avoid serving as "critical tribunals" or "cultural arbiters," legislating from on high. They simply proscribe a different list of cultural practices, including most of what theorists have done since Thales. Hoy fits this pattern. On the basis of very general, indeed *universal*, claims about the *unavoidable* historicity, linguisticality, contextuality, and so forth of rational practices, he dismisses many of the cultural practices associated with traditional philosophy or critical social theory. A "metatheory" of reason, on the same general level that philosophy usually occupies, is used as a rationale for legislating against a broad range of practices "a priori," that is, independently of examining their successes and failures in tackling particular problems. If this is so, and if that metatheory is in dispute, it is difficult to see why the refusal to elaborate it should serve the best interests of critical theory and practice.

At one point, Hoy argues that this *cannot* be done, since any attempt to explicate the background as a system of rules or the like is bound to fail (pp. 160–1). As my discussion of ethnomethodology indicates, I agree on the impossibility of spelling out "complete" systems of rules for our practices; but I do not think this warrants the conclusion that Hoy draws. The issue is not the ontological one of whether we are always "mehr Sein als Bewusstsein," but the pragmatic one of whether it is ever useful to reconstruct, as far as we can, the normative structures embodied in our practices.[6] It is a mistake to suppose that such reconstructions could be useful only if they yielded rules whose application no longer required practical reasoning and judgement. That requirement would make *all* rule systems useless, including the explicit ones that, notwithstanding their "incompleteness" and "imprecision," guide our conduct in so many areas of life from sports fields to law courts. The problem, I think, is once again the all-or-nothing forms of argument that neopragmatists persist in deploying against the philosophical tradition they reject. To borrow a phrase from Arthur Fine, they are locked in a metaphilosophical *pas-de-deux* with that tradition and ignore moves that are not part of their invariant routine: either a Theory of Reason in a foundationalist sense, or no theory of reason at all, in any sense.[7]

Hoy takes a different tack in adopting Foucault's project of showing by historical means that professedly universal conceptions of rationality are merely particular. This approach would replace the traditional search for a grand theory of what reason really is with multiple critical histories of contingent regimes of rationality (p. 146). As I am not in principle against such histories, our disagreement here comes down to whether there is *anything universal at all* to say about reason, truth, objectivity, and the like, or rather anything that would not be too "thin" to be of any use. With regard to thinness, I think one should take the same pragmatic stand as with regard to completeness or exactness: too thin for what purpose? Hoy clearly thinks that his thin "metatheory" of reason's historicity, contextuality, contingency, and so forth is thick enough to defeat the culturally significant claims of traditional philosophy and its successors, to counteract the ethnocentrism of universalist theories, and to point us in the direction of multicultural hermeneutic dialogue. These would be no mean accomplishments. Putting thinness aside, then, the issue remains whether and how a general account of rationality might still be pursued.

In my opening statement, I defended the possibility of a non-foundationalist critique of impure reason. Like grand metanarratives of historical change and big pictures of contemporary society, basic conceptions of reason and rationality can be ongoingly constructed, criticized, and revised in a naturalistic spirit (taking into account their agreement with available evidence and their coherence with other empirical theories), and with a view to the practical purposes for which they are designed (in this case, critical analyses of rationalization processes). As Peirce pointed out long ago, in most practical contexts some idea of being "true to the facts" will be of decisive importance. The stark opposition between knowledge and interest, which traditionally meant ignoring the latter the better to pursue the former and recently seems to mean the converse, also has to be superseded by critical theory.[8] The interests guiding critical theory can be identified at the most abstract level by those ideas and ideals of reason that Hoy dismisses as "utopian." He does not inquire why the classical pragmatists felt it important to invoke similar ideas in their theorizing, such as Peirce's ideas of the "faith, hope, and charity" that inform rational inquiry or Mead's idea of the "universal discourse" that serves as its normative horizon. Nor does he consider that the sorts of critique he favors are guided by utopian ideals of one sort or another, such as Rorty's dream of a "postmodernist liberalism" or Foucault's hope that "everyone's life [could] become a work of art."[9] Nor, finally, does he acknowledge that his own hermeneutic conception of a decentered "pluralistic dialogue" is another such ideal.

These utopian conceptions are surely no less "vague" than the ideas and ideals that have guided critical social theory. And like them, they are not meant to replace but to inform critical histories of the present, which like critical theories, may take their normative orientations from such ideas.[10] Hoy's objections to them are actually objections against their misuse, for example, against the dangerous illusion of a "thoroughly planned society" (p. 111). It is precisely to head off these misuses that I insisted in my statement on the regulative character of such ideas, and on their negative and critical – as well as their positive and guiding – significance. It is for the same reason that Habermas stresses their formal and procedural, in contrast to material and substantive, character. The idea of organizing our lives together on the basis of uncoerced agreements, arrived at in free and equal exchanges, by considering reasons pro and con, is not the depiction of any concrete utopia. But neither is it empty: whether individuals and societies are committed to this idea makes an enormous difference. As Hoy notes disapprovingly, Kant proposed that we act as if it were realizable in some future world and our actions could contribute to that realization (p. 117). Critical theory could do worse than retaining that practical faith and the utopian impulse that animates it.

## 7.2  Genealogy

In chapter 5 of his opening statement, Hoy plays Foucault's genealogical approach off against Habermas's reconstructive approach, much to the latter's disadvantage. His main target there is the theory of social evolution, which makes the encounter less than ideal, as that is not meant to be the *critical* edge of Habermas's enterprise. If one compares genealogical histories written with critical intent to developmental logics set out with reconstructive intent, and does so from the standpoint of critique, then the outcome is largely predecided. More to the point would be a comparison of genealogy to the sorts of theoretically informed critiques that one finds in Habermas's work from *The Structural Transformation of the Public Sphere* to the *Theory of Communicative Action*. In the latter, for instance, it is clear that developmental-logical considerations are meant in the end to serve the purposes of a critique of contemporary society. Thus the largely reconstructive treatment of rationality in chapter I is followed in chapter II by a discussion of Max Weber's account of the "iron cage" forged by rationalization processes; and the reconstructive chapter III is followed in chapter IV by a discussion of views of rationalization as reification from Lukács to Adorno. This pattern roughly continues until the work culminates in Habermas's well-known diagnosis of the ills of contemporary society in terms of a colonization of the lifeworld by the system. Along the way he indicates quite clearly just how he wants to utilize, for purposes of critique, the reconstructive and developmental considerations he introduces. For example, in his critical appropriation of the Weberian themes of the loss of meaning and freedom, his guiding idea is the *selectivity* of capitalist modernization, the failure of modern societies to actualize and institutionalize in a balanced way *all* the dimensions of reason available in modern cultures.[11] And in developing that idea, he uses his reflections on sociocultural evolution as an interpretive frame. It is this type of use for purposes of social critique that is the proper object of comparison with Foucault's genealogy.

When the comparison is made in this way, the "either/or" divides dominating the topography of Hoy's argument begin to narrow. On the one side, it becomes clear that Habermas too is interested in critically interpreting the present for the sake of identifying possibilities closed off in the past. On the other side, it begins to appear that Foucault too relies on general and abstract "metatheories" and interpretive frames to write his large-scale, critical narratives of the present. The differences between them become matters of which and how rather than whether or not. In what follows I will sketch the bare outlines of such a critical comparison, not because everything turns on "who wins, Habermas or Foucault," but because the issues Hoy raises are so diverse and complex that I couldn't hope to address them except by proposing a different comparative perspective.

Looking at the trajectory of critical social theory since its appropriation of Max Weber, we find that its basic direction is quite similar to Foucault's in an important respect: it aims to understand the ways in which reason and rationality have been socially constructed, as a means of achieving a critical self-understanding with implications for practice. From Lukács through Horkheimer and Adorno to Habermas, there has never been the slightest doubt that rationalization processes are not a story of unmitigated progress but a "dialectic of enlightenment." The real differences with Foucault concern whether there is at all a positive side to the story, an emancipatory dimension of enlightenment. I want to recall here what I argued in my opening statement concerning the many facets of rationalization that the radical critics of reason take for granted. That applies to Hoy as well. He invokes a distinction between matters for empirical research and the claims of metaphysics; he draws at every turn on the results of nineteenth-century historical enlightenment and twentieth-century anthropological enlightenment; he assumes the possibility and the right to call into question inherited beliefs, values, practices, and identities; he treats as more or less obvious the equal respect due to *all* individuals – to mention only a few of the more obvious aspects of cultural rationalization that he, if sometimes only implicitly, plainly relies upon as positive achievements. On this general issue, then, it is difficult to see how Hoy and Foucault can make sense of their critical enterprises without themselves adopting some version of the dialectic of enlightenment.

As to more specific issues, the opposition between internal and external critique that Hoy frequently invokes seems to me to cut precisely in the opposite direction from what he suggests. No one in this debate claims an extramundane, God's-eye standpoint from which to view the whole of history, society, and culture. So the opposition must turn on distinguishing critical approaches within the world. There are any number of different ways in which the key distinction may be drawn. Some of the more promising, it seems to me, build on a hermeneutic distinction that Hoy adopts: the distinction between talking about people as if they were mere objects of interpretation and talking with them as cosubjects of interpretation. In Habermas's frame of reference, this connects with the question of whether or not the interpreter takes seriously the validity claims raised by those she is trying to understand. Foucault, the genealogist, positions himself at the extreme externalist end of this spectrum. Practices in which participants raise claims to reason, truth, justice, authenticity, and the like are not merely reflectively distanced but represented in an optics of estrangement that wholly undercuts participants' spontaneous understandings of what they are up to. By contrast, Habermas, the reconstructionist, takes seriously such claims to validity and attempts to spell out their internal logics, including their pragmatic presuppositions, and their practical implications. As a critic, however, he combines this with techniques of objectification and estrangement; but, unlike Foucault's, they are never meant to be the last word. And that, it seems to me, is the central issue. Neither genealogy nor critical theory wants to cede to the participants and their traditions the only say about the significance of the practices they engage in. Both see the need for gaining some distance from "insider's" views and adopting some form of "outsider's" perspective; and both believe that historical accounts of how and why purportedly rational practices came to be taken for granted serve this purpose. But whereas the genealogist resolutely brackets the validity claims embedded in practices, the better to objectify them, the critical theorist tries to reconstruct and critically engage those claims. As Hoy himself wants in the end to combine the external perspective peculiar to genealogy with the internal perspective proper to hermeneutics, I will not belabor this point but will turn to his objections specifically against Hegelian-Marxist ways of combining them.

His disagreements with the idea of determinate negation are basically two: he rejects the claims to *necessity* and to *superiority* he sees inherent in it. As to the former, few critical social theorists would today claim any necessity for the historical developments they trace, and Habermas is certainly not among them.[12] As Hoy himself refers to passages in which Habermas explicitly renounces any such claim (p. 158), the real issue must lie elsewhere. If one examines Hoy's objections closely, they seem to target Habermas's claim that there is an underlying *logic* to patterns of sociocultural change, stages of development that have to be passed through if a society is to get from one point to another.[13] But that has to do only with *conditional* necessity. In any case, as the line of argument set out in my opening statement depends only on the "weaker" sorts of claim Hoy attributes to MacIntyre (pp. 155–6), it is not committed to necessity in any of the senses Hoy finds objectionable.

The more important disagreement concerns the progressivist implications of developmental claims. Hoy argues for dropping any and all "Whiggish" notions of superiority in favor of the less offensive notion of difference. But this is inconsistent with his larger view of the contemporary situation, as the term "postmodern" suggests. The superiority he claims for his own genealogical hermeneutics rests on taking for granted the "progressive" nature of the fruits of rationalization I mentioned above, and much else besides. It is because he is convinced that we know more and better about the historical variability and cultural diversity of forms of life, about the linguistically mediated character of thought and action, about the contingency and contextuality of rational practices, and the like, that he considers traditional metaphysics, classical rationalism, and transcendental philosophy no longer to be viable options for us. It would be impossible for him to get his argument off the ground without assuming that we had *learned* something in those respects. For, after all, the bare-bones schema for learning processes amounts to no more than this: if $y$ is superior to $x$ in some respect, and a culture, group, or individual comes to appreciate that over time, it may be said to have learned something. Neither Hoy nor any other postmodernist critic can wholly reject this notion of learning and still make sense of his critical enterprise. And if that is so, it is surely legitimate, and may well be important, for critical theorists to think seriously about the nature of socio-cultural learning processes.

This Habermas does in his theory of social evolution. As I have explained elsewhere, I have my own reservations concerning that theory.[14] But I do not think that the problems lie where Hoy sees them, and so I shall confine my remarks to refocusing the discussion.[15] As it will turn out, the points at issue are largely of an empirical-theoretical nature and thus cannot be decided by conceptual fiat. To begin with, though Habermas does say that "in a certain way it is only socialized subjects that learn," he immediately adds that "social systems can, by exploiting [individuals'] learning capacities, form new structures."[16] The main aim of his theory is precisely to comprehend how the accomplishments of individual learning processes get more widely disseminated and become part of the shared worldviews of groups in a society, how such advances in cultural knowledge can then figure in social struggles, and how, under certain circumstances, they can be drawn upon to transform the existing institutional order.[17] In a word, the theory of social evolution aims to understand broad cultural and societal developments and *not* the appearance of "higher types of individuals," and particularly not of the "rare genius" (p. 154). Moreover, it focuses only on selected aspects of large-scale changes. Thus, as Hoy notes (p. 159), it does not imply that society as a whole progresses, that life gets better and better. Rather, "progress" takes the more limited form of advances in specific cultural dimensions (e.g., in science and technology, law and morality, or art and art criticism), in the institutionalization of learning processes in those dimensions (e.g., in research laboratories, universities, legal systems, or institutions for the production, dissemination, and criticism of art), and in the exploitation of such cultural advances for social-structural transformations. Hoy does not focus his objections on these developmental claims. Rather, his most sustained criticisms target the idea that we can speak of progress in regard to *self-interpretations* (e.g., p. 202). A distinction has to be made here. Habermas does indeed regard certain epochal shifts in collective identity as advances (e.g., from clan-based through state-centered to more abstract forms of identity); but at any one of these very general "developmental-logical" levels, there is room for an indefinite proliferation of particular collective self-interpretations. To make his point against Habermas's developmental approach, Hoy would have to be willing to argue, for instance, that in-group/out-group self-understandings in terms of religious fundamentalism, ethnic purity, neonationalism, and the like are, in general, neither superior nor inferior to the sort of tolerant, live-and-let-live self-understanding he pleads for. And that would be neither theoretially consistent nor practically sound.

What does all this have to do with genealogy or with critical historiography more generally? Habermas is emphatic in rejecting the notion that particular histories could be written as *applications* of general theories, whether theories of social evolution or of contemporary society. He does, however, hold that such theories can serve as *interpretive frameworks* for writing histories.[18] Hoy rejects this in the name of Foucault's (rhetorical) insistence on the local and particular. But Foucault's (actually existing) historical studies usually deal with epochal shifts from one "age," "episteme," "regime," or the like to another, often reaching from the Renaissance to the present, and sometimes, as in the *History of Sexuality*, even spanning the distance to the Ancient World. Perhaps it will be argued that while his genealogies are not "local," they are "specific." Sweeping histories of madness, sickness, punishment, and sexuality, especially when written as keys to the history of reason, truth, subjectivity, and the like, may be more "specific" than general theories of sociocultural development, but it is hard to see that they are more specific than, say, Weber's accounts of the rationalization of religion, law, and administration, or than the Frankfurt School's studies of authority and the family, music and art, mass culture, anti-Semitism, the authoritarian state, law and legal procedure, punishment, and state capitalism, or, for that matter, than Habermas's account of the structural transformation of the public sphere. The point of this line of argument is simply to establish that the differences at issue cannot be captured by the abstract opposition "history versus theory." Critical social theorists from Marx to Habermas have aimed, in the end, at social-theoretically informed critical histories of the present.

There is, to be sure, a difference from Foucault in their explicit elaboration of social-theoretical frames of interpretation. But Foucault's genealogies are hardly theory-free. In the 1970s, for instance, his "metatheory" of the internal relations between power and knowledge served as a general framework within which his critical histories were written. Then, too, there was the vaguely functionalist perspective implicit in his scattered remarks on just why it was that new regimes came to replace the old.[19] Beyond these, there were the (abstract and general) interpretive schemes that Foucault himself proposed from time to time.[20] My point is simply that the notion of "pure" genealogy is a myth. In his historical studies Foucault routinely made use of various general schemes, frames, pictures, perspectives, and the like, which were not so different in level or function from those used in critical social theory. And this should come as no surprise, for what Foucault is after in his genealogies is a "history of reason," of "the forms of rationality and knowledge," and of "the rational subject."[21] He wants to understand how "matters stand with the history of reason, with the ascendency of reason, and with the different forms in which the ascendency operates." And this, as he notes, is "the same question" that drives "the current of thought from Max Weber to Critical Theory . . . from Max Weber to Habermas."[22] They, like him, wanted to show that "the form of rationality presented as dominant, and endowed with the status of the one-and-only reason . . . is only *one* possible form among others."[23] But he, unlike them, holds that reason is "self-created," and so "you cannot assign a point at which reason would have lost sight of its fundamental project."[24] This, I think, is a more helpful situating of his similarities to and differences from the Weberian Marxism of the Frankfurt School. The issue between them is not whether to pursue general histories of rationality or to restrict oneself instead to particular local histories, but rather how best to write general histories. In deciding that issue, we cannot avoid comparatively evaluating the different metatheories and inter-pretive schemes that inform their approaches to the history of the present. I see no inherent virtue in leaving them largely implicit rather than working them out and assessing them, in both empirical and normative respects. My own view is that Foucault's powerful insights and techniques do not require, and indeed are not even compatible with, either his ontology of power or his totalistic conceptions of society, and that they can be developed more fruitfully as a continua-tion of, rather than as an alternative to, critical social theory.[25]

## 7.3  Hermeneutics

This repositioning of Habermas vis-à-vis Foucault may serve as well to refocus his differences with Gadamer. As we saw, like Foucault he aspires to a critical history of the present written with the practical-political intent of promoting a different future. But unlike Foucault, he holds that the interpretive frames they both rely upon in practice should be made explicit and subjected to ongoing scrutiny. In his view, the latter include general accounts of reason and rationality, of societal structures and processes, and of major transformations in the history of culture and society. And this view has implications for his relation to hermeneutics as well, for it implies that there is no intrin-sic virtue in leaving the background of interpretive activity in pristine indeterminacy. Granted, as Hoy argues, that the background can never be rendered completely determinate (p. 161), we can nevertheless try to articulate some of its key elements and expose them to critical examination. And since very different assumptions on very important matters often do inform the conflicting interpretations of Foucault,

Gadamer, Habermas, and other participants in the discourse of modernity, there is every good reason to do so. Our hermeneutic starting point ineluctably figures in our selection of key phenomena, the angle of vision we adopt on them, the categorial frame in which we articulate them, the judgements of significance we make about them, the connections we draw among them, and so on. When it includes broad views of the sorts just discussed, that has consequences for the kind of future we anticipate, the standpoint we adopt on the present, the way we understand our past, and the sense of community – the "we" – that we identify with. Such systematically generalized views are meant, then, not to replace interpretation and narrative but to inform and enrich them. They are *per se* neither too empty nor too thin to make a difference. And they certainly do not restrict the historian to writing "affirmative" narratives; in fact, it was Habermas's insistence on a *critical* historiography that was at the heart of his debate with Gadamer.[26] And Hoy's present efforts to conceive a genea-logized hermeneutics might well be taken as an admission of sorts that he was right, that Gadamer's own conception of hermeneutics was conservatively slanted. But I will not pursue these intellectual-historical questions here. I want to focus instead on some of the claims Hoy raises for and about hermeneutics.

"No one," he writes, "should aspire any longer to a social theory that transcends its own socio-historical context and makes universal validity claims . . . [P]hilosophical hermeneutics . . . insists on the context-boundedness of understanding and sees theories . . . as contingent social actions themselves" (p. 172). I noted above that contingency is opposed to necessity and not to universality. (Physical theories are no less the product of contingent social actions than social theories, but that does not prevent them from plausibly claiming universal valid-ity.) I also contended that universality should not be confused with infallibility, and that claims to universal validity are especially exposed to criticism and refutation. Finally, I recommended that we distinguish the various types of theoretical knowledge that enter into our interpretive frames from the concrete interpretations they inform. The issue that remains, it seems to me, is whether interpretations or the theories that inform them can and should claim a validity beyond the context in which they are put forward. As I want to focus now on interpretation, I shall simply repeat my contention that neither the necessity nor the desirability of abandoning the type of general social theory associated with the classical tradition has been convincingly argued. If put forward in a self-consciously fallibilistic spirit, the claims of general theories to context-transcending validity are at the same time an invitation to criticism from all sides: they carry only if and insofar as they can stand up to critical discussion. The more general the claim, the broader the invitation to join the discussion, and the greater the burden of justification on the claimant. Given this non-absolutist conception of theory, it is not clear how Hoy and other contextualists could object to any theoretical practice *in advance of*, or independently of, a consideration of its viability and usefulness. In the final section of this response, I shall consider some of Hoy's objections to tying any validity claim to expections of universal consensus. For the present I will stick to issues of interpretation.

When used to cover everything from what are usually referred to as general theories to attempts at individual self-clarification, the term "interpretation" suffers greatly from indeterminacy. Analogies with "texts" and the "reading of texts" have been broadened to include just about every sort of cultural activity. This may have had some salutary effects in wringing the last gasps of life out of foundationalism, scientism, non-internal realism, ahistorical logocentrism, and the like, but it has also brought on a night in which everything appears an indistinguishable grey. Properly to assess the claims Hoy raises concerning the logic of interpretation – and they are, it should be noted, quite general claims – we would have to distinguish among very different types of interpretation – for instance, those dealing literally with texts from those dealing with various sorts of text analogues, within the former among religious, legal, philosophical, scientific, fictional, etc. texts, within the latter among historical, social, cultural, economic, political, psychological, etc. text analogues, and so on and so forth. And then in each type we would have to distinguish further the different sorts of interpretations constructed in different contexts for different purposes. At present, I shall confine myself to a few remarks on two broad types of interpretation Hoy singles out: critical history and self-understanding. The points I wish to stress are, first, that such interpretations are susceptible to critical-reflective examination and, second, that they can be examined under different aspects.

With regard to the former, the notions of "proliferation" and "multiplicity" that Hoy opposes to the idea of "one right interpretation" should be taken to mean not that "anything goes" but rather that "more than one thing goes" (p. 201). Since he retains the regulative idea of consistency in interpretation (p. 178), he will have to allow for conflicts of interpretation and for critical-reflective discourses dealing with them. If we were to understand those discourses, broadly speaking, in MacIntyre's terms, which Hoy does not rule out (p. 156), the conflicts would be expressed in familiar types of argument concerning the pros and cons of competing interpretations. In the case of historical interpretations, the burdens of such argument are not light, for one of the principal aspects under which historians debate their differences is a concern with truth. Denied the appeal to truth, with its attendant prescriptions concerning a critical use of sources and the like, historiographical discourse would be immensely impoverished, if not rendered simply incoherent.[27] Nevertheless, experience has shown that that appeal often does not suffice to eliminate all but "one right interpretation." And philosophical hermeneutics, with its rich elaborations of effective-historical consciousness, the hermeneutic circle, the interpretive standpoint with its preconceptions and pre-judgements, and the like, has contributed mightily to our understanding of why this should be the case. As for my disagreements with Hoy, they do not turn on denying the possibility, desirability, or even necessity of offering ever-new interpretations of the past from ever-changing points of view in the present and orientations toward the future. They have to do, rather, with the conditions under which this sort of proliferation should transpire. Relatively few historical interpretations manage to stand up to the pressures of critical-reflective examination. And the differences among those that do are often differences of perspective, interest, emphasis, and the like, that is, the sorts of differences that might possibly be reconciled in a more comprehensive interpretation. According to Gadamer, it is some such regulative idea of completeness, of an ideal unity of sense, that structures historiographical discourse.

Hoy allows that such a "critical monism" regarding interpretations might reasonably be held, but he regards its regulative ideas as "empty" and thus prefers to adopt a "critical pluralism" (p. 200). At least in the field of historical interpretation, which he singles out, the ideas of completeness and unity or coherence seem anything but empty. For one thing, they are an important impetus to the proliferation that Hoy espouses. They spur historians ongoingly to examine and re-examine materials from ever-changing points of view and thereby to produce new historical accounts, ongoingly to test the consistency of those accounts against the expanses of historical research regarded as "well established" and to adjust for inconsistencies in one way or another, and ongoingly to construct more comprehensive accounts that integrate novel insights into a coherent sense of the whole. They also serve to instigate the sorts of challenge to claimed unity and completeness characteristic of genealogical and deconstructionist historiography. Hegel taught us long ago that the dialectic lives from such claims. Without them, I am afraid, we would likely drift into an uncritical pluralism of "whatever serves your purposes, whatever they may be." The point of stressing the regulative character of these ideas is to turn attention away from metaphysical issues and toward questions of

historiographical practice: with what idealizing assumptions do historians normally work and what would their discourses look like if they
tried to do without them? Can we write *history* – in contrast, say, to
fiction, propaganda, or rationalization – without being oriented to the
idea of truth? And can we be so oriented without getting into just the
sorts of debates that historians, including critical historians, typically
engage in? These are the kinds of questions for which Hoy will have
to find convincing answers if he is to persuade us to de-emphasize the
idea of truth in favor of that of usefulness, and the idea of coherent
unity in favor of that of proliferation. A more dialectical approach
might suggest that we should trace the internal relations between such
seemingly opposed pairs.

Part of the explanation for Hoy's emphasis on pluralism is the
context in which he discusses the idea of a genealogical hermeneutics.
The interest that guides him is fundamentally an ethical one: self-
understanding as a key to the good life. Unlike Aristotle, he no longer
believes that there is, in general, one right path to the good life. The
pluralism of forms of social life and the individualism of forms of
personal life have rendered that view implausible in the contemporary world. Unlike Gadamer, he is also skeptical of the idea that un-
broken traditions might be hermeneutically continued so as to furnish
culturally specific, yet normative, conceptions of the good life. He
holds instead to the (late-) Foucaultian idea that each individual's life
might be a work of art, and from that perspective he rejects the idea of
a general self-understanding that is normative for all members of the
species or of a culture. I have argued elsewhere that the aesthetics of
personal existence is an inadequate ethical-political response to a
world in which misery and injustice are rampant.[28] If aspirations to
self-invention are to be limited by considerations of justice, we have
to ask what kinds of social orders will put such limits into effect and
how those limits can be justified to those who are supposed to feel
bound by them. To be sure, Hoy is also in favor of an overarching
framework of justice; but that then demands its own reflective elaboration. We also have to investigate the social, economic, political, and
cultural conditions that perpetuate misery and injustice and render
the chances of making one's life into a work of art very different at
different societal locations. And for that we need a critical theory of
contemporary society at the level of Marx's *Capital* or Habermas's
*Theory of Communicative Action*, which enables us to view universal
justice and individual goods in complementary rather than opposi-
tional terms. Although Hoy does not address himself to these general
levels of practical reasoning, he cannot do without it if he does not
want his pluralism to degenerate into a war of all against all.

I have used the – admittedly vague – term "theory" to characterize some of the elements missing from Hoy's approach to critical thinking, because I want to stress that they have in principle to be defended in free and open discussion with any and all interlocutors. That is, the claims to validity of theories of justice or of contemporary society or of social evolution are not context-bound in the way that Hoy insists "social-theoretical interpretations" inevitably are (p. 172). Such theories can legitimately be contested from standpoints outside the context in which they originate, precisely because they claim a general validity on grounds that no competent, well-informed person could reasonably reject. The same cannot be said for the *self*-interpretations that are the crux of Hoy's argument. The self-understandings that figure in personal and collective identities are indeed context-bound in ways that general theories are not. *All* intellectual activity is, to be sure "contingent social action" (p. 172) and as such "bound" in some sense to the context in which it is carried out. But it is a fateful *non sequitur* to suppose that this ontological condition suffices to show that the meaning and validity of the claims that arise from the various activities are all tied *in the same way* to their contexts of origin – as if there were not important differences between such "contingent" activities as doing mathematics, physics, history, or criticism. We have to attend in each case to the nature of the reasoning involved, the scope of the audience intended, the sorts of considerations that are relevant, the types of criticisms that have to be faced, and so on. In the case of collective self-interpretations, there are specific ways in which deliberation remains context-bound.[29] Public discussion of such matters typically takes place within the horizons of shared histories, traditions, forms of life. The cogency or persuasive power of the considerations offered in support of different views derives in significant measure from those shared backgrounds. The intended audience is the "we" projected in the proposed self-interpretation. And the basic concern is with who "we" are and who "we" want to be. But this does not mean that there are no universalizable *aspects* of such discussions.

As Hoy notes, traditions typically comprise conflicts of interpretations; they are ambiguous and often divided legacies that can be taken up and continued in very different ways. And as Gadamer has convincingly argued, the sorts of historical self-understanding involved have practical – ethical and political – implications. The question of who "we" have been is intimately linked with those of who "we" are and who "we" want to be. In Heidegger's parlance, identity is a matter of "thrown projection," in which past, present, and future are inextricably intertwined. That our relation to the past is interpretively mediated does not mean, however, that it has nothing to do with truth claims.[30] At least since historical scholarship became animated with nationalistic aspirations in the last century, debates concerning "*wie es eigentlich gewesen war*" have been part and parcel of collective identity formation. And it has been particularly important to *critical* hermeneutics that public self-understandings can *also* be scrutinized under this aspect. To take a recent example, Habermas's intervention in the German *Historikerstreit* turned importantly on issues of truth in combatting the attempt by conservative politicians and their historian allies to rewrite German history for purposes of "putting the National Socialist past behind us."[31] Questions concerning the causes, nature, and scope of the Holocaust were central to that debate, as were questions concerning the extent of support enjoyed by the National Socialist regime, its main war aims (particularly as regards the Soviet Union), the behavior of the German Army on the Eastern Front in 1944/45, the ways in which the German citizenry did and did not "come to terms with the past" in the 1950s, and so on. It was absolutely crucial to blocking the effort to "normalize" the past for purposes of reestablishing continuity with a superseded political identity that it could be thematized under the aspect of historical truth: did it or did it not measure up to international standards of historical scholarship.

It was also important that the revisionary undertaking could be discussed under context-transcending aspects of right; for the identity the revisionist historians aimed to shore up involved strongly contextualized notions of responsibility. Is it right, for example, to interpret the events of that period from the perspective of daily life, personal experience, local community, and the like, so as to cramp the vision of nationally organized horrors? Is it right to place the sufferings of the Jews on a moral par with that of the Germans? Is it right to put the fascist past behind us now the better to get on with the business of the present? Is it right to project a future centered on German exceptionalism, its "middle-European" geopolitical position, and its "cultural" distance from the "civilization" of the West and its heritage of universal rights and principles? These questions are illustrative of the important role that aspects of moral, legal, and political right can, do, and should play in public processes of collective self-interpretation. Projected group identities can be criticized not only for lies, distortions, and half-truths about the past, but also for the unfairness they show and the harm they do to minorities within and strangers without. The power of the critical interpretations developed in connection with the contemporary politics of identity, it seems to me, also depends crucially on the context-transcending import of these two aspects of self-understanding, truth and rightness.

Though viable group-identities have to respect claims to truth and justice – if for no other reason than to avoid making themselves easy targets in the public conflicts of interpretation that are increasingly typical of ethical-political deliberations in pluralistic and democratic societies – they certainly cannot be derived from them. For identities are as Hoy says irreducibly plural, and that plurality is bound up with the incalculable diversity of individual and group life-histories and forms of life. This is also the case with "truthful" and "righteous" identities, that is, those incorporating a respect for and orientation to truth and justice. These are not the only publicly debatable aspects of self-interpretations. Questions of well-being, self-fulfillment, and authenticity, while not context-transcending in the same way, are no less arguable. The fact that we no longer expect them to have one right answer for everybody, does not render public deliberation about them pointless. Practical reasoning in a particular context is still practical *reasoning*; and insofar as the context is common to the parties to the discussion, the cogency of reasons or their lack of it is an intersubjective matter. While Hoy acknowledges the conflicts of interpretation at the heart of virtually every tradition, he tends, like most contextualists, to treat the recognition of difference as the end of the story rather than as the beginning of discussion and debate, which, as Mill famously reminded us, are the lifeblood of cultural and political affairs in a democratic society. Public disagreements are played out in the public sphere. Members of the "we" assumed or projected in public discussion can enter the fray, contest the ideals and strong evaluations appealed to, argue that a proposed arrangement is not, all things considered, good for "us" in the long run, criticize the conception of who "we" are and want to be that is behind it, unmask the illusions or self-deceptions involved in it, and so on. Thus, in the German historians debate, in addition to questions of truth and justice, issues of these latter sorts figured prominently. Do we (Germans) really want to reestablish continuity with *those* aspects of our heritage? Or with others? And how? Should German identity center around particularities of German culture and tradition or be oriented more strongly to values and principles shared with other democratic, pluralistic societies? Should the anti-Communism Germans share with the latter be taken as more basic to their identity than commitments to the rule of law, popular sovereignty, or international justice? Should post-War generations spend less time talking about the past and get on with their lives, or should they somehow assume responsibility for it and try to come to terms with it? The notion of responsibility does not figure centrally in the aesthetics of self-making, particularly not that of our responsibilities to others. This is a fatal flaw.

Individual identities are formed in and through social relations, group identities are shaped in complex webs of cultural interaction and social interdependency, and local identities are increasingly refracted through global networks. In a world in which larger and larger waves of politically and economically driven migrants press or are pressed against the walls of national identities, eighteenth-century cosmopolitanism seems a better starting point for thinking about collective identity.

## 7.4  Pluralism

It should be evident by now that critical theory of the Habermasian sort is in no way "opposed to pluralism" (p. 200). It simply refuses to equate it with "anything goes" and insists that an acceptable pluralism requires an overarching framework of justice, so that one group's well-being does not come at the expense of another's. In Hoy's argument, the suggestion that critical social theory is somehow unfriendly to pluralism is tied to Habermas's explication of the meaning of validity in terms of rationally motivated consensus. Once again, it will be important to resituate the issues before addressing them. To begin with, Habermas has consistently restricted the focus of his analysis of justification to *discourse* – critical, reflective, argumentative dialogue – *about questions of truth and justice*. He does not claim, and in fact explicitly denies, that suppositions of like universality attach to critique or textual interpretation, or to discussions of ethics, politics, identity, and the good life. In such matters, differences in context and perspective do influence the form and substance of deliberation in ways that restrict the scope of claims to validity – for instance, to claims about who *we* are and want to be, about what is good *for us* in the long run, or the like.[32] Furthermore, even in those types of discourse which Habermas does see as structured by a supposition of there being one right answer – so that two conflicting views cannot both be correct – he does not treat consensus as *determining* validity.[33] "Social agreement" is not the "arbitrator of validity" (p. 174), nor is validity "founded on consensus" (p. 177). Thus the contrast that Hoy draws between Gadamer's privileging of *die Sache*, what is being talked about, and Habermas's privileging of agreement among those talking is misleading (pp. 189–90). Both *Verständigung* and *die Sache* figure centrally in *both* analyses: dialogue and discourse are oriented toward achieving mutual understanding *concerning* the matter under discussion.

Habermas's discourse theory of validity is not meant to *define* either truth or moral rightness but to offer an account of what is involved in "redeeming" or *justifying* truth and rightness claims.[34] Cast in epistemic rather than in ontological terms, it attempts to elucidate the pragmatic presuppositions of the critical-reflective discourses in which such claims are debated. And it is in that context that notions like rational assertability, rational acceptability, and agreement under ideal conditions figure. Hoy asks us to choose between the view that "agreeing to something makes it true" – "truth as the result of agreement" – and the view that "we agree to something because it is true" – "agreement as the result of truth" (p. 189). But there is quite a bit of space between these two poles, and it is there that we will find Habermas. As Hoy himself acknowledges, our only access to the *Sache* and the truth about it is through language. Thus neither can be set over against agreement in language, either the global sorts of agreement that Wittgenstein held to be presuppositions of making sense at all, or the more domain-specific sorts of agreement that we rely on in regard to this or that subject matter. In domains of inquiry in which critical-reflective discourse has been institutionalized, the achievement of agreement rests on an argumentative weighing of reasons pro and con. There, it is not because we agree that we judge a claim to be valid; rather, we agree because we have grounds for granting its validity. It is not the agreement that warrants the claim but the warrants for the claim that ground the agreement. To make his case against Habermas on this point, Hoy would have to explain how truth can produce agreement in a way that is not epistemically mediated through evidence and argument. But that would be inconsistent with his own hermeneutic position.

Where does this leave us? The real issue, it seems to me, is whether critical-reflective discourse about claims to truth and justice rests on the pragmatic presupposition of there being one right answer, to which any reasonable, well-informed person could rationally agree under ideal conditions. Spelling out such conditions is, of course, notoriously problematic.[35] But that is not my concern here, since Hoy objects to the very idea of there being an internal relation between truth or rightness and universal acceptability, no matter under what conditions. I argued in my opening statement that scientific discourse about the objective world is guided by the supposition of there being one truth about the world, and I will not repeat that argument here. The challenge it presents to Hoy is to provide an alternative, more plausible reconstruction of scientific discourse that does not include that supposition. The more difficult cases for my position are truth claims about the *human* world, and many of the difficulties lie parallel to two questions that Hoy analytically distinguishes and then ("contingently") reconnects: (1) whether there is only one right understanding of a sociohistorical "text," and (2) whether sociocultural differences call for a higher community with shared principles (p. 178). I will follow his analytical distinction in my response.

(a) The key issue in what Hoy calls the "hermeneutical question" is one that divided Habermas and Gadamer in their influential exchange. Habermas aspired to a *theory* of communicative action, by which he meant at least the following: a coherent set of truth claims about the social world, which have to be defended against reasoned criticism from whatever quarter. The latter is part of what is meant by saying that their validity is context-transcending. Does Hoy think we can do without theoretical, context-transcending truth claims altogether? Not entirely. He acknowledges the "paradoxical" nature of the "metatheoretical" claims that make up the core of his reply, for they are themselves context-transcending claims about the nature of truth, meaning, interpretation, historicity, and the like. As we saw, that paradox is typical of contextualist arguments generally. Hoy handles the appearance of contradiction by distinguishing metatheories from first-order theories or interpretations. While the former may properly claim context-transcending validity, the latter may not (p. 201). But this claim itself depends on his metatheory being the right one, and thus is not the end but the beginning of disagreement. Moreover, the considerations that Hoy advances in defense of his metatheory look suspiciously like *substantive* claims about language, interpretation, and so forth. That should come as no surprise, for there is a long history of failed attempts to distinguish "meta" from "object" languages. What we in fact have are two competing, substantive accounts of certain aspects of sociocultural life, each claiming to be not just "true for us" but "true, period." And if those substantive claims can legitimately aspire to context-transcending validity, there is no obvious reason why others may not as well. Nor is Hoy's metatheory neutral with respect to "first-order" interpretations. It implies, for instance, that any interpretation which fails to recognize the variability of forms of life or the interpretational nature of worldviews and self-understanding is inadequate, for it conflicts with central insights of the (one right) metatheory.

The fact that postmodernist thinkers invariably suppose much of what they are denying is of particular significance in an argument *about* unavoidable presuppositions. Be that as it may, Hoy might want to argue that whatever presuppositions the genealogical hermeneut does rely upon, they do not include the expectation of rationally motivated consensus. And here, it seems to me, we have the nub of his criticism of Habermas. Reasoned discourse about the human world has, since Socrates, been structured around the assumption that one view of a given matter (*Sache*) is better than competing views, and that argumentation, if carried out properly, will show us in the long run which it is – which has the preponderance of reasons on its side. If this supposition were dropped, the nature of discursive activity would change significantly; and that would have practical consequences, for in many areas of life there are no clear alternatives to reasoned discourse of the familiar sorts. At the same time, discussions about the human world often seem interminable. We have gotten used to living with unresolved disagreements in all the "human sciences," where what Kuhn calls the "preparadigmatic" stage seems never to be superseded by "normal science," as regularly happens in the natural sciences. We even have plausible explanations of why this should be the case, and they turn on the ineliminable interpretive dimension of social inquiry and the standpoint-bound character of interpretation.[36] Hoy insists on these same features and concludes that we have to drop the supposition that there is a unique truth about the human world. Is there no alternative?

I argued above that historical interpretations can and should be critically examined under the aspect of their truth to the facts.[37] The same holds for interpretations of the social world generally. Hoy will point out that this is normally not sufficient to eliminate all but one interpretation of a given domain of phenomena, precisely because of the standpoint-boundness or contextuality of interpretive activity. "An interpretation," he notes, "can only illuminate at the cost of shading over or leaving out. . . . [This] does not imply . . . that all interpretations misrepresent what they are about. They capture aspects of the *Sache* correctly, but the *Sache* is more complex than any single interpretation can possibly be" (p. 191). This is true. But if one adds the regulative constraints of consistency and coherence, then the space for an "irreducible plurality" of equally good interpretations considerably narrows: for an interpretation to stand up over time to critical scrutiny, it will have not only to square with the agreed upon facts and the accepted methods for determining them, but will have to be internally consistent and cohere with everything else we think we know about the domain under consideration, or it will have to defend its failure to do so by challenging elements (including purported facts) of the established consensus. The conflict of interpretations in history and the social sciences is normally carried out under just such constraints. They are what structure the conflict as a reasoned discourse, as a debate about which is the best interpretation, all things considered. And yet, the debate frequently fails to end in consensus;

there often remains a plurality of viable candidates for "the best interpretation." But the pragmatically important point is not that discourse should always lead to rational agreement, but that it should be carried out *as if* rational agreement about which is the right, or at least the best, interpretation were possible. The pluralism that then remains is not that of self-encapsulated, incommensurable points of view, but of different voices in an ongoing discursive consideration of the reasons for and against competing views. That is to say, it is a critical pluralism closer to what John Stuart Mill espoused than to the cultural archipelagos envisioned by radical contextualists.

(*b*) It is not clear to me in which of these directions Hoy wants to go. He expressly recommends a critical pluralism (p. 200). But some of his arguments seem to undercut it, for instance, the suggestion that to claim one's views are right or better than competing views borders on intolerance, disrespect, and ethnocentrism (p. 203). If rational discourse about what is true or morally right presupposes an ideal of uncoerced consensus, and if we believe we have good reasons for our beliefs, then, he argues, we have to suppose that ideally others should agree with us – and that is ethnocentric. But *all* parties come to the discussion thinking they have good reasons for holding the beliefs they do. Respect for opposing views is shown not by granting, prior to any discussion, that they are just as good as one's own but by listening carefully to them, trying honestly to understand them, weighing fairly the grounds on which they are held, and being open to the possibility that they *may* prove superior to one's own. This is what one expects, ideally, from all parties to a rational discourse. It is the sort of respect we show to those we regard as our moral and intellectual equals.[38] Lack of respect is not, then, endemic to the very idea of argumentative discourse, but only to some of the ways it has been put into practice. Hoy's contention that Habermas's way belongs among these rests on attributing to him a principle of charity in interpretation which supposes that "most of our beliefs must be true" (p. 203). But Habermas's position on that is much closer to the one I sketched in section 3.2 of my opening statement: the interpreter must suppose that the views she wants to understand are by and large held for reasons that make sense in their context. And, as I argued in section 3.4, the question of whether they are reasons that could convince her in the end must be left to critical-reflective dialogue. The "charity" required for understanding other views requires neither, *pace* Davidson, supposing most of their beliefs to be true (from our perspective) nor, *pace* Hoy's reading of Habermas, supposing most of our own to be true. It means supposing that they hold their views for reasons that have to be understood, appreciated, and discursively weighed. This model of interpretive understanding leaves open the question of whose views will turn out to be superior in a given respect.

But not entirely open, Hoy might well reply, since the social-evolutionary components of Habermas's interpretive frame ensure that the interpretation of some types of traditional views will represent them from the start as "premodern" and hence not up to discursive par (p. 204). Here I can only refer back to what I argued at some length in my statement. All the participants in the discourse of modernity, including Hoy, rely on presuppositions that mark their standpoints as post-traditional. There is no getting round that. He is committed for instance, to regarding putatively timeless, necessary truths as in need of "unmasking" (p. 207). His target is traditional metaphysics and its disguised continuations; but of course a similar "unself-consciousness of contingency" applies to much vaster domains of traditional *and* – hermeneutically and genealogically unenlightened – contemporary thought. He insists that unmasking not be understood as "seeing through illusions" or "showing us how society really is" (p. 207), but he clearly does hold that timelessness and necessity (really) are illusions that have to be dispelled or "deconstructed." And he clearly does believe that critical historiography discloses reality in important ways: "genealogical research will show that self-understandings that are taken as universal, eternal, and necessary [really] have a history with a [real] beginning and therefore, possibly, an end" (p. 207, my additions) In these respects, at least, new interpretations may be better interpretations because, being historically and hermeneutically enlightened, they capture better the way things really are.

I agree with Hoy that "things" should not be understood here to refer to "things in themselves" or even to *Gegenstände* in the sense of the objects of the natural sciences (p. 193). Inquiry in the human sciences has to do with *Sachen* that are always already interpreted; it aims at interpretations of interpretations. As interpretations are always from a point of view, and as interpretive points of view are themselves variable, "no interpretation is ever final (even ideally) . . . new interpretations will always be needed" (p. 190). This holds for our conception of what it is we have to understand no less than for our understanding of it: "the *Sache* is not eternal, but is itself evolving with the history of interpretation" (p. 190). This internal historicity of the objects of the human science means that even "the ideal of a complete or final representation" is out of place there (p. 190). As Gadamer has put it, "whereas the object of the natural sciences can be described *idealiter* as what would be known in the perfect, complete knowledge of nature, it is senseless to speak of a perfect or complete knowledge of history. . . . [or] of an object in itself toward which

research is directed" (quoted on p. 193). Picking up on the same line
of thought, Albrecht Wellmer has argued that while the notion of an
ideal language of unified science seems to make sense, the notion of a
single, ideal language of interpretation does not.[39] Our finitude and
historicity mean that we have unendingly to construct new interpretations from ever-changing points of view.

On this point I am in agreement with Hoy. Even if we grant with
Habermas the possibility of incorporating general theories and metatheories into our interpretive frames, and thus of reducing to some
extent their contextuality, that will not eliminate the need to adopt
particular points of view on particular phenomena. A structural description of "post-traditional" modes of consciousness, for example,
does not of itself capture the myriad, different, concrete shapes of
consciousness compatible with it. Nor can a general model of the
basic structures and dynamics of developed capitalist societies itself
explain the different historical shapes they take. As a result, there is
every reason to expect the conflict of interpretations to be a permanent
feature of human studies. But the consequences of this need not be
those Hoy envisions. If interpretations can *also* be assessed under the
aspects of truth, internal consistency, and coherence with other bodies
of knowledge and interpretation, then, this conflict can take the form
of critical-reflective discourse. Hoy sets dialogue in opposition to the
regulative ideas of universality and consensus; in reality, those ideas
are often its driving force. Dialogue in the form of discourse lives from
the effort to persuade interlocutors of the validity of one's claims. And
if they are claims to truth or rightness *tout court*, the circle of potential
interlocutors is in principle without limits. I suggested in my opening
statement that this has to be given a pragmatic formulation. The
rhetorical occasions for reasoned persuasion are constantly changing,
and with them the partners, contexts, and purposes of dialogue. Thus,
I argued, we have to see the vindication of universal validity claims
through the reasoned agreement of a universal audience as something
that is always only ongoingly accomplished, in ever-changing circumstances, and for all practical purposes. At the same time, the discourses
that serve as the vehicle for this are guided by ideas of truth and justice,
*foci imaginaria*, without which these types of communicative activity
would be impossible. Of course, it would be an error or, as Kant would
say, a transcendental illusion to take these "subjective necessities" (i.e.
pragmatic presuppositions) of discourse to be "objective necessities in
things," and then either to affirm or to deny them as such. What is at
stake here are the requirements of a certain type of activity.

Hoy sometimes seems to be suggesting that we could do without
them. He writes, for instance, that while Habermas's "meta-procedural"

ideal of uncoerced consensus may be hard to disagree with, it is too "empty" to be of consequence, and in any case is not "necessary" (p. 176). Against the charge of emptiness and lack of "epistemological or normative import" (p. 179), I will simply reaffirm the (pragmatist) view that the idea of settling cognitive and moral disagreements by reasoned discourse and uncoerced consensus rather than by force, authority, dogma, or the like is perhaps without equal in its consequences for civilization.[40] The fact that this idea has a history seems to indicate that it is not necessary. But what is the sense of necessity at issue here? Neither side is arguing for metaphysical or transcendental necessity. Habermas's claim is that the idea of uncoerced, reasoned agreement is a pragmatic presupposition of certain types of discursive practice which are central to modern forms of life and to which we have no viable alternatives. So what Hoy has to argue is that we could do without practices, like the one in which we are presently engaged, in which claims are advanced on grounds meant to persuade any competent and reasonable judge. I will leave the very considerable burden of that proof to him.

## NOTES

1 The lack of elaborated foundations in Marx explains the repeated attempts by "*praxis* philosophers," beginning with the young – Heideggerian – Marcuse, to flesh out Marx's notion of social practice.

2 See Jürgen Habermas, *Communication and the Evolution of Society*, trans. T. McCarthy (Cambridge, MA: The MIT Press, 1976), pp. 95–177.

3 George E. Marcus and Michael M. J. Fischer, *Anthropology as Cultural Critique* (Chicago: The University of Chicago Press, 1986), p. 77.

4 *The Theory of Communicative Action*, 2 vols, trans. by T. McCarthy (Boston: Beacon Press, 1984, 1987), vol. 1, p. 6.

5 Ibid., pp. 137–40.

6 The German phrase is Gadamer's, from "Rhetorik, Hermeneutik und Ideologiekritik," in K. O. Apel et al., *Hermeneutik und Ideologiekritik* (Frankfurt: Suhrkamp Verlag, 1971), pp. 57–82, here p. 78.

7 Fine applies this image to the realism/anti-realism debates in "And Not Anti-Realism Either," *Nous* 18 (1984): 51–65.

8 See Jürgen Habermas, *Knowledge and Human Interests*, trans. J. J. Shapiro (Boston: Beacon Press, 1971).

9 See Richard Rorty, "Postmodernist Bourgeois Liberalism," in Rorty, *Objectivity, Relativism, and Truth* (Cambridge, UK: Cambridge University Press, 1991), pp. 197–202; and Michel Foucault, "On the Genealogy of Ethics," in P. Rabinow (ed.), *The Foucault Reader* (New York: Pantheon, 1984), p. 350.

10 Cf. Nancy Fraser, "Foucault on Modern Power: Empirical Insights and Normative Confusions," in Fraser, *Unruly Practices* (Minneapolis: University of Minnesota Press, 1989), pp. 17–34. Like postmodernists generally, Hoy implicitly ties his hopes for a better world to "genuine" enlightenment – in his case, genealogical and hermeneutic self-understanding – though in discussing Horkheimer and Adorno he dismisses any such tie as an "utopian illusion" (p. 115).

11 See *The Theory of Communicative Action*, vol. 1, pp. 235–42.

12 Thus in *Communication and the Evolution of Society* he clearly distinguishes developmental logics from learning processes under contingent conditions, on pp. 140ff.

13 Claims of this kind are pervasive in developmental studies of linguistic, cognitive, interpersonal, and moral learning processes. For a naturalist, whether they are justified can only be a matter of which are the best empirical theories of the domains in question – and not a matter for conceptual legislation.

14 See Thomas McCarthy, *Ideals and Illusions* (Cambridge, MA: The MIT Press, 1991), chapter 5.

15 One source of our differences is Hoy's focus on Habermas's "Geschichte und Evolution" (in J. Habermas, *Zur Rekonstruktion des Historischen Materialismus* [Frankfurt: Suhrkamp Verlag, 1976], pp. 200–59, an essay written to counter Niklas Luhmann's systems-theoretic approach to history. It contains formulations that can be misleading when taken out of that context. There are more straightforward formulations in *Communication and the Evolution of Society* and *The Theory of Communicative Action*.

16 *Communication and the Evolution of Society*, p. 154.

17 For an overview, see Thomas McCarthy, *The Critical Theory of Jürgen Habermas*, (Cambridge, MA: The MIT Press, 1978), pp. 232–71.

18 That is, the "narrative perspective" of the critical historian may include an "interpretive frame" informed by such theories. ("Geschichte und Evolution," pp. 203–7). In an interview with Perry Anderson and Peter Dews, Habermas goes so far as to say that theories of the type that interest him "prove their worth in the end only by contributing to the explanation of concrete historical processes." Peter Dews (ed.), *Habermas: Autonomy and Solidarity* (London: Verso, 1986), p. 167.

19 Cf. Axel Honneth, *The Critique of Power*, trans. by K. Baynes (Cambridge, MA: The MIT Press, 1991), chapter 6.

20 Some of these are discussed in T. McCarthy, *Ideals and Illusions*, chapter 2.

21 Michel Foucault, "Structuralism and Post-Structuralism: An Interview with Gérard Raulet," *Telos* 55 (1983): 195–211, here pp. 198ff.

22 Ibid., p. 200.

23 Ibid., p. 201.

24 Ibid., p. 202.

25 There are many passages in which Foucault even sounds like a neo-Marxist. For instance, in *Power/Knowledge*, trans. Colin Gordon et al.

(New York: Pantheon, 1980), he says that we have to understand how low-level mechanisms of power became "economically advantageous and politically useful" to the "real interests" of the bourgeois "system" and how, "as a natural consequence, all of a sudden they came to be colonized and maintained by global mechanisms and the entire State system. It is only if we grasp these techniques of power and demonstrate the economic advantages or political utility that derives from them in a given context for specific reasons, that we can understand how these mechanisms come to be incorporated into the social whole" (p. 101). Indications of some sort of materialist functionalism can be found in his historical studies as well. See, for instance, *Discipline and Punish*, trans. A. Sheridan (New York: Vintage, 1979), pp. 220–2, where he cites Marx's *Capital*.

26 See Georgia Warnke, *Gadamer: Hermeneutics, Tradition and Reason* (Oxford: Polity, 1987), chapter 4. The passage from Habermas Hoy cites concerning the "affirmative" character of history ("Geschichte und Evolution," p. 245) has to be read in context. That it is not meant to deny the "critical potential" of historical writing becomes evident on the following page, where Habermas discusses "critically oriented history" that aims not to reaffirm an established tradition but to foster a different one, such as "a history of blocked liberalization, of suppressed social struggles, [or] of missed emancipation, a Benjaminian history from the standpoint of the victims" (p. 246).

27 The idea of truth is equally important to *critical* discourse. Removing the appeal to truth from the "weapons of critique" risks delivering up the conflict of interpretation to the balance of power.

28 See *Ideals and Illusions*, pp. 67–75.

29 See Jürgen Habermas, "On the Pragmatic, the Ethical, and the Moral Employments of Practical Reason," in *Justification and Application: Remarks on Discourse Ethics*, trans. by Ciaran Cronin (Cambridge, MA: The MIT Press, 1993), pp. 1–17.

30 On p. 191 Hoy seems to endorse a similar view, when he writes that though interpretations do not "mirror an independent reality" they can "capture aspects of the *Sache* correctly." Since the *Sache* is always linguistically mediated, this amounts, he notes (212, n. 35), to a kind of "internal realism" not unlike the one that Hilary Putnam sketches in *Reason, Truth, and History* (Cambridge, UK: Cambridge University Press, 1981). He does not consider, however, that Putnam explicates the notion of truth basic to his internal realism in terms of "idealized rational acceptability" or "rational acceptability under ideal conditions" (p. 55). This comes very close to Habermas's version of an internal realism tied to rational consensus under ideal conditions.

31 On what follows see chapters 9 and 10 of Jürgen Habermas, *The New Conservatism*, trans. S. Nicholsen (Cambridge, MA: The MIT Press, 1989). For a brief overview of the controversy, see Robert Holub, *Jürgen Habermas: Critic in the Public Sphere* (New York: Routledge, 1991), pp. 162–89. For a broader treatment, see Charles Maier, *The Unmasterable Past* (Cambridge, MA: Harvard University Press, 1988).

32 By and large, these are the matters that concern Hoy in chapter 6. The difference in focus may account for some of the differences in views. Habermas discusses the varying scope of the different types of critical reflection and the claims that issue from them in *The Theory of Communicative Action*, vol. 1, pp. 20–4, and in *Justification and Application*, *passim*.

33 Some of his earliest formulations of the discourse theory of truth might be read in that way, especially those in "Wahrheitstheorien," in H. Fahrenbach (ed.), *Wirklichkeit und Reflexion* (Pfullingen: Neske, 1973), pp. 211–66. But his subsequent formulations are clear on this point. See, for instance, *The Theory of Communicative Action*, vol. 1, pp. 316–18.

34 Again, the later formulations are clearer on this point than the earlier. See the previous footnote and Habermas's "Reply," in A. Honneth and H. Joas (eds), *Communicative Action* (Cambridge, MA: The MIT Press, 1991), pp. 231ff.

35 Habermas's earliest efforts issued in the notion of an "ideal speech situation," which has been a magnet for criticism ever since. See "Wahrheitstheorien."

36 Cf. the essays collected in *Understanding and Social Inquiry*, F. Dallmayer and T. McCarthy (eds), (Notre Dame: University of Notre Dame Press, 1977); and *The Interpretive Turn*, D. Hiley, J. Bohman and R. Shusterman (eds), (Ithaca: Cornell University Press, 1991).

37 To say that there are no uninterpreted facts is not to say that there are no facts. And to say that factual claims are inherently contestable does not mean that agreement on facts is impossible. These two common errors indicate that we need a new theory of facts.

38 Compare the "politics of mutual respect" discussed by Amy Gutmann and Dennis Thompson, "Moral Conflict and Political Consensus," in R. Douglass, G. Mara, and H. Richardson (eds), *Liberalism and the Good* (New York: Routledge, 1990), pp. 125–47.

39 Albrecht Wellmer, *The Persistence of Modernity* (Cambridge, MA: The MIT Press, 1991), pp. 168–82.

40 Cf. C. S. Peirce, "The Fixation Belief," in P. Wiener (ed.), *Charles S. Peirce: Selected Writings* (New York: Dover, 1958), pp. 91–112.

# 8

# Rejoinder to Thomas McCarthy

The debate format of this book puts me in a peculiar rhetorical predicament. My position as the opponent of the Habermasian conception of critical theory as defended by Thomas McCarthy seems to require me to disagree with Habermas's central claim. This claim is roughly that genuine discursive disagreement is not possible unless the parties are rationally aiming at agreement on the one, right account. I am therefore caught in a "performative contradiction" if I disagree with this claim. For if I disagree, apparently I must be presupposing that I am right and that he must agree with me. But then I am aiming at agreement, which is what this debate positions me to be denying. Of course, I might be disagreeing simply for the sake of disagreeing, but then I am not really debating, at least not rationally. However, my rhetorical predicament keeps me from agreeing with Professor McCarthy, for if I were simply to agree that agreement is the necessary *telos* of genuine debate, there would seem to be nothing left to debate. That dissolution of the debate might seem to be the triumph of the Habermasian defense of enlightenment and modernity. However, I doubt that McCarthy would welcome such ready acquiescence, because if the thesis were so readily granted, it would appear to be *trivially* true, and so thin as to be of no philosophical interest.

Right from the start, then, let me resist being put on the "other" side from truth, rationality, and freedom. Neither do I want to be forced to attack these notions, nor do I want to read either Foucault or Gadamer, the two theorists whom I have tried to amalgamate and defend, as subverting them. What is at stake are particular *conceptions* of truth, rationality, and freedom, and the arguments for them. In challenging the arguments for Habermas's program I am not saying that these concepts should be given up altogether. Instead, I am maintaining that the classic critical theorists' arguments are not convincing, or that the conceptions do not have the force attributed to them. More specifically,

I have been trying to show that the writing of concrete "critical history" does not require the strong "theory of theory" of the Habermasian approach to critical theory.

In the opening chapters, however, Professor McCarthy has offered a more pragmatic and less transcendental reading of critical theory than Habermas and his Frankfurt School mentors. McCarthy's reconstruction of Habermas downplays some parts that I have criticized (such as the developmental learning theory or the ideal speech situation), while seeking to retain the central kernel. While there is much that I find attractive in this less transcendental version of classic critical theory, I do not find it completely de-transcendentalized. Indeed, I suspect that it contains the same "theory of theory." So although I find McCarthy's reconstruction of critical theory plausible and even congenial, there are suggestions that I still find myself resisting. Let me therefore not linger over the points on which we agree, but instead, focus the issues about which we disagree. In brief, I still am not fully persuaded that the aspiration to "universal validity" does much work, or that, as explained here, it is needed to make "critical history" possible.

To highlight our differences, let me raise four questions that focus some contrasts used in McCarthy's account. (1) Are socialized individuals better conceived as rational agents than as cultural dopes? (2) Do these social beings need to aspire beyond local solidarities to universal agreement? (3) Is non-violent social pluralism possible only if there is transcultural validity? (4) Is the pragmatic transformation of the real made more effective by the supposition of counterfactual ideals? I have phrased these questions as I do because I think that McCarthy would expect the answer of yes to all of them. My intuitions are, in contrast, either to answer no in each case, or at least to challenge the terms in which the questions are posed. I will address these four questions as they are answered in McCarthy's opening three chapters. (At the time of writing this response to those chapters I have not yet seen his response to my chapters.)

## 8.1  Rational Agents or Cultural Dopes?

No one wants to be thought of as a cultural dope, of course. One prefers to think of oneself as a rational agent. That is the attractiveness of Thomas McCarthy's insistence that being able to give reasons for what we do is an essential component of social interaction, and is constitutive of our understanding of ourselves as accountable social agents. His picture of agency in social contexts sees us as "knowl-edgeable agents who are acting accountably in those contexts, that is, of agents who by and large know what they are doing and why they are doing it" (§3.4, p. 91). McCarthy makes this picture sound much more plausible than the "deconstructionist" picture of cultural dopes who are socially constructed to such an extent that they do not know at all what they are doing or why. Indeed, if genealogy describes social practices without any attention at all to subjects' self-understandings, it makes human agents not merely into cultural dopes but social zombies.

I do not believe that genealogy has this effect. I grant that when Foucault was working on his history of the prison, he did work with a model of power that de-emphasized the priority of individual self-understandings and that suggested instead that such self-understandings are largely constructed by impersonal social practices. However, his later studies of sexual ethics acknowledge not only that self-understandings are shaped by these social practices, but also that social subjects are themselves complicit in this social conditioning, often consciously doing it to themselves. So Foucault is not an in-visible-hand theorist who believes that social conditioning is entirely subliminal. Individuals learn to discipline or fashion themselves, and Foucault never asserts that this socialization is always bad. So I would resist reading Foucault in particular or the critical activity of geneal-ogy in general as the "deconstructionist" denial of social agency in McCarthy's contrast between deconstruction and reconstruction.[1]

However, I also resist McCarthy's "reconstructionist" picture of rational agency. The quote above stated that we have to think of rational social agents as "by and large" knowing what they are doing and why. This phrase does not say that we are rational only if we *completely* know what we are doing or are *fully* rational. But it does imply that we should try to approach that ideal. I take the suggestion as being more than that we must assume simply that most of our beliefs are true. We could assume this without assuming that we could ever articulate most of our beliefs, which remain for the most part in the background. So McCarthy's notion of accountable rational agency seems to require the stronger claim that we be able to *state and justify* most of our beliefs. I infer this stronger claim because on his picture agents have to *know* what they are doing and *why*.

This picture strikes me as being too strong because I do not think that we can aspire to the self-transparency of making most of what we believe fully articulate. We also do not need to believe that insofar as we lack such self-transparency we fail to be rational. The idea of fully articulating most of our beliefs may even involve an unintelligible picture of belief. However, I will not dwell on the problems here because McCarthy also rejects the ideal of self-transparency (§3.2, p. 77), and I have shown in chapter 5 that Habermas has himself recognized that understanding is always conditioned by a larger, unarticulated background. I will only add that this recognition of the impossibility of self-transparency and the ineliminability of the background suggests to me that there is no *unconditional* understanding. Words like "unconditional" and "unlimited" validity still feature frequently in McCarthy's model, however, and are centrally tied to his insistence on the "universal." I would have thought that since philosophy has, on his own account, moved away from foundationalism and "metaphysics," it could also move away from the ideal of the unconditional. Perhaps I would have fewer misgivings about the appeal to "universality" if it were uncoupled from "unconditionality," a term that does not have a genuine use outside the foundationalist enterprise.

Even the classic version of critical theory might not accept McCarthy's account of rational agency and accountability, which seems more reminiscent of "traditional theory." Critical theory maintains, after all, that for the most part agents do not know what they are doing or why. These agents would give reasons, but they are the wrong reasons because they represent a misperception of the agents' real interests, a misperception that is caused by massively repressive social institutions. I hasten to add that McCarthy does recognize the value of macrosociological frameworks that condition action in ways that are "beyond the ken of participants" (§3.3, p. 84). So at the same time that he believes that individual rational agents can "by and large" know what they are doing and why, he also grants that there is much that is beyond their ken.

Although there might appear to be some tension here, I do not find this view of social agency implausible because hermeneutics has been arguing all along that social agents' self-descriptions must be taken seriously even if finally they are not the whole story. The hermeneutical view is that social agents find themselves acculturated within a social background. (I note that the term "background" connotes a more amorphous, less theoretically demarcated field than "macroframework.") Social agents cannot and need not make this background fully explicit to themselves. But no particular part of the background is in principle hidden, because when there is a social breakdown or "problematization," relevant parts of the background can be discerned. Genealogical histories achieve this hermeneutical effect by contrasting present practices to past practices that are no longer live options for us. But at least our recognition that there once were different options may lead us to become cognizant of what options are real for us now, even if we cannot go back to the past. For this reason I believe that McCarthy and I are in agreement that the stories produced by such "histories of the present" need not always be stories of loss, as they perhaps tend to be in French hands, but neither do they need to be stories of gain. We agree that they will be mostly stories of both, especially since there is "no gain without loss" (§3.3, pp. 83–4).

I think that we would also agree that social agents are neither simply social zombies nor fully self-transparent rational agents. These extremes leave room for a wide range of ways of studying the middle ground. But if we can agree on this particular point, that only brings us to the next problem. On the hermeneutical model the self-understandings of individual agents must be taken into account, but such self-understandings need not be full or correct explanations of social action, and therefore may need to be criticized. The next question is, then, from what position does such criticism come? Does such criticism necessarily presuppose some agreements that are universal and that transcend the different cultural backgrounds forming local solidarities? Or is criticism possible only from within some local solidarity, and therefore inevitably ethnocentric?

## 8.2 Local Solidarity or Universal Audience?

Thomas McCarthy has explained why he believes that local solidarity is not sufficient to explain how social and moral criticism of agents' self-understanding is possible. He agrees that we cannot aspire to making conscious all the unconscious determinants of thought, but only to making particular factors evident. Thus, complete self-transparency is not an intelligible ideal. But even though analysis always presupposes a background that conditions the validity of critical explanations, McCarthy thinks that pluralistic, hermeneutical theorists like Gadamer, Foucault, and Richard Rorty insist too much on the context-bounded-ness of validity claims. He stresses that the activity of discussing which assessments are right involves giving reasons pro and con. He fears that the hermeneutic theory of interpretation entails that such intersubjective assessment of reasons "gets downgraded to a capacity to serve as carriers of the dominant social and cultural forms" (§2.1, p. 37). So the danger is that hermeneutics makes genuine criticism impossible. He thus thinks that Gadamer is a conservative proponent of "traditionalism" (§2.2, p. 41). Foucault is a crypto-normativist who seems to be attacking universal values like freedom and truth, when the attack itself tacitly relies on these same values (§2.1, p. 34). Finally, Richard Rorty's frank ethnocentrism is found to commit the following performative contradiction: to be ethnocentric about Western liberal culture is tacitly to favor universal values because, on McCarthy's account, that culture is and has long been universalist (§2.1, pp. 32–3).

I have tried to show in my previous chapters and in other places how these readings of Gadamer and Foucault can be countered by more sympathetic interpretations. McCarthy has, of course, read the texts closely, and in *Ideals and Illusions* and other places he has supported his interpretations meticulously. Now is not the time for a war of exegesis, so for detailed rebuttals of such criticisms of these pluralists let me refer readers to my previous chapters. There I argue that Gadamer is not a reactionary defender of tradition, but on the contrary, is showing how the tradition can be criticized by drawing on other resources suppressed within the tradition, which is never monolithic. I do not see Foucault as a crypto-normativist because I do not see him saying that truth and freedom are simply effects of power. Instead, I see him as firmly opposing domination by his critical activity of unmasking historical instances where claims of supposed progress toward superior knowledge and more humane freedom concealed highly repressive social practices. Finally, McCarthy's discovery of a performative contradiction in Rorty depends on McCarthy's assessment of Western culture as universalist, when that assessment is what is at issue.

## (i)  Universal audience?

Instead of skirmishing around these other theorists, let me engage directly with McCarthy's well-articulated position. He starts from a claim that we both accept, namely, that social discussion and criticism involve warranting and contesting reasons. On his view, this weighing of reasons will only be a sham unless we presuppose that ideally the validity of these reasons could be agreed to by everyone, whether in this culture or any other culture, who was uncoerced and who had all the relevant information. Validity claims transcend their contexts of origin. How far does this context-transcendence go? McCarthy uses words like "universality" and "unconditionality" to insist that ideally the claims would be seen as valid from any and every context. While he does not put much rhetorical weight on Habermas's notion of the ideal speech situation, McCarthy himself speaks of a *universal audience*. Not only must some original audience assent to the truth claims, one audience after another must agree that the claims are the result of the best possible argument. Although this sequence is "in principle never-ending," the universal audience at the end of the sequence is implied by the provisional acceptance of truth claims by any intermediate audience. The universality and unconditionality of the truth claims thus comes down to "the implicit promise they contain to convince a universal audience" (§3.2, p. 76).

I find myself unconvinced by this account for many of the same reasons that I gave earlier against Habermas's account. For one thing, I think that it would be irrational for one to aim at an ideal if one knew that in principle it could never be attained. Just as no one could really aim to discover the last value of $\pi$ because there is no last number, so no one could really be trying to complete the endless task of convincing a universal audience. I do not think it even makes sense to think of coming *closer* to what the universal audience would find convincing. McCarthy suggests that the pragmatic value of this ideal is to warn us not to treat any interpretive or evaluative scheme as "finished, final, complete" (§3.2, p. 77). But his admission that "warrants which suffice to convince one audience in one set of circumstances will not suffice to convince all other audiences in all other circumstances" (§3.2, p. 77) seems right to me. Moreover, it strikes me as a good reason for thinking that we do *not* presuppose the possibility of an ideal universal audience when we engage in dialogue.

Because McCarthy offers this same claim as a reason for the necessity of presupposing the universal audience, I have to ask myself why he and I draw opposite conclusions from this point. A worry that I have is that despite McCarthy's denial, his picture of the universal audience might be bringing back the ideal of self-transparency. One reason that *real* audiences disagree is because their interpretive background practices contain unarticulated assumptions that lead to differing readings of premises and thus differing inferences. When McCarthy posits the one universal audience, I do not see how this ideal oneness would be possible unless the universal audience had attained self-transparency.

I do not want to suggest that McCarthy's ideal is a God's-eye point of view. That position is a form of what I have called in chapter 6 metaphysical monism. I find this position unintelligible, given the paradox that the aperspectival point of view that supposedly sees all points of view would itself no longer be a possible point of view. I do not ascribe that position to McCarthy, but instead the position that I have called *critical monism*. Monism, in my terms, insists that there is only one right interpretation. This interpretation might only be an ideal limit where all the possible questions about all the features of the object of interpretation would be resolved, but however defined, monism thinks of interpreters as presupposing the possibility of converging on this limit. Pluralists, in contrast, hold that there can be rational disagreements that do not presuppose ideal convergence or consensus. Monism or pluralism are *metaphysical*, in my terms, when the unity or plurality are asserted to be necessary features of the interpretation-transcending object. In their *critical* versions monism or pluralism follow not from the nature of mind-independent reality, but from the requirements of the activity of understanding and interpreting.[2]

While I respect critical monism, I do not find it convincing because it goes farther than is necessary and seems like philosophical overkill. I ascribe the position to McCarthy because his universal audience would seem to have achieved the "one right interpretation." Indeed, there would be no need to speak of interpretation at all, and what the universal audience would have ascertained is, in McCarthy's phrase, the *"unique truth"* about the world (§3.4, p. 91). This supposition of the uniquely true account is what makes him a critical monist, in my terms.

More specifically, I take it that he is a monist not only about (1) objective scientific descriptions of the physical world but also about (2) normative arrangements of the social world. To respond briefly to the first point let me suggest a reservation about the monistic view of science. McCarthy argued for the supposition of a unique truth from the supposition of an objective physical world or "an independent reality that is intersubjectively available" (§3.4, p. 91). But from the supposition of the objectivity of the world it does not follow automatically that there is only one complete theory that could be true about it (if that is what he means by a "unique truth"). The world might be objective, but infinitely complex, such that no single theory could map it entirely or uniquely.

On the second point, I hesitate about the way the model of the universal audience is extended from the scientific to the social domain. On McCarthy's own view there are differences between the natural and the social sciences. A central difference is that social reality, unlike physical reality, includes what people think is real (for instance, about themselves). How they see others will both condition and be conditioned by how they see themselves. So a particular self-understanding, or the story a particular group tells about itself, is never complete, but will depend on specific contrasts. There would always seem to be a further story to be told about any given audience than it could tell about itself. Presumably this would be true of the universal audience itself, at least if it still includes real people (who are said to be neither featureless nor self-transparent). McCarthy insists that the universal audience would not necessarily be homogenized and uniform, and if he also grants that the universal audience does not have self-transparency, then there is always more to say about even a universal audience than it can say about itself. So once again, if the idea of a universal audience is at all intelligible, I do not see why it would follow that there is only one true account about even this ideal audience.

Kant is famous for his distinction between the questions about what I must believe and what I can hope. The universal audience strikes me as at most an ideal for which one can hope (if it is at all intelligible), but not as a necessary supposition for belief and action. I have sketched some conceptual difficulties that I find in this notion, but McCarthy has raised some equally difficult problems about the idea of solidarity. So let me turn to that notion, which features more explicitly in Richard Rorty's pragmatism than in either Gadamer or Foucault.[3] While the term is thus not a central one for either hermeneutics or genealogy, the issue is a general one, for anything short of a universal audience seems to rely on distinguishing "us" from "them." But who, then, are "we"?

## (ii) Solidarities

Solidarity is a difficult notion. At first it might seem to be an admirable social ideal insofar as it brings well-intentioned people together in a tolerant community. The feeling of community is also a welcome antidote to the alienation and isolation experienced by individuals in a competitive society. Solidarity recognizes that the social glue that holds groups together runs deeper than conscious decisions and surface structures. However, for that reason solidarity can also be regarded suspiciously. Recently, for instance, Thomas Nagel in *Equality and Partiality* (Oxford: Oxford University Press, 1991) grants the political reality of solidarity. But he also sees its sinister side, which follows if the formation of a "we" depends on the exclusion of others.

> Solidarity requires identification with those with whom one feels it. For that reason there is always a potentially sinister side to it: It is essentially exclusive. Solidarity with a particular group means lack of identification with, and less sympathy for, those who are not members of that group, and often it means active hostility to outsiders; but to some extent this is inevitable, and it is such a powerful source of political allegiance to institutions which deal equitably with members of the

group that it must be relied on. By the same token, its absence will weaken the support for cooperative efforts in certain collectivities, particularly if they contain subgroups whose solidarity is strong. I myself find solidarity which depends on racial, linguistic, or religious identification distasteful, but there is no denying its politically cohesive, and disruptive, power. (178)

The first thing that the hermeneutic turn does is to challenge this widespread understanding of the "we" as primarily exclusive. For Gadamer the "we" is not formed by *excluding* others, but is itself primitive, not derivative. The minimal structure required for language use (or "dialogue," in Gadamer's terminology) is the triangulation (to use Donald Davidson's term) between two conspecific creatures and a common object (or *Sache*).[4] In dialogue the "we" that links a conspecific "I" and "Thou" is not a relation of exclusion, but a condition of communication without which a subsequent perception of difference and otherness would not be possible. So on Gadamer's hermeneutic theory of communicative solidarity, the dialogical "we" is formed by an initial act not of exclusion, but of inclusion.

Foucault does not address the question of what Gadamer calls the ontology of language and of the "we," but one interesting remark he did make about the "we" also suggests that he sees the "we" as a matter more of community-formation than of exclusion. This remark was made in response to a criticism of him by Richard Rorty:

R. Rorty points out that in these analyses I do not appeal to any "we" – to any of those "we's" whose consensus, whose values, whose traditions constitute the framework for a thought and define the conditions in which it can be validated. But the problem is, precisely, to decide if it is actually suitable to place oneself within a "we" in order to assert the principles one recognizes and the values one accepts; or if it is not, rather, necessary to make the future formation of a "we" possible, by elaborating the question. Because it seems to me that the "we" must not be previous to the question; it can only be the result – and the necessarily temporary result – of the question as it is posed in the new terms in which one formulates it.[5]

The example he gives is his own book, *Madness and Civilization*, which did not get an immediate response because there seemed to be no audience for it at first, but which finally caught the attention of others (like Laing, Cooper, and Basaglia) and led to effective reforms in the treatment of the mentally ill. So Foucault's view about the "we" is more forward-looking than backward-looking. The backward-looking tendency is to tie action back to a tradition in which the values that guide the action are rooted. The forward-looking tendency is to try to create a "we" that would be likely to form, in Foucault's words, "a community of action."

Contrary, perhaps, to Foucault's own rhetoric, I do not see that there is necessarily a tension between these two tendencies. The backward-looking or "hermeneutical" tendency is not necessarily "traditional-ist" in a reactionary sense since the point can be to challenge the status quo, not simply to maintain it. The forward-looking or "genea-logical" tendency would not be effective unless it found an audience, and thus it depends on the contingencies of the particular situation in which it strikes a chord. However, I do not believe that the forward-looking direction must look as far forward as McCarthy's final univer-sal audience. The "we" that is formed does not have to think of itself as final, but as responding to needs that it hopes are only temporary because correctable. New needs and contingencies will always arise. The backward-looking direction can serve the forward-looking direc-tion by helping to understand how the needs arose and why they went unperceived, or if perceived, why they were fatalistically taken to be inevitable rather than historically contingent.

The solidarity resulting from this formation of a "we" should not be construed as homogenizing social differences. If solidarity is the for-mation of a community of action to correct specific social problems, this solidarity goes only so far and does not bridge all social distinc-tions. Any particular individual can feel solidarity with several or even many social groups. Thomas McCarthy raises an excellent point, however, in his critique of Horkheimer's claim that solidarity with the wretched of the earth is the compassionate root of morality. McCarthy suggests that this claim does not answer questions such as, solidarity with which side, or sympathy with whom? So on his view solidarity cannot substitute for the need for rational criticism and justification, but on the contrary, such a feeling would require communicative exchange and reasoning (§1.3, p. 26).

In §2.4 (p. 54), however, McCarthy goes farther and urges us to accept Habermas's extension of solidarity into a universal. Habermas sees soli-darity as "the realization that each person must take responsibility for the other because as consociates all must have an interest in the integrity of their shared life context in the same way."[6] Solidarity and justice are said to be two aspects of the same thing insofar as giving reasons and coming to discursive agreement requires giving arguments that transcend par-ticular lifeworlds and that presuppose the ideal communication com-munity of "all subjects capable of speech and action."[7]

The question that immediately comes to my mind here, however, is whether this extension of solidarity does not make it so thin as to be empty. Horkheimer's original idea of compassion for the suffering seems to have now been redefined so that solidarity is with all humanity. One might share Hegel's concern that such a generalized sense of solidarity will lead to inaction instead of action, since any particular individual can do little to help all humanity. That may be why Richard Rorty believes that the notion of solidarity can have content only for those closer to home. That is, it is enough to help those closer to us whom we can help, as long as we really do help them.

However, if solidarity is not universal but local, do we fall back into a dangerous relativism where we become unable to criticize ourselves or our own moral practices and social arrangements? Here again I recall what I said about this issue in chapter 6. As Alexander Nehamas has also pointed out, each of us belongs to several communities. So if criticism requires us to step outside our community, we do so not by transcending to the standpoint of the ideal communication community or the universal audience, but simply by seeing a particular context in which we inhere from other contexts in which we also inhere.

Is it really necessary to add to this model the idea of getting *agreement* between all these different social self-understandings? Certainly we should not close ourselves off from self-understandings other than our own. Indeed, I think that for the most part we are interested in other people (and other peoples) precisely because they are so different from us. We feel *enriched* by getting to know them better, without necessarily feeling that we would want to be like them. In chapter 6 I argued that one can learn more about others and about oneself without the formation of consensus and convergence. Georgia Warnke calls this process a hermeneutic conversation, and in her recent book, *Justice and Interpretation* (Cambridge, UK: Polity Press, 1992), she argues that such a pluralistic model is adequate for the specific needs of political theory. The task of political theory, she suggests,

> perhaps should not be to adjudicate between different interpretations of the meaning of our political heritage. Perhaps it should not be trying to forge a consensus or synthesis of interpretations. Perhaps it should be trying, rather, to discover what each interpretation can learn from the others and to encourage a kind of hermeneutic conversation in which different interpretations can become more educated, refined and sophisticated through their "contest" with the others. In a conversation of this kind each interpretive stance may retain its distinctiveness; it can also help to develop and enrich the others and, in turn, be developed and transformed by them. We need not agree with each other in the end, but we can all come to recognize the partial and one-sided character of our

initial positions and incorporate into our more considered views the insights we have come to learn by trying to understand other interpretations of our history and experience. The important question, then, is no longer which interpretation of our history and experience is correct because none is exhaustively correct. The important question is, rather, how or why our interpretations differ and what new insights into the meaning of our traditions we might glean from the attempt to understand the cogency of interpretations different from our own. (132)

If communication is modeled on Gadamerian conversation instead of Habermasian argumentation, rationality can be preserved without a philosophical insistence on monism. Interpreting texts, other people, or ourselves does not seem to be simply a matter of arguments winning out over other arguments, but of expanding our ideas, altering our practices, and, in general, educating ourselves. There is no need to think that there is only one way to realize these interpretive aims.

To this hermeneutic insistence on pluralism Thomas McCarthy might well raise the question whether hermeneutics is being inconsistent in insisting on pluralism and openness to many interpretations at the same time that it seems so adamantly opposed to one particular interpretation, namely, the one that sees things from a universal and impartial perspective. My response is not to deny the desirability of learning to view matters not only from a personal perspective but also from one that increasingly disregards oneself and approaches impartiality. But the point at issue is not impartiality, but monism. Even if impartiality were attainable, it does not follow that there would be a uniquely true account. More to the point, even if one grants the need to see things from an impartial as well as from a personal perspective, it does not follow either that these two perspectives can be reconciled with each other harmoniously, or that when they conflict, that the only reasonable solution is for the impartial standpoint to trump the personal standpoint. In *Equality and Partiality* Thomas Nagel shows poignantly not only the desirability of both standpoints but also the difficulty in reconciling them. He resists the utopianism that suggests that the impartial must always trump or even eliminate the personal. While one can often shift to an impartial standpoint when one's preferences conflict with another person's, sometimes that is not possible. For instance, I might want the last life jacket for my child and Thomas McCarthy might want it for his. Yet each of us would be acting perfectly reasonably in letting the personal standpoint take priority over the impartial perspective. Indeed, there might be something irrational in either of us even trying to take the impartial standpoint in this case.[8]

In the social and political sphere Nagel is similarly pessimistic about reconciling the two standpoints. We may all behave reasonably and still not find a solution that no one could reasonably reject. So even a theorist like Nagel who respects both the impartial and the personal standpoints does not necessarily conclude that following reasonable procedures will lead to unanimity and convergence on a reasonable solution:

> [P]erspective enters into what is reasonable, in ways that can sometimes make reasonable unanimity impossible. Each party is assumed in such a case to be subject to three distinct types of reasons: (a) egalitarian impartiality, (b) personal interests and commitments, and (c) consideration for what can reasonably be asked of others. Together these may fail to pick out any solution on which all reasonable persons must converge.(172)

A compelling example is the appalling discrepancy in standards of living between the prosperous and the poorest countries around the world. Given extreme economic inequality and radical value differences, there seems to be no solution to which all nations could reasonably be expected to agree (which is not to say that the prosperous nations could not reasonably be expected to do more to aid the poorest ones).

I raise this example not only to illustrate how impartiality and rationality do not necessarily lead to convergence and unanimity, but also to suggest the emptiness of invocations of universal solidarity in the face of bitter need both abroad and at home. Indeed, in view of such inhumane differences, expressions by rich Western nations of solidarity with all humanity might well be received by the poorer nations with varying degrees of suspicion, resentment, and hostility. Solidarity, if the notion is to have any content, should start closer to home. But this is not to say that it is exclusionary. If solidarity starts locally, it can be expanded as we widen our interpretations through forward-looking encounters with others. But there is no reason to posit a single, universal solidarity at the end of the process. Solidarities should also not be taken as natural kinds or closed mind-sets. If each of us participates in several communities, if everyone is starting from a variety of social roles and group identities, then there is no reason to think of solidarities as anything more than possible interpretations of how these various starting-points can be integrated. On the hermeneutical-genealogical model, thinking of solidarities as interpretations has the pragmatic advantage of making them more likely to be actively forward-looking and tolerantly open-ended.

## 8.3  Pluralism or Consensus?

Thomas McCarthy and I share the desire to take cultural difference into account without homogenizing it or reducing it to what Thomas Nagel calls the "view from nowhere," where these differences no longer make any difference. Habermas's discourse ethics is said not to be such a view precisely because it insists that all would have to talk with one another and to reach mutual agreement. In the previous sections I raised some conceptual difficulties about this model, which seems to abstract so much from what real participants in real discourse situations could really be doing that the viewpoint of the ideal, counterfactual universal audience would seem to be such a view from nowhere. However, I recognize that McCarthy denies this equation and in this section I will focus on the issue of the limits of pluralism. The issue is whether diversity does or does not have limits, and whether there must be a minimal amount of shared agreement no matter how wide the range of substantive and normative disagreement is.

In contesting the Habermasian model I do not mean to deny that there are limits to the diversity that can be tolerated. The issue for me is whether the Habermasian model either establishes what those limits are or whether it is correct about why there are limits. I suspect that our efforts to tolerate as much diversity as possible will be limited only by contingent cases where violence erupts and toleration is suspended for the sake of self-protection. The Habermasian model asks more of philosophy. Philosophy is expected to specify the a priori limits of diversity, the common ground that must be respected by any individual or group that communicates discursively. The hesitations I raise rely on a sense that philosophy on this model tries to accomplish too much and succeeds only in establishing too little.

The differences between McCarthy and myself are not political, but meta-philosophical. I could accept much of what he says in the following quotation, but I still resist his argument less because of its universalism than because of its implied monism:

> If there are important divergences in the beliefs and outlooks, desires and feelings, norms and values of peoples who have nevertheless to live together, and if there is no "view from nowhere" from which neutrally to adjudicate such differences, then there is in the end no non-coercive alternative to finding or constructing common ground in and across the diverse "views from somewhere." And the only reasonable way of doing that is through reciprocal understanding and symmetrical discussion of differences (§3.4, p. 90).

In our multicultural world McCarthy believes that local solidarities are not enough to ground mutual intelligibility, which requires "the background of our common humanity" (§3.4, p. 91). In his last sentence of chapter 3 he therefore invokes the "cosmopolitan" ideal of Kant and Schiller that the "boundless claims of reason" would transcend the divisions of nation-states and all natural communities to form a global perspective that recognizes everyone's common humanity.[9]

Of course I agree that discussion is better than coercion and violence. But if one can reasonably be skeptical about this cosmopolitan ideal – if, for instance, one agrees with Thomas Nagel's pessimism about forming a world community that would legitimate a global government – then there may be no impartial solution to which even fully reasonable parties could be expected to agree. The "common ground" that the Habermasian model calls for seems too thin in the face of the extreme discrepancies that face the world today. The ideal that everyone should agree to everyone's interpretations of their needs and to the principles that should be followed for meeting these needs posits an endless task that no real group could emulate in real time (which implies that trying to act on this impossible ideal would in fact be irrational). In practice, such a discussion would appear only to perpetuate the status quo and the existent power relations with their attendant economic inequalities.

So does denying the Habermasian program leave the dissenting pluralist in the position of advocating violent coercion? That is the rhetorical alternative that McCarthy offers. But again I propose that the issue is more about what can be expected of philosophy, and I think that to expect philosophy to come up with a social theory that necessarily prevents coercion and violence is to ask too much of it. The question is whether the model of a hermeneutic conversation does not do a better job of characterizing *real* dialogues, without adding the supposition of a never-realized universal audience.

The hermeneutic model calls for enlarging one's interpretations, and enriching them by holding them open to other interpretations. Differences between interpretations can be recognized without necessarily being assimilated. How much difference can be tolerated is thus an unanswerable question. All that can be said is that the expectation of convergence on a final, single consensus is *not* a presupposition that anyone is committed to in the act of interpreting. An interpreter can offer an interpretation to others and expect them to find it reasonable and insightful without also expecting them to drop their differing interpretations. Furthermore, in limiting cases where two interpretations conflict to such an extent that both cannot be true, coercive violence is not the only alternative. Particular defenders of these conflicting interpretations may go to their deaths without giving in, but the more usual outcome is that yet another interpretation will come along that will reconfigure the interpretive scene in a way that either resolves or dissolves this conflict. There is no a priori way to say how this happens or even that it must happen. But the reminder that it *does* happen at least should help the contestants to recall that they are interpreting, and that interpretations are, and should remain, expandable and open to other views.

Hermeneutics does not deny the value of consensus, but it does not make consensus the only game in town, as McCarthy suggests in his assessment that contemporary societies have "very little else to appeal to in legitimating their laws, institutions, and policies than the free and reasoned agreement of their members" (§1.3, p. 27). But I wish to note that even McCarthy believes that the thrust of Habermas's position has been "obscured by the stress Habermas places on agreement and consensus" (§3.2, p. 78). The standard reading of Habermas sees him as defending a "consensus theory of truth" whereby, to put the point bluntly, something is true (or morally right) because everyone would agree to it (under ideal, uncoerced, unconstrained conditions). McCarthy de-emphasizes the role of agreement by stressing instead that participants in real-time discussions agree to the validity of a claim because it seems right, or well-supported by evidence and inference: "It is because validity claims are redeemed by the grounds or reasons offered in support of them, *and not by agreement as such*, that any existing consensus is open to reconsideration" (§3.2, pp. 75–6; emphasis added). *Real* consensus has no validating function at all: "In general, it is not *because* we agree that we hold a claim to be valid; rather, we agree because we have grounds for granting its validity" (§2.2, p. 42). He also adds in the same paragraph that "it is not the reported agreement that warrants the claim, but the warrant for the claim that grounds the agreement."

These remarks strike me as being correct about real discussion, and they also suggest to me that in seeking understanding, I am not necessarily positing the agreement of a universal audience or ideal communication community. In real inquiries agreement does not appear to be the essential telos of understanding, but a fortunate by-product. Or is agreement always fortunate? Actually I am a little disappointed to see this much rapprochement with Thomas McCarthy. I like to imagine that even in the ideal speech situation there would still be philosophical debates between the likes of Habermas, Gadamer, Foucault, and Rorty. If there would not be such debate, then it is really Habermas's ideal speech situation that would be the end of philosophy, not Rorty's edifying conversations.

With this reformulation there is in any case much less distance between Thomas McCarthy and myself than between the Habermasian model and the hermeneutical-genealogical model as I portrayed them in chapter 6. On the pluralistic hermeneutic account as I reconstruct it, what one aims at is an understanding of the subject matter and not agreement as such. When one's understanding of the subject matter is not reciprocated by others, one should wonder why. Dissent is worth investigating because it might lead to new insights into the issues under investigation. Nevertheless, the telos of understanding is the subject matter (or what Gadamer calls the *Sache*), not the agreement for the sake of agreement. To my mind, however, McCarthy's shift away from a stress on consensus should be accompanied by a shift away from monism and toward interpretive pluralism. McCarthy does not draw the same conclusion, but instead argues for the pragmatic value of maintaining Habermas's split between the real and the ideal. So fortunately there is still some disagreement between us, and in the final section I will continue the Hegelian tradition of criticizing this Kantian split between the real and the ideal by arguing instead for the pragmatic value of the critique of actuality in the hermeneutical-genealogical "history of the present."

## 8.4 Identity in Difference?

A charge that I raised in the earlier chapters against Habermas's model of the ideal was that it is so utopian that real dialogues cannot and should not take it as their measure. On my hermeneutic view, dialogues occur in real time, and should not take their measure from an ideal that always and necessarily remains contrary to fact. Thomas McCarthy argues against this view by urging that ideals have pragmatic value even if they are neither ever realized in practice nor realizable in principle. I will summarize his pragmatic arguments, but then I will argue that similar pragmatic results follow from hermeneutic pluralism. My strategy is to maintain that if similar pragmatic advantages follow from both positions, then there is no need to take on the extra philosophical baggage of an idealization that inevitably transcends any real, practical situation. A pluralistic hermeneutics is enough and the supposition of a monistic universal audience or ideal speech situation becomes unnecessary.

A pragmatic argument works differently than a transcendental argument. The transcendental strategy of argumentation tries to establish the necessary conditions for engaging in a certain type of activity.

Thus, Habermas tries to show that giving reasons for one's conclusions and challenging opposing reasons presupposes that ideally every rational person who had all the evidence would agree in the end. The pragmatic strategy of argumentation does not seek to show the necessity of such an ideal supposition, but only its desirability. Trying to realize the ideal is said to serve the practice better, and not doing so hinders the practice. An advantage of the pragmatic argument is that it does not rely on a dubious model of how rational agents would perform under ideal conditions, but it settles for a model that starts from where we are now and tries to establish what is "practically indispensable" (§2.4, p. 47). So McCarthy restricts the scope of the discussion to what obtains "for us" practically, without attempting to establish transcendentally what obtains everywhere and always "in itself."

However, is there much difference between a condition that turns out to be indispensable for *us* in *our* cognitive or normative inquiries, and one that would be indispensable for anyone and everyone? I believe that McCarthy thinks not, and that the difference is more in the path of argument than in the necessity of the conclusion. My worry, however, is that in a conclusion about, in my words, "what we *must* believe if we are to think and act as we do," there can easily be a slide from a weaker, pragmatic sense of "must" to a stronger, transcendental sense of "must." The pluralist hears the first sense and infers that an interpretation can be believed rationally without being thereby believed to be the only possible one. The monist moves to the second sense and infers that in accepting an interpretation, the interpreter also accepts that only one of the possible interpretations of the same domain (although not necessarily that particular interpretation) can be right. I read McCarthy as using his pragmatic argumentation to establish this stronger, monistic sense of necessity insofar as he hopes to establish his entitlement to terms like *unlimited*, *unconditional*, and *universal* validity.

On his account the pragmatic value of these monistic notions is that without them nothing could "force us to expand our horizons and learn to see things in new ways" (§3.1, p. 74). The argument is that without this stronger notion of reason and necessity there could never be any "self- and situation-transcendence" (§3.2, p. 74). For McCarthy it is not enough to assume that one context is transcended only by seeing it from another context, for that context will itself be transcended. The assumption must be the stronger one that if anything is believed to be correct in any one interpretation, then it must also be believed that there is only one coherent account that captures all that is correct in the various competing accounts. McCarthy cites with approval the view that independent reality is unitary and coherent, and "so too all the correct accounts of it must add up in the end to one coherent account" (§3.1, p. 73). Without the context-transcendent import of truth, he maintains, no one would critically examine the validity of their beliefs: "The claim to a validity that carries beyond the particular circumstances of utterance, indeed a validity that could be rationally acknowledged by all competent judges under ideal epistemic conditions, is precisely what opens up assertions to ongoing discursive examination" (§3.1, p. 74).

My hermeneutic intuitions are that this ideal is too contextless, and that what opens assertions to critical evaluation are more empirical events, such as finding some conflicting evidence, encountering someone who disagrees, or learning that one's outlook is either too narrow or too broad. Thinking about what all ideal judges would say is such an empty notion that it strikes me as being more likely to be used simply to reinforce one's existing beliefs. If I were asked why I thought my assertions were correct and I answered that all ideal judges would corroborate them, I think that I could well be accused of dogmatism. So my reaction is that even Thomas McCarthy's monistic idealization is not pragmatically relevant enough to be the motivation for challenging one's own assertions.

What seems more useful to me than thinking of the one true account and assuming that one's own account is approximating it is the hermeneutic reminder that one's account is an interpretation. Reminding oneself that one's account is an interpretation blocks dogmatism because it reminds one of the partiality of one's perspective. Interpretations also are pragmatic in the sense that they serve certain purposes and arise from specific needs. As these purposes and needs change, so will the pragmatic circumstances of interpretation. So interpretation does not necessarily aspire to McCarthy's degree of context-transcendence, since it more modestly recognizes its historical specificity and the limits of its utility. In what follows, then, I pick out three pragmatic arguments that McCarthy gives for the ideal of transcending all particular contexts, and I show that the hermeneutic context-boundedness has the same practical consequences. In this way I hope to undermine McCarthy's argument for the necessity of presupposing critical monism as a regulative ideal by showing that the ideal is pragmatically unnecessary.

(1) The first argument that I will challenge is that the ideal of rational acceptance by all competent judges can serve as an ongoing corrective to "actually accepted validity claims" (§3.2, p. 75). Right away I note that McCarthy grants that this ideal never in fact obtains and is "never more than potential" (§3.2, p. 75). So his argument seems to be that

since we never do know that our assertions are true, we should always hold ourselves open to the possibility that they are false. This thought does resist dogmatism by allowing for the possible fallibility of our theories. But it buys this laudable fallibilism at the cost of an apparent skepticism. The insistence that the warrants that serve as promissory notes for our beliefs can never be cashed in strikes me as undermining belief, not reinforcing it. The hermeneutic model, in contrast, does not hold belief hostage to a future that can never be present. It insists, instead, that beliefs are checked only against other actual beliefs, not against some ideal panel of judges. We are ourselves the judges, and what we do is continually to reexamine the assumptions and methods of our interpretations against other evidence and other interpretations. In real time the best corrective to an actually accepted validity claim might well be another actually accepted validity claim. Ideal judges are not needed to tell us when there is an actual inconsistency, so I do not see where the idealization does any real work. Interpretation just is the process of unfolding and articulating beliefs and practices, and it involves testing what we find ourselves saying or doing against other things that we also say and do.

(2) Of course, we might be deceiving ourselves and hiding certain facts or attitudes from ourselves. McCarthy's second major argument is, therefore, that we need the ideal of unconditional truth to discover "hidden conditions" and to become "conscious of unconscious determinants of our thought and action" (§3.2, p. 77). While he grants that we could never achieve the self-transparency of making all these hidden factors conscious, he thinks that without the ideal of making some of them conscious, argumentation would never be more than an unbridgeable contrast between what "I think" and what "you think." Here again, however, insofar as McCarthy allows for the inevitability of some indeterminacy in the background of argumentation, that indeterminacy weakens the ideal of the "best argument" winning in the end and warranting the unconditionality of truth. An argument never wins unless everyone interprets the premises in the same way, and this admission of indeterminacy (even in the ideal situation) suggests that there will always be hidden factors that might lead to differences of interpretation.

Does hermeneutics never suspect hidden conditions and unconscious determinants? Does it always have to take a given self-interpretation at face value? A brief answer is that its willingness to admit differences of interpretation suggests on the contrary that it has to grant a high priority to uncovering these hidden factors. If a conflict of interpretation is encountered, then among the first things to do is to start investigating the background for divergent practices or assumptions that might be leading to the surface conflict over particular beliefs or values. So I see no reason for thinking either that hermeneutics is prevented methodologically from ferreting out hidden factors, or that its main reason for doing so is a commitment to counterfactual universal agreement or unconditional truth.

(*3*) Behind this quasi-epistemological second argument lies a more political third argument. The question is, are there limits to how much difference in interpretation can be reasonably tolerated? McCarthy's strongest argument against the hermeneutical pluralism that I have proposed is, in my opinion, that pluralism is enabled, not disabled, by the harmony provided by a single framework. This framework may come down to the agreement to disagree, and to the procedural guarantees that make disagreement and difference possible. McCarthy thinks, therefore, that the formation of abstract, universal norms has served the pragmatic function of making social pluralism possible. His strongest argument for his universalism, as I read him, is that "abstract generality is not a threat to difference but a licence for it" (§3.2, p. 80). He insists correctly that "abstraction *need* not mean homogenization nor universality uniformity" (§3.2, p. 80).[10] Context-transcendent universalism is not necessarily utopian, furthermore, but also has what he calls a "subversive" potential (§1.2, p. 21; §2.1, p. 37). His argument for this is double-edged: any claims to unconditional validity are "permanently exposed to criticism from all sides," and any claims that we agree to here and now must be challenged to see if they could also be agreed to under other circumstances (§2.1, p. 37).

I say this argument for the pragmatic value of the ideal of harmonizing social pluralities within a single procedural framework is double-edged because it guards against two dangers, (i) complacency and (ii) parochialism. On the first point, the claim is that the ideal of unlimited validity is needed to prevent us from sinking into the complacency of thinking that however bad our present social arrangements are, they are still the best that we can do for now, so we should learn to live with them. Certainly McCarthy is right to criticize complacency, but once again I suggest that the model that I have presented is sufficient to make the same critique without the unnecessary monistic idealization. Sometimes hermeneutics and poststructuralism are accused of condoning this social complacency precisely because of their apparent lack of enthusiasm for context-transcendent universals like freedom and truth. I have argued, however, that neither Foucault nor Gadamer are opposed to these abstract concepts in principle, but are more interested in how various enriched conceptions are interpreted concretely in practice.[11] Gadamer's theory is not traditionalist and does not condone complacency about the status quo. Hermeneutics does not have to condone the dominant interpretation of the tradition but can instead look for possibilities in the complex tradition that have been concealed by this dominating interpretation. Foucault puts this method into practice by writing the history of the present and showing some surprising contrasts between what people intended and what the actual historical effects were. This method of critical history strikes me as effectively subverting complacency. If subverting complacency is a social benefit in itself, as McCarthy seems to be granting, then I see no need to ground it in the further idealizations of unlimited validity or counterfactual consensus.

The second edge of McCarthy's attack challenges the parochialism that might result from the hermeneutic insistence that understanding and interpretation always grow out of and are tied to a context. McCarthy's idealization of reason implies ideally that to believe something reasonably is to have reasons that make not believing it unreasonable or irrational. This ideal of the reasonable as what no one could rationally reject guards against the parochialism of reasons being relative to contextual self-understandings. Hermeneutics could respond in turn, however, that to assume that belief is reasonable only when it is based on conclusive evidence and valid arguments, or generally on reasoning that no one could reject, is an unnecessary idealization of belief.[12] Too much middle ground is lost by calling all belief that falls short of this ideal unreasonable or merely parochial. In practice understanding often results from inconclusive evidence and judgemental insight (or *phronesis*) that cannot be reduced to rules. Understanding arrived at in this way is reasonable, even if it is interpretive.

Moreover, explicitly admitting to the interpretive character of our understanding does not commit us to parochialism. On the contrary, it reminds us that because our understanding is interpretive, we must be alert to its partial character and open to other perspectives. Parochialism is not simply a matter of not having complete knowledge of everything that needs to be known. No one has that. Instead, it is a matter of thinking that one does know all or even most of what needs to be known, and thus of being closed to other interpretations. The hermeneutic insistence on the openness of interpretation strikes me as being at least as good an antidote to parochialism as Habermas's idealizations.

This conclusion leaves McCarthy and me agreeing that the plurality of social differences needs to be respected. We disagree, however, on which philosophical perspective best respects those differences. Do we agree on the more important practical point, then, and disagree only on the less important meta-philosophical one? I am inclined to say yes, but my guess is that he will think that this assessment minimizes the import of philosophy and its abstractions. Either way, I hope to have established from within our considerable range of agreement at least enough disagreement not only to support my stand, but also to generate future debate among as many as care to take part.

NOTES

1 For a more detailed defense of Foucault against this line of interpretation see my introduction to *Foucault: A Critical Reader* (Oxford and Cambridge, MA: Blackwell, 1986), especially pp. 14–23.
2 I develop these distinctions in several recent essays, particularly in "Is Hermeneutics Ethnocentric?" in *The Interpretive Turn: Philosophy, Science, Culture*, eds David R. Hiley, James F. Bohman, and Richard Shusterman (Ithaca: Cornell University Press, 1991).
3 See Richard Rorty, "Solidarity," in *Contingency, Irony, and Solidarity* (Cambridge, UK: Cambridge University Press, 1989); "Solidarity or Objectivity?" in *Post-Analytic Philosophy*, ed. John Rajchman and Cornel West (New York: Columbia University Press, 1985); "On Ethnocentrism: A Reply to Clifford Geertz," *Michigan Quarterly Review* 25 (1986): 525–34.
4 See my article, "Post-Cartesian Interpretation: Hans-Georg Gadamer and Donald Davidson," forthcoming in the Library of Living Philosophers volume on *The Philosophy of Hans-Georg Gadamer* (LaSalle, IL: Open Court Publishing Company).
5 Michel Foucault, "Polemics, Politics, and Problematizations: An Interview," in Paul Rabinow's *Foucault Reader* (New York: Pantheon, 1984), p. 385.
6 J. Habermas, "Justice and Solidarity: On the Discussion Concerning Stage 6," in *The Moral Domain*, ed. Thomas E. Wren (Cambridge, MA: MIT Press, 1990), p. 244.
7 Ibid., p. 245.
8 For further discussion of the life jacket example see Thomas Nagel, *Equality and Partiality*, pp. 24–5 and 172.
9 In the previously cited essay, "Justice and Solidarity" (p. 246), Habermas also invokes this cosmopolitan ideal as part of his universalization of solidarity:

Justice is inconceivable without at least an element of reconciliation. Even in the cosmopolitan ideas of the close of the eighteenth century, the archaic bonding energies of kinship were not extinguished but only refined into solidarity with everything wearing a human face. "*All* men become brothers," Schiller could say in his "Ode to Joy." This double aspect also characterizes the communicative form of practical discourse: the bonds of social integration remain intact despite the fact that the agreement required of all transcends the bounds of every natural community.

The cosmopolitan ideal is clearly articulated in Kant's essay, "Idea for a Universal History from a Cosmopolitan Point of View."

10 Foucault is sometimes read as saying that modernization has only brought about increased social homogenization (through what Foucault calls "normalization") and thus has suppressed individualism and difference. In *Discipline and Punish: The Birth of the Prison* (trans. Alan Sheridan; New York: Random House, 1977; p. 184) Foucault, however, makes exactly the point that at the same time that normalization homogenizes society, it individualizes:

> In a sense, the power of normalization imposes homogeneity; but it individualizes by making it possible to measure gaps, to determine levels, to fix specialities and to render the differences useful by fitting them one to another. It is easy to understand how the power of the norm functions within a system of formal equality, since within a homogeneity that is the rule, the norm introduces, as a useful imperative and as a result of measurement, all the shading of individual differences.

11 Here I follow the distinction that Rawls has made familiar between a general *concept* (for instance, of justice) and differing *conceptions* of it. McCarthy seems to rely on this distinction at the end of §3.2 when he distinguishes thin, abstract universals from their differing, thicker, situated contextualizations, and insists that their "concrete meaning-in-action is inherently open to discussion, that is to say, essentially contestable" (81). With this admission of the essential contestability of the meaning of universals he seems to me to come over to the pluralist camp. To say that a basic concept is essentially contestable, in the technical sense defined by W. B. Gallie or Steven Lukes, is to say that disputes about it are endless, and without resolution, even ideally. This is a risky admission by McCarthy or any universalist, for proponents of essential contestability are often accused of relativism.

12 See Thomas Nagel in *Equality and Partiality* (pp. 161–2):

> Belief is reasonable when grounded on inconclusive evidence plus judgement. In such a case one usually acknowledges the possibility of some further standard to which impersonal appeal can be made, even though it cannot settle existing disagreements at the moment. But even without such a standard, belief may not be unreasonable. In any case, it would be absurd to claim that individuals should decide what to do in their own lives only on grounds which they believe it would be unreasonable for anyone else to reject, including grounds having to do with fundamental values they believe to be objectively correct.

# Index

absolutism  42, 132, 136, 218
accountability  34, 44, 45, 63, 65–6, 70,
    71, 72, 75, 91, 252
action  9, 27, 46, 67, 68, 78, 136, 166,
    195
Adorno, Theodor W.  3, 14, 112,
    114–30, 131, 132, 135, 137, 139,
    144, 146, 147, 152, 158, 166, 225
    *Dialectic of Enlightenment*  114, 117,
    118, 119, 124, 128, 131, 134, 136
    'Kritik'  136
    *Minima Moralia*  135
    *Negative Dialectics*  116, 120, 124,
    127, 132
aesthetic, the  186, 187
aesthetics  124, 234, 237
agency  34, 40, 78
alienation  111, 257
anthropology  40, 86–7, 88, 89, 174,
    204, 225–6
anticipation of completeness (*Vorgriff
    der Vollkommenheit*)  196, 197–200
antirationalism  9, 11
anti-Semitism  115, 229
argument  43, 45, 53, 76, 148, 161, 207,
    239, 241, 261, 266, 269, 271
argumentative discourse  76, 242
Aristotle  28, 53, 54, 160, 194–5, 234
art  120, 218, 228, 229, 234
    criticism  45, 228
authenticity  226, 237
authority  45, 49, 74, 82, 191, 194,
    195–7, 229, 245
autonomy  2, 14, 37, 43, 44, 45, 46, 50,
    54, 56–7, 66, 74, 78, 91, 113, 150, 202

background  161, 185–6, 191, 194, 195,
    252, 253, 269
    of knowledge  197
Bacon, Francis  115, 129, 130
barbarism  113, 114, 116, 146, 152
Barthes, Roland  198
Baudelaire, Charles  135, 136
belief(s)  32, 44, 47, 48, 49, 75, 87, 90,
    91, 122, 123, 132, 133, 183, 184,
    194, 195, 203, 226, 242, 251, 256,
    268, 269, 270, 271
Benjamin, Walter  135, 145, 165
bias  21, 105
Buck-Morss, Susan  133, 136

capitalism  19, 24, 55, 229, 244
categorical imperative  50, 53, 79
certainty  123, 125, 172, 207
Chomsky, Noam  160, 187
civil rights  56, 162
cognition  132, 146, 152, 166, 186, 187,
    196, 267
coherence  3, 111, 233, 234, 241, 244
collective decision-making  24, 25, 28
collective identity  92, 228, 235, 236,
    238
commensurability  128, 154
common will  79, 187
communication  44, 45, 51, 67, 83, 148,
    159, 180, 187, 191, 206, 207, 258,
    259, 260, 265
communicative action  28, 38, 44, 46,
    47, 50, 54, 71, 73, 77, 78, 91, 152,
    161, 173, 177, 179, 180, 181, 193,
    200, 203, 218, 244
communicative rationality  32, 39, 45,
    64, 72, 73, 75, 180, 183, 184, 187,
    221, 258, 259
community  52, 201, 202, 203, 257
complacency  4, 270, 271
completeness  200, 223, 233
    anticipation of *see* anticipation of
    completeness
conflict  183, 270
conflict of interpretations,  237, 244, 269
conformism  67, 118, 128, 130
consciousness  8, 16, 31, 41, 50, 74, 77,
    114, 132, 133, 152, 179, 187, 199,
    233, 244
    false  10, 41
    shapes of  122, 123
    true  10
consensus  3, 14, 51, 74, 76, 78, 79, 161,
    165, 166, 167, 174, 175, 176, 177,

180, 182, 184, 188, 189, 190, 194,
195, 198, 200, 201, 203, 209, 221,
223, 224, 225, 227, 232, 234, 238,
240, 241, 242, 244, 245, 256, 258,
260, 263–6, 271
theory of truth 189, 265
*see also* nonconsensuality
context 107, 172, 185, 189, 190, 194,
197, 204, 205, 231, 235, 238, 267,
271
transcendence 21, 39, 40, 72, 74, 231,
236, 240, 254, 268, 270
contextualism 20, 37, 40, 68, 72, 193,
222, 227, 232, 237, 240, 241, 242,
244, 271
contextualization 36, 67, 69, 81
contingency 13, 27, 33, 107, 159, 166,
172, 178, 180, 181, 193, 201, 207,
219, 227, 231, 243
contingent social actions 172, 231, 235
convention 32, 41, 44, 74, 137
convergence 201, 203, 204, 205, 206,
207, 209, 256, 260, 262, 264
conversation 68, 89, 261, 265
cooperation 38, 39, 63, 65, 72
counterenlightenment 1, 2, 153, 202
critical activity 3, 35, 93, 106–7, 114,
115, 124, 133, 136, 137, 139, 145,
202, 223, 231, 254
evaluation 12, 76, 81, 82, 268
historiography 119, 158, 162, 228,
231, 243
history 3, 119–20, 124, 126, 131,
134–6, 138, 155, 158, 160, 161, 164,
166, 167, 177, 202, 203, 208, 217,
219, 223, 224, 229, 232, 250, 271
monism 200, 233, 255, 268
pluralism 200, 233, 242
reflective dialogue 44, 46, 50, 66, 75,
81, 91, 232, 233, 239, 242, 244
social theory 3, 8, 20, 22, 23, 24, 31,
57, 74, 137, 138, 152, 218, 219, 221,
222, 224, 225, 227, 229, 230, 238
criticism 18, 44, 74, 75, 103, 127, 137,
152, 154, 197, 203, 235
critique 18, 84, 119, 173, 218, 224, 226,
238
of enlightenment 119, 123, 125, 131,
152, 195
of reason *see* reason, critique of
cross-cultural dialogue/discourse 88,
90, 91
interpretation 85, 89
representation 88, 90
cultural change 48, 205, 218
difference 178, 263, 227
dopes 38, 250–3
practices 40, 222
relativism 32, 88
reproduction 46, 55
studies 14, 31, 40
culture 8, 12, 16, 36, 38, 40, 73, 119,
122, 192, 193, 197, 218, 222, 226
holistic conceptions of 78

Darwin, Charles 8, 49, 150
Davidson, Donald 242, 258
deconstruction 7, 8, 14, 15, 20, 21, 34,
35, 36, 37, 74, 77, 82, 83, 123, 145,
149, 178, 184, 188, 189, 193, 200,
207, 208, 218, 243, 251
democracy 24, 28, 55, 56
Derrida, Jacques 14, 34, 35, 123, 145,
149, 153, 187, 189, 198
Descartes, René 2, 27, 104, 111, 113,
133, 172, 179, 208
desire 45, 51, 90, 218
determinacy/indeterminacy 68, 78, 269
determinate negation 8, 122, 132, 136,
227
detranscendentalization 8, 10, 43
development 23, 118, 120, 150, 152,
153, 155, 156, 157, 158, 160, 162,
164, 204, 218, 221, 224, 228, 229
developmental theory 157, 164, 167,
250
dialectic 35, 76, 120, 121, 122, 123,
124, 126, 127, 132, 233
of enlightenment 117, 146, 225, 226
of the general and the particular 68,
77, 80
of the ideal and the real 77
dialectical critique 20, 25, 125
dialectical thinking 120, 126
dialogue 87, 238, 244, 258, 266
*différance* 35, 36, 37, 74
difference 2, 36, 80, 227, 266–72
dignity 53, 91
Dilthey, Wilhelm 133, 199
disagreement 175, 245, 249, 256
discipline 165, 178
discontinuity 125, 127, 128
in history 119, 130
discourse 45, 75, 76, 80, 90, 148, 180,
181, 182, 187, 188, 198, 203, 223,
233, 238, 239, 241, 242, 245, 268
argumentative *see* argumentative
discourse
critical-reflective *see* critical-reflective
discourse
ethics 50, 52, 53, 54, 56, 263
practical *see* practical discourse
rational *see* rational discourse
scientific *see* scientific discourse
discursive practices 46, 196–7
discussion 45, 90, 176, 254, 265
dissent 166, 184, 201, 265
divergence 205, 206, 207
diversity 21, 80, 193, 263
dogmatism 21, 37, 125, 268, 269
Dreyfus, Hubert 194, 195
Droysen, Gustav 193, 197
Durkheim, Émile 14, 129, 220

economic inequality 262, 264
economic system 88, 130, 159
education 56, 57, 73
*Einverständnis* 180, 182, 188
emancipation 3, 113, 219

empathy 12, 53
empirical science 48, 90, 149, 150
enlightenment 1, 2, 3, 8, 13, 34, 41,
 106, 114–16, 118, 120, 121, 123,
 124, 125, 127, 128, 130, 131, 146,
 151, 153, 154, 155, 166, 179, 225,
 249
 critique of *see* critique of
 enlightenment
Enlightenment, the 21, 42, 124, 128,
 131, 191, 194, 195
epistemology 8, 40, 41, 87, 104, 122,
 133, 138–9, 179, 192, 207, 245
equality 25, 54
ethics 24, 25, 49, 52, 57, 63, 79, 106,
 150, 160, 161, 173, 237, 238
 discourse *see* discourse ethics
*ethnos* 32, 41
ethnocentrism 3, 32, 33, 157, 161, 203,
 205, 223, 242, 253, 254
ethnography 82, 83, 86, 174
ethnomethodology 63, 64, 65, 68, 72,
 75, 82, 222
evaluative schemes 77, 91, 255
evidence 43, 239, 265, 267, 268, 269,
 271
evolution 149, 150, 154, 155, 156, 157,
 158, 177, 182, 200, 202, 206, 225
evolutionary theory 151, 153, 157, 158,
 159, 160, 161, 162, 164, 165, 167,
 204
Existence 12, 13

fallibilism 10, 218, 219, 220, 231, 269
fascism 134, 236
fatalism 113, 137
Fichte, Johann Gottlieb 113
Fine, Arthur 222
first-order interpretations 201, 240
first-order theories 201, 221, 240
first-person point of view 73, 92
force 33, 71, 80, 206, 245
form of life 2, 162, 181
Foucault, Michel 1, 3, 7, 8, 14, 19,
 33–4, 63, 78, 79, 83, 85, 107, 115,
 119, 127, 131, 139, 144–9, 153, 158,
 159, 162, 163, 164, 165, 166, 167,
 173, 176, 177, 178, 179, 182, 188,
 202, 222, 223, 224, 225, 226, 228,
 229, 230, 234, 249, 251, 253, 254,
 256, 258, 259, 265, 270, 271
 *Discipline and Punish* 128, 145
 *History of Sexuality* 229
 *Madness and Civilization* 258
 'practical critique' 7
 'What is Enlightenment?' 202
foundationalism 14, 42, 161, 172, 218,
 222, 232, 252
Frankfurt School 1, 19, 74, 107, 128,
 144, 145, 146, 151, 162, 164, 180,
 183, 219, 229, 230, 250
freedom/unfreedom 12, 16, 17, 20, 22,
 23, 25, 42, 54, 78, 79, 112, 113, 115,
 146, 225, 249, 253, 254, 270

Freud, Sigmund 8, 77, 83
fusion of horizons
 *(Horizontverschmelzung)* 191–3, 197

Gadamer, Hans-Georg 1, 2, 3, 41, 83,
 177, 180, 184, 188–200, 203, 204,
 206, 222, 230, 233, 234, 235, 238,
 240, 243, 249, 253, 254, 256, 258,
 261, 265, 266, 270
 *Truth and Method* 183, 188, 195, 196,
 197, 199
Garfinkel, Harold 38, 63, 64, 66, 67, 69,
 71, 72, 75, 80
*Gegenstand* 193, 243
gender 82, 88, 90
genealogical hermeneutics 3, 4, 177,
 178, 200–9, 227, 234, 240, 265
genealogical history 159, 161, 164, 167,
 203, 207, 208, 224, 233, 252
genealogy 3, 33, 34, 55, 83, 147–8, 149,
 150, 155, 158–64, 165, 166, 167,
 173, 174, 178, 179, 183, 202, 207,
 208, 219, 222, 224–30, 243, 251,
 257, 259
German Idealism 77, 111, 178, 217
Geuss, Raymond 120
globalization 37, 88, 92
God's-eye-view 10, 32, 40, 43, 81, 199,
 220, 226, 255
Gramsci, Antonio 130
group identity 236, 237

Habermas, Jürgen 1, 2, 3, 17, 24, 26, 28,
 32, 37, 38, 39, 43, 44, 45, 46, 47, 50,
 51, 52, 53, 55, 56, 71–2, 73, 75, 76,
 78, 79, 83, 85, 104–5, 144, 146, 147,
 148, 149, 150, 151, 152, 153, 154,
 155, 156, 158–64, 165, 166, 167,
 173, 175, 176, 177–88, 193, 195,
 196, 200, 202, 203, 204, 206, 208,
 218, 220, 221, 222, 224, 225, 226,
 227, 228, 229, 230, 236, 238, 239,
 240, 241, 242, 243, 244, 245, 249,
 250, 252, 254, 255, 261, 263, 265,
 266, 267, 271
 'Geschichte und Evolution' 151
 *Knowledge and Human Interests* 104
 *Legitimation Crisis* 55
 *The Philosophical Discourse of
 Modernity* 144, 205
 'The New Obscurity' 159
 *The Structural Transformation of the
 Public Sphere* 55, 224
 *Theory of Communicative Action* 177,
 180, 203, 224, 234
Hegel, Georg Wilhelm Friedrich 8, 13,
 28, 31, 92, 106, 117, 119–20, 121,
 122, 123, 127, 128, 148, 149, 152,
 153, 155–6, 187, 199, 218, 226, 233,
 260, 266
 *Logic* 122
 *Phenomenology of Spirit
 (Phänomenologie des Geistes)* 122,
 128

Heidegger, Martin 37, 120, 126–7, 130, 131, 132, 134, 137, 139, 191, 192, 195, 197, 217, 235
  *Being and Time (Sein und Zeit)* 129, 134, 183
hermeneutics 1, 2, 77, 83, 86, 108, 177–8, 181, 184, 189, 192, 193, 194, 196, 198, 199, 200, 204, 222, 226, 231–8, 240, 252, 253, 257, 261, 265, 266, 269–70, 271
  genealogical *see* genealogical hermeneutics
  pluralism 182, 183, 184, 188–9, 202, 266, 270
historical interpretations 232, 233, 241
historical necessity 130, 158
historical progress 117, 151, 152, 153, 158
historicism 3, 8, 9, 10, 11, 32, 40, 42, 131, 189, 222, 240, 243, 244
*Historikerstreit* 236
historiography 119, 120, 136, 148, 151, 155, 159, 164, 165, 167, 184, 199, 233
history 40
  critical *see* critical history
  Hegel's approach to 121
  of rationality 145, 230
  of reason 146, 229
  of science 83, 145
  of subjectivity 229
  of the present 165, 230, 252, 266, 271
  totalizing conception of 117–18
Hobbes, Thomas 27
holism 3, 78, 194, 198, 217
Holocaust, the 236
horizon 192, 193, 267
  fusion of *see* fusion of horizons
Horkheimer, Max 3, 8–18, 21, 23–8, 31, 37, 54, 56, 75, 81, 103–14, 115–16, 119–24, 126, 128, 129, 130, 137, 144, 146, 152, 158, 166, 173, 181, 182, 225, 259, 260
  *Dialectic of Enlightenment* 114, 116, 117, 124, 128, 131, 134, 136
  'Materialism and Morality' 24
  'On the Problem of Truth' 10, 11
  'The Social Function of Philosophy' 11
  'Traditional and Critical Theory' 20, 103, 104, 108, 113
human sciences 82, 105, 162, 163, 193, 241, 243
humanism 34, 111, 114
humanity/inhumanity 79, 112, 184
Hume, David 186

ideal, the 10, 37, 38, 46, 73, 77, 80, 107, 188, 266, 267
ideal epistemic conditions 73, 74, 268
ideal speech situation 46, 159, 162, 177, 181, 182, 196, 201, 250, 254, 265, 266
idealism 17, 22, 111, 113, 114, 179

German *see* German Idealism
idealizing assumptions 75, 234
identity 2, 13, 36, 46, 47, 53, 92, 132, 137, 157, 226, 235, 237, 238, 266–72
ideology 23, 73, 113
  critique 82, 105
immanent criticism 121, 124, 125, 132, 136, 139
impartiality 54, 80, 261, 262
  of laws 53
incommensurability 128, 130, 154, 206
  in history 119, 127
independent reality 172, 192, 256, 268
indeterminacy *see* determinacy
indexicality 67, 68, 72
individualism 22, 24, 47, 56, 128, 234
  rationalist 12, 36, 37
individuation 46, 79
Ingram, David 175
Institute for Social Research 8, 10, 75
intelligibility 36, 48, 70, 71, 91, 132
interactive competence 65, 69
intercultural dialogue 91, 92
interest(s) 2, 24, 25, 27, 52, 54, 55, 71, 138, 223
interpretation 46, 80, 82, 91, 124, 172, 183, 184, 189, 190, 195, 196, 198, 199, 202, 204, 207, 208, 217, 226, 231, 232, 235, 238, 240, 241, 242, 243, 244, 255–6, 260–1, 264–5, 267, 268, 269, 270, 271
  conflict of *see* conflict of interpretations
  errors in 39, 72
interpretive pluralism 4, 266
  schemes 38, 77, 91, 255
intersubjective
  recognition 45, 51
  understanding 70, 180
  validity 39, 51, 86
intersubjectivism 44, 54, 71, 179, 189
irony 77, 92, 136, 137
irrationality 26, 125, 146, 148, 201

Jameson, Fredric 120
Jay, Martin 112, 120, 145
judgement 67, 78, 80, 175, 194, 222
justice/injustice 3, 12, 23, 24, 25, 27, 32, 37, 52, 54, 55, 56, 166, 207, 226, 234, 237, 238, 244, 259
justification 16, 32, 40, 42, 44, 46, 53, 74, 173, 208, 231, 238, 259

Kant, Immanuel 2, 8, 9, 14, 16, 24, 25, 26, 35–6, 38, 39, 40, 43, 44, 46, 50, 52, 53, 54, 56, 63, 71, 79, 104, 106, 111, 116, 117, 130, 132, 139, 146–7, 152, 153, 160, 178, 179, 180, 182, 186, 187, 200, 217, 221, 224, 244, 257, 264, 266
  *Critique of Pure Reason* 7, 146, 221
  *Groundwork* 42
  'The History of Pure Reason' 146
  'What is Enlightenment?' 146

*see also* neo-Kantianism
Kohlberg, Lawrence  153, 167, 177
Kuhn, Thomas  162, 241

Laclau, Ernesto  179, 205, 206
language  34, 35, 36, 38, 42, 68, 69, 74,
    78, 131, 137, 159, 166, 179, 181,
    183, 192, 196, 198, 204, 206, 218,
    227, 239, 240, 244, 258
  philosophy of *see* philosophy of
    language
law  27, 50, 51, 228, 229
*Lebensphilosophie*  9
liberalism  79
lifeworld  2, 45, 51, 52, 78, 160, 161,
    164, 173, 179, 184, 240, 259
linguistic competence  160
linguistic understanding  191
linguistics  2, 153, 160, 187
local solidarity  253–62, 264
logic  2, 21, 120, 122, 185, 187, 226, 227
logical necessity  108, 120
logocentrism  2, 21, 34, 35, 36, 78, 232
loss  83, 84, 253
Lyotard, Jean-François  147, 153, 158,
    166
  *The Postmodern Condition*  158, 166

MacIntyre, Alasdair  47, 83, 155, 227,
    232
  *After Virtue*  155
Mannheim, Karl  9, 11, 104
  *Ideology and Utopia*  10
Marcuse, Herbert  23, 24
  'Philosophy and Critical Theory'  20,
    22
market  24, 25, 129
Marx, Karl  3, 8, 13, 14, 15, 17, 18, 19,
    22, 31, 74, 77, 85, 218, 220, 226, 229
  *Capital*  234
  *The Eighteenth Brumaire*  219
materialism  9, 24, 56, 127
Mead, George Herbert  28, 64, 217, 223
meaning  21, 36, 39, 46, 91, 192, 198,
    199, 225, 240
means-ends reasoning  183, 221
meta-narrative  158, 217, 218, 220, 223
metaphysics  9, 36, 48, 52, 90, 113, 114,
    148, 149, 150, 151, 156, 163, 179,
    198, 199, 217, 219, 221, 225, 227,
    233, 243, 245, 252
meta-procedural idealizations  175, 202,
    244–5
metatheory  3, 104, 165, 173, 175, 179,
    201, 202, 208, 225, 229, 230, 240,
    244
methodology  90, 121, 124, 196, 197
Mill, John Stuart  220, 237, 242
modernism  92, 119, 135, 136, 147, 152,
    203, 218, 231, 243, 249
monism  4, 200, 255–6, 261, 263, 266,
    267, 268, 270
  critical *see* critical monism
moral agent  117, 150

philosophy  150, 152, 156
  principles  152, 160, 178
  right  177, 203, 236
  theory  3, 24, 25, 52, 53, 56, 155
morality  24, 25, 26, 27, 32, 42, 47, 48,
    53, 54, 56, 106, 116, 118, 119, 122,
    152, 154, 156, 186, 187, 228, 259
mutual intelligibility  67, 78, 91, 264
mutual understanding  54, 69, 70–1, 78,
    91, 183, 238

Nagel, Thomas  262, 263, 264
  *Equality and Partiality*  257, 261
natural science(s)  14, 15, 82, 104, 105,
    131, 150, 162, 194, 241, 243, 256
naturalism  149, 150, 153, 155, 217,
    218, 219, 220
nature  48, 80, 110–11, 113, 115, 132,
    133, 137–8, 153, 157, 193, 218
necessity  108, 121, 123, 124, 127, 130,
    136, 147, 175, 207, 218, 219, 227,
    231, 244, 243, 245, 267
negative history  117–18
neo-Kantianism  24, 28, 162
Nietzsche, Friedrich Wilhelm  3, 7, 8,
    37, 39, 119–20, 121, 123, 125, 130,
    134, 135, 139, 147, 149, 150, 151,
    153, 154, 155–7, 158, 206, 217
  'The Use and Abuse of History for
    Life'  119, 134
nihilism  3, 154, 157, 194, 201
nonconsensuality  78–9, 176, 201
non-identity  132, 137

objectivity  2, 14, 36, 39, 40, 51, 63, 72,
    80, 86, 87, 132, 133, 223
Offe, Claus  56
ontology  41, 74, 75, 126, 199, 221, 222,
    230, 258

Peirce, Charles Sanders  28, 217, 223
performative
  contradiction/self-contradiction  33,
    173, 175, 221, 249, 254
perspective  238, 261
philosophical theory  124, 137, 156
philosophy
  Continental *see* Continental philosophy
  dialectical  123
  enlightenment  123, 152
  of history  112, 113, 117, 139, 151,
    152, 158, 162, 177, 181, 206, 218,
    219
  of language  152, 158, 177, 183
phronesis  52, 160, 194, 195, 271
Piaget, Jean  153, 159, 160, 167, 177
Plato  38, 146
pluralism  3, 13, 17, 21, 48, 50, 52, 80,
    123, 174, 175, 176, 177, 178, 182,
    184, 185, 191, 193, 197, 200, 201,
    202, 206, 223, 233, 234, 238–45,
    253, 256, 260, 261, 263–6, 267
pluralistic societies  81, 237
poetics  90

Poincaré, Henri 103
political action 154, 165, 219
politics 25, 42, 55, 56, 63, 80, 83, 87,
    88, 90, 126, 178, 179, 216, 238
  of identity 236
  of truth 33
Pollner, Melvin 72
positivism 16, 33, 125, 131, 137, 163,
    172
postmetaphysicalism 36, 77, 149
postmodernism 13, 17, 37, 136, 144,
    147, 153, 158, 218, 227, 240,
poststructuralism 1, 2, 64, 78, 108,
    119–39, 144, 148, 149, 150, 151,
    153, 162, 163, 166, 179, 217, 270
post-traditionalism 46, 47, 50, 243, 244
power 2, 27, 33, 74, 80, 89, 129–30,
    131, 154, 165, 173, 182, 183, 222,
    229, 251, 254
  relations 38, 113, 115
  *see also* will to power
practical discourse 50, 51, 53, 55, 56
practical reason 23, 25, 26, 28, 43, 44,
    52, 54–5, 56, 63, 64, 67, 69, 71, 75,
    78, 80, 178, 195, 222, 237
pragmatic presuppositions 47, 226,
    244, 245
pragmatics 160, 177,
  of communication 36
pragmatism 2, 3, 8, 17, 72, 83, 107, 108,
    217–24, 245, 254, 257, 266
  American 8, 217
prejudice 32, 41, 191, 194, 195, 196,
    197
principle of charity 183, 184, 203, 242
  of insufficient reason 76
prisons 33, 145, 158, 166
progress 113, 115–16, 117, 118, 127,
    129, 130, 151, 152, 153, 154, 156,
    159, 217, 218, 228, 254
provinciality 180, 204, 206
pure reason 2, 55, 180, 182
Putnam, Hilary 28

race 49, 88
Ranke, Leopold von 195
rational acceptability 51, 73, 75, 76,
    239, 268
  agency 43, 44, 68, 250–3, 267
  choice 63, 71, 221
  discourse 26, 49, 201
  reconstruction 83, 149, 150, 152, 154,
    155, 157, 158, 160, 164
  subject 2, 8, 229
rationalism 9, 12, 21, 37, 64, 75, 114,
    115, 128, 131, 138, 154, 179, 222, 227
Raulet, Gérard 145, 147
Rawls, John 24, 28, 53
real interests 138, 139, 252
real, the 10, 37, 38, 73, 77, 188, 250, 266
realism 87, 189, 192, 199, 217, 232
reason
  critique of 206; pure 7, 14, 20, 21–2,
    31, 35, 50, 64; impure 81, 92, 223

practical *see* practical reason
reconstruction 14, 21, 82, 164, 222,
    224, 226, 251
recontextualization 25, 34
reductionism 9, 149
reflection 134, 195
reflexivity 15, 16, 47, 66
relativism 2, 3, 10, 12, 86, 131, 132,
    133, 137, 155, 204, 260
religion 27, 48, 90, 119, 228, 229
representation 2, 16, 88, 89, 190
repression 137, 252, 254
responsibility 12, 38, 236, 237, 259
Ricoeur, Paul 82
rightness 236, 239, 244
rights 37, 79, 138, 236
Rorty, Richard 2, 14, 33, 40, 41, 42, 76,
    149, 217, 222, 223, 253, 254, 256,
    258, 260, 265
  *Philosophy and the Mirror of Nature*
    32

*Sache* 180, 189, 190, 191, 193, 238,
    239, 241, 243, 258, 266
science 45, 63, 76, 80, 90, 103, 114,
    128, 137, 162, 163, 196, 197, 217,
    228, 239, 241, 256
  history of *see* history of science
self-consciousness 2, 17, 31, 34, 35, 43
self-criticism 137, 203, 220
self-interpretation 167, 190, 207, 208,
    228, 235, 236, 237, 269
self-reference 35, 201, 202
self-reflection 116, 120, 219
self-transparency 4, 251–2, 253, 255,
    256, 269
self-understanding 8, 19, 34, 40, 52, 82,
    130, 131, 146, 190, 195, 199, 202,
    203, 207, 221, 225, 228, 232, 234,
    236, 240, 243, 251, 253, 256, 260,
    271
sexuality 158, 229, 251
*Sittlichkeit* 56, 79
situation-transcendence 74, 267
skepticism 12, 23, 37, 124, 184, 269
social action 64, 65, 66, 67, 69, 71, 154,
    165, 173, 219, 221, 253
  agency 3, 250–3
  change 17, 113, 137, 162, 218
  criticism 4, 106, 116, 155, 167, 174,
    225, 254
  Darwinism 150, 153
  difference 174, 259, 271
  interaction 54, 64, 69, 113, 120, 187,
    250
  organization 64, 111, 112, 152
  pluralism 181, 188, 200–1, 250, 270
  practice 34, 38, 40, 42, 63, 110, 148,
    174, 180, 184, 196, 203, 208, 251
  reality 38, 126, 172, 256
  sciences 14, 56, 82, 105, 128, 151,
    163, 241, 256
  solidarity 70–1, 129, 202
  structure 38, 77, 78, 137, 228

theory 104, 124, 151, 152, 153, 155, 158, 161, 163, 172, 173, 177–8, 205, 208, 220–1, 231, 238, 264
socialization 44, 46, 53, 55, 56, 57, 64, 65, 67, 78, 79, 150, 250, 251
society 8, 12, 16, 31, 55, 107, 129, 134, 150, 153, 159, 184, 197, 201, 207, 219, 220, 226
sociology 64, 109, 138, 148, 152
of knowledge 9, 11, 20, 23, 104
Socrates 11, 45, 74, 154, 241
solidarity 26, 54, 201, 202, 256, 257–62
speech 68, 78, 183
speech act theory 187, 202
spirit 31, 121, 157
standards 68, 73, 75, 80, 82, 107, 152, 196
subject–object distinction 132, 133, 138
subjectivity 14, 50, 133, 179, 187, 189
suffering 17, 107, 135
sympathy (*Mitleid*) 26, 259
systematic philosophy 178, 186

Taylor, Charles 122, 150
'Understanding and Ethnocentricity' 204
technology 80, 90, 115, 118, 159
teleology 63, 71, 151, 158, 205, 228
textuality 87, 90, 194, 196, 198, 200, 203, 204, 206, 232, 238, 240, 261
theory of communicative action 240
of contemporary society 228, 235
of language 181, 184, 188
of social evolution 218, 219, 224, 228, 229, 235
of theory 104, 124, 131, 156, 160, 161, 250
third-person point of view 73, 92
time 74, 147, 192
tolerance 21, 54, 91, 263
totalization 108, 112–13, 127
tradition 12, 41, 46, 47, 52, 53, 74, 131, 157, 193, 194, 195, 196, 197, 199, 204, 234, 235, 254, 258, 271
traditional theory 104–5, 108, 109, 110, 112, 119, 127, 144, 145, 172, 173, 182, 207, 252
traditionalism 41, 253, 259, 270
transcendence 32, 72, 73, 221
transcendental philosophy 150, 152, 227
transcultural validity 32, 207, 250
truth
claims 39, 51, 73, 75, 76, 185, 186, 236, 239, 240, 254
conditions 185, 187

unanimity 73, 262
uncoerced consensus 175, 176, 201, 203, 242, 245
unconditional validity 21, 74, 252, 267, 270

unconditionality 37, 254–5, 269
unity 129, 181, 200, 233
universal, the 13, 24, 25, 36, 252
universal audience 76, 253–62, 263, 264, 265, 266
claims 167, 172, 222
history 117–18, 119, 127, 151, 154, 155, 158, 165, 199
norms 196, 197, 270
validity 161, 173, 180, 231, 244, 250, 267
values 207, 253
universality 2, 3, 20, 27, 33, 39, 40, 50, 80, 89, 108, 147, 148, 172–8, 187, 191, 197, 200–1, 205, 206, 208, 217, 223, 231, 238, 244, 254–5, 263, 270
unlimited validity 74, 252, 267, 270, 271
utopianism 23, 56, 107–8, 115, 116, 126, 127, 129, 135, 137, 139, 151, 159, 217, 219, 261, 266, 270

validity 12, 37, 39, 40, 42, 46, 50, 69, 72, 73, 74, 91, 184, 185, 186, 207, 238, 239, 254, 265, 267, 268
claims 75, 77, 78, 81, 89, 90, 166, 172, 174, 177, 180, 184, 185, 187, 204, 205, 226, 230, 235, 238, 253, 254, 268
intersubjective *see* intersubjective validity
unconditional *see* unconditional validity
unlimited *see* unlimited validity
values 32, 44, 45, 49, 50, 64, 75, 80, 81, 90, 149, 175, 202, 226, 258, 270
*Verständigung* 39, 44, 45, 47, 180, 182, 183, 188, 238
*Verstehen* 81, 182
view from nowhere 14, 90, 263
violence 89, 118, 130, 263, 264

Warnke, Georgia 196, 260
*Justice and Interpretation* 260
warranted assertability 51, 73, 75, 76
Weber, Max 14, 85, 145, 220, 221, 224, 225, 229, 230
well-being 237, 238
Wellmer, Albrecht 79, 244
West, the 205, 262
Whiggism 146, 147, 156, 157, 161, 204, 205, 227
will-formation 50, 79
will to power 39
Williams, Bernard 150, 160
Wittgenstein, Ludwig 40, 63, 66, 160, 239
women 49, 89, 218
Wright Mills, C. 16

*Zeitschrift für Sozialforschung* 20

# VOLUME SIX:
# THE INFERNAL P

Shadowline®

image

**FIRST PRINTING: MAY 2019**

**ISBN: 978-1-5343-1069-8**

RAT QUEENS, VOL. 6: THE INFERNAL PATH. Published by Image Comics, Inc. Office of publication: 2701 NW Vaughn St., Suite 780, Portland, OR 97210. Copyright © 2019 KURTIS WIEBE & JOHN UPCHURCH. Contains material originally published in single magazine form as RAT QUEENS Vol. 2 #11-15 and RAT QUEENS SPECIAL: NEON STATIC #1. All rights reserved. "Rat Queens," its logos, and the likenesses of all characters herein are trademarks of Kurtis Wiebe & John Upchurch, unless otherwise noted. "Image" and the Image Comics logos are registered trademarks of Image Comics, Inc. Shadowline® and its logos are registered trademarks of Jim Valentino. No part of this publication may be reproduced or transmitted, in any form or by any means (except for short excerpts for review purposes), without the express written permission of Mr. Wiebe. All names, characters, events, and locales in this publication are entirely fictional. Any resemblance to actual persons (living or dead), events, or places, without satiric intent, is coincidental. Printed in the USA. For information regarding the CPSIA on this printed material call: 203-595-3636. For international rights, contact: foreignlicensing@imagecomics.com.

**KURTIS J. WIEBE**
story
**OWEN GIENI**
art, colors,
covers

**RYAN FERRIER**
letters
**TIM DANIEL**
frame

**JIM VALENTINO and
OWEN GIENI**
B covers

**PRISCILLA PETRAITES
MARCO LESKO**
art & colors page 118

® **IMAGE COMICS, INC.**
Robert Kirkman—Chief Operating Officer
Erik Larsen—Chief Financial Officer
Todd McFarlane—President
Marc Silvestri—Chief Executive Officer
Jim Valentino—Vice President
Eric Stephenson—Publisher/Chief Creative Officer
Corey Hart—Director of Sales
Jeff Boison—Director of Publishing Planning
& Book Trade Sales
Chris Ross—Director of Digital Sales
Jeff Stang—Director of Specialty Sales
Kat Salazar—Director of PR & Marketing
Drew Gill—Art Director
Heather Doornink—Production Director
Nicole Lapalme—Controller
IMAGECOMICS.COM

**MELANIE HACKETT**
edits
**MARC LOMBARDI**
communications
**JIM VALENTINO**
publisher/book design

**RAT QUEENS created by KURTIS J. WIEBE and ROC UPCHURCH**

A

PRODUCTION

SORRY ABOUT THE TARTS. YOU DON'T HAVE TO EAT IT, HONESTLY.

THIS IS THE BEST I'VE EATEN IN MONTHS. BURNT TARTS INCLUDED.

USUALLY GET THE TIMING RIGHT, BUT... WAS WORKING ON TOO FUCKING MANY THINGS AT ONCE, I GUESS.

HOW'RE YA HOLDIN' UP?

GOOD. WELL, AS CAN BE, YOU KNOW?

BARRIE LEFT THIS MORNING, SAID HE'D HELP MOTHER TAKE CARE OF THE BUSINESS. ASKED HIM TO STAY HERE, BUT, I MEAN...I UNDERSTAND.

WHY DIDN'T YOU GO WITH?

MY PROMISE TO DAVE. HE ACTUALLY INSISTED I GO, THAT HE HAD MORE THAN ENOUGH FRIENDS HERE TO HELP HIM.

I MADE HIM A DEAL. WHEN WE FIND HIS SON, WE'LL ALL GO BACK TO SEE MY FAMILY. INTRODUCE HIM TO MOTHER.

BUT...YOU'RE COMING BACK, RIGHT?

...

I DON'T KNOW. HAVEN'T THOUGHT THAT FAR DOWN THE ROAD YET.

WE'VE ALL BEEN THROUGH A LOT. WITH EVERYTHING...

HOW ARE YOU DOING?

ME?

GOOD.

I MEAN, BEING AN UNORTHODOX MAGE, YOU KIND OF EXPECT TO MEET AN EVIL MANIFESTATION OF YOURSELF *SOME* DAY.

JUST... MAYBE NOT SO SOON, IS ALL. HEH.

NEVER HAD A FRIEND WAKE A DORMANT MONSTER GOD TO REWRITE HISTORY AND SAVE ME BEFORE. YOU KNOW HOW TO MAKE A GIRL FEEL PRETTY FUCKING SPECIAL.

HEH. YEAH. WELL...

AND ON THAT AWKWARD NOTE, CAN WE PLEASE GET BACK TO A NORMAL FUCKING LIFE FOR--

KSH

LOOK. I GET IT. THIS IS AWKWARD. WE DIDN'T LEAVE ON THE BEST OF TERMS.

AND I COULDN'T STAND HANNAH, TO BE PERFECTLY HONEST.

I'VE CHANGED. I'M A MUCH BETTER PERSON NOW, FUCKING BITCH.

I AIN'T BEEN A QUEEN FOR A LONG TIME, BUT...YA'LL MADE A PROMISE TO ME THAT I COULD COME BACK ANY TIME.

TRUTH IS, I NEED YOUR HELP.

YOU KNOW YOU'RE ALWAYS WELCOME BACK, SADIE. AND THERE'S NO SHAME IN ADMITTING THAT SOMETIMES YOU CAN'T DO EVERYTHING ON YOUR OWN.

WE'LL DO WHATEVER WE CAN TO FIND THE PEOPLE RESPONSIBLE FOR TURNING YOU INTO THIS HORRIBLE CREATURE.

WHAT? YOU KIDDING ME? BEING AN OWL IS FUCKING AWESOME! HONESTLY, DON'T WORRY ABOUT THAT, I JUST PISSED OFF THE WRONG OWL'S ALL.

MORNING, LADIES. AND NEW STRANGER.

GODSDAMN. GOOD MORNING, FOR REAL.

I SMELL GOOD FOOD.

IT'S ALL OVER THE FLOOR THANKS TO CAPTAIN OWLTITS HERE. BUT YOU'RE WELCOME TO HELP YOURSELF.

YES, I WILL MAKE UP FOR THAT BY BEING AS BRIEF AS POSSIBLE. NOT LONG AFTER WE PARTED WAYS, I BECAME THE PROTECTOR OF THE BURNING REACH. YOU KNOW IT?

MY DRUIDIC POWERS WERE MODEST THEN, BUT NOW? I'M A NATURE-FUCKING, STORM-LAYING MOTHER-FUCKER.

SO, WHEN I TELL YOU I WAS FORCED TO SURRENDER CARE OF *MY* LAND TO AN INVADING ARMY OF MONSTERS, I WANT YOU TO FULLY COMPREHEND HOW DIRE THE SITUATION IS.

I FOUGHT, MILE BY MILE, SOAKED THE SOIL RED WITH MY OWN BLOOD TIL' I COULDN'T HOLD ANY LONGER.

TIL' THE BURNING REACH BECAME A LAND FAR OFF IN THE DISTANCE.

IT'S WHAT YOU'D EXPECT. ORCS. TROLLS. THE DEGENERATES THAT ASSOCIATE WITH THEM.

NO OFFENSE TO THE ORCS AND THOSE THAT LOVE THEM...IN THIS ROOM. SORRY, DIDN'T THINK ABOUT IT TIL' I SAID IT OUT LOUD.

DID THEY FLY BANNERS?

YOU'RE REALLY MESSING ME ALL UP OVER HERE. SWORE OFF ORCS AFTER I HAD TO KILL A THOUSAND OF 'EM. AND LOOK AT YOU. GODSDAMN...

UM, WELL. THANK YOU. BUT...YOU WERE GOING TO SAY?

YEAH, YEAH, GETTING TO THAT HANDSOME.

AS WITH ALL THINGS, IT STARTED SMALL...

WHY DO PEOPLE DO GOOD THINGS, EVEN WHEN IT'S TO THE DETRIMENT OF THEIR OWN HAPPINESS OR SAFETY?

MAYBE NOT GOOD SO MUCH...

MORE... SELFLESS?

HEAVY QUESTION TO ANSWER BEFORE LUNCH.

THAT'S WHERE I LIVE.

I SUPPOSE EVERYONE HAS THEIR OWN REASONS, THEIR OWN MOTIVATIONS. EVERY CHOICE. EVERY PATH A PERSON TAKES. EACH IS AS UNIQUE AS THE NEXT.

WHY DID YOU BACK HANNAH AFTER SHE ATTACKED THE COUNCIL OF NINE?

THAT'S...COMPLICATED. ON THE SURFACE, IT WOULD LIKELY APPEAR TO BE OUT OF SELF-PRESERVATION. SHE WAS MY ADOPTED DAUGHTER, AFTER ALL. I HAD TO OWN MY MISTAKES, OF WHICH MANY WERE CONVINCED HANNAH WAS AT THE TOP OF THE LIST.

OTHERS MIGHT'VE ASSUMED I WAS BEHOLDEN TO OBLIGATION. I LOVED HER MOTHER, AND SO FELT IT IMPORTANT TO PASS THAT ON TO HANNAH. AND, THERE IS TRUTH IN THAT, BUT... IT IS NOT THE WHOLE OF IT.

I ACTED TO FORGE A LEGACY. NOT ONLY OF MY PROGENY, WHICH I COMPLETELY CONSIDER HANNAH TO BE, BUT IN MY MARK ON THE WORLD WHEN I LEAVE IT BEHIND.

I STOOD BY HER, AND FOR HER, BECAUSE IT WAS IMPORTANT THAT ONE COULD BE RECOGNIZED FOR THEIR MISTAKES AND IN TURN GRANTED FORGIVENESS.

WHAT ARE WE BUT A LEDGER OF MISTAKES MADE AND LESSONS LEARNED?

I WANT THE WORLD TO BE A PLACE WHERE THAT CAN HAPPEN FOR ANYONE. EVEN THE DAUGHTER OF A NECROMANCER AND A DEMON.

IT'S WONDERFUL, REALLY, HOW MUCH I SEE THAT IN YOUR LOVELY LITTLE CREW.

IN THE END, THE QUEENS WERE THE BEST THING TO HAPPEN TO HANNAH. THAT WILL BE THE LEGACY OF THE RAT QUEENS...AN ACCEPTING PLACE FOR THOSE WHO HAVE NO HOME. UNTIL THEY DO.

...
I'M LEAVING.

YES. I HAD THAT SENSE.

YOU'RE RIGHT, THOUGH. ABOUT WHAT DETERMINES INTENT.

THERE'S AN INFINITE NUMBER OF REASONS WHY...

I'M ONLY LOOKING FOR ONE.

HELLO?

HELLO, DELILAH.

YOU'VE REALLY GONE AND DONE IT, HAVEN'T YOU?

YOU'LL BE COMING WITH ME.

SNAP

WOOOOOSH

LET THEM GO. WE HAVE NO QUARREL HERE. IF YOU WANT US TO LEAVE...

I'M NOT WILLING TO LET YOU BRING HARM TO MY FRIENDS. SO--

I'VE OTHER MEANS OF NEGOTIATION IF YOU'D RATHER GO DOWN THAT PATH.

...

RIGHT THEN.

HERE'S MY OFFER!

CLANG

# CHAPTER TWELVE

"...AT LEAST WE'RE ALL TOGETHER!"

...

WHAT THE...

YOU...UH, AROUND HERE, NAKED SMIDGEN... LADY?

WELCOME, DELILAH!

THIS MUST BE ALL VERY CONFUSING FOR YOU.

AS IT SHOULD BE! YOU HAVE PASSED INTO THE REALM OF THE DEAD.

YES. IT'S TRUE. BECAUSE YOU'RE QUITE DEAD.

DEAD?

WHAT HAPPENED TO NAKED SMIDGEN LADY?

HARBINGER OF DEATH, THAT ONE.

OH YES, AND WE HAVE WARNED HER ABOUT THAT SORT OF THING BEFORE. THE WHOLE SHEER GOWN GETUP. WE DO NOT APPROVE.

SHE REALLY OUGHT TO COVER UP.

SHE SHOULD BE ALLOWED TO WEAR WHAT SHE WANTS.

RIGHT. EXACTLY. UNLESS WE SAY OTHERWISE.

OF COURSE!

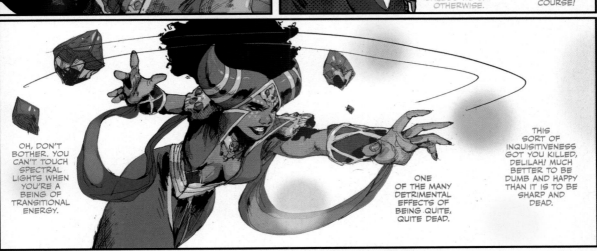

OH, DON'T BOTHER. YOU CAN'T TOUCH SPECTRAL LIGHTS WHEN YOU'RE A BEING OF TRANSITIONAL ENERGY.

ONE OF THE MANY DETRIMENTAL EFFECTS OF BEING QUITE, QUITE DEAD.

THIS SORT OF INQUISITIVENESS GOT YOU KILLED, DELILAH! MUCH BETTER TO BE DUMB AND HAPPY THAN IT IS TO BE SHARP AND DEAD.

IF I'M ALREADY DEAD, WHAT'S THE RISK?

OH, GOOD LOGIC, THAT. I LIKE HER ALREADY.

DON'T GET ME WRONG, I APPRECIATE YOUR KINDNESS... I GUESS I'M JUST A LITTLE LOST...

THIS IS EXPERMENTIA, MY LITTLE CORNER OF THE UNIVERSE. WE'RE A VERY OPEN AND WELCOMING GROUP HERE.

WE KEEP A PRETTY REGULAR SCHEDULE. AN ACTIVE MIND IS A HEALTHY MIND AND ALL THAT.

YEAH, I... I GET THAT I'M IN THE GOD REALM. WHICH...IT'S A LITTLE OVERWHELMING. BUT I DON'T EVEN KNOW WHO YOU ARE. OR WHY YOU BROUGHT ME HERE.

OH, RIGHT! I GET SO CAUGHT UP IN OVERSEEING ALL THE SEX IN THE UNIVERSE I FORGET THE SMALL DETAILS.

I'M LADY LOVE, GODDESS OF LOVE AND OTHER LOVE RELATED DOMAINS.

OKAY. AND WHY DID YOU KIDNAP ME?

KIDNAP? OH, SWEET CHILD. I DID NO SUCH THING. I ASSISTED IN YOUR ASCENSION.

I DIDN'T ASK TO COME HERE.

YEAH, I KNOW, LOVE. I REMEMBER ALL TOO WELL. I FELT THE SAME. THERE'S REALLY NOTHING YOU CAN DO. YOU INVOKED THE GREAT THREE.

SEE THE WORLD THROUGH ANCIENT EYES. MAKE A HORRIBLE MISTAKE THAT ALTERS THE UNIVERSE IN SOME WAY. HEAR A PRAYER SENT IN YOUR NAME.

SO, AS AN OFFICIAL DELEGATE, AND ON BEHALF OF ALL DEITIES ACROSS REALITY...

...WELCOME TO THE GOD CLUB.

ALRIGHT, ALRIGHT. I'LL GO FIRST. MY WORST CHILDHOOD MEMORY?

ME AND MY BROTHER VOON USED TO BE INSEPARABLE. WHEREVER I WENT, HE FOLLOWED. IT WAS LIKE THAT FOR YEARS, EVERYTHING BETWEEN US WAS...WELL, REAL FRIENDSHIP.

THINGS GOT COMPLICATED AS WE GOT OLDER. WE BOTH FELL FOR THE SAME PERSON. I MEAN, WE WEREN'T EVEN BLOODED THEN, BUT, EVEN THE YOUNG GET CRAZY IDEAS ABOUT LOVE.

WE FOUGHT. I BROKE HIS ARM. AND FROM THAT DAY FORWARD WE WERE ENEMIES. IF I COULD GO BACK...

HOW ABOUT YOU, HANNAH?

HMMMM. EITHER LOSING MR. HOPS, THE BEST BUNNY STUFFY IN THE UNIVERSE, ORRRRRR MY MOTHER BEING SLAUGHTERED IN FRONT OF ME.

GODS. MINE WAS I ATE SHIT FOR GOLD.

DO NOT RECOMMEND.

I HAD NO IDEA YOU ENDURED THAT KIND OF TRAUMA, HANNAH. I'M GENUINELY SORRY...

OH, UH... THANKS, SADIE. TO BE HONEST, I ALWAYS THOUGHT YOU MIGHT BE THE KIND OF PERSON WHO ATE SHIT FOR GOLD...

AND EVEN THOUGH THAT TURNS OUT TO BE TRUE, YOUR INFLUENCE WAS THE MAIN REASON I STOPPED GIVING A SHIT WHAT PEOPLE THOUGHT ABOUT ME.

I'M COOL LIKE THAT.

EVERYONE STAY QUIET! THERE'S AN ENCAMPMENT AHEAD!

KEEP LOW, FOLLOW ME!

FUCKING DISGUSTING ORCS.

C'MON, SADIE.

PRESENT COMPANY EXCLUDED. Y'ALL ARE EXTREMELY FUCKABLE.

WE HAVE TO DO SOMETHING.

WE WOULD BE UP AGAINST A POWERFUL ENEMY. BUT I AGREE. ANY IDEAS?

THE BEST PLAN WOULD BE TO AVOID CONFRONTATION. BETTY, COULD YOU SNEAK INTO THE CAMP, GET TO THOSE CAGES AND WORK ON QUIETLY GETTING THEM OUT?

OBVIOUSLY. BUT THERE'S A LOT OF BAD GUYS TO AVOID. COULD USE A DISTRACTION.

FUCK...

MORE?

PEOPLE WORSHIP ME.

AND CAN YOU PUT A DAMN SHIRT ON? GODS!

I GET THE WHOLE SEX GOD THING, BUT THERE'S A TIME AND PLACE...

WHICH IS EVERY WAKING HOUR IN THIS PLACE, APPARENTLY!

I'M A LOVE GOD, DEAR.

I THINK YOU MIGHT'VE SWAPPED PORTFOLIOS WITHOUT REALIZING.

SO...WHAT? THE GODS JUST HANG AROUND HERE AND BANG AWAY ON EACH OTHER ALL DAY LONG?

OH NO, IT'S NOT AT ALL LIKE THAT. WE ALSO MAKE LOVE TO THE SPIRITS OF THE DEAD. THIS *IS* THE AFTERLIFE, HUN.

≈SIGH≈

I DON'T WANT ANY GOD POWERS. I DON'T WANT NAIVE PEOPLE PRAYING TO ME.

WHO SAID ANYTHING ABOUT GOD POWERS?

ISN'T THAT THE WHOLE POINT? GODS BLESS THE WEAK WITH MAGICAL IMBUEMENTS?

I MEAN, IF THAT'S WHAT YOU BELIEVE.

I THOUGHT YOU WERE THE EXPERT HERE, BEING A GOD AND ALL.

I HONESTLY HAVE NO IDEA HOW THIS WORKS. I HEAR VOICES IN MY HEAD. I CONCENTRATE REALLY HARD ON THOSE VOICES. WISH THEM WELL. CARRY ON WITH MY DAY.

I...

HOW DID WE GET TO THE GOD SPOT? YOU SNAPPED YOUR FINGERS AND I WAS TRANSPORTED TO...WHAT, ANOTHER PLANE?

OH, THAT'S JUST MAGIC. LOTS OF WIZARDS AROUND HERE. THEY MAKE AMAZING LITTLE CONTRAPTIONS THAT WHISK US AROUND. MAKES TRAVEL SOOOO WONDERFUL.

HOW DO YOU HEAR THE VOICES?

I REALLY DON'T KNOW.

EVER THINK THAT MAYBE YOU'D BEEN UNDER A LOT OF PRESSURE AND YOUR BRAIN JUST POPPED?

BECAUSE I HEARD A VOICE. AND LET ME TELL YOU, SISTER. I'VE BEEN A LITTLE STRESSED LATELY.

YOU KNOW, I FEEL A LOT BETTER ALREADY.

MAKES A LOT OF SENSE TO ME THAT ALL OF THIS, IT'S JUST REGULAR FOLK ESCAPING TO ANOTHER PLANE TO GET THEIR ROCKS OFF AND HARASS PEOPLE.

EXACTLY WHAT I IMAGINED THE GODS TO BE.

YOU CAN DISMISS ME. THE GODS. ALL OF IT. I DO NOT UNDERSTAND HOW THIS WORKS, BUT I KNOW IT'S TRUE. YOU HAVE ELEVATED BEYOND THE MORTAL REALM.

YEAH. HOW'S THAT?

BECAUSE IT WAS MY VOICE THAT CALLED OUT TO YOU.

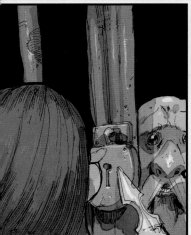

HELLO THERE, FRESH LITTLE LAMB. YOU'VE STUMBLED INTO THE WRONG CAMP.

NAH, YOU'VE STUMBLED INTO THE WRONG WOMAN.

EVOKAR ENSI-

NECRIUS
ENFILE.

SHLK

# CHAPTER THIRTEEN

WHAT REALM IS THIS?

MINE. A LONG TIME AGO.

THE GODS ARE IN DANGER... A SICKNESS IS SPREADING. I BELIEVE YOU CAN HELP.

HOW? YOU'RE A GOD, MORE THAN I AM OR WILL BE.

"I DON'T UNDERSTAND ANY MORE THAN YOU AND I'VE BEEN AT IT A LONG TIME. I'VE TRIED TO FIX...THIS."

"I HAD NO IDEA WHO WOULD HEAR MY PRAYER. IT CONNECTED WITH YOU. SO HERE WE ARE. I DON'T KNOW HOW YOU CAN MAKE A DIFFERENCE..."

...ALL I ASK IS THAT YOU TRY.

TELL YOU WHAT. I'M GOING TO MAKE MYSELF COMFORTABLE.

I'M GOING TO SIT RIGHT HERE UNTIL YOU TELL ME WHAT'S GOING ON.

AND I'LL WARN YOU, IF I AM A GOD, I'M PRETTY DAMN SURE MY SLICE OF DIVINITY IS AWKWARDNESS.

SPLASH OF ANXIETY. DIVERSIFY MY PORTFOLIO.

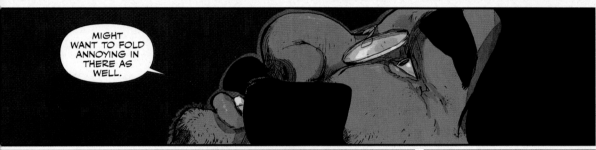

MIGHT WANT TO FOLD ANNOYING IN THERE AS WELL.

HEY. SO, I ACTUALLY HAVE IMPORTANT THINGS TO DO. GOTTA FIGURE OUT WHAT TO DO ABOUT N'RYGOTH BEING AWAKENED, HAVE AN EVIL VERSION OF MY BEST FRIEND FLOATING AROUND REALITY...

WOW. HOW INTERESTING.

REAL GOD MATERIAL HERE.

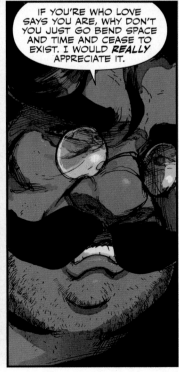

IF YOU'RE WHO LOVE SAYS YOU ARE, WHY DON'T YOU JUST GO BEND SPACE AND TIME AND CEASE TO EXIST. I WOULD *REALLY* APPRECIATE IT.

WHAT DO YOU MEAN YOU DON'T KNOW WHO I AM?

IT'S NOT PERSONAL, BILFORD. I GREW UP WITH A VERY SPECIFIC RELIGION AND THEY WEREN'T EXACTLY OPEN TO NEW IDEAS. IT WAS N'RYGOTH ALL DAY, EVERY DAY.

WHEN I LEFT, THE LAST THING I WANTED TO WASTE TIME ON WAS ANOTHER RELIGION. I WAS FIGURING MYSELF OUT. DIDN'T NEED ANOTHER ARBITRARY SYSTEM OF MORALS TELLING ME HOW TO LIVE AND BREATHE.

LIFE'S COMPLICATED ENOUGH.

I GAVE EVERYTHING FOR WHAT I BELIEVED! EVERYONE THINKS SMIDGENS ARE ADORABLE, LOVABLE LITTLE SHITS.

BUT NO ONE CARES ABOUT HISTORY, ABOUT WHERE WE COME FROM.

SO WHY DON'T YOU TELL ME?

...

WE WERE LOST.

I'M LISTENING.

"NOT SO LONG AGO, WE WERE DIVIDED. SEPARATED BY THE BELIEF THAT EACH TRIBE WAS SUPERIOR. THAT THEIR CONVICTIONS WERE THE RIGHT."

"ENTITLEMENT TO THE BRINK OF MADNESS."

"WHAT WE FAILED TO SEE WAS THE CONNECTION. ALL THE BEAUTIFUL THINGS THAT BONDED US. IN THE DEEP FABRIC OF THE SMIDGEN PEOPLE, WHAT MADE US MORE ALIKE THAN DIFFERENT..."

"IT WAS DIVINE."

# CHAPTER FOURTEEN

BE STRONG. YOU MIGHT BE FROM A DEVIANT STRAIN OF ORC, BUT I SUSPECT YOU WILL SURVIVE THIS.

THERE IS HONOUR IN THAT. RARE FEW SPECIES SURVIVE THE EXPERIMENTATION...THE *TRANSFORMATION.*

MY CHILDREN OF THE FLESH. THEY WERE MUCH LIKE YOU. ORDINARY ORCS, BORING RANK AND FILE SOLDIERS BEFORE THEY MET ME.

I GAVE THEM *POWER.* NOT ONLY OF THIS PHYSICAL FORM, BUT AN ELEVATION OF CEREBRAL ECSTASY IN THE SHIFT.

ONLY ONE OF US REMAINS UNSHAPED. A STILLBORN.

"YOU WILL BE HIS REBIRTH."

NO...NOT HIM...

...NOT MY BOY!

LOOK AT YOU. THE PUREST EXPRESSION OF THE ORCISH STRENGTH. BONE AND MUSCLE WITH A BRAIN.

A STUNTED, EMOTIONALLY DRIVEN BRAIN, TRUE...BUT I CAN WORK WITH IT.

...

SUCH A PERFECT SPECIMEN. I'M TEMPTED TO GUESS THAT YOU MIGHT EVEN BE FROM MY TRIBE, AS FLAWLESS AS YOU ARE.

I'M NO FUCKING FLESHER.

I'VE SEEN YOUR FUCKING AFTERMATH. YOU SPARED NONE. FEMALES. CHILDREN. YOU TURNED THEM INTO LIVING MONUMENTS OF YOUR INSANE CULT.

I'M NOTHING LIKE YOU.

I REMEMBER THINKING THE SAME WHEN THE FLESHERS DESCENDED ON US. LIKE ALL THE OTHER TRIBES, WE FELL EASILY TO THEIR POWER.

WHAT CHANCE DOES ONE STAND AGAINST AN ANCIENT MAGIC THAT SHAPES MUSCLE AND BONE INTO THE LIVING STRINGS FOR A MAD PUPPETEER?

I AM NOT A FLESHER. I BECAME ONE.

# CHAPTER FIFTEEN

WHAT HAVE I DONE?

HE WAS TAKEN FROM YOU, LOVE. STOLEN.

I CAN'T FIX THIS.

YOU'RE A HEALER, REMEMBER?

OH, LOVE, WHAT HAPPENED TO YOU?

SHE TRIED TO BE A HERO.

TRIED TO BE? BITCH, SHE IS A HERO. TRYING TO PULL YOUR ASS OUT OF THE FIRE. GODS.

DAMN.

HEY...YOU'RE BACK... AND YOU LOOK REALLY...FUCKING GOOD.

THANKS, HUN. I'VE PATCHED YOU UP BEST I CAN. BUT... EVEN I HAVE MY LIMITS.

WHOEVER DID THIS...THEY USED SOME KIND OF DEEP, ANCIENT, CORRUPTED MAGIC AND I CAN'T--

WHOA. NEW HANNAH.

YOU OKAY?

YEAH. FUCKING WEIRD, RIGHT? I DON'T KNOW...YEAH, I--

NEW HANNAH.

AH, BROOG. I THOUGHT I RECOGNIZED YOU.

TO BE FAIR, WE'VE BOTH CHANGED.

MY NAME IS BRAGA. AND I'M THE SAME FUCKING PERSON I'VE ALWAYS BEEN, BROTHER.

DO YOU PROMISE TO BE GOOD?

NOPE.

I WANT TO FULLY ENJOY THIS. I WOULD HAVE YOU AT YOUR BEST.

YOU USE SUCH FANCY LANGUAGE NOW. DON'T TELL ME YOU'VE ACTUALLY BEEN READING.

READING? OH, MY, NO.

SWISH

YOU WOULDN'T BELIEVE WHAT I'VE LEARNED THROUGH THE SHIFT. THE CRAFT NOT ONLY EXPANDED MY PHYSICAL SELF, BUT THAT SPARK OF...CREATIVITY IN THE REALIGNING OF FLESH...

IT LED ME TO DESTROY MY MASTER, OUTMANOEUVERED HIM TO HIS DEATH, AND IN HIS SUFFERING...I LEARNED EVERYTHING ABOUT THE FLESH.

OH YES, MY MIND IS MY GREATEST ALLY NOW--MY BODY ITS SLAVE.

I HAVE YOU TO THANK FOR THAT, BRAGA.

...

OF ALL THE PLACES TO FIND YOU...HERE ON MY DOORSTEP. I'M AN AVID PROPONENT THAT EXISTENCE IS ASTOUNDING CHAOS, BUT...

...I CAN'T HELP BUT MARVEL AT THE FATES, HERE AND NOW.

LET'S GET ON WITH IT THEN.

FUNNY. I'M JUST REALIZING HOW UNSATISFYING THIS WILL BE. YOU DON'T STAND A CHANCE.

I WANTED YOU TO STAND A CHANCE.

TRY ME.

IT'S NOT MY PLACE. YOUR FATE SHOULD BE CHOSEN BY THE TRIBE YOU KILLED.

WHAT?

FATHER BEGGED YOU TO TAKE HIS PLACE. OUR PEOPLE RESPECTED YOU. YOU WERE A FORMIDABLE WARRIOR, SKILL FAR EXCEEDING MY OWN. YOU, ONE BERSERKER, TOOK OUT ALL MY MEN AND CHOPPED OFF MY ARM.

THEN YOU LEFT.

WHAT DID YOU THINK WOULD HAPPEN TO OUR PEOPLE? LEAVING IT IN THE HANDS OF FATHER? OF ME? TWO ORCS, SHAMED IN BATTLE, HONOURLESS VERMIN. THAT'S WHAT THE TRIBE CALLED US BEFORE THE END...

OUR PEOPLE ARE ALL BUT DEAD. YOU AND I... THE LAST.

YOU'RE NOT MY BROTHER. NOT MY TRIBE. THIS...FACE YOU WEAR. YOU SAID IT YOURSELF...

THE SHIFT REVEALS THE TRUE MIND THROUGH THE BODY.

LOOK AT YOU, VOON. YOU'RE A FUCKING MONSTER. YOU ALWAYS HAVE BEEN.

I'VE HAD A LIFETIME'S FILL OF YOUR JUDGEMENTS!

NEON STATIC SPECIAL cover by WILLIAM KIRKBY

# NEON STATIC SPECIAL

## KURTIS J. WIEBE
**story**

## WILLIAM KIRKBY
**art**

## RYAN FERRIER
**lettering**

--FOR SO MANY YEARS. SHE WAS THE ONE QUIET PLACE IN THIS MESSY STORM OF A LIFE.

AND, LIKE HER NOW, I WAS ADRIFT THEN. I WANT SO DESPERATELY TO GIVE HER AN ANCHOR...

Jitterbug Mine was a very special woman.
1

Stake My grandmother was so important to me. I hope I helped!
3

AND BY ANCHOR, I MEAN A PROPER BURIAL. I'M NOT WORRIED ABOUT HER BECOMING A GHOST AND GOING CRAZY OR ANYTHING. HEH.

=SNIFF= THAT WOULD BE SO GRANDMA, THOUGH.

WELCOME TO SAVEME
FUNDS RAISED FOR: "GRANDMA'S DEAD...HELP!" 1,253 GOLDYEN

NiceShade Lost my gran, too, chum. Hope this helps!
1

I KNOW THE PERFECT PLACE. A BEAUTIFUL ALCOVE ON THE COAST. SHE ALWAYS LOVED THE OCEAN.

...

BETTER GET TO WORK.

GRANDMA ALWAYS TOLD ME, "THE OCEAN IS GREAT." THAT'S HOW I KNOW SHE LOVED THE OCEAN, YOU KNOW?

# Palisade

DING

LAY DOWN ANY ARMS AND STEP INTO THE HALL!

HERE WE GO!

RATA TAT TAT TAT TAT

OH... SHIT.

FUCKING PHASE DRAGON.

LADIES. IT'S ABOUT TO GET COMPLICATED.

BLAM
BLAM
BLAM

A FUCKING DRAGON? AGAIN?

WE HURT THIS ONE A BIT FOR YOU. IF THAT HELPS?

GET INSIDE, I'LL HANDLE THIS.

**Later**

YOU'RE SURE ABOUT THIS?

LAST THING WE WANT IS SAWYER AND HIS P.C.D. CRONIES BREATHING DOWN OUR NECKS ALL DAY.

STILL DON'T UNDERSTAND WHY THE PALISADE CYBERCRIME DIVISION ISN'T HANDLING THIS CASE ON THEIR OWN.

WELL BELOW THEIR PAY GRADE AND FUCKING PERFECT FOR US.

HAS NOTHING TO DO WITH YOU AND SAWYER'S FREQUENT TRIPS TO BONE TOWN?

I CUT HIM A DISCOUNT FOR SERVICES RENDERED. HEHE.

TEN SAVEME FUNDRAISERS, SPOOFED THROUGH DOZENS OF RELAY NODES, ALL LEADING TO ONE IP. A SINGLE USER WHO LOGS INTO THIS ALLEY TERMINAL ONCE A DAY.

SAWYER'S RIGHT, THERE'S A SCAMMER. WE'VE COMPLETED THE HARDEST PART OF THE MISSION, NOW WE WAIT.

WHAT SORT OF PERSON ARE WE DEALING WITH?

A CRIMINAL.

YEAHHHH, BUT...I MEAN, WHAT IF THEY'RE JUST...HAVING A TOUGH TIME?

I DIDN'T ACCESS THEIR LIFE HISTORY, BETTY. AND WE'RE NOT BEING PAID ENOUGH TO CARE. AT THE END OF THE DAY, SOMEONE'S PREYING ON SYMPATHETIC PEOPLE.

YEAH. AND THAT'S *OUR* TURF.

YOU BETTER BEHAVE, MISTER! I DON'T WANT ANY UNNECESSARY VIOLENCE!

HEY! WE GOT A GUY!

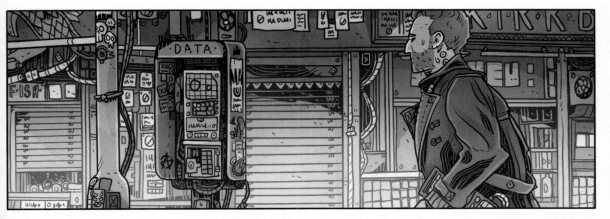

I SAID NO UNNECESSARY--

VIOLENCE IS ALWAYS NECESSARY.

MY FRIEND WAS SIMPLY TRYING TO MAKE IT CLEAR THAT WE MEAN BUSINESS.

BUT I ALSO WANT IT TO BE CLEAR THAT WE'RE REASONABLE FOLKS WHO PREFER TO NEGOTIATE!

I THINK SHE BROKE MOST OF MY BONES.

A NEW RECORD!

LET'S KEEP THIS CIVIL, LADIES!

THAT'S UP TO MR. DEAD GRANDMA HERE...

CARE TO FILL US IN ON YOUR LITTLE OPERATION?

UM...I...JUST NEEDED SOME GOLDYEN...TO, YOU KNOW--

THWAK

I BOUGHT YOU TIME, MISTER! STOP WASTING MINE!

OK. OK! LOOK...THE GOLDYEN AIN'T FOR ME, ALRIGHT? THERE'S THIS GUY...CASTIWYR. YOU KNOW THE NAME?

DON'T TELL ME PIXEL-DICK IS SECRETLY A SHADY GUY. I COULDN'T COPE.

WHAT'S HE GOT TO DO WITH THIS?

HE'S BLACKMAILING ME! I DON'T KNOW HOW, BUT... HE GOT HIS HANDS ON PRIVATE INFORMATION. STUFF...I- I CAN'T HAVE LEAKED TO THE PUBLIC.

AS LONG AS I KEEP PAYING HIM 1,000 GOLDYEN A WEEK, HE'LL HANG ONTO IT...OR SO HE SAYS.

WHEN DID THIS HAPPEN?

CASTIWYR'S DONE THIS TO OTHERS. WE COVERTLY MESSAGE EACH OTHER ON A PRIVATE FORUM.

A FEW WEEKS AGO...

ANYTHING IN YOUR ONLINE ROUTINE CHANGE AROUND THEN?

UH, WELL... SEE, I'D STARTED USING THIS...VIRTUAL DATING PROGRAM... LOVEME. TRYING TO FIND THE ONE, YOU KNOW?

AWWWWW.

WEIRD THING IS...EVEN IF PEOPLE MISS THEIR PAYMENTS, HE DOESN'T MAKE ANY SECRETS PUBLIC. JUST GIVES A WARNING...

IT CAN'T BE ABOUT THE MONEY. HE'S THE RICHEST, MOST HANDSOME HACKER HUMANITARIAN IN PALISADE. MY QUESTION IS...

"WHY?"

LOVE ME

YOU KNOW... THIS IS *YOUR* NATURAL PLAYGROUND, BETTY. EVER THINK THAT *YOU* SHOULD GET A HARDWIRE IMPLANT?

⸞SIGH⸞

GOOD MORROW TO YOU, M'LADY. WOULD--

CHECK MY BALL. THAT'S A 'KINDLY FUCK OFF' BALL.

I DIDN'T THINK IT WAS POSSIBLE TO CRINGE SO HARD THAT YOUR DIGITAL FACE HURTS.

--FIND IT REALLY HARD TO BELIEVE, SADIE, CONSIDERING *I'M* THE MOST SOCIALLY AWKWARD BEING IN THIS ROOM.

THAT'S VERY SWEET. BUT...I REALLY DO FIND THIS DIFFICULT. HATE IT EVEN. HONESTLY, I'M JUST LOOKING FOR A BIT OF COMPANY.

YEAH, I TOTALLY GET YOU. FEELS LIKE EVERYONE ON THIS SITE'S JUST HERE FOR ONE THING, RIGHT?

GANGBANGS.

...

FUCK. LIGHTEN YOUR BALL, CHUMMER! I'M JUST MESSIN' WITH YA!

RIGHT. RIGHT!

AH, I'M BEING HARD ON YOU. I SHOULDN'T BE. THIS DATING GAME IS A ROUGH RACKET. YOU WANT TO GO SOMEWHERE PRIVATE? GET TO KNOW EACH OTHER?

...

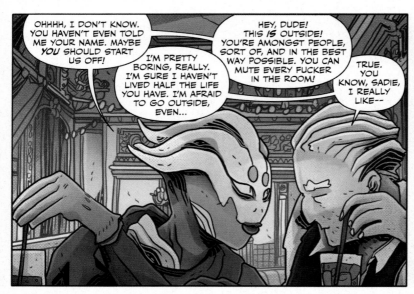

OHHHH, I DON'T KNOW. YOU HAVEN'T EVEN TOLD ME YOUR NAME. MAYBE *YOU* SHOULD START US OFF!

I'M PRETTY BORING, REALLY. I'M SURE I HAVEN'T LIVED HALF THE LIFE YOU HAVE. I'M AFRAID TO GO OUTSIDE, EVEN...

HEY, DUDE! THIS *IS* OUTSIDE! YOU'RE AMONGST PEOPLE, SORT OF, AND IN THE BEST WAY POSSIBLE. YOU CAN MUTE EVERY FUCKER IN THE ROOM!

TRUE. YOU KNOW, SADIE, I REALLY LIKE--

DND

BZZZT

DND

DON'T WORRY. YOU'RE SAFE.

SORRY ABOUT THIS. LOOKS LIKE YOU WERE HAVING A HOT DATE WITH PHISHING AI.

WELL, SHIT. GUESS THAT EXPLAINS WHY HE WANTED TO KNOW MY DIRTIEST SECRET...

ALSO EXPLAINS WHY I WAS MAKING SUCH A QUICK CONNECTION. IS THERE SOMETHING WRONG WITH ME?

THERE'S SOMETHING WRONG WITH ALL OF US.

TRUE.

WELL... I'M ALREADY OF A MOOD. WANT TO MAKE OUT A LITTLE?

...

GOT WORK TO DO.

BEEP

WHAT A STRANGE PLACE FOR THE RICHEST, MOST HANDSOME HACKER HUMANITARIAN IN PALISADE TO LIVE.

I THOUGHT THIS IS WHERE PALISADE DUMPED ALL THEIR DEAD BODIES.

COULD'VE FOOLED ME.

BIG DIFFERENCE BETWEEN A POOR NEIGHBORHOOD AND A CEMETERY, HANNAH.

LET'S GO CATCH US THE REAL BAD GUY!

SEEMS TOO QUIET. SURE YOU CAN'T GIVE US AN IDEA OF SECURITY?

I TOLD YOU, I'M NOT IN HIS NETWORK. UNLESS YOU WANT ME TO RISK MY BRAIN WITH A BLACK I.C. BOMB?

LIFE IS RISK, DEE. JUST...FUCKING MITIGATE OURS, IS ALL I'M ASKING.

WHIRRR

CRACK

GO, GO, GO!

UH....

WHAT THE FUCKAHAHAHAHAH?

I THINK IT'S TIME CASTIWYR MADE HIS PUBLIC DEBUT.

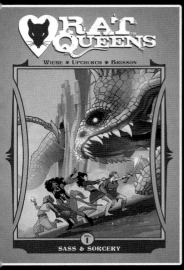
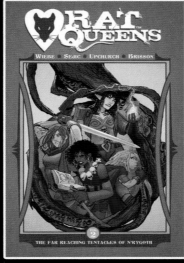

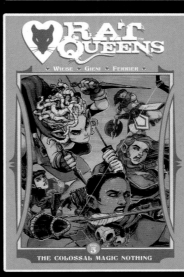

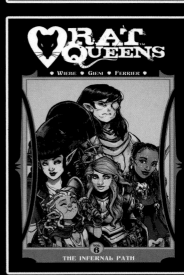

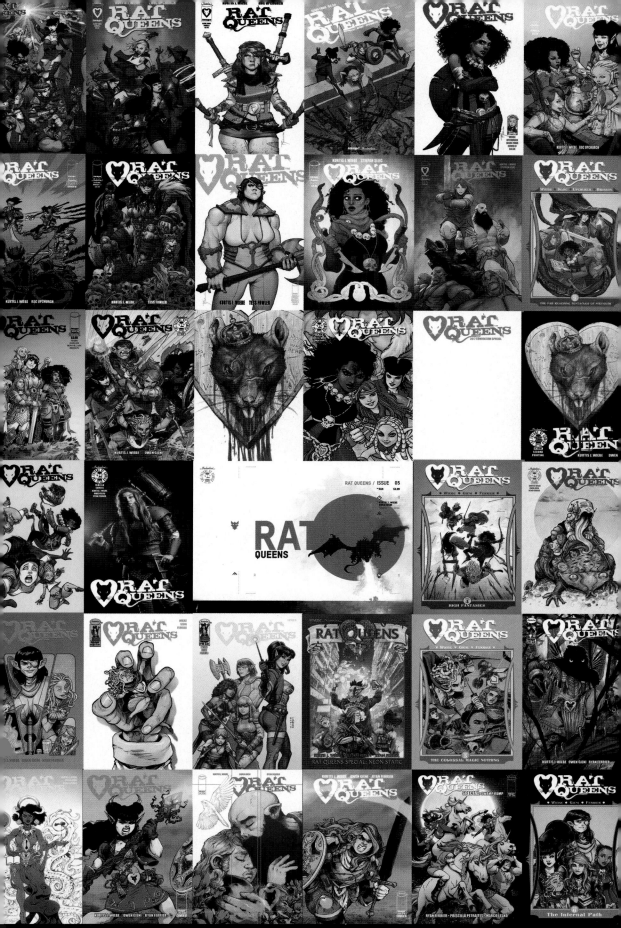

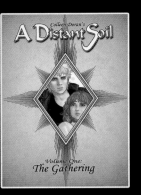

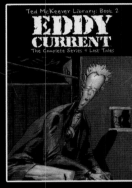

# WHERE DIVERSITY THRIVES

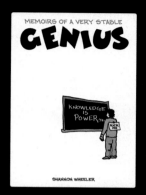

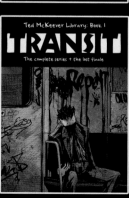